CRIMINAL JUSTICE HISTORY

CRIMINAL JUSTICE HISTORY is an international forum for the history and analysis of crime and criminal justice. It annually publishes research and historiographical articles, comparative and interpretive essays, conference assessments, research notes, book review essays, and reviews. The annual encourages submissions from authors in any part of the world in disciplines such as history, law, anthropology, sociology, political science, and the criminal justice sciences that relate specifically to the history of crime and criminal justice and to its broader social, historical, legal, and institutional contexts in any geographical area or period.

CRIMINAL JUSTICE HISTORY

AN INTERNATIONAL ANNUAL

Volume 13

1992

Greenwood Press
Westport, Connecticut • London

ISBN: 0–313–28319–2

First published in 1993

Greenwood Press, 88 Post Road West, Westport, CT 06881
An imprint of Greenwood Publishing Group, Inc.

Printed in the United States of America

The paper used in this book complies with the Permanent Paper Standard issued by the National Information Standards Organization (Z39.48–1984).

10 9 8 7 6 5 4 3 2 1

Contents

Preface

Nuance has become the watchword of current writing in criminal justice history, and nowhere has this become more evident than in the subject area of prisons and regimes of punishment. The literature in the area has come to rival that of the social history of crime, and has been attested to by the work, among many others, of John Stack, David Smith, Philip Priestley, Massimo Pavarini, Dario Mellossi, Michael Ignatieff, Christopher Harding, Michel Foucault, John Conley and Rainer Baehre. The movement to integrate the history of prisons and punishment into the social, economic, political, and cultural fabric of society is reflected in the major book of Roger Hood and Leon Radzinowicz on *The Emergence of Penal Policy* (1986), the capstone of Radzinowicz's history of English criminal law. The history of prisons, like that of crime, is in the midst of being written from the bottom up.

Dr. Stack engages the reader to address the extent to which historians have not yet explored the perceptions and experiences of prisoners and their local vernacular environment, even with the new social history that ostensibly looks at history from the ground up. Examining the levels of imprisonment for children in Victorian England, Stack arrives at several interesting conclusions. The rise of the new, urban police courts led to increasing rates of child prosecution, but without any clear pattern of sentencing. While few children were actually incarcerated, those who were, comprised males from working class, Irish families in the most urbanized counties. Thus, the old stereotype of the Irish in the evil cities comes back into play, but with significant differences. Questions involving the role of the Irish in criminal prosecutions, of rural and urban communities and their support group networks, and of the relationship of victims-to-offenders, and local authorities-to children, should repay future research.

Similar nuances were at work with the one million Pacific Island laborers, largely from Melanesia, who went to Australia and New Zealand for work in the second half of the nineteenth century. Examining the police watch-house and bench books for Queensland, Mark Finnane and Clive Moore study arrests in several districts from the 1860s to the early 1900s within the social, economic, and demographic structures of the colony. The findings reveal that these workers had, like the Irish in England, a higher rate of arrest than the resident population, and were prosecuted more for personal and public offenses than for property crimes. Their use of the strike and riot as forms of protest was not dissimilar to the Englishman's use of arson in the same century, as noted in Malcolm Chase's review of a recent work on maiming and poaching in East Anglia. By the 1890s the Melanesians were not only becoming proletarianized, they were also serving as victims as well as the perpetrators. They were, however, treated differently in the various communities. The suggestion is that broader changes in their position at law may be related to changes in their social and working life in their respective communities.

While the Melanesians of Queensland were stigmatized to varying degrees, and conducted numerous strikes and several wide scale disturbances which led in part to their eventual deportation, the indigenous peoples of Mexico faced even deeper labeling. Paul Vanderwood's narrative account of the millenarian movement among the indigenous people of Tomochic, Mexico, in the 1890s, is a moving story of a people who preferred the preaching of a teenage girl, Teresa, for the moral regeneration of their society, to the established Roman Catholic Church and a government that perceived the movement as subverting the foundations of society and the state. Labeling them as *fanáticos* and *bandidoes*, and characterizing them as rebels and revolutionaries, liberal reformers used miscegenation against their indigenous society. Drawing upon the ideas of Eric Hobsbawm, Vanderwood sees the ruling Porfirian elites using this ideology to create a national political legitimacy and invent a Mexican community that did not exist. In so doing, the elites not only suspended civil rights in the prosecution of various crimes, but also caused splits within communities and prompted later bandits to pose as revolutionaries. The plight of people thus stigmatized, and their attempts to replicate the structures they have left, is discussed in David McCreery's review of a recent work on bandits in Peru.

Religious ideals also shaped the views of evangelical social reformers who challenged the institutions of corporal and capital punishment in the early republican period of the United States. In previous volumes of this *Annual*(1987), Randall McGowan revealed how they affected the movement for the reform of capital punishment in Great Britain, and Paul Cromwell charted the influence of the Quakers (1989). Here Christopher Adamson explores the work of Arminians, Methodists, and Wesleyans, particularly in the northern states, who challenged the criminal justice system. Perceiving prisoners as saints who could be saved for Christ, these men drew upon their theology and the gathered facts concerning death, insanity, and recidivism to promote the reform of penal policies and practices. As reformers, however, Adamson reveals the practices and conservative nature of their ideas. They were not against the existence of corporal or capital punishment, nor were they for social reform or a stronger role for government. Preferring private to public action, the prison reform societies which emerged became a conservative, modernizing force in American society.

The penal institutions and criminal justice systems in the United States became models for other countries in the nineteenth century. Following World War I, German jurists, criminologists and penologists visited various states to learn how Americans handled the problems of street and professional crime in industrial cities for the new Weimar Republic. Robert Waite presents a fascinating account of what the Germans perceived and learned in the 1920s and 1930s. They were appalled by the political influence, protectionism, and corruption which existed in the police forces, courts, and prisons. They attacked the institutions of jury trial, plea bargaining, the law profession, and sentencing, which they ascribed all to the evils of democracy. However, they liked the Federal Bureau of Investigation, the use of the "lineup" and fingerprinting, and experiments with sterilization. Adopting a tougher approach to the crime problem with the advent of the Nazi government in 1933, the knowledge which these expert visitors acquired in the United States forms an intriguing window into the early history of the Fascist State.

The history of crime in Germany, which has developed somewhat slower than that in other European countries, is the focus of two chapters in this volume. Martin Schüssler's analysis of the Nuremberg outlawry books 1285–1400 is a major work in medieval quantitative history. Using the methodology of Marvin Wolfgang, Schüssler assesses the typology of criminal prosecutions, trials and punishments, places them within the context of social and economic structure, and compares the results with other major European towns from Italy to England. He concludes that the typology and rates of recorded crime in Nuremberg were similar to other medieval towns, with some notable exceptions. Most of the perpetrators were of the middle class, and many prosecutions were socially motivated. In addition, the rise of prosecutions over the period caused private prosecutions to supplant public ones, leading to a more repressive government campaign against offenders.

The use of local judicial records to provide insights into the criminal justice system and the larger society is also the focus of Maria Boes' study of the treatment of women in Frankfurt am Main in the early modern era. A small, but politically important imperial city, Frankfurt experienced a structural economic change from agriculture to commerce and manufacturing, and an accompanying transformation of its social structure, from the mid-sixteenth to the late seventeenth centuries. In contrast to medieval

Nuremberg, criminal justice fell largely on the heads of the poor and impoverished, and women were used in crime reporting, bringing accusations, and as expert witnesses. Moreover, as accused, they faced judicial torture and corporal punishment without the alternative of fines, and had little protection when their husbands were convicted as culprits. Therefore, women remained disadvantaged members of this economically progressive community. The similar status of women and children in England is apparent from Roget Swift's review of a recent work on criminal justice in Victorian Kent.

The purpose of law, as Bernard Porter writes (p. 252), could be seen as imposing a simplistic order on what is otherwise a complex and disordered reality. It is in this vein that the better research and writing in criminal justice history explores the nuances and complexities rather than following the more traditional path of singular explanations. As Clive Emsley reminds us in his review essay of recent books on police history, in our modern society the police function is becoming blurred with the military, and the people who are rounded up are not always the dregs. The increasing discovery and availability of police records may allow us, as Robert Storch writes, to see the police from within their own perspective. Such records might also assist us in discovering why legislation against "vice,"as Mark Clapson notes, often fails. This bottom-up approach must also infuse, as Christopher Harding emphasizes, the history of prisons by giving more attention to the prisoners themselves. The law is created for people, and as David Garland states in his most recent book reviewed here, punishment not only just happens to offenders, but it forms and deforms (as James Sharpe puts it) our social and political outlook as well as reflecting our changing sensibilities.

CRIMINAL JUSTICE HISTORY

German Crime in the Later Middle Ages: A Statistical Analysis of the Nuremberg Outlawry Books, 1285–1400

Martin K. Schüssler
Birkenfeld, Germany

This chapter is a study of crime in Nuremberg between the end of the thirteenth century and 1400. The data on which it is based are derived from *Acht-, Verbots- und Fehdebücher Nürnbergs von 1285–1400*, published by Werner Schultheiss in 1960. The chapter will focus on what types of crime were committed in this important German city during the later Middle Ages, how Nuremberg's crime rate compared to those of other medieval areas, the origins and class background of criminals, and how the repression of crime and the punishment of criminals were organized.

Statistical research into medieval legal records is often difficult. Such investigations into German legal records have been few in number; most were carried out more than a century ago.[1] More recently, only half-hearted efforts have been made in this field by German scholars.[2] In the last twenty years, however, English and American scholars, following the example of Marvin E. Wolfgang, who in the 1950s conducted a quantitative study of Philadelphia criminal records,[3] have used the so-called statistical approach to the study of medieval records.[4] Among scholars of the Anglo-Saxon world the "statistical approach" has come to be seen in a positive light, while the older "impressionistic approach," in which opinions of the records were based only on a scholar's subjective "impressions," has come to be viewed negatively.[5]

In earlier work I conducted some quantitative investigations in English legal records of the thirteenth and fourteenth centuries.[6] Based on this experience, I have come to believe that such methods can also be used in examining German records. Since other European legal records have shown themselves suitable for quantitative investigation, German records should be no exception.[7] European records, however, represent different legal systems, and are not exactly comparable. England, for example, experienced an early centralization of judicial activity. From the time of Henry II, crown justice comprised prosecuting felons.[8] But such centralization of judicial activity never took place in the German Empire. In England, there are coroners' rolls and rolls of the justices in eyre, prepared by royal civil servants and containing all those criminal cases the scribes who drew up the documents were aware of. With their aid, it is possible to estimate fairly accurately England's homicide rate in the later Middle Ages.[9]

By way of contrast, the German records—books of outlawry, of prohibitions, and of feuds—are not as complete. They do not contain all the crimes known to the police authorities, nor do they record all criminals tried in court. Instead, they primarily contain records of felons who were expelled, outlawed, or required to abjure the realm, and some other indications of punishment.[10] Therefore, it is impossible to calculate crime rates or conviction rates for thirteenth- and fourteenth-century Nuremberg. Finally, these German records are not very informative. We cannot learn as much about the details of criminal deeds from them as we can from the rolls of the English coroners and justices in eyre. The German outlawry books, however, record not only felonies, as do the coroners' and the eyre rolls, but also simple transgressions. Thus for certain purposes the German records are more illuminating than the English ones.

This study is based on the premise that the Nuremberg outlawry books, although deficient in some regards, are suitable for a quantitative investigation. They make it possible for the medieval criminologist to form a picture of crime in later medieval Germany, and to compare this picture to what is known from other countries during the same period. The reader should be aware that, in categorizing this data, "political crimes" are defined to include not only political revolutions, but also trade unionism and refusal to accept the verdict of a court.[11] The category of "religious crimes" includes not only heresy and witchcraft, but also perjury.

CRIME RATES

Since crime rates are commonly expressed in the form of *x* number of crimes per 100,000 population per year, the first step in calculating a crime rate is to determine the population of the region under study. In the period in question, Nuremberg had a population of approximately 20,000. This figure fluctuated over time, depending on such things as the famines of the early fourteenth century and the pestilence of 1348.[12] The latter may have caused the population to decrease in size, although after 1350 the city's population may have grown.[13] These fluctuations cannot be precisely calculated, so it is assumed that the population of Nuremberg averaged 20,000 throughout the fourteenth century.

Even a cursory survey of the sources reveals that an overall crime rate for Nuremberg cannot be calculated. The number of crimes recorded every year was generally small, ranging between one and sixty-seven.[14] But these are only *recorded* crimes. In a populous medieval city like Nuremberg, there were surely hundreds of crimes committed. But the Nuremberg outlawry books record only those crimes for which felons were expelled from the city. There were many other felons who were not expelled by the city authorities, but were either executed or punished in some other way. Therefore, one can estimate *minimum* rates for certain types of crime, but not the overall crime rate. And, given the fact that we must assume a stable population, we cannot determine whether the crime rate increased or declined between 1285 and 1400.[15]

Of the crimes recorded in the *Achtbücher*, homicide is the best documented. The figures are as follows: in the years 1292–97, 30 homicide cases were recorded, or 5 per annum. This would indicate that the minimum homicide rate for Nuremberg during this period was 25/100,000. Similar numbers of homicides are recorded in 1310, 1316, 1319, 1320, 1333, 1382, and 1384. In 1391, 8 homicides were recorded; in 1392, 13. The homicide rates would thus have been 40 and 65/100,000. The years just mentioned appear to be those for which crime in general is best documented.[16] The Nuremberg homicide rates thus ranged between 20 and 65/100,000, with the higher number probably being a more accurate reflection of the real homicide rate.

Comparing these rates with data from other regions reveals the following. An analysis of Buff's Augsburg data[17] reveals homicide rates of from 50 to 70/100,000 for the years 1352–68. Frauenstädt,[18] Kriegk,[19] and Demandt[20] have found similar patterns, although their figures are not very exact. English homicide rates have been found to range between 7 and 28/100,000 in rural areas, and up to 110/100,000 in urban areas.[21] Data from the south of France are very inaccurately recorded; hence it is impossible to calculate crime rates for this region. But the rolls of the *Registre criminel du Châtelet de Paris* give us enough material with which to calculate a homicide rate of 8/100,000 for the areas of Paris under royal jurisdiction at the end of the fourteenth century. As in the case of Nuremberg, this figure should be treated as a minimum rate.[22]

Several scholars have investigated Italian criminal records. Their work reveals homicide rates in Florence of 152/100,000 in 1352–55. In 1382–85, after the introduction of a reformed police and judicial system, the homicide rate was 68/100,000.[23] In Bologna between 1281 and 1290, 58 homicides were recorded, an average of about 6 a year, which would give a rate of 18/100,000.[24] Finally, in Venice the homicide rate appears to have been 9/100,000, which once again should be regarded as a minimum rate.[25]

If these rates are compared with those from Nuremberg, where the homicide rate ranged from 20 to 65/100,000, it appears that Nuremberg's homicide rate was close to the mean of all recorded European ones. Nuremberg never equaled Florence's rate of 152/100,000, the highest recorded (outdistancing even the high rate of 110/100,000 in Oxford); but its rate also never fell as low as the rate recorded in Paris. Nuremberg seems to fall right in the middle of the range of recorded homicide rates. Six to twenty cases of assault and violence were registered every year in Nuremberg,[26] giving an assault rate of 30 to 100 cases per 100,000 population per annum. By way of comparison, Buff finds a rate of approximately 35 recorded cases per 100,000 in Augsburg.[27] In Bologna, 30 cases of assault were recorded in the period between January and March 1319,[28] an annual rate of 350 recorded cases per 100,000 population. In the period between 1281 and 1290, however, only 99 cases of violence were recorded for an average of 10 a year, or 30/100,000. Compared with these rates, that of Nuremberg does not appear too high.[29]

In regard to property crimes (here defined as robbery, burglary, larceny, and receiving of stolen goods), the data in Nuremberg seem completely recorded only for the years 1381–84 and 1391–92. The number of cases recorded annually ranges from 4 to 27, a rate of 20 to 135/100,000.[30] In Augsburg, the rate of property crimes for the period 1369–79 was about 40/100,000.[31]

Of the 107 cases in the *Registre criminel du Chatêlet de Paris*, 61 crimes were against property. Since the record covers a period of only 19 months, there was an average of approximately 40 a year at a time when the population of the city of Paris was around 100,000.[32] In Bologna in 1281–90, there were 48 accusations of larceny for a rate of 15/100,000. In the first 3 months of 1319, however, 4 cases of theft and robbery were recorded, which produced a rate of 35 cases per 100,000.[33] In Venice in the period 1360–69, when the city's population was about 100,000, 60 thieves or robbers were tried for an average of 6 a year.[34] Once again, when these figures are compared to those from Nuremberg, the rate of property crime in Nuremberg was about average for later medieval Europe as a whole.[35]

If we compare the data from medieval Nuremberg to modern figures, the following is found. In 1984 in the Federal Republic of Germany, there were 2,722 homicides (involving 2,959 murderers) for an annual homicide rate of 4.4/100,000.[36] In Nuremberg in 1988 there were 70 homicide cases for an annual rate of 14.7/100,000.[37] Thus, the homicide rate in Nuremberg in the later Middle Ages appears to have been much higher than that in the late twentieth century. We might assume that all other types of crime were committed much more frequently in the Middle Ages than today, as contemporary Germany does not have a particularly high crime rate. The industrialized country with the highest crime rate is the United States, while the United Kingdom has lower rates.[38] In the medieval, as in the modern period, Germany thus appears to have had rates of crime that were about average for Europe as a whole, and Nuremberg had crime rates that were typical of cities in western Europe.

TYPES OF CRIME

This section discusses the relative proportion of different types of crime. The source for this section is the Nuremberg *Achtbücher*. The reader should note that, in calculating the following figures, only those crimes whose nature is clearly specified have been counted. Crimes whose nature is not specified in the records have been omitted from the following figures. The Nuremberg records contain a total of 704 cases.[39] Of these 704 cases, 148 were homicides (c. 21%), 110 assaults (c. 16%), 173 property crimes (c. 25%),[40] and 52 frauds (7.5%).[41] Arson accounted for less than one percent of the total, while political crimes made up fifteen percent, Religious crimes 5.5 percent, sexual offenses six percent, and miscellaneous (labeled as "other") four percent.[42]

In the criminal records of Augsburg for 1338–69, Buff has found 169 homicide cases, 120 assaults, but only 88 property crimes.[43] Demandt unfortunately did not collect any statistical evidence concerning the prevalence of different crimes.[44]

Bellamy's investigation of crime in five English counties in the fourteenth and fifteenth centuries found that about one-quarter of all recorded felonies were homicides,[45] while about half were property crimes.[46] Hanawalt, using records for eight English counties in the period from 1300 to 1348, found that larceny made up thirty-nine percent of all recorded crimes, burglary twenty-four percent, homicide ten percent, and robbery ten percent.[47] Pugh's investigations revealed that two percent of those detained in Newgate gaol had committed fraud, thirty-four percent larceny, twenty-two percent homicide, and six percent had received felons. Rape and arson were very rare.[48] In the Lincolnshire eyre rolls, Langbein found that twenty-five percent of the offenses listed were homicides and twenty percent were robberies.[49] The DeWindts discovered that twenty-five percent of all cases in the Huntingdonshire eyre roll involved homicide, and about fifty percent were crimes against property.[50]

In Venice, homicides, robberies, and larcenies seem to have accounted for the majority of crimes.[51] In Bologna, the percentage of homicides and assaults was larger than that of property crimes.[52] In Florence, the number of homicides and crimes against property was almost equal.[53] And of the cases recorded in the *Registre criminel du Châtelet de Paris*, twenty percent were homicides, fifty-seven percent crimes against property, and twenty-three percent crimes against public order.[54]

Thus it seems that in western Europe as a whole about one-quarter of all felonies recorded were homicides, and approximately half were crimes against property. True, the pattern in Nuremberg, Augsburg, and the northern Italian communes differs, with the recorded number of crimes against property making up a smaller proportion of all recorded crime. But it is possible that some of this difference may be accounted for by the fact that thieves were not outlawed, but punished in a different fashion, perhaps being executed; thus they would not be recorded in the outlawry books. On the other hand, it appears that capital punishment was only rarely imposed on murderers. One might also speculate that thieves were generally members of the lower classes, whereas murderers were "good burghers," members of the upper or middle classes, and who, it was felt, should receive lighter sentences. In regard to other types of crime, the pattern in Nuremberg seems remarkably similar to that common in the other areas. In conclusion, it appears that the pattern of crime in Nuremberg, in the medieval period as in the modern, was not very different from that typical of western Europe as a whole.[55]

TYPES OF CRIMINAL BEHAVIOR

The evidence in the Nuremberg *Achtbücher* makes it clear that in all types of crime the great majority of felons acted alone, without any accomplices. This was especially so in the case of homicides and assaults. It was less so in the case of robbery, for the obvious reason that a single felon could seldom successfully stop and rob a guarded convoy of merchants' wagons. In cases of burglary, larceny, the receiving of stolen goods, gambling, and fraud, however, individual action was common, as it was in the case of religious crimes, sexual offenses, and the categories labeled "other" and "unspecified" crimes. Collective action was more common in cases of arson and political crime.[56] Those criminal associations that did exist were not very large, only occasionally having more than four people. Only gangs of robbers were differently organized.[57]

In the records of homicide and assault cases, one does not find mention of professional criminals. However, thirty professional criminals are recorded in the robbery cases.[58] No professional criminals are mentioned in the burglary and larceny cases. One professional criminal is mentioned as receiving stolen goods[59] ten are mentioned in gambling cases but none are found in fraud or arson cases,[60] or connected with political or religious crimes. But several professional criminals committed sexual offenses, among them panderers, procurers, and prostitutes.[61] In total, forty-one professional criminals appear in the sources. Like the "amateur" felons, they either acted alone or with only a few accomplices.[62] Large gangs are mentioned only in connection with cases of robbery; and it was only in such cases that felons were named as having committed more than one crime.[63] Criminals probably recruited accomplices among people whom they could trust, such as close relatives. In eleven of the homicide cases and in seventeen of the robbery ones, the perpetrators were related. In cases involving larceny, receiving of stolen goods, fraud, and arson, it was rare for groups of accomplices to act together. But groups of relatives acting together frequently committed political and religious crimes, as well as crimes the nature of which is not exactly specified.[64]

In the cases involving homicide, larceny, gambling, fraud, arson, political and sexual offenses, and unspecified offenses, groups of accomplices often included people who had originally come from the same settlement outside Nuremberg.[65] Groups of criminals on occasion included masters and servants, husbands and wives, fellow guild members, and acquaintances and friends.[66] Unlike the modern pattern of criminal behavior, relatives and friends committed crimes together, rather than committing them against one another. Criminals and victims were rarely related to or acquainted with one another. The only exception to this pattern was the case of quarrels between spouses, which could lead to violence and even homicide. But of this last category of crime, there are only seven cases recorded in the Nuremberg outlawry books.[67] Members of the same guild, or masters and servants, also committed relatively few crimes against each other; indeed, guild members mainly committed crimes against one another only if they were members of rival guilds, in incidents counted as political crimes. Three sexual offenses involving a master and a servant were also recorded.[68]

Bellamy, Given, and Hanawalt agree[69] that in England in the thirteenth and fourteenth centuries the typical criminal acted alone. If felons had accomplices, these were often relatives or acquaintances. Cooperation among family members in committing crime was common. One can even speak of "family gangs," in which fathers were ordinarily, but not exclusively, the leaders. In later medieval England, the proportion of all criminals who can be classified as "professional" was less than twenty-five percent. Many professional criminals were members of gangs, which frequently included in their ranks members of the gentry or nobility. Even clerics were often members of such gangs.[70]

The pattern of crime in northern France seems to have been very similar. Most criminals were amateurs, professionals being only a minority of all felons; most crimes were committed by men acting alone, and gangs organized around family ties were common.[71] Such "family gangs" were even more common in the cities of northern Italy. Obviously, the amateur criminal acting alone could, in the case of partial skirmishes or crimes of revenge, expect support from the family.[72]

The pattern of crime in Nuremberg, therefore, appears to have been typical of later medieval western Europe as a whole, with most crimes being committed by amateurs acting alone, occasionally united in gangs that were often organized around familial ties. In Nuremberg there seem to have been fewer "family gangs," especially in comparison to northern Italy. The percentage of professional criminals seems to have been below that of England and the other areas studied, where it hovered around twenty to twenty-five percent. This pattern, however, may be an artifact of the way in which the Nuremberg *Achtbücher* were composed; professional gangsters were probably more likely to be executed than "good burghers," and thus are not mentioned in the records.[73] Even if we take this factor into consideration, it can be argued that the pattern of criminal behavior in Nuremberg was very similar to that found elsewhere in western Europe in the later Middle Ages.

ORIGIN AND SOCIAL BACKGROUND OF CRIMINALS AND THEIR VICTIMS

Criminals

Most felons recorded in the Nuremberg *Achtbücher* were inhabitants of the city, as shown in Appendix 4. The city's inhabitants perpetuated 173 of 243 homicides, 99 of 141 assaults, 51 of 69 larcenies, 275 of 338 religious offenses, 43 of 69 sexual offenses, 49 of 58 "other" crimes, and 509 of 916 unspecified crimes. Moreover, the majority of professional criminals (159 of 203) were inhabitants of Nuremberg.[74] Thus it appears that the policy followed by the city council of expelling from the city outsiders who had committed crimes, a policy adopted in other cities such as Augsburg,[75] was not an effective means of restraining criminality. Only a small percentage of the criminals active within the city, about one-third of the total, could be neutralized in this fashion.[76]

There were some exceptions to this pattern of criminality. Most robbers, for example, were not inhabitants of Nuremberg. Only eleven were local people, the other 425 originating elsewhere.[77] An explanation for this phenomenon may lie in the fact that most robbers were noblemen and their henchmen—inhabitants of the Franconian region, but not citizens of Nuremberg, who were waging feuds against the city.[78] In the case of burglary, the two recorded felons were not native to the city, which suggests that burglars who were inhabitants of the city were punished in some fashion other than by expulsion, and hence were not mentioned in the records.[79] Most gamblers, perpetrators of fraud, and coiners of false money were not natives of the city. Most of these may have been itinerant professional criminals, but the evidence is inconclusive.[80] The fact that a majority of those who committed political crimes were not citizens of Nuremberg may be explained either by the fact that during periods of feuds or wars Nuremberg's enemies were usually outsiders, or by the fact that the city's internal enemies were noncitizen revolutionaries who, having been denied citizenship by the city council, were trying to acquire it by means of force.[81] In general, it appears that more than two-thirds of the criminals recorded in the outlawry books were natives of the city of Nuremberg.

Similarly, Buff found that in Augsburg outsiders only rarely engaged in criminal activity,[82] a pattern that Demandt also found in Eschwege in Hessia.[83] But Bellamy, Morris, and Rye all believe that the "outsider criminal" was the most common type of felon in later medieval England; in most cases felons did not originate in the areas where they committed their crimes but were often vagrants.[84] They base their conclusions, however, not on statistical analysis of the records, but on an impressionistic "reading" of the sources. It is therefore not surprising that Hanawalt, basing her opinion on statistical analysis, found that about eighty percent of all criminals lived in the area where they committed their crimes, and that strangers are infrequently recorded as felons.[85]

Coopland and Lavoie[86] argue that in late fourteenth-century Paris most criminals were outsiders. Geremek,[87] however, on the basis of quantitative investigation rather than an impressionistic survey of the records, came to the opposite conclusion, a position also supported by the work of Lanhers.[88] The same conclusion as to the relative frequency of "outsider-criminals" emerges from the Italian material.[89] Therefore, it seems that throughout western Europe crimes were committed primarily by felons who either lived in, or originated not very far from, the places where they committed their offenses. This pattern also seems to be characteristic of modern crime. In Nuremberg in 1988, the percentage of outsiders who committed either homicide, robbery, or larceny was about forty percent.[90]

Victims

Inhabitants of Nuremberg also made up the majority of all victims recorded in the *Achtbücher*. As documented in Appendix 4, inhabitants of Nuremberg comprised 124 of 140 homicides, 59 of 65 assaults, 164 of 197 robberies, and 51 of 69 unspecified and "other" crimes.[91] It should be remembered that, since the purpose of the *Achtbücher* was to record the names of those who were denied entry to the city, the clerks who composed them were primarily interested in recording the names of people who had been outlawed or expelled. Therefore, they were not particularly interested in the names of victims and only rarely recorded them. But from those victims' names that are recorded, eighty percent were citizens of Nuremberg, and this is an accurate indication of the overall pattern of victimization in the city. The pattern of victimization is also similar to that which emerges from English legal records.[92]

Sex of Criminals and Victims

The Nuremberg *Achtbücher* indicate that men made up the majority of both criminals and victims. In almost all types of crimes women were mentioned as either victims or perpetrators in less than five percent of the cases. In only a few types was their percentage higher, as in larceny cases where women made up about a third of the total. Indeed, in the cases of receiving stolen goods women outnumbered men (although since so few cases of this type are recorded, not too much weight should be given to this figure). In the religious and political crimes women also made up about a third of the total. Only in the cases of sex crimes did women victims outnumber male victims; one, therefore, must assume that most of these cases must be incidents of rape.[93] Only three children are recorded as victims, two being homicide victims and one the victim of a sexual assault. No children are recorded as having committed crimes. Modern data also reveal a striking difference in the rates of involvement of men and women. In Nuremberg in 1988, with the exception of sex crimes, fewer women than men were victims of all types of crime.[94] Similarly, male offenders outnumbered female offenders, by a figure of 24,887 to 7,935. In larceny cases, women accounted for 37.3 percent of the offenders. Of the recorded offenders, 24,887 were adults, and 7,357 were juveniles. It thus appears that most crimes were committed by men in both medieval and modern Nuremberg. One normally attributes the preponderance of male criminals in the Middle Ages to the patriarchal social conditions that then prevailed, but it is nevertheless striking that males made up the majority of criminals in both the medieval and the modern eras.

Buff found that the percentage of women committing crimes in Augsburg was also low.[95] In England women were also only rarely criminals or victims of crime. The percentage of female criminals and victims seems usually to have been around ten percent with some variation depending on the type of crime and the region under study. In some areas up to eighteen percent of victims of homicides were women, while in others, such as the town of Oxford, all victims were male. Poor women were more likely to commit crimes than rich ones. Professional gangs had female members, but these usually carried out only menial tasks. The female domain was primarily that of the nonviolent crime, such as larceny or fraud. A striking observation is the fact that in medieval England one-third of those named as receiving felons were female. Obviously, it was regarded as a duty of the mistress of the house to hide a relative or friend who was pursued by royal justice. Despite this, it is clear that women were only rarely perpetrators or victims of crime in medieval England.[96] The same observation seems to apply generally to all of western Europe, medieval and modern.

Noble and Clerical Criminals

Offenders of noble or clerical background are only rarely recorded in the Nuremberg outlawry books; victims of this social background are even rarer. Only in the case of robbery were noble offenders common, making up more than a third of recorded offenders (149 out of 436). Clerics seem to have been more active in committing robbery than other crimes, with four offenders in this category listed in the records.[97] In the case of political crimes, nobles were registered as offenders in about a third of the cases, apparently as a result of the fact that noblemen often waged feuds against the city. Otherwise, noblemen and clerics seldom appear in the records either as perpetrators or as victims.[98]

City patricians were seldom recorded as perpetrators of crime, making up only 1.8 percent of the total. They were much more frequently recorded as victims, accounting for 12.4 percent, a rather high figure. It should be remembered, however, that the clerks who composed the documents only rarely mentioned victims. And it is possible that they were ordered to record every patrician who was a victim of a crime, perhaps as a way of justifying the policy of expelling "outsider-criminals" in the face of criticism of this policy by other cities or the emperor.[99] Fifty-nine patrician felons were recorded in some fifty-one cases, seven of whom were women, and all but one of sixty-six patrician victims were male.[100] Seven of the patrician criminals committed homicide, twelve were involved in political offenses, four in assault, three in robbery, six in religious offenses. Patricians were also seldom listed as victims except in robberies, where fifty-five were the victims chiefly through their convoys being waylaid outside the city limits. In five of these cases patricians were captured and held for ransom. Apart from a few homicides, assaults, and larcenies, members of this class were recorded as victims in no other types of crime.[101]

A striking observation is the fact that, whereas most patrician families are seldom mentioned in the records, a few families figure frequently with their members listed as either perpetrators or victims. Members of the Beheim and Gostenhofer families are listed in the outlawry books as criminals six times, members of the Heiden family seven, and members of the Imhof family three. No other family is mentioned more than once or twice. As victims the Beheims are mentioned three times, the Imhofs five, the Maurers, Männleins, and Rummels four times each, and the Stromeyers five. No other patrician family is mentioned more than twice.[102] We can thus conclude that Nuremberg patricians were infrequently involved in crime, either as perpetrators or victims. They were occasionally the victims of robbery. As criminals, they typically engaged in violent crimes. Some families seem to have had a greater disposition to violent crime than others. Because of their wealth and their trading activity, some families were more frequently the victims of crime.

Sterns discovered that in the Order of the Teutonic Knights, a definitely noble organization, criminal behavior was not unknown.[103] Buff found that Augsburg patricians and nobles from the city's immediate hinterland were seldom recorded as criminals or victims, the same observation applying to clerics. Here the city's middle class figured most often as criminals or victims.[104] Demandt's investigation of Eschwege records established that, in contrast to the middle classes, the city's upper classes appeared infrequently in the records. Here also some families displayed a greater propensity to engage in crime than others.[105]

In thirteenth- and fourteenth-century England, criminous clerics were very common, accounting for fifteen to twenty percent of those recorded as criminals, a figure that far exceeded their proportion in the population as a whole.[106] Towns with an uncommonly high number of clerics, such as Oxford, experienced extremely high crime rates. With the exception of Hammer, most scholars agree that in later medieval England clerks committed crimes more frequently than other groups in the population.[107] They often used their special knowledge of reading and writing to engage in fraud; but there were also gangs of monks that specialized in robbery and the holding of captives for ransom. It is clear that the criminal behavior of clerics was not limited to the less violent crimes, an observation supported by the town of Oxford's high homicide rate.

The English gentry and nobility were only infrequently mentioned as engaging in criminal acts. It is possible, however, that they engaged in criminal behavior more frequently than the records indicate. Their acts, which, if done by others, might have been prosecuted as felonies, may have been regarded as legitimate exercises of the right of self-help. The fact that they committed few crimes may thus be due to the fact that they did not have to do so for economic reasons, and because their acts, no matter what they were, were often regarded as legitimate.[108]

Coopland and Lavoie argued that in late fourteenth-century Paris criminals tended to be either very poor or of noble or clerical origin.[109] But Geremek demonstrated that this conclusion was the result of an impressionistic reading of the sources. A statistical analysis indicated that in most cases criminals came from the middle classes.[110] Lanhers's work supports Geremek's conclusions.[111] Those who have investigated the Italian archives have also concluded that the very poor and the very rich, vagrants on the one hand and *nobili* on the other, predominated among the ranks of criminals. It is possible that these conclusions, based on largely impressionistic surveys of the evidence, may be misleading.[112] To conclude, it appears that throughout western Europe clerics and nobles were rare among the ranks of criminals, with the notable exception of the clergy of England.

Occupations of Criminals and Victims

In the Nuremberg records one frequently finds mentioned as criminals grocers, dyers, weavers, tailors, cobblers, metalworkers, scribes, millers, bathkeepers, butchers, bakers, innkeepers, and servants. All the crafts typical of Nuremberg in the later Middle Ages are well represented among those recorded as criminals.[113] There appears to have been no specialization by crafts in particular types of criminal behavior. This can be seen clearly in the case of the cobblers, smiths, butchers, and bakers. The latter two crafts seem to have been especially prone to crime.[114] Those who committed crimes were usually apprentices or journeymen; only rarely were they masters or shop owners. The only employers who appeared in the records as criminals were merchants and traders. Interestingly, urban civil servants frequently appeared as criminals, especially in cases of assault.[115] One town officer even became a professional criminal. Perhaps this pattern can be explained by the fact that town employees often found it necessary to resort to violence in carrying out their duties.

The city's Jews were never named as criminals in cases involving violence. Rather they appeared in cases involving sex offenses and crimes of an unspecified nature. One might suspect that many of the accusations against them were false. On the other hand, they were frequently named as victims of violent crimes.[116] It thus appears that the citizens and employees of the city sought to find reasons to expel Jews from the city or to coerce them to leave; the city council, however, seems to have protected Jews more often than it prosecuted them.[117] Jews, however, were more frequently victims rather than perpetrators in felony cases.

In general, wealthy victims, merchants, and estate owners, as well as their servants, appear in cases of robbery. Not surprisingly, civil servants were frequently the victims of political crimes. In the case of homicide, it does not seem that a single social class or craft group was especially likely to produce victims. Although the fact that the outlawry books are concerned with listing offenders, and only rarely list victims, all classes of the population were likely to be victims of violent crimes, while only the rich were victims of property crimes.[118] In Augsburg, Buff found that bakers, butchers, bath-keepers, and tailors were frequently mentioned as criminals. This is the same pattern found in Nuremberg.[119] Demandt also mentions craftsmen such as smiths, butchers, millers, and carpenters as criminals in Eschwege.[120]

Given's investigation of English legal records found that, of those criminals whose occupations are known, most were craftsmen.[121] The next largest groups were composed of servants, who in most cases committed their crimes on their masters' orders, and civil servants, whose homicides were committed in the course of carrying out their official duties. Hanawalt argues that the majority of English felons were recruited among the upper and middle levels of village society, while in the towns felons were often craftsmen and servants.[122] Hammer found that in the town of Oxford many criminals were students and scholars as well as servants.[123] While Given has found that the majority of English victims were craftsmen—bakers, butchers, weavers, and smiths—and servants,[124] Hanawalt has found a similar pattern in fourteenth-century England,[125] as has Geremek in Paris.[126]

Summary

Quantitative investigations of medieval legal records indicate that all over western Europe the social backgrounds of criminals and victims were quite similar. Crimes were committed by local people who were often members

68. Richtſtätte mit Rad und Galgen.

Fakſimile eines Holzſchnittes von Hans Burgkmaier im „Theuerdank“.

Execution site. From a woodcut by Burgkmaier, early sixteenth century.

79. Raubritter überfallen ein Dorf.
Nach dem „Mittelalterl. Hausbuch", Bilderhandschrift aus dem Ende des 15. Jahrhunderts.

Robber knights attacking a village. From a woodcut, late fifteenth century.

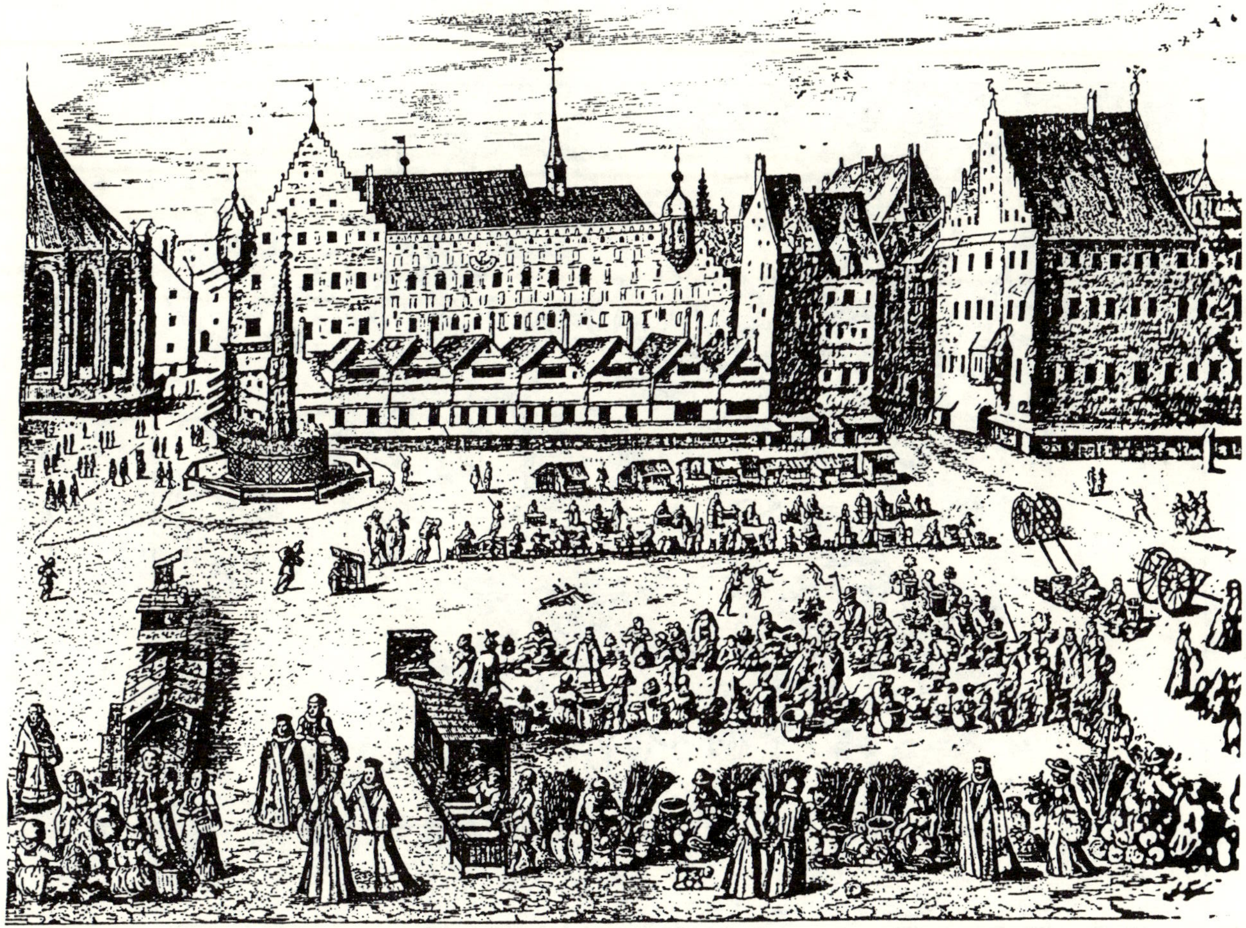

Nuremberg market square and city hall (background center). From a woodcut by Lorenz Strauch, 1599.

Nuremberg market square and St. Sebaldus' Church (background right). From a woodcut by Lorenz Strauch, 1599.

Nuremberg market square and Our Lady's Church. From a woodcut by Lorenz Strauch, 1599.

of the middle classes; victims were also local people, frequently from the middle classes. Men comprised the majority of both criminals and victims. With the remarkable exception of English clerics, the ecclesiastics, nobles, knights, and urban patricians were seldom mentioned as either criminals or victims. The occupations of criminals and victims seem to have been similar everywhere, not merely in German cities, but throughout western Europe as a whole. Thus the social origins and background of criminals in Nuremberg seem quite similar to that found elsewhere.

CAUSES AND MOTIVES OF CRIMINAL BEHAVIOR

Since the Nuremberg clerks of the later Middle Ages did not think it important to record motives for criminal behavior, there is only a limited number of cases where a possible motive is indicated.

In homicide cases the records indicate only three kinds of motivation: gain (i.e., the illegal appropriation of goods, as in robbery), arguments of an unspecified nature, and, in one instance, sexual desire. Arguments and desire for gain are thus the two principal motives recorded for murder.[127]

In assault cases a greater variety of motives is recorded. In these instances gain is only a minor motivation. Arguments are once again an important factor, but political motivations, intra-familial arguments, and jealousy are also present. In one case prejudice against Jews also figured. In many cases the scribes could not discern any concrete motivation for violent behavior, making such notations as "crime committed without any cause"; at times they attributed crimes to the "bad reputation of the criminal."[128] Gain, of course, figured as an important motive for robbery. Here the objects taken were not so much cash as trade goods and cattle. People were also abducted and held for ransom. It appears that crime often paid in the vicinity of Nuremberg; but within the city itself such crimes were only infrequently committed.[129]

Larceny was also committed for gain. But in these instances the value of stolen goods was much lower than in the robbery cases. In five instances only money was stolen; in all the other cases various trade goods like cloth and dresses were taken. The value of the objects stolen in larceny cases was quite low compared to those in robbery;[130] the two cases of the receipt of stolen goods in which the value of the stolen objects is recorded also reveal that the value of the goods involved was lower than in those of robbery.[131] In the arson cases, which are very few in number, the motives listed included arguments in general and intrafamilial quarrels.[132] It thus appears that the primary motive for arson was revenge.

The motives for political crimes were not merely "political," that is, a desire to change the government through violent revolution. Frequently political crimes grew out of disagreements between citizens or between the city and neighboring nobles, disagreements that resulted in feuds. Several other motives are also listed—such as gain,[133] racial hatred, trade union activity, resistance to judicial decisions, and the "bad reputation" of the criminal. The dominant motives in these cases seem to have been arguments in general, political machinations, and resistance to judicial decisions.[134]

Among the motives for religious crime, is not only religious zeal, which was the main motive, but also the desire for gain and political reasons.[135] In the sex offense cases, two motives were recorded: sexual desire in cases of ravishment and rape, and gain in cases of procuring or prostitution.[136] In other types of criminal behavior the main motives given were gain and arguments in general.[137] But there are also alcohol abuse and the bearing of arms. Indeed, among the punishments handed out are frequent injunctions forbidding the visiting of inns or the bearing of arms.[138]

In general, it appears that the most frequent motive listed for all crimes recorded in the Nuremberg outlawry books was gain, followed by arguments in general. Gain, however, was quite clearly the dominant motive, even, surprisingly enough, in such categories of crime as homicide and political offenses. Alcohol abuse and the bearing of arms, while they may have worsened the crime situation in medieval Nuremberg, were not important causes in themselves of criminal behavior. Buff has argued that in Augsburg the principal cause of criminal activity was the abuse of alcohol, as well as the bearing of arms in a society prone to belligerence. But Buff also thought that the desire for gain was at work. He also felt that changes in the price of food could have caused changes in the crime rate, especially among the vagrant population.[139] Demandt believed that in Eschwege crimes were caused mainly by arguments, but with gain figuring as a motive in cases of larceny, robbery, and infringements of trade regulations. Alcohol abuse also seems to have been a factor, since inns were frequently mentioned in connection with crime. Finally, guild strife seems also to have been a motivating force.[140] Frauenstädt believed that the bearing of arms and abuse of alcohol must have caused many crimes.[141] Kriegk was of the opinion that the generally belligerent nature of society was the cause of many crimes, with desire for gain being the major, specific motivating factor.[142] Bellamy and Rye felt that most crimes in the later Middle Ages were not the result of premeditation, but grew out of sudden quarrels, with the practice of bearing arms leading to violence.[143] Given felt that alcohol abuse played a major role in turning arguments violent.[144] Hanawalt argues that in two-thirds of the homicide cases she examined arguments were the principal cause; intrafamilial quarrels, however, were rare. In ten percent of her homicide cases revenge was the motive, in twenty percent robbery. Alcohol abuse was a factor in only five percent.[145] Gain often figured as the direct motive for a crime, or as a motive for a quarrel that resulted in a crime. Hanawalt also found that during periods of famine there was a general increase in crime in England. During these periods the majority of criminals came not from the lower classes, but from the middle and upper orders, the same classes that committed most crimes during nonfamine periods. But even during famine periods the percentage of thefts that involved food was no higher than in normal years.[146]

Crimes of passion seem to have been rare in England. Economic considerations seem to have been paramount.[147] Pugh found that half of those prisoners awaiting trial at the end of the thirteenth century in Newgate faced accusations of robbery or larceny.[148] Hanawalt felt that the value of goods involved in cases of theft and robbery was not especially high. The most common object of theft was cloth, followed by small articles of value, food, and cattle. Money was only occasionally stolen. The value of seventy percent of those objects stolen was less than 10s.[149] Chojnacki speculated that in later medieval Venice motivations such as jealousy or revenge were common. Therefore, one finds more intrafamilial homicides than in the northern countries. Arguments over money often led to homicides, which Chojnacki believed to be typical of the belligerent social conditions of the age.[150]

Lanhers and Geremek have found similar patterns in northern France. Homicides prompted by strong emotional states, such as those produced during arguments or arising out of desire for revenge, were common. As for more deliberate motives, these, when they can be established, seem mostly economic in nature; but once again the objects desired seem to be of little value. In property crimes the objects stolen were usually cattle and small articles of value, only rarely money.[151] Lavoie and Grava think that in the south of France the chief motives for crime were poverty, the belligerence of society, hate, and revenge.[152]

It thus appears that in Nuremberg, and throughout much of Europe, the basic causes and motives of crime were remarkably similar, with the sole exception of Italy. In Italy crimes of passion and intrafamilial crimes, relatively uncommon elsewhere, were frequent. The basic causes of crime seem not so much to have derived from the abuse of alcohol and the carrying of arms, as from the deeply rooted belief that all problems could be solved with violence. The dominant motive for crime was gain. In almost all cases where a motive is specified, it was almost invariably the desire to accumulate property.[153] And it seems that the majority of criminals were recruited not from the ranks of the poor but from the wealthier middle classes. These patterns were found throughout western Europe. In Nuremberg, the causes and motivations of crime can be seen as typical of medieval Europe as a whole.

CRIMINALS AND THEIR MODUS OPERANDI

The weapons used to commit homicides and assaults in thirteenth- and fourteenth-century Nuremberg were primarily knives. Swords and other weapons were used less commonly, probably as a result of the city's ordinances prohibiting the carrying of swords and "peaked" knives.[154] More injuries were caused by blunt instruments than by "sharp" instruments. Some blunt instruments, such as fists, wooden clubs, and similar weapons, were not recorded as weapons per se. Most wounds recorded were to the head and neck, perhaps indicating that assailants were well aware of how best to inflict injury on their victims.

In only one report of theft is there information on the modus operandi. In this case fishing-rods were used to catch birds.[155] In gambling cases the use of false dice was mentioned in five cases;[156] in cases of fraud a false weight was used once; and, of course, in counterfeiting cases false coins were disseminated.[157] Religious crimes mainly took the form of cursing and perjury; but two cases of witchcraft were also mentioned.[158]

Sexual offenses did not ordinarily consist of rape (only eight such cases are extant), but primarily took the form of procuring, deviant behavior, and intercourse with "prohibited" groups, such as Jews.[159] The other crimes mentioned were minor transgressions such as insults and defamations, as well as economic offenses, which were especially obnoxious in a mercantile center such as Nuremberg.[160]

In Augsburg Buff found that in the commission of violent crimes use was made primarily of swords and knives. Pikes were infrequently used. Arrows were also employed, but only, as in England, for stabbing victims rather than shooting them. Therefore, it is not surprising that in Augsburg there was a general prohibition of the bearing of arms, which (unlike the case in Nuremberg) extended to instruments of daily use. As in Nuremberg, rape cases in Augsburg were rare; by way of contrast, other sexual offenses were common. The production of falsified records and fake coins was frequently mentioned.[161] In Eschwege, Demandt observed many minor transgressions and petty offenses; but he also enumerated cases of counterfeiting, as well as ravishing, arguments, insults, and offenses against public order and the regulations governing trade. In violent crimes, knives and axes were the most important weapons, although the throwing of stones was also recorded.[162] In Frankfurt im Main Frauenstädt found that hoes, daggers, swords, and knives were the most commonly employed weapons.[163]

In rural England knives and axes were the commonly used weapons, making up more than fifty percent of the instruments used in violent incidents.[164] As in Nuremberg, most wounds recorded were to the head and neck, but the abdominal region was also the site of injuries. The death of victims from minor wounds that worsened from the lack of adequate treatment seems to have been very rare.[165] Knives and axes, regarded in England not as weapons but as tools of daily use, were not included in bans against the carrying of arms. Such prohibitions included only arms of war, which were usually carried only by members of the gentry or nobility. Therefore, knives and axes were used by members of the English lower classes to commit crimes.[166] In England robberies frequently took place in the forests or in the fields surrounding villages.[167] Burglaries were uncommon, but those that took place seem to have been carefully planned and executed.[168] The dominant forms of sex crimes did not include rape but other forms of deviance.[169] The pattern of crime in France[170] and Italy[171] seems to have been similar to that in Germany and England.

So once again there is a striking similarity between the modus operandi of criminals in Nuremberg and in other western European regions: Weapons were used in similar fashions in the commission of crimes virtually everywhere; governmental efforts to restrict the use of such weapons were also similar throughout Europe; and most criminals seem to have been amateurs, who acted spontaneously and opportunistically, without premeditation.

THE LOCATION OF CRIMES

Excluding robberies from consideration, most crimes in Nuremberg whose locations are recorded took place indoors. If robberies are included, however, more crimes took place outdoors.[172] Since most recorded robberies took place outside the city walls, it thus appears that most crime within the city took place indoors while that outside the city walls was primarily committed in open country.

More urban crimes were committed in Nuremberg's northern district (in the ward of St. Sebaldus) than in the city's southern district on the other side of the River Pegnitz (in the ward of St. Laurence). The area between the castle and the town hall seems to have been infested with criminal activity. There were also some other areas where crime was very common: around the Laufer Gate in the northwest and around the Hospital Gate in the southeast.[173] There were thus areas of the city more liable to criminal activity than others. The various markets and open squares were also nuclei of criminal behavior. In Nuremberg in 1988 there was much crime in the streets, with the rate even increasing for robbery, but with larceny being committed mainly indoors.[174]

In Augsburg, Buff argues that inns were often the scenes of crimes, but that crimes also took place in the streets, gardens, and bath-houses. Home burglaries were rare. In Buff's opinion the most crime-ridden part of the city was the area around the town hall, the so-called Perlachberg.[175] Demandt also concluded that in Eschwege the principal locales of crime were the streets, inns, and bath-houses (bath attendants, both male and female, seem to have had a particularly bad reputation).[176] Bellamy has argued that in England most crimes were committed in urban areas or in the forests,[177] a pattern that seems to echo that of the Nuremberg region. Hanawalt has argued that most homicides and robberies were committed outdoors, with burglaries and arson, not surprisingly, being indoor crimes. She explains the fact that most crimes took place outside by the fact that medieval men were accustomed to meet in the open air.[178] Her conclusion does not parallel mine about the location of crime in Nuremberg. Hammer, too, finds that

Sites of Criminal Activity in Nuremberg

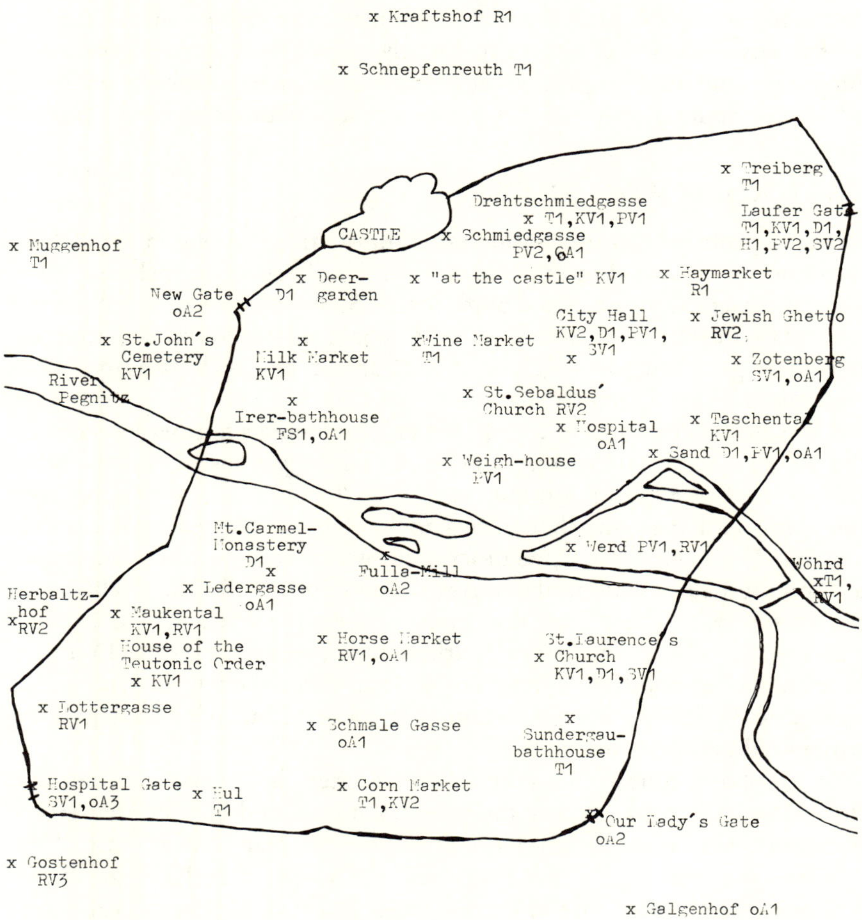

NUREMBERG CITY MAP

showing places where crimes were committed

Abbreviations as above - numbers after letters T,KV, etc. mean the number of crimes which have been committed at this place and which are known

homicides in Oxford were localized in certain precincts of the town, and occurred largely in the streets.[179] In this respect, at least, the eastern districts of the town of Oxford seem rather like the area below the castle in Nuremberg.[180] In Italy, most crimes seem also to have been committed outdoors, in the streets of the region's cities.[181] In Paris, as in Oxford and Nuremberg, certain regions within the town were regarded as peculiarly prone to criminal behavior.[182] Most crimes were committed within cities, but outdoors.

The data from Nuremberg diverge from this pattern. Most crimes were located indoors, but there may be some distortion introduced into the figures by the fact that few cases give an indication of where a crime was committed. Nuremberg seems like other cities in possessing areas where crime was unusually prevalent. In Nuremberg these districts were, unlike those in Oxford and Paris, not situated on the city's periphery and inhabited by the poorer elements of the population, but, as in Augsburg and Italy, lay at the center of the city close by the town hall and the homes of the well-to-do. Nuremberg thus shows some strong similarities to other European cities, as well as some interesting differences. Considering the topographical distribution of crime in Nuremberg, one is tempted to hypothesize that crimes were typically not committed by the very poor against the rich, but by members of the middle and upper classes against one another.

TEMPORAL DISTRIBUTION OF CRIMINAL ACTIVITY

The Nuremberg outlawry books only rarely record the time of day or day of the week when a crime was committed. The clerks were obviously not interested in recording such information. But they were interested in the date on which a criminal was outlawed, expelled, or banned, since the recording of such information was the main purpose of the outlawry books. Hence there is frequent mention of the date of a criminal's conviction, but only rare indications of the date of the crime. The two dates, however, seem to have been relatively close to one another.[183] It is thus possible to make inferences about at least the time of year when a crime was committed.

Different types of crime were committed at different times of the year. Homicides took place mainly in spring and summer. Assault showed a similar pattern, with a drop-off in winter. Robberies seem almost never to have taken place in the winter; they were most common in spring and summer. Burglaries, larcenies, and the receiving of stolen goods show no strong seasonal variation, being dispersed throughout the year. Illegal gambling shows a clear rise during the summer. There was no favorite season for the commission of fraud, arson, and political crimes. But in the case of religious crimes there is a clear drop in their frequency during the autumn. Sexual offenses usually took place during the warmer months of the year, although some cases are recorded during the winter. Crimes categorized as "other" were mainly committed in summer and autumn; those in the "unspecified" category were most common in winter and spring.[184]

These seasonal variations can often be readily explained. In the case of robbery it is obvious that merchants' convoys were not moving across the country in autumn and winter. The tendency for violent crimes to be committed during the warmer seasons may be linked to certain nearly universal psychological factors. In modern society violent crimes tend to cluster in the warm seasons.[185] Crimes against property, political crimes, and religious crimes were more independent of the seasons. Crimes were more common at night than during the day, and, with the exception of violent crimes, more common during the week than on weekends. But since the data on which these generalizations are based are very scanty, one should not ascribe undue validity to these conclusions.[186]

In Augsburg, Buff did not investigate either the days of the week or the seasons when crimes were committed, but he did find that night was the most common time for criminal activity.[187] Hanawalt believed that in England violent crimes, such as homicide and assault, usually took place on weekends while property crimes were committed mainly on weekdays. The most common times of day for crime were dawn and night. Violent crimes were committed primarily during the warmer months between March and August. There were, however, some regional variations. In rural areas crime appears to have been linked to the seasonal occupations of the agricultural year, such as sowing and harvesting; in the university town of Oxford, however, crime was linked to the university's calendar,[188] a conclusion supported by Hammer.[189] In Paris, Geremek found that crimes were mostly committed at night.[190]

Some general European patterns emerge from these studies. Most crimes in western Europe were committed at night or at daybreak. The Nuremberg data accord with this pattern. Violent crimes took place more frequently on weekends, when people gathered together and had opportunity to get into disputes. Once again Nuremberg fits into this general pattern. In the Nuremberg region, most violent crimes and crimes committed outside the city walls (which were mostly robberies) took place during the warm seasons. Once again Nuremberg's pattern is typical of that of western Europe as a whole.

ACCUSATION AND PROSECUTION

Private Accusations

Private accusations were most common in Nuremberg at the end of the thirteenth and the beginning of the fourteenth centuries. During the fourteenth century they were almost completely supplanted by accusations ex officio. In most cases, with the obvious exception of homicides, the victims themselves accused the felons. In only a few types of crimes did individuals other than the victim bring accusations. One of these was assault, where perhaps the victims were too seriously injured to prosecute themselves; the other type in which this was common were sexual offenses, that is, rape, where a similar factor may have been at work. And in the category of "unspecified crimes" many accusations were brought by people other than the victims themselves.[191]

An examination of private accusations reveals that the accusers were often victims' fathers, brothers, or wives; nonrelatives also made accusations. Among relatives, brothers were more common than wives.[192] This may be due to the fact that many victims were young men who had not yet married. If this supposition proves correct, it would give a very interesting image of the age distribution of criminals and victims.

In England, the Crown mistrusted such private accusations, known in common law as "appeals." They were frequently quashed with the result that their number decreased during the thirteenth century.[193] The courts seem to have believed that private appeals were often misused by those who wished to attack their enemies, even if they were innocent of the commission of any felonies. In England most appellants were either the victims themselves or their close relatives, often their wives.[194]

In Bologna, private accusations were frequently misused for political purposes. The town government, when it was controlled by the *nobili*, therefore opposed such accusations, while the *popolo* favored them. (This is similar to the situation in England, where the Crown opposed private accusations while the nobility, gentry, and the common people favored them.)[195]

It is possible that similar misgivings in Nuremberg about the abuse of private accusations led to their decrease and the growing resort to public indictment. But it is perhaps not coincidental that it is around 1325 that the first prosecutions ex officio are recorded in the outlawry books, in the same period when political crimes begin for the first time to be recorded in the *Achtbücher*.[196]

Prosecution Ex Officio

In the Nuremberg outlawry books examples of prosecutions ex officio in homicide cases appear from 1381; in other cases the use of such procedures appeared around 1325. One is tempted to believe that a rise in the crime rate led the city government to make use of this procedure to more effectively repress crime.[197] The relative lack of public prosecution in homicide cases is probably due to the fact that victims' relatives frequently brought private accusations. There are, however, relatively many public accusations in cases of assault. Victims of assaults may not have regarded such acts as felonious, or they may have preferred to exact private vengeance. In cases of robbery it appears that the victims, the merchants of Nuremberg, themselves accused those who had despoiled them. In contrast, cases of larceny, gambling, sexual offenses, and political and religious crimes were frequently prosecuted ex officio. It appears that the city council regarded these crimes, particularly the political ones, as sufficiently dangerous to warrant governmental prosecution. The city council may also have had something to do with the large number of appeals lodged by approvers, that is, indictments brought by accomplices against their fellow criminals, promising either not to prosecute approvers or to pardon them outright. Such appeals by approvers were frequent in cases of robbery (not surprising given the high importance attached by the city council to the town's trade), and in political crimes, where major plots against the city's government were discovered by this means.[198] The seriousness with which robbery and political crimes were viewed is underlined by the fact that it was only in the prosecution of these offenses and the expulsion of professional criminals that the armed police forces of the city were brought into play.[199] The giving of pledges for good conduct was found only in the category of unspecified crimes, indicating that these were probably petty offenses.[200]

Buff has argued that there was a similar movement from private accusations to *ex officio* prosecutions in Augsburg. Indeed, this seems to be a common pattern throughout western Europe.[201] England had long known forms of public accusation through the presentments offered by tithings.[202] But the concealments of crimes were common. Presenting juries, evidently to protect their fellow villagers or townsmen, often indicted strangers or "persons unknown."[203] This led the Crown to want to restrict this type of indictment, along with private appeals of felony,[204] and to introduce appeals by approvers. But this type of procedure was successfully blocked by the nobility, the gentry, and other subjects, thus keeping the Crown from employing it on a wider scale.[205] Venice and Bologna also knew public prosecutions, where they were fairly unpopular, even being openly opposed by the *popolo* of Bologna.[206] In the cities of the county of Flanders, under the control of the duke of Burgundy from 1384, the political authorities from the end of the fourteenth century sought to counteract crime through repressive means: by indictments ex officio, appeals of approvers, speedy trials, and immediate execution of sentences without possibility of appeal.[207]

Therefore, continental Europe during this era witnessed a common development leading away from private accusations and toward greater use of public prosecution. In England, where jury trials predominated, this trend could be counteracted by jurors who were free to decide the guilt or innocence of the accused. Thus the Crown's efforts to repress crime could be obstructed. The second half of the fourteenth century was thus a period in which governments, with the exception of that of England, tried increasingly to suppress crime by means of public indictment and prosecution. This development can be observed not only in Nuremberg, but also throughout Germany, Italy, France, and Flanders.

ESCAPE AND OUTLAWRY

Criminals in Nuremberg often fled before they could be arrested and brought to trial. The records contain 141 cases involving 202 criminals in which this happened. In homicide cases most of the criminals fled,[208] but flight was common in all categories of crime. Schultheiss observed that most cases of flight were recorded in *Achtbuch I*, between 1285 and 1337; after this period the number of such cases decreased rapidly.[209] This decrease seems to be linked to an intensified prosecution of crime in Nuremberg after 1325, with a larger proportion of criminals being apprehended after that date than before.[210]

At Augsburg between 1338 and 1400, approximately 3,000 people were outlawed, with 420 of these sentences being imposed between 1338 and 1368. For this thirty-one year period, Buff believes this to be a minimum figure; he estimates that about 1,000 outlawries took place during this period. After 1368, when the guilds had taken over power in the city, the number of outlawries rapidly decreased, as the new government set about to repress crime by arresting and trying criminals. Thus, after 1368 the crime rate in Augsburg decreased, with the exception of crimes against property; at the same time the rate of arrests increased and the rates of escape and outlawry decreased.[211]

In thirteenth- and fourteenth-century England felons regularly escaped the clutches of the law. English common law did not allow convictions *in contumaciam*. Thus fugitives were exacted three times; if they did not surrender to the court at the fourth exaction, they were outlawed. It appears that about eighty percent of all felons fled. Of those who were exacted, about 60 to 70 percent were outlawed.[212] This pattern changed at the end of the fourteenth century. This change was not due to more effective efforts by government agents to prevent escapes, but to the fact that in certain areas of England felons entered into private compacts, known as peace bonds, not to flee but to stand trial. The pledges for these peace bonds were usually members of the gentry class. It appears that the people respected these men more than Crown officials, because in regions where these bonds were used rates of flight decreased rapidly.[213]

In Italy, it was also common for felons to flee. Thus in Venice the number of outlaws living in the inner city became such a serious problem that the government allowed them to be killed with impunity; it also endeavored to get them to denounce their accomplices.[214] In Florence, the resort to flight was restrained only upon the introduction of a form of personal liability. Citizens pledged a certain sum of money with the government to guarantee their good behavior; this sum was confiscated by the city treasury if a citizen committed a crime and fled from prosecution.[215] In Paris, the government took steps similar to those employed in Venice, with government officials trying to prevent escapes and arresting felons so that they could stand trial.[216]

Nuremberg once again seems to display a pattern similar to that found throughout western Europe. At the end of the thirteenth and the beginning of the fourteenth centuries it was quite common for felons to escape justice. Rates of arrest and conviction were low, and outlawry rates were accordingly high. This situation changed in the second half of the fourteenth century, when governments began to repress crime by police measures, preventing, if possible, the flight of felons. England was an exception to this pattern, since its legal system did not permit measures such as were employed elsewhere. But on the Continent, European governments sought to suppress crime through repressive means. In this respect Nuremberg did not differ from most other European cities and regions, with the exception of Florence and the privileged cities of Flanders.

PUNISHMENT AND PARDON

Three classes of punishment were meted out in late medieval Nuremberg: first, punishments similar to those found in modern legal systems, such as execution, corporal punishment, fines, prohibitions on entry of inns and gambling, and imprisonment;[217] second, perpetual or temporary banishment at a prescribed distance from the city;[218] and, third, self-banishment.[219]

The punishments formally prescribed by the law were almost never imposed; instead the city council varied the nature of its penalties and even imposed some that were not contained in the law.[220] Punishment during the fourteenth century was intended to deter potential criminals; but the punishments actually handed down could succeed only partially in accomplishing this goal. Executions were rare. The outlawry books mention only eighty-seven, plus nine criminals sentenced to death who received pardons.[221] Execution as a penalty is found primarily in cases of robbery and political crime, although it was also imposed at a rate above the average in religious cases.[222]

Corporal punishment was also rare. It was imposed only in cases of assault, larceny, and religious and sexual offenses.[223] Confiscations and fines were rare.[224] Frequently criminals were only menaced with fines, or were forbidden to carry arms, to enter inns, or to gamble. These "punishments" must be regarded more as preventative measures than as punishments proper. Similarly, the threat of imprisonment was more common than imprisonment itself.[225] And, finally, compensation of the victim by the criminal, at which point prosecution ceased, also took place.[226] Thus it appears that punishments were almost never imposed in the way the formal law envisaged. Punishment seems to have often been regarded by the Nuremberg town councilors as too severe, leading to a general tendency to mitigate or convert punishments, or to pardon. Nuremberg citizens, especially, were not treated with the severity required by the law.[227] This is illustrated by examining the ways in which criminals were banished from the city. Banishments were seldom imposed in accordance with the strict letter of the law.[228] In some cases, where the crimes recorded appear to be equally blameworthy, very different sentences of banishment were imposed. In other cases the individual banished from the city had to compensate the victims or pay a fine upon his eventual return. The severity of banishments varied, ranging from sentences of permanent exile at a distance of thirty miles from the city, to sentences of temporary banishment of a half-year's duration at a distance of less than one mile.[229] And one should always remember that sentences of banishment already represent a mitigation of the law; criminals were not punished, but simply excluded from the city, frequently for only short periods of time.

In the cases involving "self-banishment," criminals had a degree of control over deciding the duration and the distance of their exile from the city.[230] The terms of these self-banishments also varied markedly, ranging from permanent exile at a distance of twenty miles from the city, to a half-year within two miles of Nuremberg. There appears to be no correlation between the length of the period of banishment or self-banishment and the nature or severity of the crime. In homicide cases, sentences of banishment ranged from perpetual exclusion at a distance of ten miles to less than a year with no distance from the city specified. One wonders whether banishment was effective in repressing crime, since those exiled from the city may simply have turned to committing crimes in the surrounding hinterland.[231]

In fourteenth-century Augsburg, Buff found that, in addition to corporal punishments, there were about ten executions a year. He argues that although felons were often threatened with punishment, punishments were seldom inflicted. It seems that the Augsburg town councilors often found the law too rigorous, and hence pardoned or banned criminals, requiring that they pay compensation. Those who had influential pledges of money were, as in Nuremberg, pardoned.[232]

In Demandt's opinion most punishments, even those for very grave crimes, could be bought off with money at Eschwege. For the town council compensating victims was more important than inflicting punishment on criminals.[233] In Frankfurt am Main four to five people were executed every year during the last third of the fourteenth century. But here, too, the number executed constituted only a very low proportion of all criminals punished.[234]

In England, the practice known as "abjuring the realm" was similar to the German institution of banishment or self-banishment. Felons who had fled into sanctuary could take an oath to leave the kingdom forever. The county coroner thereupon assigned them a port, often Dover, whence they could take passage out of the kingdom. But it appears that most abjurers failed to reach their assigned ports, taking refuge in the forests or someplace else. Very few abjurers actually left the kingdom.[235] Hence abjuration failed to remove felons from the realm. In England, as in Germany, felons thus remained near the places from which they had been banished, doing so legally in Germany but illegally in England. In both cases they probably were able to continue their criminal careers. The only punishment for felony recognized in later medieval English law was death by hanging. In the case of trespasses, however, corporal punishments such as the pillory were inflicted.[236] Fines and amercements, confiscations and imprisonment, were also employed.[237] The weapons used to commit crimes as well as the objects that caused fatal accidents were considered deodands, and were confiscated by the Crown.[238]

For felonies the only punishment was death. Many jurors seem to have found this unpalatable, being reluctant to convict even those who were obviously guilty. The conviction rate for felons was only around twenty percent.[239] But only some of those convicted were actually executed, the jurors frequently recommending mercy for them and the Crown granting them pardons. The Crown, ever in need of money, was willing to grant pardons to those able to pay for them. In some cases political motives prompted the Crown to issue a pardon. And, finally, jurors for personal reasons often requested that a pardon be granted. Thus, of those actually tried, less than five percent were ever executed. Of the larger number of people suspected of having committed felonies, about eighty percent fled, never to be tried.[240] Thus it appears that in England only a very low percentage of felons was ever convicted, and an even smaller percentage executed. The primary cause for this was probably the fact that jurors regarded the only punishment available for felonies—death—as too harsh, and, having the legal ability to mitigate the imposition of such punishments, did so. The Crown as well often engaged in practices that help explain the low execution rate for felons.

But it does seem that throughout western Europe courts of law were more interested in compensating victims than in punishing convicted criminals.[241] In southern France it was common for punishments to be limited and compensation given victims. In northern France, however, where the Crown appears to have desired to repress crime rather than ameliorate its effects, rates of conviction and execution were higher.[242] In the privileged cities of Flanders, where good burghers could not be tried in comitial courts but only in urban ones, there was an open system involving compensation of victims and non-punishment of criminals.[243] In Bologna and Florence there were similar systems characterized by victim compensation and non-punishment of criminals,[244] whereas at Venice the republic tried to repress crime through governmental action.[245]

After this survey of Europe, one conclusion seems clear: Where criminals were judged in local courts, they were not "punished" in a sense that modern Europeans would understand; instead they were able to ransom themselves by compensating their victims and going into exile. In places where criminals were not tried in local courts, but in those of a centralizing, regional political authority, a very different situation existed. Here the chances of a criminal being executed were much higher. Nuremberg fits into the first rather than the second pattern.

CONCLUSION

Patterns of criminal activity and repression in Nuremberg seem basically similar to those found throughout continental Europe. This is probably the most important conclusion reached by this investigation. The one area that does not fit easily into this general European pattern is England, with its individualistic legal system. This legal system not only had procedures and rules that differed from those on the Continent; but it also gave jurors room to manipulate the rules in accordance with their own wishes and values. But, with the exception of England, the way in which crime was prosecuted was basically the same in western Europe.

Nuremberg's crime rate seems similar to those found elsewhere in western Europe, and the mix of crimes recorded seems typical of most medieval societies.[246] Most crimes involved a single perpetrator acting alone. Criminal associations seem to have been largely amateur in nature, and often organized around kinship ties. The criminals recorded did not come mainly from the poorer ranks of society, but from the middle classes. Members of the nobility engaged in feuds and robbery, but members of the urban patriciate were only rarely involved in crime, either as criminals or as victims. Unlike the situation in England, clerics were seldom involved in crime.[247] The chief causes of crime seem to have been arguments, a generally belligerent social tone, the common practice of bearing arms, and the desire for gain. Indeed, where consciously articulated motives are reported in the records, most seem to have been economic in nature.[248]

Methods of committing crimes, the places where they were committed, and the times when they were committed all seem to have been similar to the patterns found elsewhere. Most crimes, with the possible exception of robberies, often planned and committed by nobles, seem to have been spontaneous, unplanned phenomena.[249] Nuremberg also seems typical of Europe as a whole, in that the fourteenth-century increase in criminal activity led to the development of a repressive governmental campaign against crime. Private accusation was replaced by ex officio proceedings, with governments taking over the task of prosecuting crime as well as judging it. Escape and outlawry rates decreased, and the menace of "real," afflictive punishments hung increasingly over the heads of criminals. But the punishments available often seemed too harsh to jurors, who preferred to pardon or excuse felons, if they were "good burghers," while providing, if possible, compensation to the victims.[250]

NOTES

This chapter is a revised version, in English, of my "Statistische Untersuchung des Verbrechens in Nürnberg im Zeitraum von 1285–1400", which was published in *Zeitschrift der Savigny-Stiftung für Rechtsgeschichte, Germanistische Abteilung* 108 (1991): 117–93. I am indebted very much to J. B. Given of the University of California, Irvine, for rereading a translation of this chapter and for giving advice on its presentation.

1. See O. Buff, "Verbrechen und Verbrecher zu Augsburg in der zweiten Hälfte des 14.Jahrhunderts," *Zeitschrift des Historischen Vereins für Schwaben und Neuburg* 4 (1877): 160–231; Paul Frauenstädt, *Blutrache und Totschlagsühne im deutschen Mittelalter* (Leipzig, 1881), 44–47; G. L. Kriegk, *Bürgertum im Mittelalter* (Frankfurt am Main, 1868), 1:197–222.

2. Karl E. Demandt, "Recht und Gesellschaft—Rechts-, sozial- und sittengeschichtliche Studien zur strafrechtlichen Praxis in einer hessischen Stadt des 15.Jahrhunderts," *Zeitschrift für Hessische Geschichte* 83 (1972): 9–56; H. P. Hils, "Zum Stand der hauptberuflichen Fechter nach mittelalterlichen Rechtsquellen," *Zeitschrift der Savigny-Stiftung für Rechtsgeschichte, Germanistische Abteilung* 102 (1985): 328–40; Indrikis Sterns, "Crime and Punishment among the Teutonic Knights," *Speculum* 57 (1982): 84–111. A notable exception is Herta Mandl-Neumann, "Aspekte des Rechtsalltags im spätmittelalterlichen Krems," *Rechtsgeschichtliche Schriften vom Österreichischen Historikertag* (Krems, 1983): 312–27.

3. Marvin E. Wolfgang, *Patterns in Criminal Homicide* (Philadelphia, 1955).

4. See Alfred Soman, "Deviance and Criminal Justice in Western Europe," *Criminal Justice History* 1 (1980): 1–28; Barbara A. Hanawalt, *Crime and Conflict in English Communities, 1300–1348* (Cambridge, Mass., 1979), together with R. F. Hunnisett's review in *Criminal Justice History* 2 (1981): 161–63; James B. Given, *Society and Homicide in Thirteenth-Century England* (Stanford, 1977); Carl I. Hammer, Jr., "Patterns of Homicide in a Medieval University Town: Fourteenth-Century Oxford," *Past & Present* 78 (1978): 3–23; Richard W. Kaeuper, "Law and Order in Fourteenth-Century England: The Evidence of Special Commissions of Oyer and Terminer," *Speculum* 54 (1979): 734–84; Edward Powell, "Social Research and the Use of Medieval Criminal Records," *Michigan Law Review* 79 (1981): 967–78.

5. J. B. Post, "The Evidential Value of Approvers' Appeals: The Case of William Rose, 1389," *Law and History Review* 3 (1985): 91–100.

6. Martin Schüssler, "Vergleich von Theorien der Historischen Kriminologie zum Verbrechensanstieg und zum hohen Niveau der Verbrechensrate im England des 13. und 14.Jahrhunderts," *Monatsschrift für Kriminologie und Strafrechtsreform* 71(4) (1988): 246–54; idem, *Die Gentry und das Verbrechen im England des 13. und 14.Jahrhunderts*, (inaug. diss., Stuttgart, 1989).

7. Marvin B. Becker, "Changing Patterns of Violence and Justice in 14th and 15th Century Florence," *Comparative Studies in Society and History* 18 (1976): 281–96; S. R. Blanshei, "Crime and Law Enforcement in Medieval Bologna," *Journal of Social History* 16 (1982): 121–38; W. M. Bowsky, "The Medieval Commune and Internal Violence: Police Power and Public Safety in Siena, 1287–1355," *American Historical Review* 73 (1967): 1–17; Robert Brentano, "Violence, Disorder, and Order in Thirteenth-Century Rome," in *Violence and Civil Disorder in Italian Cities,*

1200–1500, ed. Lauro Martines (Berkeley, 1972), 308–30; Stanley Chojnacki, "Crime, Punishment, and the Trecento Venetian State," in ibid., 184–228; G. W. Coopland, "Crime and Punishment in Paris, September 6, 1389, to May 18, 1390," in *Medieval and Middle Eastern Studies*, ed. Sami E. Hannah (Leyden, 1972), 64–85; Gaetano Cozzi, "Authority and the Law in Renaissance Venice," in *Renaissance Venice*, ed. J. R. Hale (London, 1973), 293–345; Bronislaw Geremek, *The Margins of Society in Late Medieval Paris* (Warsaw, 1970/Cambridge, 1987); Yves Grava, "Justice et pouvoirs à Martigues au XIVe siécle," *Provence historique* 28 (1978): 305–22; Yvonne Lanhers, "Crimes et criminels au XIVe siécle," *Revue Historique* 240 (1968): 325–38; Rodrigue Lavoie, "Justice, criminalité et peine de mort en France au Moyen Age," in *Le sentiment de la mort en Moyen Age*, ed. Claude Sutto (Quebec, 1979), 31–55; idem, "Les statistiques criminelles et le visage du justicier," *Provence historique* 29 (1979): 3–20; Guido Ruggiero, "Excusable Murder: Insanity and Reason in Early Renaissance Venice," *Journal of Social History* 16 (1982): 109–19.

8. Felonies include the following acts: high treason, mutiny in the royal army, embezzlement from the Exchequer, counterfeiting, homicide, assault, robbery, burglary, larceny, receiving of felons, arson, and, from 1285, rape.

9. See Hunnisett, Book Review of Hanawalt, "Norfolk Delivery Rolls", *American Journal of Legal History* 22 (1978): 257–59.

10. See Karl Kroeschell, *Deutsche Rechtsgeschichte* (Reinbek/Hamburg, 1972), 2:208, 214; Werner Schultheiss, *Die Acht-, Verbots- und Fehdebücher Nürnbergs von 1285–1400* (Nuremberg, 1960), 1:98, 119, 186. See App. 1, *passim*.

11. Defining political crimes is difficult. Indeed, almost any definition, including that advanced here, is by its nature arbitrary. See S. L. Waugh, "The Profits of Violence: The Minor Gentry in the Rebellion of 1321–1322 in Gloucestershire and Herefordshire," *Speculum* 52 (1977): 843–69; E. J. Hobsbawm, "Distinctions between Socio-Political and Other Forms of Crime," *Society for the Study of Labour History Bulletin* 25 (1972): 5–6. It should be noted that the actions of the Nuremberg "Riot Council" of 1348–49 were not too revolutionary. Its members included patricians, and, after 1349 some members of the Riot Council sat on the more conservative council then in power. See Schultheiss, *Achtbücher*, 1:34, 44–46, 76, 156, 165, 216. Schultheiss argues that the *Achtbücher* (written in German from 1334 to 1335) were the only judicial records kept in the city of Nuremberg.

12. See John B. Hennemann, Jr., "Black Death and Royal Taxation in France, 1347–1351," *Speculum* 43 (1968): 405–27; Henry S. Lucas, "The Great European Famine of 1315, 1316, and 1317," *Speculum* 5 (1930): 343–77.

13. Karl von Hegel, "Über Nürnbergs Bevölkerungszahl und Handwerkerverhältnisse im 14. und 15.Jahrhundert," *Chroniken der deutschen Städte, Nürnberg* (Mayence, 1864), 2:502–3.

14. App. 2.b., col. 5 = crimes in general.

15. See Schultheiss, *Achtbücher*, 1:54.

16. App. 2.b., col. T = homicides.

17. Buff, "Augsburg," 167–68.

18. Frauenstädt, *Blutrache*, 45–46, n. 32. The data are as follows: Speyer (Palatinate) 1333–40 = 15 homicides = 30 per 100,000 per annum (p.a.); Lahr (Baden) 1356 = 19 homicides; Stralsund (Pomerania) 1310–99 = 121 homicides = 9 per 100,000 p.a.; Liegnitz (Silesia) 1339–54 = 76 homicides = 70 per 100,000 p.a.;

Breslau (Silesia) 1357–99 = 243 homicides = 40 per 100,000 p.a. (Homicide rates are approximate data, the number of inhabitants being taken from Putzger, *Historischer Weltatlas* [Bielefeld, 1969], 70–71.)

19. Kriegk, *Bürgertum*, 202–3 (very inaccurate data).

20. Demandt, "Recht," 23, has 1,200 criminal cases in 20 years, or 60 p.a., the population of Eschwege (Hessia) approximated by him as 2,500.

21. See Given, *Society and Homicide*, 36–38; Hanawalt, *Crime and Conflict*, 98; idem, "Violent Death in 14th and Early 15th Century England," *Comparative Studies in Society and History* 18 (1976): 302; Hammer, "Oxford," 11; E. B. DeWindt and A. R. DeWindt, *Royal Justice and the Medieval English Countryside* (Toronto, 1981), 110. (The highest number of 110 homicides per 100,000 inhabitants p.a. is reached in Oxford.)

22. Lavoie, "Statistiques," 4–6; idem, "Justice," 36–37, 41; Geremek, *Margins*, 7, 15, 49–51, 55, 57, 58, 60, 61.

23. Becker, "Florence," 287.

24. Blanshei, "Bologna," 127–29. (Population taken from Putzger, *Historischer Weltatlas*, 70–71.)

25. Chojnacki, "Venice," 198, 215.

26. App. 2.b., s.v. KV = assault. (In 1348 there were 6, in 1381 16, and in 1392 20 cases p.a..)

27. Buff, "Augsburg," 121–22. Frauenstädt, *Blutrache*, 45–46, n. 32, has some inaccurate data: Stralsund 1310–99 = 103 cases of assault = 8 per 100,000 p.a.; Liegnitz 1339–54 = 67 cases of assault = 60 per 100,000 p.a.; Breslau 1357–99 = 242 cases of assault = 40 per 100,000 p.a.; Kriegk, *Bürgertum*, 202–3, also has quite inaccurate data.

28. Blanshei, "Bologna," 127–29.

29. Other data not available.

30. App. 2.b., s.v. R = robbery, E = burglary, D = larceny, and H = receiving of stolen goods.

31. Buff, "Augsburg," 212–13.

32. Lavoie, "Justice," 36–37; Geremek, *Margins*, 49–51.

33. Blanshei, "Bologna," 127–29.

34. Chojnacki, "Venice," 198, 215.

35. Other data not available.

36. Bundeskriminalamt, ed., *Polizeiliche Kriminalstatistik für die Bundesrepublik Deutschland* (Wiesbaden, 1985), 67–71.

37. Polizeipräsidium Mittelfranken, ed., *Kriminalstatistik, Jahresbericht 1988* (Nuremberg, 1989), 5, 12.

38. Her Majesty's Stationery Office, ed., *Criminal Statistics of England and Wales* (London, 1983), 34–36; Lawrence Stone, "The History of Violence in England: A Rejoinder," *Past & Present* 108 (1985): 224; J. H. Gaute and R. Odell, *The Murderer's Who's Who* (London, 1979), 18; Giles Playfair, *Crime in Our Century* (London, 1977), 21.

39. App. 2.b., s.v. col. T = homicides, to col. sV = other crimes (=13 cols.). See Hermann Knapp, *Das alte Nürnberger Kriminalrecht* (Berlin, 1896), 170–97.

40. Crimes against property are defined as robbery, burglary, larceny, and receiving of stolen goods. See App. 2.b., s.v. R, E, D, H. See Knapp, *Kriminalrecht*, 141–70.

41. Cases of fraud are defined as prohibited gambling, fraud, and counterfeiting. See App. 2.b., s.v. FS and BF.

42. Robberies are differentiated from political crimes or feuds in that way that, if during combats there was made any booty, it is defined as robbery, if not, as political crime.

43. Buff, "Augsburg," 212–13.

44. Demandt, "Recht," 14–17.

45. For a definition of felonies, see above, n. 8.

46. John G. Bellamy, *Crime and Public Order in England in the Later Middle Ages* (Toronto, 1973), 33.

47. Hanawalt, *Crime and Conflict*, 10, 66, 237; idem, "Economic Influences on the Pattern of Crime in England, 1300–1348," *American Journal of Legal History* 18 (1974): 294.

48. R. B. Pugh, *Imprisonment in Medieval England* (Cambridge, 1968), 84; idem, *Calendar of London Trailbaston Trials under Commissions of 1305 and 1306* (London, 1975), 6–8, 26.

49. I. L. Langbein, "The Jury of Presentment and the Coroner," *Columbia Law Review* 33 (1933): 1337.

50. DeWindt and DeWindt, *Royal Justice*, 51.

51. Chojnacki, "Venice," 211, 215; Cozzi, "Venice," 332.

52. Blanshei, "Bologna," 130. Also in Nuremberg and Augsburg.

53. Becker, "Florence," 287–88.

54. Lavoie, "Justice," 41–43; Geremek, *Margins*, 49–51, 55–57, 58–61.

55. In 1988 there were recorded the following percentages of crimes in Nuremberg: larceny 50.2; fraud 11.8; assault 10.9; sexual offenses 1.2; homicide .1. See *Kriminalstatistik* (Nuremberg, 1988), 11–17, 51–53, 59–60, 76–78.

56. See App. 3 (Criminal Actions), *passim.*

57. Ibid.

58. See 3.a.

59. See 3.b.

60. See 3.c.

61. See 3.d.

62. See 3.e.

63. See 3.a.

64. See 3, *passim.*

65. *Loc. cit.*

66. *Loc. cit.*

67. See 3.a. The modern phenomenon of the frequent acquaintance of the criminal and victim is discussed by K. Sessar, "The Familial Character of Criminal Homicide," *Victimology* 4 (1975): 29–42.

68. See App. 3.d.

69. Bellamy, *Crime and Public Order*, 37; Given, *Society and Homicide*, 42, 45, 54, 135–36, 153, 156; Hanawalt, "The Peasant Family and Crime in Fourteenth-Century England," *Journal of British Studies* 13 (1973): 12–14; idem, *Crime and Conflict*, 61, 123, 189, 193.

70. Bellamy, *Crime and Public Order*, 37; idem, "The Coterel Gang: An Anatomy of a Band of 14th Century Criminals," *English Historical Review* 79 (1964): 698–717; L. O. Pike, *A History of Crime in England* (London, 1873), 1:242–43;

Walter Rye, "Notes on Crime and Accident in Norfolk, Temp. Edward Ist," *Archaeological Review* 2 (1889): 215; M. Weinbaum, *London unter Eduard I. und Eduard II.* (Stuttgart, 1933), 87, 117, 126–29, 155–56; T. F. Tout, "A Medieval Burglary," *Collected Papers* 3 (1934): 112; Hammer, "Oxford," 20; C. Austin Beard, "The Office of Justice of the Peace in England," *Columbia University Studies in History, Economics, and Public Law* 20 (1904): 37; M. Keen, *The Outlaws of Medieval Legend* (London, 1961), 194–200; R. B. Pugh, "Some Reflexions of a Medieval Criminologist," *Proceedings of the British Academy* 59 (1975): 101–2; Colin Platt, *Medieval England* (London, 1978), 109; R. H. Hilton, *A Medieval Society: The West Midlands at the End of the Thirteenth Century* (Cambridge, 1983), 257; idem, *The English Peasantry in the Later Middle Ages* (Oxford, 1975), 92–93; Alan Harding, *The Law Courts of Medieval England* (London, 1973), 91; Given, *Society and Homicide*, 42, 93; Hanawalt, *Crime and Conflict*, 186, 189, 191, 193, 237; idem, "The Female Felon in Fourteenth-Century England," *Viator* 5 (1974): 263.

71. Lavoie, "Justice," 45; Coopland, "Crime and Punishment," 69; Geremek, *Margins*, 21, 30–37, 109–34, 192–210, 211.

72. Becker, "Florence," 292–94. Other data not available.

73. See below, nn. 227–28.

74. App. 4, s.v. Local origins and social backgrounds of criminals and victims, *passim*; see Schultheiss, *Achtbücher*, 1:101–5, 167.

75. See Buff, "Augsburg," 182, 213, where he describes the annual expulsion of criminous strangers from the city on 16 October. See below, nn. 227–28.

76. Karl Kroeschell, *Deutsche Rechtsgeschichte* 2 (Reinbek/Hamburg, 1972), 207–8, 214.

77. App. 4, s.v. robbery.

78. *Loc. cit.*, s.v. criminals of noble origin; see above, n. 42, about differentiation of robbery and political crimes.

79. App. 4, s.v. burglary.

80. *Loc. cit.*, s.v. gambling, fraud, coining of false money.

81. *Loc. cit.*, s.v. political crimes. See above, n. 11.

82. Buff, "Augsburg," 172–73.

83. Demandt, "Recht," 14, 21–22, 29–32.

84. W. A. Morris, *The Frankpledge System* (New York, 1910), 152; Bellamy, *Crime and Public Order*, 30; Rye, "Notes," 206.

85. Hanawalt, *Crime and Conflict*, 129, 169; A. DeWindt, "Peasant Power Structures," *Medieval Studies* 38 (1976): 263.

86. Coopland, "Crime and Punishment," 67, 72–77, 79–83; Lavoie, "Justice," 43.

87. Geremek, *Margins*, 30, 37, 97, 244.

88. Lanhers, "Crimes et criminels," 325–26.

89. D. Waley, "A Commune and Its Subject-territory in the Thirteenth Century: Law and Power in the Sienese Contado," in *Diritto e potere nella storia Europea*, ed. L. S. Olschki (Florence, 1982), 309; Brentano, "Rome," 316, 324; Blanshei, "Bologna," 123–28; Becker, "Florence," 286–92; Chojnacki, "Venice," 189, 203–4, 213–16; Cozzi, "Venice," 311–12, 319, 323.

90. See *Kriminalstatistik* (Nuremberg, 1988), 23, 30, 43.

91. App. 4, *passim*. No victims were recorded in the religious offense or in cases involving gambling, fraud, and counterfeiting.

92. Hanawalt, *Crime and Conflict*, 55, 60–61; Given, *Society and Homicide*, 168–69. Other data regarding crime on the Continent not available.

93. App. 4, s.v. sexes.

94. *Loc. cit.*, s.v. children. See *Kriminalstatistik* (Nuremberg, 1988), 23, 25, 30, 46.

95. Buff, "Augsburg," 172–73.

96. Hanawalt, *Crime and Conflict*, 83, 115, 118, 120, 123, 153; idem, "Female Felon," 253–67; idem, "Economic Influences," 290–94, 296; idem, "Violent Death," 305–7; Given, *Society and Homicide*, 42, 55, 118–21, 135–43, 147, 166; Pugh, "Reflexions," 103; K. Casey, "Women in Norman and Plantagenet England," in *The Women of England*, ed. B. Kanner 101; R. Kittel, "Women under the Law in Medieval England," *loc. cit.*, 130; Hammer, "Oxford," 13–14. See Schultheiss, *Achtbücher*, 1:75.

97. App. 4, s.v. offenders and victims with a noble or clerical origin.

98. *Loc. cit.* Perhaps the Nuremberg clergy did not figure among criminal offenders because of its wealth, comprised of extensive properties both in and around the city. See Schultheiss, *Achtbücher*, 1:112, 115–16, 125, 132, 136, 152–53 (Monastery of St. Aegidius, convent of St. Catherine [Dominican], convent of St. Clare [since 1314], monastery of Heilsbronn, convent of the Teutonic Knights, convent of Engelthal, Hospital of the Holy Spirit, monastery of St. Francis, and the monastery of St. Dominic). But members of the clergy, despite their wealth, also do not figure very often as victims of criminal activity.

99. App. 4, s.v. Nuremberg patricians as offenders and victims.

100. *Loc. cit.*, s.v. list of cases.

101. *Loc. cit.*

102. *Loc. cit.*, s.v. patrician families mentioned.

103. I. Sterns, "Crime and Punishment among the Teutonic Knights," *Speculum* 57 (1982): 84–111.

104. Buff, "Augsburg," 172–73.

105. Demandt, "Recht," 14, 21–22, 29–32. See Kriegk, *Bürgertum*, 199, where, in contrast, nobility and clergy are introduced as frequently mentioned classes of criminals.

106. Bellamy, *Crime and Public Order*, 73.

107. Ibid., 35–40; idem, *Criminal Law and Society in Later Medieval and Tudor England* (New York, 1984), 115–23; Rye, "Notes," 204–5, 212–13; Pike, *History*, 297–98, 301, 307; Pugh, "Reflexions," 89, 93–94, 100, 104; Hammer, "Oxford," 3ff. 18–20; Hanawalt, *Crime and Conflict*, 136–38, 178; J. R. Wright, *The Church and the English Crown* (Toronto, 1980), 220; F. J. Pegues, "A Monastic Society at Law in the Kent Eyre of 1313/14," *EHR* 87 (1972): 548–64; T. F. Tout, "A Medieval Burglary," *Collected Papers* 3 (1934), 93–114.

108. Bellamy, "The Coterel Gang: An Anatomy of a Band of 14th Century Criminals," *EHR* 79 (1964): 698–717; E. L. G. Stones, "The Folvilles of Ashby-Folville, Leicestershire, and their Associates in Crime, 1326–1347," *TRHS* (7) (1957): 117–36; Keen, *Outlaws*, 84; Rye, "Notes," 214; C. M. Fraser and K. Emsley, "Justice in North East England, 1256–1356," *American Journal of Legal History* 15 (1971): 174–75; Morris, *Frankpledge*, 73–75; S. L. Waugh, "Reluctant Knights

and Jurors," *Speculum* 58 (1983): 941–52; R. F. Trehearne, "The Knights in the Period of Reform and Rebellion," *Bulletin of the Institute of Historical Research* 21 (1946): 1–4; A. Harding, *Plaints and Bills in the History of English Law* (Cardiff, 1975), 79; K. B. MacLane, "A Case Study of Violence and Litigation in Early 14th Century: The Disputes of Robert Godfield of Sutton-le-Marsh," *Nottingham Medieval Studies* 28 (1984): 22–37; Beard, "Justice of the Peace," 23–25; F. M. Powicke, *King Henry and the Lord Edward* 1 (Oxford, 1947), 507–44; Tout, "Medieval Burglary," 93; Nathalie Fryde, "Robber Barons," in *Medieval Legal Records*, R. F. Hunnisett and J. B. Post ed. (London, 1978), 198–206; Given, *Society and Homicide*, 237; S. S. Walker, "Violence and the Exercise of Feudal Guardianship," *American Journal of Legal History* 16 (1972): 320–32; G. Lapsley, "Knights of the Shires in the Parliaments of Edward II," *EHR* 34 (1919):36–42; W. R. Jones, "Keeping the Peace," *American Journal of Legal History* 18 (1974): 316; B. A. Hanawalt, "Fur-Collar Crime," *Journal of Social History* 7 (1975): 1–17; Chr. Carpenter, "Law, Justice, and Landowners in Late Medieval England," *Law and History Review* 1 (1983): 205–37; Edward Powell, "The Restoration of Law and Order," in *Henry V: The Practice of Kingship* ed. G. L. Harriss (Oxford, 1985), 53–74; S. L. Waugh, "For King, Country, and Patron," *Journal of British Studies* 22 (1983): 23–58; idem, "The Profits of Violence," *Speculum* 52 (1977): 843–869. See above, n. 42, for a definition of political crimes.

109. Coopland, "Crime and Punishment," 67, 72–77, 79–83; Lavoie, "Justice," 43.

110. In northern France members of the nobility constituted only two percent of the criminals recorded. See Geremek, *Margins*, 253.

111. Lanhers, "Crimes et criminels," 325–26.

112. Waley, "Commune," 309; Brentano, "Rome," 316, 324; Blanshei, "Bologna," 123–28; Becker, "Florence," 286–92; Chojnacki, "Venice," 189, 203–4, 213–16; Cozzi, "Venice", 311–12, 319, 323. The same problems of interpretation apply to the "Zoendinc"-books of Ghent, which frequently mention patricians. Nicholas argues that disputes involving nonpatricians were generally not settled by arbitration of the "Paysierders," and that therefore cases mentioning their involvement were not recorded in the surviving records. See D. M. Nicholas, "Crime and Punishment in Fourteenth-Century Ghent," *Revue Belge de Philologie et d'Histoire* 48 (1970): 289–334, 1141–76, esp. 1171–72.

113. Hegel, "Nürnberg," 507–10. The origins of family names and their use for the determination of occupations are debated by Schultheiss, *Achtbücher*, 1:167.

114. App. 4, s.v. occupations.

115. *Loc. cit.* See Schultheiss, *Achtbücher*, 1:101–5, 167.

116. App. 4, s.v. occupations. Schultheiss, *Achtbücher*, 1:103f.

117. Schultheiss, *Achtbücher*, 2:718, 723. *Loc. cit.*, 1:30 (pogrome of 1298), 73, 74, 76, 81 (pogrome of 1384).

118. App. 4, s.v. occupations of victims. See Willi Rüger, "Mittelalterliches Almosenwesen," *Nürnberger Beiträge zu den Wirtschafts- und Sozialwissenschaften* 31 (1932): 1–36.

119. Buff, "Augsburg," 172.

120. Demandt, "Recht," 21–31.

121. Given, *Society and Homicide*, 83.

122. Hanawalt, *Crime and Conflict*, 132, 136; idem, "Economic Influences," 296; idem, "Violent Death," 308–9.

123. Hammer, "Oxford," 14–19.

124. Given, *Society and Homicide*, 86.

125. Hanawalt, *Crime and Conflict*, 55, 60, 61.

126. Geremek, *Margins*, 253, relates the following data: craftsmen forty percent, peasants seventeen percent, servants twenty-one percent, rural workers thirty-one percent.

127. App. 5 (Causes and motivations for committing crimes), s.v. T = homicides.

128. *Loc. cit.*, s.v. KV = assault.

129. *Loc. cit.*, s.v. R = robbery.

130. *Loc. cit.*, s.v. D = larceny.

131. *Loc. cit.*, s.v. H = receiving of stolen goods. We have to assume economic motivations for committing crimes like gambling, fraud, and counterfeiting, but there are no data to prove this.

132. *Loc. cit.*, s.v. Br = arson.

133. *Loc. cit.*, s.v. PV = political crimes.

134. *Loc. cit.*, s.v. PV = political crimes/value of booty.

135. *Loc. cit.*, s.v. RV = religious crimes.

136. *Loc. cit.*, s.v. SV = sexual offenses.

137. *Loc. cit.*, s.v. SV = other crimes.

138. App. 12 (Punishments and Pardons), s.v. "other punishments."

139. Buff, "Augsburg," 174–75, 198, 207–8. See Hanawalt, "Economic Influences," 281ff.

140. Demandt, "Recht," 35–43.

141. Frauenstädt, *Blutrache*, 44–45.

142. Kriegk, *Bürgertum*, 202.

143. Rye, "Notes," 206; Bellamy, *Crime and Public Order*, 37.

144. Given, *Society and Homicide*, 193.

145. Hanawalt, *Crime and Conflict*, 162, 171; idem, "Peasant Families," 3–10; idem, "Violent Death," 311–13.

146. Idem, "Economic Influences," 281–97.

147. Given, *Society and Homicide*, 38; Hunnisett, Book Review, *History* 63 (1978): 445, Hammer, "Oxford," 14, 18–20.

148. Pugh, "Reflexions," 87.

149. Hanawalt, *Crime and Conflict*, 71, 72, 75, 120–21, 191, 256–58. See Pugh, "Reflexions," 87, 103 (in opposition).

150. Chojnacki, "Venice," 210–13.

151. Lanhers, "Crimes et criminels," 326, 329, 331, 338; Geremek, *Margins*, 100.

152. Lavoie, "Statistiques," 17; grava, "Justice," 308–9.

153. See K. Sessar, "Familial Character," 29ff. See above, n. 67.

154. App. 6, s.v. homicides and assault. See Josef Baader, ed., "Nürnberger Polizeiordnungen," *Bibliothek des Litterarischen Vereins zu Stuttgart* 57 (2) (1861): 38–39; Schultheiss, *Achtbücher*, 2:55–60 (Laws against bearing of arms).

155. App. 6, s.v. larceny.

156. *Loc. cit.*, s.v. gambling.

157. *Loc. cit.*, s.v. fraud and coining of false money.

158. *Loc. cit.*, s.v. religious crimes. See also Schultheiss, *Achtbücher*, 1:94; 2:192, 619; Richard Kieckheffer, *European Witch Trials, 1300–1500* (London, 1976), 108, 114, 117, has three similar cases from Nuremberg (i.e., the two cases in Schultheiss and another in the year 1392, taken from "Stadtrechnungen," Staatsarchiv Nürnberg, No. 4, fol. 26b). See also Baader, "Polizeiordnungen," 68–69; H. H. Kunstmann, "Zauberwahn und Hexenprozess in der Reichsstadt Nürnberg" (inaug. diss., Mayence, 1970), 26, J. Monballyu, "Schadelijke Toverji te Brugge en te Ieper in de 15de Eeuw," *Handelingen van het Genootschap voor Geschiedenis* 121 (1983): 265–69, states that this low number of witch trials was typical for the fourteenth century. The fifteenth century also produced very few witch trials. Such trials were conducted like all other trials then: Conclusive evidence had to be produced; the defendant had the right to defend himself, and the punishments imposed were in accordance with the severity of the damage done. In the case of prosecution of witchcraft, Nuremberg thus seems to have been a typical late medieval city. Given, by contrast, has found a very high number of heresy cases from the single inquisitorial tribunal of Toulouse in southern France. In the period between 1308 and 1323, 930 sentences were imposed here, approximately 37 per year. But, of course, the prosecution of witches and heretics is not exactly analogous. See James B. Given, "The Inquisitors of Languedoc and the Medieval Technology of Power," *American Historical Review* 94 (1989): 336–59, esp. 340, 353.

159. App. 6, s.v. sexual offenses.

160. *Loc. cit.*, s.v. other crimes; see Baader, "Polizeiordnungen," 124–57.

161. Buff, "Augsburg," 173, 175, 177, 183–86, 198.

162. Demandt, "Recht," 15–16, 32–43.

163. Frauenstädt, *Blutrache*, 45.

164. Rye, "Notes," 206, 208; Given, *Society and Homicide*, 189; Hanawalt, *Crime and Conflict*, 100; idem, "Violent Death," 310–11; Hammer, "Oxford," 20–21.

165. See T.A. Green, "The Jury and the English Law of Homicide," *Michigan Law Review* 74 (1976): 41 (in opposition).

166. Hanawalt, "Violent Death," 310–11; Hammer, "Oxford," 20–21.

167. *Victoria History of the Counties of England, History of Hampshire and the Isle of Wight* 2 (London, 1905), 473; *loc. cit.* 5 (1908):39.

168. Tout, "Medieval Burglary," 93–115.

169. Hanawalt, *Crime and Conflict*, 100.

170. Grava, Justice," 308; Lanhers, "Crimes et criminels," 336.

171. Chojnacki, "Venice," 189–99; Cozzi, "Venice," 311–23; Brentano, "Rome," 316, 324.

172. App. 7, s.v. places indoors and outdoors where crimes were committed. Robberies frequently took place in the forests. *Loc. cit.*, s.v. robbery.

173. App. 7, *passim* (places crimes were committed within the walls of Nuremberg). See Schultheiss, *Achtbücher*, 2: 228–31, with register of Nuremberg localities; and App. 13, city map.

174. *Kriminalstatistiken* (Nuremberg, 1988), 42, 45.

175. Buff, "Augsburg," 174, 199, 205–6.

176. Demandt, "Recht," 36, 39. Also in Nuremberg bath-houses were mentioned very frequently as places where crimes were committed.

177. Bellamy, *Crime and Public Order*, 59.

178. Hanawalt, *Crime and Conflict*, 77, 101; idem, "Violent Death," 314.

179. Hammer, "Oxford," 20–21 (with city map).

180. *Loc. cit.*, 4.

181. Blanshei, "Bologna," 127.

182. Geremek, *Margins*, 21, 30, 68–94, 99.

183. See Schultheiss, *Achtbücher*, 1: 48–56.

184. App. 8.

185. See Bundeskriminalamt, ed., *Kriminalstatistik 1984 für die Bundesrepublik Deutschland* (Wiesbaden, 1985), list 08, p. 1 (statistics of periods crimes were committed).

186. App. 8.

187. Buff, "Augsburg," 174.

188. Hanawalt, *Crime and Conflict*, 78, 99, 100, 284; idem, "Violent Death," 304–5.

189. Hammer, "Oxford," 21–22.

190. Geremek, *Margins*, 26.

191. App. 9, s.v. private indictments. S. S. Walker, "Punishing Ravishers," *Journal of Medieval History* 13 (1987): 239, 242–43, argues that the relatives of a ravished woman felt it more important to be compensated than to see the felon punished. The crime itself was viewed as, to use Walker's term, "sexually neutral." J. B. Post is of the same opinion; see "Ravishment of Women and the Statutes of Westminster," in *Legal Records and the Historian*, ed. J. H. Baker (London, 1978), 160. Post believes that the Crown's interest in such cases derived from its desire "to maintain the integrity of family estates" (pp. 154, 160).

192. App. 9, s.v. T = homicides.

193. Alan Harding, *The Law Courts of Medieval England* (London, 1973), 57–68; Jane M. Kaye, "Gaol Delivery Jurisdiction and the Writ 'de Bono et Malo'," *Law Quarterly Review* 93 (1977): 270–71; Hunnisett, *Medieval Coroner* (Cambridge, 1961), 255–60; Langbein, "Jury of Presentment and the Coroner," *Columbia Law Review* 33 (1933): 1337; Hanus, "Certiorari," *American Journal of Legal History* 12 (1968): 63ff.

194. M. J. Russell, "Trial by Battle and the Appeals of Felony," *Journal of Legal History* 2 (1980): 135–45; Hunnisett, *Medieval Coroner*, 55–60; D. R. Ernst, "The Moribund Appeal of Death," *American Journal of Legal History* 28 (1984): 164–67; Pike, *History*, 289–92; Bellamy, *Crime and Public Order*, 125–31; Post, "Ravishment," 152–53.

195. Blanshei, "Bologna," 121–22, 129–30.

196. See Schultheiss, *Achtbücher*, 2:489; Baader, "Polizeiordnungen," 14–15.

197. App. 10, s.v. public indictments. See Baader, "Polizeiordnungen," 14–15. Given, Inquisitors," 347, argues that the recording of cases was in itself an effort on the part of governmental officials to repress crime. The city of Nuremberg from 1287 was exempt from the jurisdiction of foreign courts. In 1313 the settling of cases by the verdict of jurors (*Schöffen*) was introduced. In 1320 the city acquired jurisdiction over all criminals. Between 1323 and 1339 the post of mayor of the city passed from the hands of Franconian knights, chosen by the emperor, to those of citizens of the city. From 1355 peasants belonging to Nuremberg citizens had to sue at the city court. In 1377, with the city now having a high court of justice, the office of "questioners" (*Frager*) was introduced. From 1385 the mayor of the city

(*Schultheiss*) lost his position as a justice. See Schultheiss, *Achtbücher*, 1:30–40, 42–44, 46–47, 65 (prosecution ex officio by the city), 88 (conviction of wrongdoers), 111 (jurisdiction over the city's hinterland), 127, 132, 155.

198. App. 10, s.v. appeals of approvers.

199. *Loc. cit.*, s.v. police action.

200. *Loc. cit.*, s.v. pledges found.

201. Buff, "Augsburg," 210.

202. Sir F. Pollock and F. W. Maitland, *The History of English Law*, 1:151; F. W. Maitland, *Justice and Police* (London, 1885), p. 136; Harding, *Law Courts*, 56; Hanawalt, *Crime and Conflict*, 66–67; Bellamy, *Crime and Public Order*, 121, 124; Pike, *History*, 120; Morris, *Frankpledge*, 94–106, 117, 123–28, 161–63; H. R. T. Summerson, "Law Enforcement in Thirteenth-Century England," *American Journal of Legal History* 22 (1979): 313–27.

203. Summerson, "Law Enforcement," 322–26; Anne R. DeWindt, "Peasant Power Structures in Fourteenth-Century King's Ripton," *Medieval Studies* 38 (1976): 244 ff.; J. A. Raftis, "The Concentration of Responsibility in Five Villages," *Medieval Studies* 28 (1966): 92–108.

204. See above, n. 193.

205. Hunnisett, *Medieval Coroner*, 69–75; H. G. Richardson, "Year Books and Plea Rolls as Sources of Historical Information," *TRHS* 4 (5) (1922): 35–36; Kaye, "Gaol Delivery," 263; M. T. Clanchey, "Highway Robbery and Trial by Battle in the Hants. Eyre of 1249," in *Medieval Legal Records*, ed. R. F. Hunnisett and J. B. Post (London, 1978), 29–30; Hanawalt, *Crime and Conflict*, 283; F. C. Hamil, "The King's Approvers," *Speculum* 11 (1936): 238–58; J. B. Post, "Evidential Value of Approvers' Appeals," 93–100.

206. Cozzi, "Venice," 332; Blanshei, "Bologna," 121, 127.

207. Coopland, "Punishment," 373; Geremek, *Margins*, 48–61; Monique Mestayer, "La procedure criminelle à Douai a la fin du XIVe siècle," in *Cornua Legum*, ed. G. Macours (Bruges, 1987), 111–20.

208. App. 11, s.v. escape and outlawry.

209. Schultheiss, *Achtbücher*, 1:88, 89, 97. The Nuremberg Outlawry Book No. I contains a total of 1,020 cases, in 155 of which (15.2%) people were outlawed. On outlawry in general, see Schultheiss, *loc. cit.*, 49–53. On p. 54 he argues that outlawries decreased because of a decrease in crime rates, a decrease that in turn was caused by the greater piety of the people and the infliction of more severe punishments by the governments. This thesis is, to say the least, debatable. The property of those outlawed was not confiscated (see p. 55). On pp. 80–81 Schultheiss argues that the number of banishments from the city increased at the end of the fourteenth century, as a result of a period of warfare.

210. See above, n. 196.

211. Buff, "Augsburg," 160, 178, 186, 208–10, 212–16.

212. Hunnisett, *Medieval Coroner*, 59; Pike, *History*, 293; Hilton, "Medieval Society," 250–52; Morris, *Frankpledge*, 153; Richardson, "Year Books," 37; Raftis, "Concentration of Responsibility," 108, 116; Fraser and Emsley, "Justice," 178; Pugh, "Reflexions," 104; Rye, "Notes," 210; Bellamy, *Crime and Public Order*, 187; Given, *Society and Homicide*, 207; Summerson, "Law Enforcement," 313.

213. D. J. Clayton, "Peace Bonds and the Maintenance of Law in Late Medieval

England—The Example of Cheshire," *Bulletin of the Institute of Historical Research* 58 (1985): 133–48.

214. Blanshei, "Bologna," 121–22; Becker, "Florence," 287, 289; Cozzi, "Venice," 293–94, 311–12, 323, 339.

215. Becker, "Florence," 287–89.

216. Geremek, *Margins*, 25–37.

217. App. 12.

218. *Loc. cit.*, s.v. banishments.

219. *Loc. cit.*, s.v. self-banishments. Since our source is an outlawry book, it is to be expected that most punishments recorded are outlawries, banishments, and self-banishments. Only rarely are other types of punishment recorded.

220. See Baader, "Polizeiordnungen," 14–23; Kroeschell, *Rechtsgeschichte*, 2:209, 213.

221. App. 12, s.v. executions.

222. See Given, "Inquisidors," 340 ff.

223. App. 12, s.v. corporal punishment; see Schultheiss, *Achtbücher*, 1:78.

224. App. 12, s.v. confiscations and fines. See Schultheiss, *Achtbücher*, 1:62, 75, 79. A large fine of 30 pounds was rare. The city clerks earned, according to their importance, either 5, 8, 32 1/2, or 60 florins a year, or 12 or 20 pounds a year. See ibid., 143–50. In constructing my statistics, I have counted the destruction of a castle as a confiscation.

225. App. 12, s.v. other punishments; see Schultheiss, *Achtbücher*, 1:78.

226. App. 12, s.v. compensation; see S. S. Walker, "Punishing Convicted Ravishers," *Journal of Medieval History* 13 (1987): 237, 242, 243.

227. From 1313 there were trial juries (*Schöffengerichte*) in Nuremberg; from 1377 the office of questioner (*Frager*) is found. See Schultheiss, *Achtbücher*, 1:31, 37. Schultheiss argues (pp. 64, 69) that abjurations should be regarded as pretrial proceedings. The city authorities tried to avoid accusing and trying their citizens, being primarily concerned to see victims compensated. Nicholas, in "Crime and Punishment," 1162 ff., offers a similar argument about legal proceedings in Ghent. In Nuremberg, foreigners were treated much more severely than citizens; they were prosecuted energetically and were subjected to torture during their interrogations. See 1:88–94.

228. See Baader, "Polizeiordnungen," 14; Hermann Knapp, *Das alte Nürnberger Kriminalrecht* (Berlin, 1896), 52–130; Schultheiss, *Achtbücher*, 1:56–72. Abjuration was also known in northern Germany, Flanders, Würzburg, Regensburg, and Frankfurt am Main. It was most commonly imposed in cases of larceny, primarily against foreigners rather than against citizens. Abjurations made up only about ten percent of all banishments, and became progressively more rare.

229. App. 12, s.v. banishments. See Schultheiss, *Achtbücher*, 1:79–81, 97. In Outlawry Book No. I there are recorded 1,020 cases, 282 of which (27.6 percent) are self-banishments, 583 (57.1 percent) banishments.

230. App. 12, s.v. self-banishments. The banned person took the oath of *Urfehde*, promising not to be the city's enemy in times to come because of punishment by its officers. See Schultheiss, *Achtbücher*, 1:82–86 (from 1323 on).

231. Foreigners were even banned from the city on mere suspicion. See Schultheiss, *Achtbücher*, 1:54, 76–77, 79.

232. Buff, "Augsburg," 163–64, 166, 176, 178–80. See App. 12, s.v. pardons; Schultheiss, *Achtbücher*, 2:772, 1113; Knapp, *Nürnberger Kriminalrecht*, 132–37.

233. Demandt, "Recht," 14–17.

234. Kriegk, *Bürgertum*, 200–203.

235. Rye, "Notes," 204; Fraser and Emsley, "Justice," 178; Rev. J. C. Cox, *The Sanctuaries and Sanctury Seekers of Medieval England* (London, 1911), 12–24, 271–76; Hunnisett, *Medieval Coroner*, 37–54; N. M. Trenholme, *The Right of Sanctuary in England* (St. Louis, 1901), 313–36.

236. Rye, "Notes," 207; Hanawalt, "Female Felon," 265–66; Pollock and Maitland, *History*, 2:452, 461.

237. Ibid., 2:488; Bellamy, *Crime and Public Order*, 169; DeWindt and DeWindt, *Royal Justice*, 101–3; Pike, *History*, 137–39; Given, *Society and Homicide*, 10; Morris, *Frankpledge*, 152–53; Hanawalt, "Violent Death," 308; F. W. Maitland, "Liability of the Hundred," *Collected Papers* (Cambridge, 1911), 246.

238. Pollock and Maitland *History*, 1:533; Hunnisett, *Medieval Coroner*, 192; P. R. Hyams, *King, Lords, and Peasants* (Oxford, 1980), 131–32; R. H. Hilton, *The English Peasantry in the Later Middle Ages* (Oxford, 1975), 21.

239. Fraser and Emsley, "Justice," 177; Stones, "Folville," 130; Pugh, "Reflexions," 84–92; Bellamy, *Crime and Public Order*, 158–59; Given, *Society and Homicide*, 93–140; Hanawalt, "Female Felon," 256, 266; idem, *Crime and Conflict*, 44–63; idem, "Economic Influences," 295; idem, "Violent Death," 315–16; Hammer, "Oxford," 4; DeWindt and DeWindt, *Royal Justice*, 59; Edward Powell, "Social Research and the Use of Criminal Records," *Michigan Law Review* 79 (1981): 967–78.

240. Bellamy, *Crime and Public Order*, 162; Pollock and Maitland, *History*, 2:481; Hunnisett, *Medieval Coroner*, 78; N. D. Hurnard, *The King's Pardon for Homicide before A.D. 1307* (Oxford, 1969), 194–213; Cox, *Sanctuaries*, 16; Stones, "Folville," 120, 128; Bellamy, "Coterel," 700, 705; Given, *Society and Homicide*, 207; Simon J. Payling, "Law and Arbitration in Nottinghamshire, 1399–1461," in *People, Politics and Community in the Later Middle Ages*, ed. Joel Rosenthal and Colin Richmond (New York, 1987), 140–60.

241. Becker, "Florence," 290–91; D. M. Nicholas, "Crime and Punishment in 14th Century Ghent," *Revue belge de philologie et d'histoire* 48 (1970): 1162–76; Walker, "Ravishers," 237–43.

242. Geremek, *Margins*, 48; Lavoie, "Statistiques," 6–18; Grava, "Justice," 305–12; F. W. Maitland, "Malice Aforethought," *Collected Papers* (Cambridge, 1911), 320–23. In southern France there was even a tendency to limit punishment in the case of heresy. See Given, "Inquisitors," 340, 353, where the author states that of the 930 punishments imposed on heretics, only forty-two amounted to death by burning.

243. See Nicholas, *Ghent*, 289–334, 1141–76. But not so in the comital cities: See Mestayer, *Procedure criminelle à Douai*, 111 ff.

244. Blanshei, "Bologna," 121–26; Becker, "Florence," 281–91.

245. Chojnacki, "Venice," 200–201, 225–27; G. Ruggiero, "Excusable Murder: Insanity and Reason in Early Renaissance Venice," *Journal of Social History* 16 (1984): 109–14.

246. See above, sections II and III.

247. See above, sections IV and V.

248. See above, Nuremberg is an example of what might be called a "northern-type" of criminal motivation. In Italy, however, a "southern-type," with crimes of passion, is more common.

249. See above, sections VII to IX.

250. See above, sections X to XII.

APPENDIX

Statistics

Source: Die Acht-,Verbots- und Fehdebücher Nürnbergs,1285-1400,
ed. Werner Schultheiss,Nuremberg 1960.

1.List of cases per annum

1285 - No.151-53
1286 - 154-64,173-75
1287 - nil
1288 - nil
1289 - nil
1290 - No.165-72,176-78
1291 - 179-83
1292-1297 (six years) - No.1-62
1298 - No.63-64,184-86,495
1299 - 187-91
1300 - 192-95
1301 - 65-67,196-97
1302 - 68,198
1303 - 69,583-85
1304 - 70-71,586-89
1305 - 91-107
1306 - 108-10
1307 - 72-74,111-12,199
1308 - 75-79,200-09,595
1309 - 80-90,113,210-13
1310 - 214-15,223-39
1311 - 240-47,595-98
1312 - 216,248,599
1313 - 217,249,600-01
1314 - 218,250-52
1315 - 114-25,253-58
1316 - 126-29,259-68,602
1317 - 130-33,269-81
1318 - 282-87,603
1319 - 134-38,288-95,590,604
1320 - 139-40,219-21,296-309
1321 - 141,222,310-22,605-07
1322 - 142-49,323-26
1323 - 150,327-39
1324 - 340-49
1325 - 350-53
1326 - 354-68,608
1327 - 369-70,594
1328 - 371-72
1329 - 373-90
1330 - 391-99
1331 - 400-14
1332 - 415-31,591-93
1333 - 432-56
1334 - 457-59
1335 - 460-86
1336 - 487-94,496-514,609
1337 - 515-39,548-52
1338 - 540-47,610

1339 - No.553-59
1340 - 560-61
1341 - 562-70,611,691
1342 - 571-72
1343 - 573-77,612-14,743-57
1344 - 578-80,692
1345 - 581-82,615-16,693-96
1346 - 617-18,697-700
1348 - 627-28,702-30,742
1349 - 629-33,634-38,731-41
1350 - 639-64
1351 - 633,665-78
1352 - nil
1353 - No.679-81,758
1354 - 682,684-86
1355 - 683
1356 - nil
1357 - No.687-90
1358 - nil
1359 - nil
1360 - nil
1361 - nil
1362 - No.1079
1363 - 1080
1364 - nil
1365 - nil
1366 - nil
1367 - No.1081
1368 - 1082
1369 - 1083-84
1370 - 1085-86
1371 - 1087-88
1372 - 1089-92
1373 - 1093
1374 - 1094 a-e
1375 - 1095 a-e
1376 - 1096 a-f
1377 - 1097 a-b
1378 - 1098-99
1379 - 1100-02
1380 - 1103
1381 - 759-809,1024,1026-30 b,1032-35,1104 a-i
1382 - 810-50,1036-48e,1049-50,1105
1383 - 851-89,1048 f-g,1051-64,1106-07
1384 - 890-929 c,1065-71,1107-08
1385 - 1109
1386 - 1110
1387 - 1111
1388 - nil
1389 - No.1112
1390 - nil
1391 - No.930-51,1103
1392 - 952-1017,1114-18
1393 - 1119-21
1394 - 1030 c-1031 b,1072-74,1122-23
1395 - 1124
1396 - 1125-27
1397 - 1128-32 b,1132 d-e
1398 - 1075-78,1132 c,1133-36

1399 - No.1025,1137-39
1400 - nil
1401 - nil
1402 - nil
1403 - No.1018-23
(*)

2.Criminal Statistics (**)
a.Abbreviations:
No. = number;V = crimes in total (cases);T = homicide;KV = assault and violence against persons;R = robbery;E = burglary;D = larceny; H = receiving of stolen goods;FS = prohibited gambling;BF = fraud and coining of false money;Br = arson;PV = political crimes;RV = religious crimes;SV = sexual offenses;sV = other crimes;oA = unspecified crimes;EV = mentioning of professional criminals (cases)

b.list of crimes per years

years	V	T	KV	R	E	D	H	FS	BF	Br	PV	RV	SV	sV	oA	EV
1285-86	17	1	-	-	-	7	-	-	-	-	-	-	-	-	9	2
1290-91	16	-	-	-	-	3	-	1	-	-	-	-	-	-	12	-
1292-97	61	30	8	1	-	-	-	-	-	-	-	-	1	1	20	1
1298-99	11	2	-	-	-	-	-	-	-	1	1	-	-	1	6	2
1300-10	94	18	2	-	-	1	-	-	1	-	1	1	1	3	66	3
1311-20	112	30	1	-	-	5	-	2	-	-	1	-	-	1	72	12
1321-30	105	10	3	-	-	8	-	-	-	1	-	1	1	-	81	3
1331-40	164	13	1	-	-	3	2	2	-	-	2	7	4	1	129	5
1341-47	51	2	1	-	1	4	-	-	-	-	3	2	10	1	27	-
1348-51	95	6	11	5	1	7	-	1	-	2	34	6	9	2	11	5
1353-55	6	2	-	-	-	-	-	-	-	-	1	1	-	-	2	-
1357	3	1	-	-	-	-	-	-	-	-	-	-	-	-	2	-
1362-63	2	-	-	-	-	-	-	1	-	-	-	1	-	-	-	-
1367-80	42	-	-	30	-	-	-	-	1	-	9	2	-	-	-	-
1381	66	2	16	12	-	2	-	8	1	1	7	5	5	5	2	4
1382	59	4	10	11	-	1	-	6	1	-	10	6	4	3	3	3
1383	63	-	11	22	-	5	-	5	1	-	4	2	1	4	8	1
1384	45	5	11	7	-	1	-	1	-	-	5	2	5	6	2	2
1385-87	4	-	-	3	-	-	-	-	-	-	-	-	-	1	-	-
1389	1	-	-	-	-	-	-	-	-	-	1	-	-	-	-	-
1391	22	8	9	1	-	-	-	2	-	1	1	-	-	-	-	-
1392	67	13	20	3	-	3	1	6	10	-	3	2	-	-	6	-
1393-99	50	1	2	22	-	-	-	-	2	-	22	-	1	-	-	-
1403	6	-	4	-	-	1	-	-	-	-	-	-	-	1	-	-
total	V	T	KV	R	E	D	H	FS	BF	Br	PV	RV	SV	sV	oA	EV
	1162	148	110	117	2	51	3	35	17	6	105	38	42	30	458	43

(*) 1285-1403 = 118 years,but only cases of 102 years are recorded in the source
(**) The numbers in brackets or in the footnotes are the numbers of the cases in the Nuremberg outlawry books in Schultheiss' edition.

	T	KV	R	E	D	H	FS	BF	Br	PV	RV	SV	sV	oA	EV
criminals															
professional	-	-	30	-	-	1&	10	-	-	-	-	18	-	-	-
"gangs"	-	-	39	-	-	-	-	-	-	-	-	-	-	-	-
more than 1 case	-	-	13*	-	-	-	-	-	-	-	-	-	-	-	-
related	11	1	17	-	1	1	-	2	1	17	7	1	1	20	4
same place	1	-	-	-	1	-	3	1	1	6	-	1	-	10	-
master/servant	1	1	-	-	1	-	-	-	-	9	-	-	-	-	-
couple	2	1	1+	-	4	1	-	-	-	2	4	2	7	23	4
unmarried couple	-	-	-	-	-	-	-	-	-	-	-	5	-	-	-
friends	-	-	-	-	-	-	-	-	-	-	-	8	-	-	-
same guild	4	8	-	-	2	-	-	-	-	6	-	-	-	8	-
crim./victim															
related	5	1	-	-	1§	-	-	1a	1b	-	-	-	-	-	-
neighbours	-	-	-	-	-	-	-	-	1c	-	-	-	-	-	-
same place	1	-	-	-	-	-	-	-	-	-	-	-	-	-	-
married	6	1	-	-	-	-	-	-	-	-	-	1	-	-	-
victim wife	5	1	-	-	-	-	-	-	-	-	-	-	-	-	-
victim husband	1	-	-	-	-	-	-	-	-	-	-	1	-	-	-
unacquainted	-	-	-	-	-	-	-	-	-	-	-	9	-	-	-
same guild	2	-	-	-	-	-	-	-	-	-	-	-	1	-	-
rivaling guild	-	8	-	-	1#	-	-	-	-	5	-	-	-	-	-
servant victim	2	-	-	-	1ß	-	-	-	-	1d	-	3e	1	-	-

& 952
* 662,1032-34,1049,1050-55,1058,1102,1104a
+ 1062
§ 1023
a 889
b 944
c 637
799
ß 856
d 802-04
e 801,811. 1137

4.Local origins and social backgrounds of criminals and victims

a.-f.	T	KV	R	E	D	H	FS	BF	Br	PV	RV*	SV	sV	oA	EVx
city-criminals	173	99	11	-	51	5	36	10	6	246	275	43	49	509	159
non-city	70	42	425	2	18	-	45	17	4	703	63	26	9	407	44
city-victims	124	59	164	2	14	-	-	-	3	52	-	22	8	21	-
non-city	16	6	33	1	2	-	-	-	-	5	-	-	-	-	-
sex/crim. m	239	139	434	2	49	2	80	23	8	941	238	44	41	721	157
f	4	2	2	-	20	3	1	4	2	18	100	25	17	195	46
sex/victims m	121	49	181	2	12	-	-	-	4	12	-	5	3	17	-
f	12	9	2	-	2	-	-	-	-	1	-	17	1	4	-
children	2	-	-	-	-	-	-	-	-	-	-	1k	-	-	-
nobles/crim.	1a	-	149	-	-	-	-	-	-	301	-	2l	1q	2r	-
victims	3b	-	2c	-	-	-	-	-	-	1m	-	2n	-	-	-
crim.clerks	-	1d	4e	-	1j	-	-	-	-	1o	4	1p	-	6s	-
cleric.vict.	1f	2g	1h	1	2k	-	-	-	-	-	-	-	-	1t	-
patrician crim.	7	4	3	-	1	-	-	1	-	12	6	-	1	16	-
vict.	6	2	55i	-	1	-	-	-	-	-	-	-	-	-	-
jews/criminals	-	-	1	-	-	-	1	-	-	2	-	4	-	10	-
victims	-	2	4	-	1	-	-	-	-	2	-	-	-	-	-

---

* religious crimes are cases No. 192,387,437,591-93,617,619,664,685, 707,725,730,731,760,761,763,770,779,822,823,827,830,831,844,874,876, 893,920,971,1002,1079,1099,1100.

x Terms used in the records for describing professional criminals:
ruffiani: No.30,125,134,201,360,399,413,463.
malefactores: No.82,218,228,241,244,246,263,265,279,280,294,315.
infamia: No.123,156,163,186,495.
Unendlichkeit:No.765.
Ungeratenheit:No.646.
Ungezogenheit:No.764,893.
Übeltätigkeit:No.832.
böser Leumund:No.479,724,726,738,760,800,839,841,851,917.
Bube: No.451.
schädliche Leute: No.598.
pedellus suspectorum: No.433.
k 624
a 1041
l 620,627
q 1019
r 337,393
b 53,56,256
c 1076,1138
m 1030b
n 594,615
d 1071
e 1076,1086,1095c,1096e
j 295
o 1024
p 625
s criminous clerks in No.91,124,161,166,282,469
f 519
g 776
h 1096f
k 614,856
t 965
i 5 of those 55 Nuremberg patricians were ransomed.

4.g.
1. Occupations of criminals

criminals	T	KV	R	E	D	H	FS	BF	Br	PV	RV	SV	sV	oA	EV
civil servants	2	-	5	-	-	-	-	-	-	-	1	1	1	3	1
shopkeepers	-	-	-	-	-	1	1	3	-	5	3	-	5	8	2
furriers	1	-	-	1	1	-	1	-	-	1	2	-	1	5	-
dyers	2	2	-	-	-	-	-	-	-	1	12	-	-	-	-
coopers	-	-	-	-	-	-	-	-	-	-	-	1	-	2	-
painters	-	3	-	-	-	-	-	-	-	-	-	-	-	-	-
wool-pickers	2	1	-	-	-	-	-	-	-	-	-	-	-	2	-
purse-makers	-	1	-	-	-	-	-	-	-	1	2	1	-	1	-
weavers	1	1	-	-	2	-	-	-	-	4	4	-	-	3	-
silk spinners	-	-	1	-	-	-	-	-	-	2	-	-	-	-	-
tailors	5	5	-	-	-	-	2	-	-	21	1	-	1	8	-
mantlers	-	2	-	-	-	-	-	-	-	2	2	-	-	1	-
saddlers	5	-	-	-	-	-	-	-	-	4	-	-	-	2	-
glovers	-	-	-	-	-	-	-	-	-	-	-	-	-	3	-
leatherworkers	-	-	-	-	3	-	-	-	-	-	-	-	-	11	3
cobblers	1	3	-	-	2	-	3	-	-	12	-	-	1	7	3
ropers	2	-	1	-	-	-	2	-	-	1	-	-	-	-	-
cartwrights	1	-	-	-	1	-	2	-	-	1	-	-	-	1	-
joiners	1	2	-	-	-	-	-	-	-	1	-	-	-	3	2
masons	-	-	1	-	-	-	-	-	-	-	-	-	-	-	-
stone-masons	1	1	-	-	1	-	-	-	-	1	-	-	-	-	-
carpenters	-	3	1	-	-	-	-	-	-	1	2	-	1	3	1
blacksmiths	2	4	-	-	1	-	4	-	-	25	2	2	1	16	-
wire-smiths	-	2	-	-	-	-	-	-	-	5	-	-	-	3	-
cutlers	2	1	-	-	-	-	-	-	-	13	-	-	-	4	-
brass-smiths	-	1	1	-	-	-	-	-	-	6	-	-	-	6	-
blade-smiths	3	2	-	-	-	-	-	-	-	1	-	-	-	-	-
arrow-smiths	-	1	-	-	-	-	-	-	-	1	-	-	-	-	-
brass-founders	3	1	-	-	1	-	-	-	-	3	-	-	-	-	-
needleworkers	-	-	-	-	-	-	1	-	-	-	-	-	-	-	-
locksmiths	-	1	-	-	-	-	-	-	-	2	-	-	-	1	-
goldsmiths	1	2	-	-	-	-	-	-	-	2	-	1	-	2	-
mirror-makers	-	1	-	-	-	-	-	-	-	-	-	-	-	-	-
herdsmen	1	-	-	-	2	-	-	-	-	-	-	-	1	5	1
hunters	1	-	-	-	-	-	-	-	-	2	4	-	-	-	-
scriveners	1	2	-	-	-	-	-	-	-	3	1	-	-	6	1
stewards	1	-	-	-	-	-	-	-	-	1	2	-	-	1	-
farmers	1	1	-	-	-	-	1	-	-	1	-	-	-	3	-
millers	3	-	-	-	1	-	-	3	-	1	1	-	-	12	5
fishers	1	-	-	-	-	-	2	-	-	-	1	-	-	3	-
bath-keepers	3	3	-	-	-	-	1	-	-	-	-	3	-	7	1
waiters	2	2	-	-	-	-	4	-	-	-	2	-	-	5	1
cooks	-	-	1	-	3	-	-	-	-	-	-	-	-	4	3
butchers	2	3	-	-	-	-	2	-	-	8	1	1	-	13	-
bakers	8	8	-	-	-	1	3	-	-	2	2	1	2	36	2
inn-keepers	1	-	5	-	-	-	-	-	-	4	-	2	1	-	-
carters	-	1	-	-	-	-	-	-	-	-	-	-	-	3	-
porters	2	-	-	-	-	-	-	-	-	-	-	1	-	-	-
brickmakers	-	3	-	-	-	-	-	-	-	-	-	-	-	1	-
servants	15	9	18	-	2	1	1	-	-	33	5	5	-	13	-

2. Occupations of victims

victims	T	KV	R	E	D	H	FS	BF	Br	PV	RV	SV	sV	oA	EV
furriers	1	-	-	-	-	-	-	-	-	-	-	-	1	-	-
dyers	1	-	-	-	1	-	-	-	-	-	-	-	-	-	-
painters	-	1	-	-	-	-	-	-	-	-	-	-	-	-	-
tailors	1	-	-	-	-	-	-	-	-	-	-	-	-	-	-
leatherworkers	2	-	-	-	1	-	-	-	-	-	-	1	-	-	-
weavers	1	-	-	-	1	-	-	-	-	-	-	-	-	-	-
needleworkers	1	-	-	-	-	-	-	-	-	-	-	-	-	1	-
wool-pickers	-	-	-	-	-	-	-	-	-	-	-	-	-	1	-
coopers	1	-	-	-	-	-	-	-	-	-	-	-	-	-	-
cartwrights	-	-	-	-	-	-	-	-	-	-	-	-	1	-	-
blade-smiths	1	-	-	-	-	-	-	-	-	-	-	-	-	-	-
cutlers	1	-	-	-	-	-	-	-	-	-	-	-	-	1	-
brass-smiths	1	-	-	-	-	-	-	-	-	-	-	-	-	1	-
goldsmiths	-	-	1	-	-	-	-	-	-	-	-	-	-	-	-
stove-fitters	1	-	-	-	-	-	-	-	-	-	-	-	-	-	-
tin-smiths	-	2	-	-	-	-	-	-	-	-	-	-	-	-	-
bath-keepers	1	3	1	-	-	-	-	-	-	-	-	2	-	-	-
fishers	1	-	-	-	-	-	-	-	-	-	-	-	-	-	-
carters	-	-	3	-	-	-	-	-	-	-	-	-	-	-	-
millers	2	-	-	-	-	-	-	-	-	-	-	-	-	-	-
pawnbrokers	-	1	-	-	-	-	-	-	-	-	-	-	-	-	-
merchants	1	-	102	-	-	-	-	-	-	-	-	-	-	-	-
scriveners	-	1	1	-	1	-	-	-	-	-	-	-	-	-	-
bakers	1	-	-	-	-	-	-	-	-	-	-	-	1	-	-
butchers	-	-	1	-	-	-	-	-	-	-	-	-	-	-	-
porters	1	-	-	-	-	-	-	-	-	-	-	-	-	-	-
hunters	-	1	-	-	-	-	-	-	-	-	-	-	-	-	-
servants	3	2	10	-	-	-	-	-	-	-	-	-	-	-	-
estate owners	-	1	15	-	-	-	-	-	3	5	-	-	-	-	-
civil servants	-	3	7	-	-	-	-	-	-	15	-	-	-	1	-

4.h. Nuremberg patricians as criminals and victims

criminals
crimes: 51
criminals: 59 (7 female)
criminals in toto: 3344
patricians = 1.76 percent

victims
crimes: 64
victims: 66 (1 female)
victims in toto: 532
patricians = 12.4 percent

list of cases:

criminals:
No.52,54,64,73,125,127,134,141,194, 196,197,202,216,316,320,336,337,382, 386,511,560,591,592,593,606,616,632, 633,634,642,655,704,731,792,810,812, 842,861,905,908,945,1024,1031a-b, 1096a,1099,1104e,1114,1132c.

victims:
No.2,256,289,292,390,661,662, 668,673,677,682,683,797,1029, 1032,1033,1036,1048,1o48a,1052, 1066,1068,1081,1082,1085,1086, 1089,1093,1094,1094a-b,1095, 1095b+d,1096,1096b,1097a,1098b, 1104f,1106,1119,1129,1133.

Nuremberg patrician families mentioned in records:

criminals:		**victims:**	
Aichacher	2		
Ackermann	1	Ammann	1
Baumgartner	1		
Behaim	1	Behaim	3
Böhmer	1		
Bürgler	2		
Dörrer	1	Deichsler	2
Ebner	1	Ebner	2
Eisenhuter	1	Eisenhuter	1
		Eisvogel	1
Eseler	1	Eseler	1
		Flextorfer	1
Fürer	2	Fürer	1
Geusmid	1		
Gostenhofer	6		
Graser	2	Graser	2
		Grolant	2
		Gross	2
Gruntherr	1	Gruntherr	2
		Haller	2
Heiden	7	Heiden	2
Imhof	3	Imhof	5
Kohler	1	Kohler	2
		Krauter	1
Kress	2	Kress	1
Kuhdorfer	1	Lochheim	1
Maurer	1	Maurer	4
Maler	2	Männlein	4
Muffel	2	Muffel	2
Nützel	2		
Ortlieb	1	Ortlieb	1
Pfinzing	1		
Pilgram	1	Pilgram	1
		Pirckheimer	2
Rater	1	Rümelein	1
Rieter	2	Rummel	4
Schürstab	1	Sailer	1
		Schopper	1
Teufel	1	Seckendorfer	1
Tucher	1	Stromeyer	5
		Volckamer	2
		Vorchtel	2

5. Causes and motivations for committing crimes

homicide: gain 3, arguments 4, sexual 1
assault: gain 1, arguments 14, political 6, jealousy 3, ill fame 2, racism 1, unknown 3
arson: arguments 2 (1)
political crimes: gain 6, arguments 38, political 13, treason 6, ill fame 6, racism 2, trade unionism 3, contempt of court 9 (2)
religious crimes: gain 2, political 6, religion 12
sexual offenses: gain 13, sexual 29
other crimes: gain 11, arguments 6

Illegal acquiring of property

robbery (3)
ransom - 21 cases
booty - 232 horses
135 cattle
money: 6798 pounds of hellers, 119 fl., 1 threescore of Meissen pennies (10 cases)
goods: nails, 4 merchant carts, bales of fustian, cloth, 1 barrel of copper, spices and sugar, 1 shipsload of iron
arms: 6
clothes: 13
jewels: 2

larceny:
booty - cloth, etc. - value: 8 1/2 pounds of hellers (4)
cloth, etc. - value unknown (5)
money, etc. - value unknown (6)
money - value: 14 pounds of hellers (7)
bowls, mugs - value unknown (8)
animals - value unknown (9)

political crimes: (10)
value of booty: 500 pounds of hellers, 7500 florins, horses, cattle, money

---

(1) No.944,1026
(2) No.652,656,666,718,802-04
(3) No.661-62,676-77,981,1027-28,1032-37,1039,1043-45,1048g,1049,1051, 1054-55,1057-59,1066,1069,1076,1078,1084-85,1087,1093,1094b,1095c-d, 1096f,1098a,1104a,1104e-g,1105,1107,1110,1119,1129,1133-35,1138-39.
(4) No.471-72 - also receiving of stolen goods
(5) No.631,882-83,983
(6) No.614,740,794,799,1011
(7) No.814
(8) No.897
(9) No.692
(10) No.616,1048,1091-92,1127

6.Modus Operandi
use of weapons in T and KV: swords 9,knives 41,blunt instruments 4
stab wounds 16,blows 20 head-blows 7,wounded and mistreated 14
fishing rods used in 1 D (692)
false dice used in 5 FS
false money coined in 6 cases of BF
1 use of false weights in BF,1 opening of letters
17 cursings,6 perjuries in RV
SV: 1 homosexual assault,7 rapes,2 exhibition,3 living together unmarried,5 sexual intercourse with prohibited groups (4 jews),11 procuring,10 unchastity,2 adultery;transvestitism,incest,bigamy,prohibited prostitution 1 each
sV: 4 injuries,6 breaks of merchant law,3 non-acquiring of citizenship,2 slander

7.Places crimes were committed *

indoors:		57 V (9 T,12 KV,7 Br,16 SV)
outdoors:		142 V (5 T, 8 KV,113 R,10 sV)
inside Nuremberg:	Laufer-Gate:	8 V
	city-hall:	5 V
	Hospital-gate:	6 V
	known:	71 V
	unknown:	205 V
outside Nuremberg:	in toto	173 V (117 R,40 PV)
	forests	10 V (10 R)
	villages	11 V (6 RV)

8.Periods crimes were committed

seasons	T	KV	R	E	D	H	FS	BF	Br	PV	RV	SV	sV	oA	EV
winter	15	17	1	1	11	1	6	2	-	12	7	9	2	83	6
spring	22	22	8	-	9	2	5	2	1	11	11	5	3	82	7
summer	22	30	10	-	11	-	16	1	-	12	9	12	6	72	5
fall	16	22	5	-	9	-	5	1	2	13	3	10	6	55	5
nighttime	3	2	1	-	-	-	-	-	1	-	-	-	2	-	-
daytime	-	1	-	-	-	-	-	-	-	-	-	-	-	-	-
Sunday	-	1	-	-	-	-	-	-	-	-	-	-	-	-	-
Monday	-	-	-	-	-	-	-	-	-	1	-	1	-	-	-
Tuesday	-	-	1	-	-	-	-	-	-	-	-	-	-	-	-
Wednesday	-	-	1	-	-	-	-	-	-	-	-	-	-	-	-
Thursday	-	-	1	-	-	-	-	-	-	-	1	-	-	-	-
Friday	-	-	-	-	-	-	-	-	-	-	-	-	-	-	-
Saturday	-	-	-	-	-	-	-	-	-	-	-	-	-	-	-

* See also Appendix,No.13,Nuremberg city map

<u>9.Private indictments</u>

indictment by:

victim		6 KV,64 R,6 D,3 FS,1 BF,3 Br,1 PV,3 SV,6 sV,24 oA
victim's	father	17 T,3 SV
	mother	7 T
	brother	31 T,1 oA
	son	2 T,1 KV
	daughter	2 T
	wife	29 T,1 KV,1 oA
	husband	2 T,1 KV
	nephew	5 T
	uncle	2 T
	in-laws	1 T,1 oA
	relatives	5 T,1 KV
	friends	1 T,3 KV
	employer	1 T
	unacquainted	11 T

<u>10.Public Indictments</u>

	T	KV	R	D	H	FS	BF	Br	PV	RV	SV	sV	oA
indictments	30	88	40	45	3	30	8	4	82	33	34	16	10
appeals of approvers	-	-	9	-	-	-	1	-	4	-	-	-	-
pledges found	-	-	-	-	-	-	-	-	-	-	-	-	11
police actions	-	-	7	-	-	-	-	-	2	-	-	-	-

<u>11.Escape and Outlawry</u>

	T	KV	R	D	Br	PV	RV	SV	sV	oA	EV
persons	128	13	2	1	1	10	26	1	1	19	6

<u>12.Punishment and Pardon</u>

executions	T	KV	R	D	BF	PV	RV	SV	oA	EV
	1	2	24	4	9	38	7	-	1	1
pardoned before execution	1	2	-	-	-	3	1	1	1	-
corporal punishment	-	5	-	2	-	-	3	4	-	-

confiscation: 1 PV - castles destroyed: 9 PV

other punishments

gambling and entering of an inn prohibited:	53 oA
bearing of arms prohibited for one year:	16 oA
serving in prison:	2 KV,1 R,2 PV,1 RV,1 SV
probation granted under penalty of prison:	44 oA

compensation of victims: 39 R,28 PV,46 RV,1 sV
(and quashing of trials)

Banishments

banishment,paying of fine in case of return or compensation of victim and quashing of trial: 3 T,60 KV,48 FS,9 oA

banishment plus confiscation of goods or fine: 2 T,1 Br,2 PV

banishment,but pardoned: 1 T

banishment	T	KV	R	E	D	H	FS	BF	Br	PV	RV	SV	sV	oA	EV
permanent	19	5	-	1	13	-	-	-	2	67	205	10	2	220	10
100 years	-	-	-	-	-	-	-	-	-	-	1	-	-	2	-
20 years	-	1	-	-	-	-	-	-	-	2	-	-	-	-	-
10 years	7	10	1	-	4	-	-	1	-	12	7	4	3	27	-
9 years	-	-	-	-	-	-	-	-	-	-	-	1	-	-	-
7 years	-	-	-	-	-	-	-	-	1	1	-	-	1	-	-
6 years	-	3	-	-	-	-	-	1	-	-	-	-	-	-	-
5 years	2	13	1	1	-	-	14	1	1	37	35	6	-	206	14
4 years	-	1	-	-	-	-	-	1	-	-	-	-	-	2	-
3 years	-	8	-	-	-	-	3	-	-	11	1	18	5	23	1
2 years	6	5	-	-	2	-	8	-	-	13	4	11	4	61	1
1 year	4	11	2	-	-	-	1	2	-	13	10	7	28	57	-
1/2 year	-	2	-	-	-	-	-	-	-	-	-	-	1	-	-

self-banishment	T	KV	R	E	D	H	FS	BF	Br	PV	RV	SV	sV	oA	EV
permanent	9	-	-	-	32	2	1	-	-	-	1	2	1	181	13
10 years	2	-	-	-	6	-	3	1	-	-	-	1	-	3	1
8 years	-	1	-	-	-	-	-	-	-	-	-	-	-	-	-
6 years	-	-	-	-	-	-	-	-	-	-	-	-	-	2	-
5 years	1	-	-	-	2	-	-	-	-	-	-	1	-	21	2
4 years	-	-	-	-	1	-	-	-	-	-	-	-	-	2	-
3 years	-	-	-	-	-	-	-	-	-	-	-	-	-	5	-
2 years	-	-	-	-	1	-	-	-	-	-	-	1	-	29	-
1 year	-	-	-	-	-	-	-	-	-	-	-	-	-	4	-
1/2 year	-	-	-	-	-	1	-	-	-	-	-	-	-	-	-

Women and the Penal System in Frankfurt am Main, 1562–1696

Maria R. Boes
West Chester University, Pennsylvania

The objective of this chapter is to assess the role and treatment of women in the penal system of an early modern German town, Frankfurt am Main, from 1562 to 1696. Three distinct subjects will be probed: municipal laws, criminal court proceedings, and penal structures. The method consists of both quantitative and qualitative analyses, and comparative data will be furnished throughout in order to compare and contrast patterns of male to female penology.[1]

HISTORICAL SETTING

Frankfurt am Main was a medium-sized town averaging 17,000 to 20,000 inhabitants by the end of the sixteenth century. Despite its relatively small size, it played an important political function by hosting the imperial elections and coronations. Most important, however, Frankfurt was an imperial free city with extensive political and judicial autonomy.

By the late sixteenth century, Frankfurt's economy experienced considerable growth, which resulted in a structural change. Frankfurt changed from an agricultural to a commercial and manufacturing town.[2] This economic recovery also affected Frankfurt's social composition. Although Frankfurt was a predominantly Lutheran town, Calvinist refugees, who were credited with Frankfurt's flourishing economy, arrived in large numbers.[3] The local Jewish population also increased noticeably,[4] as did the number of skilled and unskilled workers.[5]

The administration of the city, including the judiciary, was in the hands of a city council. In criminal adjudication, the city council was empowered to initiate new laws, thereby supplementing the imperial criminal code—the *Constitutio Criminalis Carolina*. This was made possible by the salvatory clause of the *Carolina*, which allowed for local deviations. Frankfurt's criminal jurisdictional power extended over residents and foreigners alike regardless of whether they had committed their crimes locally or elsewhere.[6] The council's verdicts were final since no court of appeal existed for criminal sentences. Appeals had been abandoned during the Diet of Augsburg in 1530.

Considering the extensive powers residing in Frankfurt's city council, its social composition is of great importance. The council was divided into three benches with fourteen male members each. The first two benches were occupied by local patricians, and the third bench was composed of representatives of the local guilds. While the first bench represented the civil court, the combined three benches constituted the criminal court.[7] In other words, while for civil matters only fourteen members were responsible, all forty-two councilors were in charge of criminal adjudication.

On the surface, the evidence suggests that Frankfurt's women were excluded from any judicial say or influence. But such a deduction would be an oversimplication of a more complex operational pattern. Frankfurt's women were not a monolithic group. Patrician women were quite obviously more powerful, and exercised various degrees of influence over their husbands, including those in the city council. This is borne out by the fact that not a single patrician woman was sentenced for criminal wrongdoing in Frankfurt during the 134-year period under investigation. Thus wealth and social status did affect women's criminal adjudication pattern, and the city's municipal legislation partially accounts for that.

An analysis of various local laws reveals the existence of a double standard: the selective influence of wealth and social status on the penal structure. For various categories of crime, in particular, prostitution and fornication, monetary fines could be substituted for physical punishment depending, among other factors, on the financial and social status of the offender.[8] While such legal loopholes worked in favor of women of patrician descent, they served men even more frequently for the simple reason that men gained more wealth, influence, status, and power in the course of the sixteenth century.

Traditionally, while Frankfurt's women had been excluded from the municipal government, they at least were able to join the local guilds.[9] By the mid- to late sixteenth century, however, the city's guilds increasingly barred women from joining their ranks, resulting in lower incomes and the abolition of an alternative life-style for many local women.[10] And Frankfurt as a Protestant city with a Protestant city council seemed to accentuate this occupational gender division. One only has to cite Martin Luther's dictum that "women should remain at home, sit still, keep house, and bear and bring up children."[11] Bearing in mind these economic and social downgrading developments, women could not take advantage of Frankfurt's financial and social loopholes in the laws the same way men could. This is most clearly evidenced by an example from 1618 when an unmarried female

Table 1
Consultation of Advocates, 1562–1696

	Advocates	Sentenced Criminals	Percentage
1562-1594	46	462	9.96
1595-1627	108	415	26.02
1628-1660	66	121	54.54
1661-1689	188	340	55.29
Total	408	1,338	30.49

Source: Rathsprotokolle 1562–1625, 1627, 1629–89.

servant had sexual relations with her master, a local burgher, and became pregnant. She was charged with fornication and punished by flogging and banishment, and her master was fined.[12]

WOMEN AND CRIMINAL COURT PROCEDURES

Despite partiality in the laws, Frankfurt's women were not completely devoid of judicial influence. They played a decisive role with regard to crime reporting and criminal accusation throughout the seventeenth century. One of the most interesting cases dates from the year 1662, when an unmarried burgher's daughter started legal proceedings against a burgher with whom she had had a child.[13] She insisted that he, the father, not only pay for all the expenses incurred, but also that he take and rear the child. Frankfurt's women also resorted to indirect criminal accusations—rumors. Local arrest procedures revealed that a number of suspects were brought to trial based on rumors and hearsay.[14] And women, just like men, started and conveyed rumors.

Frankfurt's women played a role even during criminal court proceedings. The city council frequently sought the expertise of women, particularly midwives, to establish or confirm pregnancies in female suspects involved in infanticide, incest, and other reproductive-related offenses.[15] But most curiously, the last such female expert advice was registered in 1645.[16] Thereafter, only men were listed in the archives, barbers or "Medicorum, Physicorum and Chirurgis" as they were now frequently referred to.[17] Thus the evidence suggests that an emerging male medical profession was gradually displacing women in the courtroom.

This removal of female experts from criminal court proceedings is even more striking considering that it coincided with the increased employment of advocates or legal advisors by the city council (Table 1). Advocates were trained in Roman law and assisted the council in establishing the proper

Table 2
Judicial Torture Applied to Women, 1562–1696

Category	1562 to 1594	1595 to 1627	1628 to 1660	1661 to 1696	Total
"With Kindness"	18	16	1	1	36
With Pain Only	11	3	3	6	23
"With Kindness" and Pain	22	9	0	5	36
Total	51	28	4	12	95
Total Sentenced	79	113	43	80	315

Sources: Bürgermeisterbücher 1562–1625, 1627, 1629–96; Rathsprotokolle 1562–1625, 1627, 1629–89.

punishment for criminal offenses. Needless to say, no woman was to be found among such advocates. Women were not trained in Roman law, and had no access to the universities. In this connection, one can note that the verdicts suggested by Frankfurt's advocates were often influenced by social or political factors. Several soldiers sentenced to death for manslaughter had their sentences mitigated due to the influence of local advocates who suggested they fight the Turks or the French, or be banished.[18] No woman sentenced for infanticide was ever accorded a milder verdict.[19] An emerging male legal profession seemed to identify more closely with the sentencing of male suspects.

TORTURE

No gender gap existed with regard to the use of torture. The torture patterns for female criminals closely resembled those for men in both quantity and quality, especially during the 1562–94 period. Fifty-one out of seventy-nine (64.6%) female convicts were subjected to torture (Table 2). The ratio for men during the same period was 286 to 383 (74.7%). While considerably fewer female criminals were tortured from the mid-seventeenth century, this pattern reflects the general decline of the application of torture and not a milder trend toward women (Table 3). Qualitatively speaking, women were subjected to the same kind of torture as men, namely either *mit Güte*—which is translated literally (and not ironically) as tortured "with kindness"—or "with pain." The former consisted of a psychological drama by

Table 3
Male and Female Convicts Tortured, 1562–1696

Category	1562 to 1594	1595 to 1627	1628 to 1660	1661 to 1696	Total
"With Kindness"	63	49	7	19	138
With Pain Only	130	39	14	26	209
"With Kindness" and Pain	144	112	8	25	289
Total	337	200	29	70	636
Total Sentenced	462	415	121	340	1,338

Sources: Bürgermeisterbücher 1562–1625, 1627, 1629–96; Rathsprotokolle 1562–1625, 1627, 1629–89.

displaying the torture instruments in front of the suspect, while "with pain" quite obviously meant applying them.

Women by no means succumbed to speedy confessions at the mere sight of the torture instruments. Out of the total of ninety-five women tortured, only thirty-six confessed at the sight of the torture instruments.[20] Confessions made during the application of torture were valid only if they were ratified by the suspect a day or two after such an application. If the confession was not ratified, torture could be reapplied. And women, just like men, were subjected to frequent tortures. Several women were quite obstinate and did not confess under torture. In one instance, the councilors seemed to have been rather annoyed, for the records read "sie hat ihr Maul schweigen lassen also das man ihr bekanntnis nit hab könne"—she kept her mouth shut so that we could not get her confession.[21] Pregnancy affected the application of torture. Out of three registered cases of pregnant women, two were tortured "with kindness" while the third was subjected to "a little pain."[22]

PUNISHMENTS

Women, just like men, were subjected to both capital and corporal punishments. But women's capital punishments differed from those of men. Until 1618, capital punishments for women consisted of being thrown into the local Main River from a designated bridge or live burial. Out of the total of twenty-four women sentenced to death, six were drowned.[23] In contrast, out of 313 executed men, only five were handed down such a penalty.[24] And these five male culprits were not even representative because two were Jews, who were generally handed harsher punishments than other males. The other two men had been banished from Frankfurt under the threat of drowning if they returned, and the fifth was a notorious horse thief. Drowning thus seems to have been predominantly applied to women, as is most clearly demonstrated by an incest case of 1588. The stepfather was decapitated while his stepdaughter was drowned.[25]

Live burial was also a female death sentence. The only two cases of such a punishment in Frankfurt, one in 1498 and the other in 1585, were given to women.[26] The latter had murdered her former employer, and as a punishment was pinched on her arms with hot tongs in front of the house where she had committed the crime. She was then led to and placed in an open grave, her body covered with wooden branches, and a wooden pole rammed through her heart. True, no woman was ever broken on the wheel in Frankfurt, but it is an academic question which punishment was more cruel.

The harshness of the death penalties imposed on women changed in 1618, when the first woman was decapitated in Frankfurt for committing incest.[27] Hereafter, decapitation by the sword became the norm. But this milder trend cannot be ascribed to a more lenient treatment of women. It was in keeping with Frankfurt's general trend toward less cruel capital punishments. Compared to other European locations, however, Frankfurt's women received milder punishments, especially after 1618. In Frankfurt, no woman was hanged while in Amsterdam female offenders were hanged until the mid-eighteenth century, and in England until the end of that century.[28] While in Frankfurt no woman was broken on the wheel, a woman suffered such a fate in Amsterdam as late as 1746.[29]

As to corporal sentences, women again were not spared harsh physical punishments. Frankfurt's women, like men, were flogged in public, put in the pillory, and banished. Out of a total of seventy-six women sentenced for simple theft, thirty were flogged, twenty-five put in the pillory, and twenty-one banished.[30] Unlike Amsterdam, however, none lost an ear, and none was ever branded.[31] Pieter Spierenburg even states that during the 1730–50 period "a greater proportion of women than men were branded" in Amsterdam.[32] In France, women were also branded until the eighteenth century.[33] But Frankfurt's women were sentenced to physical punishments for which their male counterparts were either not convicted at all or received monetary fines only.[34] Prostitution and fornication were primarily women-oriented punishments in that only three men were sentenced for prostitution in contrast to thirty-two women. In the case of fornication sentences, the pattern changes slightly from twenty-one male versus forty-three female sentences.[35] But there exists a considerable qualitative difference between these numbers. Only three men were sentenced for simple fornication, while the rest received corporal punishments only in conjunction with other crimes. Women had a far higher rate of sentencing based on simple fornication and prostitution.[36]

MITIGATING FACTORS

There existed, however, various ways to mitigate the punishments. Again, pregnancy could have a moderating effect on the penal structure. Out of fourteen verifiable case entries, the earliest in 1573 and the latest in 1662, a total of twelve pregnant women were given a milder sentence, while in two instances the sentences were not changed but carried out after the child was born.[37] This policy was not unique to Frankfurt. In England, for example, "approximately one-half (of all those pardoned) had successfully pleaded pregnancy at assizes."[38] In Frankfurt, the mitigated sentences consisted in seven instances of life banishment and in five of the pillory and banishment.[39] No pregnant woman was flogged in Frankfurt. Yet one cannot help but wonder about the so-called leniency in these cases. Although the sentences were mitigated, the punishments—especially banishment sentences—were still harsh when one realizes that in almost all cases the woman was single and would have to care for her baby outside the protection of the city walls. In one very moving case description of a decapitation for infanticide, the female culprit even stated that she preferred the death sentence over banishment.[40]

Other mitigating factors were disease, religious conversion, extended imprisonment prior to the actual sentencing, the reimbursement of stolen goods, or young age. For these categories, there was no noticeable gender gap. But when it came to rape, the gender gap was flagrant. Most noticeably, there were only two rape cases. In both instances the stepfathers had coerced their fourteen-year-old stepdaughters. True, the stepdaughters received a milder punishment due to their young age, but they were punished, nevertheless, in that both were banished from Frankfurt.[41]

Arguably the most biased gender-related punishment consisted of sentencing women who had committed no crime whatsoever but whose husbands had been convicted of criminal offenses. In six cases women were banished simply because they were perceived as suspicious for no apparent reason other than being married to a sentenced criminal.[42] An additional eighteen women, some with their children, were ousted from Frankfurt when their husbands received the banishment sentence. In such cases, entries in the archives almost nonchalantly stated that the offender was "to have his wife" or "his wife and children to follow him."[43] These extremely unjust punishments deprived innocent women and children of the security of the town in addition to depicting wives as mere appendages of men with no personal freedom whatsoever.

This sentencing pattern is in sharp contrast to J. M. Beattie's assertion that eighteenth-century English female criminals "were not held responsible

Table 4
Distribution of Intercessions per Gender, 1562–1696

Outcome	1562 to 1594 M	F	1595 to 1627 M	F	1628 to 1660 M	F	1661 to 1696 M	F	Total M	F
Requests Granted	10	1	10	2	10	3	15	7	45	13
Requests Ignored	11	1	9	2	1	1	2	0	23	4
Outcome Unclear	5	0	4	0	1	1	5	1	15	2
Total	26	2	23	4	12	5	22	8	83	19

Sources: Bürgermeisterbücher 1562–1625, 1627, 1629–46; Rathsprotokolle 1562–1625, 1627, 1629–89.

for illegal acts done in the company of their husbands."[44] It also is in clear distinction to Nicole Castan's statement for Languedoc that married women were better protected.[45] For Frankfurt, no such assertions can be maintained.

In contrast, when it came to pleading for milder criminal punishments, Frankfurt's women had more leeway. The goal of private pleas or intercessions was to achieve a mitigation of the sentence. Commutations of sentences could take various forms such as changing death by hanging to the milder version of decapitation in addition to a speedy burial. It could even entail the acquittal of a culprit as demonstrated by various case entries.[46] While traditional historiography has it that in the majority of cases intercessions were voiced by persons of high social or political standing, this was not the case in Frankfurt.[47] Here, the vast majority of supplications originated with family members of the accused. Most remarkably, it was Frankfurt's women who played the decisive role in entering intercessions throughout the 1562–1696 period. They constituted the largest group of plea bargainers with forty-three such pleas. Wives of suspects led this list with thirty-three pleas followed by ten mothers. In contrast, fathers petitioned for a milder sentence in seventeen instances, relatives in general in sixteen, children of suspects in thirteen, and friends in thirteen cases.[48]

The high representation of women among plea bargainers seems somewhat paradoxical if one considers that very few intercessions were voiced on their behalf (nineteen female versus eighty-three male—Table 4).

Who, for example, would plead for a prostitute? In addition, women were subjected to more partial punishments than men. But the most striking aspect is the fact that many wives asking for milder punishments for their husbands were the prime victims of their husbands' criminal behavior.[49] It surely does not make sense that women whose husbands had betrayed them through incestuous relations with their own daughters or sisters, would afterwards turn around and plead for milder punishments. The answer to this riddle lies in the nature of contemporary penal structures and the socioeconomic status of women. Almost all punishments, whether capital or corporal, were meted out in public. In addition, most corporal punishments entailed banishment as well. Public exposure of the culprit entailed public exposure of the culprit's family, and male banishments often entailed the banishment of a convict's wife and children. Both the implicit punishment of the relatives via public exposure and the explicit punishment by sharing the banishment sentences prompted many wives to plead for their criminal husbands.

Contemporary women could not just leave the scene, nor their husbands or the community. Once women were turned out from the guilds they became increasingly dependent on their husbands. Therefore, while emotional reasons surely played a role in petitioning for milder sentences, women interceded out of practical concerns. They were pleading for themselves. The effectiveness of such private supplications is demonstrated by the large number of granted requests (Table 4). Considering that a suspect had no recourse to a court of appeal, the system of intercessions was of prime significance. It offered an accused access to indirect channels of appeals. Thus intercessions constituted an important extrajudicial means of reducing penalties throughout the period, and women were the most ardent and most successful of all plea bargainers.

CONCLUSION

In conclusion, while Frankfurt's partial laws allowed for preferential treatment of local patrician women, such loopholes were far more advantageous for men in general. True, while women retained a surprising amount of leeway with regard to crime reporting, their influence waned considerably in criminal court procedures. Commensurate with their general socio-economic decline, Frankfurt's female court experts, usually midwives, were phased out by mid-seventeenth century. Instead, male doctors were consulted. This trend coincided with the increased use of male legal advisors, the advocates. Reminiscent of Frankfurt's partial laws, Frankfurt's advocates exhibited social and political biases expressed in partial punishments such as for soldiers and infanticides. The application of torture, however, seems to have been the gender equalizer. Both men and women were subjected to the same treatment with the exception of pregnant women. Pregnancy also had a mitigating effect on the general penal structure. In contrast, women were given physical punishments for crimes their male counterparts paid for with monetary fines. Women were even punished simply for being married to criminal husbands. It should, therefore, not come as a surprise that women were the most ardent plea bargainers in this early modern German society.

NOTES

An earlier version of this chapter was presented at the sixteenth annual meeting of the Social Science History Association, New Orleans, 1 Nov. 1991. I wish to thank the following persons for their stimulating suggestions: Ellen Dwyer, Clive Emsley, Rosemary Gartner, Louis Knafla, Eva Österberg, Jussi Pajuoja, David Phillips, Jim Philips, Herbert Reinke, and Pieter Spierenburg. My special thanks go to Ruth Pike for her continued encouraging comments.

1. The source material consists primarily of a time series of crime sentences in the form of the *Strafenbuch*—the Book of Punishments—whose entries dictate the time frame of this study (1562–1696). This Book of Punishments contains personal characteristics of the culprits, a description of their offenses, and the presentation of the punishments in most cases accompanied by drawings showing them. It was the local *Rathschreiber*, the municipal clerks of the city council, who diligently registered the pertinent criminal information.

In addition, the *Rathsprotokolle*—the Minutes of Council Meetings—were used. These records exist for the time period of 1562 to 1689, save for the years 1626 and 1628. Each set of *Rathsprotokolle* covered one municipal calendar year from 1 May to the end of April. These records are an extremely important source because they document how the city council in its capacity as criminal court dispensed jurisdictional power. The various procedural aspects not included in the Book of Punishments, such as the use of torture and private pleas, are contained in the *Rathsprotokolle*.

These findings were supplemented by entries in the *Bürgermeisterbücher*—the Minutes of the Mayors' Meetings, or the *Protocolla Senatus* as they were called in 1672—consisting of additional daily reports of the city council meetings. These records exist, save for the years 1626 and 1628, throughout the entire time span from 1562 to 1696. They were kept in the same basic format as the *Rathsprotokolle* except that they did not include a register until the year 1689.

There exists an abundance of legislative sources in Frankfurt's municipal archives but, unfortunately, they are not codified. The sheer volume seems to have prevented the creation of any compact edition of Frankfurt's laws. For this study, a series of unpublished and published laws and edicts were consulted. The most significant were the revised local law codes, called *Reformation*, from the years 1578 and 1611, respectively. In addition, six volumes of the *Concepta Edictorum* and five volumes of the *Corpus Legum Francofurtensium* were perused. The six volumes of the *Sammlung der Verordnungen der Reichsstadt Frankfurt* represented a further legislative source. The *Rathsprotokolle* also included many municipal edicts.

The records of the guilds, the *Amts-und Zunfturkunden*, were studied in conjunction with social aspects. The following abbreviations will be used: ST for Strafenbuch, BB for Bürgermeisterbücher, RP for Ratsprotokolle.

2. Alexander Dietz, *Frankfurter Handelsgeschichte*, 2 vols. (Frankfurt am Main, 1910), 1:305; Friedrich Bothe, *Beiträge zur Wirtschafts- und Sozialgeschichte der Reichsstadt Frankfurt am Main* (Altenburg, 1906), 76.

3. Friedrich Bothe, *Geschichte der Stadt Frankfurt am Main* (Frankfurt am Main, 1913), 343.

4. I. Kracauer, *Geschichte der Juden in Frankfurt am Main, 1550–1824*, 2 vols. (Frankfurt am Main, 1925), 1:31.

5. Bothe, *Beiträge*, 156–57.

6. Johann Anton Moritz, *Versuch einer Einleitung in die Stadtverfassung der Reichsstadt Frankfurt am Main*, 2 vols. (Frankfurt am Main, 1786), 2:295; Bothe, *Stadt Frankfurt*, 226.

7. Johann Georg Rössing, *Versuch einer kurzen historischen Darstellung der allmählichen Entwicklung der heutigen Gerichtsverfassung der Stadt Frankfurt am Main* (Frankfurt am Main, 1810), 39.

8. *Sammlung der Verordnungen der Reichsstadt Frankfurt am Mayn*, ed. Johann Con. Beyerbach, 6 vols. (Frankfurt am Mayn, 1798), 1:553–55.

9. *Frankfurter Amts-und Zunfturkunden bis zum Jahre 1612*, eds. Karl Bücher and Benno Schmidt, 2 vols. (Frankfurt am Main, 1914), 1:506; 2:157; Karl Bücher, "Die soziale Gliederung der Frankfurter Bevölkerung im Mittelalter," *Berichte des Freien Deutschen Hochstifts* N.F. 3 (1887): 152.

10. *Amts und Zunfturkunden*, 1:417, 419; 2:261; Merry E. Wiesner, *Working Women in Renaissance Germany* (New Brunswick, 1986), 163, 165, 193.

11. *Martin Luther Table Talks*, ed. W. Hazlitt (London, 1857), No. 725.

12. ST 28 Feb. 1618; BB 1617, 168.

13. BB 1662, 219.

14. Out of a total of 261 verifiable cases, 46.74 percent were brought to trial based on suspicions ranging from rumors to hearsay. Captured in the act ranked second with 26.82 percent. The latter percentage seems to attest to the efficiency of the local population in apprehending a delinquent in the act. The former and considerably higher percentage testifies to the extreme vagueness of the crime-reporting system by turning sheer suspicion into a viable reason for starting criminal proceedings.

15. RP 1587, 25.

16. RP 1645, 29.

17. RP 1665, 57; RP 1687, 9.

18. ST 25 Oct. 1603; ST 17 Apr. 1634; ST 23 June 1681.

19. ST 1562–1696, series of BB and RP.

20. Series of BB and RP.

21. ST 16 Nov. 1625.

22. RP 1573, 52, 78.

23. Capital Punishments for Women, 1562–1696

Crimes	1562–94	1595–1627	1628–60	1661–96
Infant.	0	2 Drowned	0	0
	1 Drowned	1 Sword	9 Sword	2 Sword
Murder		1 Live B	0	1 Sword
Mansl.	1 Drowned	0	0	0
Incest	1 Drowned	1 Sword	0	1 Sword
Embezzl.	1 Drowned	0	0	0
Theft	0	0	1 Sword	0
Artson	0	1 Burnt	0	0
Total	4	6	10	4

Source: Strafenbuch, 1562–1696

24. ST 4 Mar. 1573; ST 20 Dec. 1587; ST 23 Apr. 1585; ST 26 Apr. 1588; ST 23 Mar. 1582.

25. ST 8 Nov. and 15 Nov. 1588.

26. Ferdinand Rau, *Beiträge zum Kriminalrecht der Freien Reichsstadt Frankfurt am Main im Mittelalter bis 1532* (Potsdam, 1916), 86; ST 11 June 1585.

27. ST 2 Jan. 1618.

28. Pieter Spierenburg, *The Spectacle of Suffering* (New York, 1984), 7; J. M. Beattie, *Crime and Courts in England, 1660–1800* (Princeton, N.J., 1986), 454, 501, 515, 536–37.

29. Spierenburg, *Spectacle*, 74.

30. ST 1562–1696.

31. Spierenburg, *Spectacle*, 75.

32. Ibid., 167.

33. Julius R. Ruff, *Crime, Justice and Public Order in Old Regime France. The Sēnēchaussēes of Libourne and Bazas, 1696–1789* (London, 1984), 113, 117.

34. BB 1607, 23; BB 1618, 168; BB 1668, 212; ST 2 Apr. 1668.

35. ST 1562–1646.

36. Women's Punishments for Simple Prostitution/Fornication, 1562–1696

Penal Category	Prostitution	Fornication
Dunking Stool and Banished	3	0
Flogged and Banished	2	3
Flogged, Pillory, and Banished	0	3
Pillory and Banished	6	5
Banished	14	11
Total	25	22

Source: Strafenbuch 1562–1696.

37. BB 1662, 87; BB 1636, 148.

38. J. S. Cockburn, *Calendar of Assize Records. Home Circuit Indictments Eliz-*

abeth I and James I. Introduction (London, 1985), 128; see also James C. Oldham, "On Pleading the Belly: A History of the Jury of Matrons," in *Criminal Justice History* 6 (Westport, 1985):1–64; Beattie, *Crime*, 431; R. J. Sharpe, *Judicial Punishment in England* (London, 1990), 41.

39. ST 23 Dec. 1573; ST 11 Feb. 1574; ST 28 Feb. 1582; ST 14 Oct. 1607; ST 19 May 1609; ST 26 Oct. 1615; ST 9 Apr. 1618; ST 10 Jan. 1618; ST 24 Oct. 1618; ST 8 Dec. 1619; ST 17 May 1625; ST 7 Dec. 1633.

40. ST 19 Jan. 1659.

41. ST 22 Nov. 1604; ST 31 Dec. 1623.

42. ST 5 May 1585; ST 7 May 1585; ST 7 Apr. 1592; ST 14 Oct. 1594; ST 24 Oct. 1618; ST 13 May 1659.

43. BB 1568, 89; BB 1586, 134; BB 1587, 201; BB 1588, 25; BB 1588, 130; BB 1595, 248; BB 1606, 35; BB 1634, 157; BB 1664, 129; BB 1674, 40; BB 1696, 13; ST 4 Nov. 1616.

44. J. M. Beattie, "The Criminality of Women in Eighteenth Century England," *Journal of Social History* 8 (Summer 1975): 95–96.

45. Nicole Castan, *Les Criminels de Languedoc: les exigences d'ordre et les voies du resentiment dans une société prérévolutionnaire, 1750–1790* (Toulouse, 1980), 29.

46. BB 1574, 188; BB 1566, 281; BB 1593, 117.

47. Beattie, *Crime*, 431; Douglas Hay, "Property, Authority and the Criminal Law," in *Albion's Fatal Tree* (New York, 1975), 43–44; Ruff, *Crime Justice*, 62.

48. Supplications from colleagues amounted to eight and entreaties from noblemen to six only (series of BB and RP).

49. BB 1611, 178; RP 1646, 33; RP 1643, 40; BB 1643, 138; RP 1662, 24; BB 1662, 87.

Wrath and Redemption: Protestant Theology and Penal Practice in the Early American Republic

Christopher Adamson
Ministry of Colleges, Toronto, Ontario

Despite the scriptural, anti-creedal character of much of American Protestantism, theology was nevertheless important in the early republic. Theological orientation was a definite guide to action for Anglicans, Congregationalists, Presbyterians, and Lutherans, while a revolt against formal theology was fostered by the preaching of the Universalists, the Methodists, and some Baptist sects, on the one hand, and by the quietistic religious vision of the Quakers and the revised Unitarianism of William Ellery Channing, on the other hand.[1] But doctrinal controversy was not only confined to the religious; it also impinged on the daily lives of Americans. Indeed theological differences of opinion were mirrored in conflicting social practices.

The purpose of this chapter is to examine the influence of contested theological views on criminal punishment. This will include an analysis of attitudes toward capital and corporal punishment, and an analysis of how conflicting theological norms shaped penal practices—specifically, the ways in which those norms were actually reflected in systems of prison discipline.

Because of the broad sweep of the evangelical revival throughout the United States during the first half of the nineteenth century, many religious leaders downplayed theological differences in order to establish a united network of benevolent associations that would rescue the country from infidelity. Evangelicalism fostered a common acknowledgment that the spread of irreligion had to be checked. The result was real cooperation among evangelical Protestants in their crusade to uplift antebellum society. Certainly the visibility of prison reform as a social movement was due in no small measure to the fact that it was a cause supported by public-spirited citizens belonging to almost every denomination. Both the Philadelphia Society for Alleviating the Miseries of Public Prisons (1787) and the Boston Prison Discipline Society (1825) were interdenominational; and the New

York Prison Association (1844) was founded by two Presbyterians, one Episcopalian, three Quakers, and two Unitarians.[2] Ecumenicism existed at the local community level too—clergymen from every denomination were invited to preach inside prison walls on the Sabbath. Writing to his mother from Sing Sing in the summer of 1831, Gustave de Beaumont expressed astonishment that "ministers belonging to different Christian communions celebrate Sundays alternately, and all the prisoners attend the service together, without perhaps knowing the difference between the sects to which their preachers belong."[3]

Most twentieth-century historians, noting the fact of ecumenicism in evangelical social reform, have minimized the significance of theological differences. Perry Miller concluded that the divisions among the Protestant sects "were of little importance before the terrific universality of the Revival."[4] Daniel Walker Howe has observed that the interdenominational cooperation that sustained the evangelical united front was facilitated by "a decline of interest in theological distinctions."[5] Although the evangelical impulse, which functioned as such a unifying force in American Christianity, did not derive from theology, it would be wrong to overlook the consequences of theological differences for the denominational structure of America's churches. The turbulence engendered by the revival actually increased the fragility of denominational identity, and the evangelical ethos intensified the competition among denominations for adherents and for cultural legitimacy.[6]

Religious reformers may have expressed a common spirit of reform, but that did not stop them from criticizing one another. Although everyone was welcome to join the different prison discipline societies, Quakers dominated the one in Philadelphia, while evangelical Calvinists controlled the one in Boston. While theological differences were ignored to the extent that doctrinal distinctions might impede interdenominational cooperation, that did not mean that theological habits of thought were entirely overlooked or that they did not have a significant effect on the process of prison reform.

EVANGELICALISM AND THE REVOLT AGAINST CALVINISM

Before charting the relationship between theological ideas and penal practices, we need to define the terms "Calvinism," "Arminianism," and "evangelicalism." Calvin's original doctrine of divine predestination asserts that human destiny—either election to heaven or reprobation in hell—depends entirely on the will of God. Faith offers no guarantee of receiving God's grace, since God's ways are inscrutable and unknowable. The Calvinist view that election and eternal damnation are foreordained by God was taken for granted by the Congregational churches in seventeenth-century New England.[7] In the eighteenth century, orthodox Calvinism was revitalized by

Jonathan Edwards (1703–58), but it was also increasingly challenged by Protestant sects operating on the basis of a theological position that is consistent with the teachings of Jacobus Arminius (1550–1609), a Dutch Reformed theologian who asserted that divine sovereignty and human freedom were compatible and that God's grace was therefore influenced by the choices that human beings made.

It was because Arminius's works were so systematic that his name is typically associated with anti-Calvinist sentiment. Nicholas Tyacke has suggested that Arminianism in early seventeenth-century England was "part of a widespread philosophical scepticism, engendered by way of reaction to the dogmatic certainties of the sixteenth-century Reformation."[8] From the outset, anti-Calvinism had a comfortable foothold in America with the presence of an established Anglican church in colonial Virginia. The rise of a liberal wing within the Congregational churches of Boston was another source of anti-Calvinism. In the 1790s, Harvard-trained ministers were defending the essential virtue of humankind and arguing that human beings were free to choose God. Tensions between liberals and the orthodox reached a climax of sorts in 1819 when William Ellery Channing (1780–1842) preached a sermon that established Unitarianism as a separate Christian fellowship.[9]

The real challenge to the Calvinist clergy derived from the teachings of John Wesley who, although he remained a priest in the Church of England all his life, argued that faith in Christ alone assured salvation. Francis Asbury, who arrived as a Methodist missionary in 1771, mobilized hundreds of ordinary Americans to serve as itinerant preachers. The central message in Methodism, that God had mitigated sin by giving every person the ability to respond to the call of the gospel, contradicted the Calvinist doctrine of predestination. Inspired by the democratization of social life that resulted from the American Revolution, Methodists and other popular religious leaders questioned the Calvinist concept of an inscrutable and arbitrary God. The idea of waiting passively to receive God's saving grace, and yet never knowing whether God had bestowed it, seemed absurd to many people in a revolutionary age governed by the spirit of reform. Thus there was an affinity between revolutionary republicanism and Arminianism in that both doctrines empowered human beings to choose their fate. To revolutionists who had fought to shape their own political destiny, the Arminian belief that human beings were also free to seek their own salvation made emotional sense, whereas the Calvinist assertion of their inability to reject sin and save themselves seemed just plain illogical.[10]

The extraordinary growth of Methodism, especially in the cities and on the frontier, was clearly an expression of a much broader evangelical revival within American Protestantism.[11] Revivalism not only challenged the orthodox Calvinist churches from the outside, however, but also transformed them from within. No segment of American Protestantism was untouched by evangelical revivalism. The Unitarian churches were caught up in the revival. But so too were the Calvinist churches. For "within the bosom of orthodox Congregationalism itself," evangelicalism engendered "certain watering-down trends which eventually led to the virtual repudiation of Calvinism in the home of its friends."[12] Congregationalist and Presbyterian ministers, inspired by the revival Timothy Dwight had begun to promote at Yale and brought closer together by the Plan of Union of 1801, set out to restore the nation's covenant with God by rescuing its people from sin. Their efforts were made possible to a significant extent by a series of important shifts in Calvinist theology.

Samuel Hopkins (1721–1803) modified Jonathan Edwards's orthodox view that human beings were morally unable to do good without divine aid by suggesting that the Calvinist God, although sovereign in all things, was a wise and benevolent ruler who had the happiness of all his subjects in mind. Hence divine law, according to Hopkins, required of all God's subjects an attitude of "disinterested benevolence" which, as we will see, was the spark that ignited various evangelical campaigns of social reform in New England. Hopkins retained the Calvinist doctrine of humankind's complete moral inability to do good and insisted that the human heart remains passive during the process of regeneration when an individual's heart is touched by the Spirit of God. The effect of the radical change in heart brought about by the Holy Spirit was, according to Hopkins, a new psychological disposition to act in such a way as to promote universal benevolence. Whereas the unregenerate will continue to be governed by self-love, the regenerate who has experienced true conversion will be driven to pursue a career of disinterested benevolence.[13]

At Yale, Nathaniel William Taylor (1786–1856) also developed a theological system that attempted to reconcile the Calvinist emphasis on moral inability with the evangelist's call to sinners to reject sin and embrace God. Whereas Hopkins insisted that spiritual regeneration was solely the work of God, Taylor defined regeneration as "that act of the will or heart which consists in a preference of God to every other object."[14] Taylor only partially embraced Arminianism in that he still insisted that the Holy Spirit influenced the human will during the act of conversion. Nevertheless, Taylor's revised Calvinism, according to which regeneration was partly the result of an act of will and partly the result of the operation of the Holy Spirit, appealed to evangelical Calvinists eager to spark revivals in their congregations.

The fires of evangelical revival burned on both sides of the theological divide within American Protestantism, disrupting the Congregational and Presbyterian churches, energizing the Methodists and Baptists, animating the Unitarians, and eventually transforming the Quakers. Evangelicalism certainly fueled efforts to humanize punishment. But while some evangelical prison reformers were ardent critics of Calvinism, others did not break away completely from Calvinism. In other words, theology continued to condition attitudes toward criminal punishment. Nowhere is this more evident than in the debates that arose over the death penalty.

CAPITAL AND CORPORAL PUNISHMENT

On the eve of the American Revolution, it was still taken for granted that felons would be hanged and perhaps mutilated, while mischievous children, idle apprentices, and disobedient animals would be flogged. Opposition to the disfiguring capital and corporal punishments enshrined in the colonial codes, however, grew rapidly during the revolutionary period. Maryland, Pennsylvania, and New Hampshire actually included clauses calling for the elimination of these codes in their constitutions.[15] Prominent revolutionists felt that the existing codes were rooted in British tyranny. "The spirit of reform revived with the Revolution," declared the wealthy Quaker philanthropist and prison reformer Thomas Eddy in 1801.[16] For public-spirited citizens like Eddy, criminal law reform was a necessary first step in the creation of a humane, Christian republic.[17]

The movement to humanize punishment in the early republic drew inspiration from both Biblical Christianity and the rationalist and humanist premises of the Enlightenment.[18] Criminal law reform was an area in which the rhetorics of Christianity and republicanism coalesced more than they conflicted. Although evangelicalism arose among the pietistic sects partly in reaction to the growing influence of rationalism in society, the language of Enlightenment humanism nevertheless had a democratizing and liberalizing influence on Christianity.[19] One indication of this influence was a willingness to revise orthodox Calvinist theological postulates. Although anti-Calvinism was less an explicit theology than a set of commonsense assumptions, the gradual metamorphosis of a jealous, vindictive God into a humane, loving one had a profound impact on attitudes toward capital and corporal punishment.[20]

Those who led the campaign to enact humane criminal laws, which would validate the norms of the new Christian republic, were typically Arminian Christians.[21] Historians have long pointed to the Quaker presence in Pennsylvania and New Jersey to explain why these states were among the first to limit the scope of capital punishment.[22] However, it was Universalists—the most radically Arminian of all denominations—who took the lead in advocating the abolition of capital punishment both in the early years of the republic and then again during the Jacksonian era. According to Universalist belief, Christ's death atoned for the sins of humanity and allowed for the possibility of universal, rather than limited, election to grace. The doctrine of everlasting punishment for sin was anathema to Philadelphia's Benjamin Rush (1746–1813), who converted to Universalism in 1790. "A belief in God's universal love to all his creatures," Rush wrote the following year, "abolishes the punishment of death for any crime and converts jails into houses of repentance and reformation."[23]

Critics of capital punishment, many of whom were, like Rush, both ardent republicans and Arminian Christians, succeeded in reducing the use of capital punishment prior to the War of 1812. Nevertheless, murder and treason remained capital crimes on the books of most northern states during the 1820s.[24] Perhaps it is significant that the Puritan states of Massachusetts and Connecticut had six capital offenses on the books in 1833, whereas Pennsylvania, Ohio, and Tennessee had only one, New Hampshire and Kentucky two, and New York, New Jersey, Maine, and Indiana three.[25]

During the 1830s Arminian Christians waged a successful campaign against public executions. Rhode Island abolished public executions in 1833, followed by Pennsylvania in 1834, and New York, New Jersey, and Massachusetts in 1835. By 1849 fifteen northern and western states were executing behind prison walls.[26] In the 1840s reformers started calling for complete abolition. Three states—Michigan in 1846, Rhode Island in 1852, and Wisconsin in 1853—abolished the death penalty for all crimes. One scholar has attributed Rhode Island's decision to the large number of Unitarians, Universalists, and Quakers in the state.[27] Another scholar has speculated that the religious pluralism of the frontier explains why Michigan eliminated the gallows.[28]

Significantly, it was the Universalist minister, Charles Spear (1801–63), who organized the campaign during the 1840s to abolish capital punishment for all crimes. Spear served as a minister to several Universalist parishes before moving to Boston in 1839 and beginning to visit local jails and prisons. Spear's efforts on behalf of criminals can easily be traced to the outlook of his mentor, Hosea Ballou, whose *Treatise on Atonement* (1805) gave Universalism a distinct theology and separate denominational identity. Whereas earlier Universalists, such as John Murray and Elhanan Winchester, had retained a concept of hell for the unrepentant, Ballou arrived at an "ultra-Universalist" position that asserted that sin was punished during the sinner's lifetime and that there was absolutely no punishment after death.[29]

A combination of religious conviction and personal ambition motivated Spear to become an advocate for the elimination of the death penalty.[30] His views on the death penalty were far from original. His bestseller, *Essays on the Punishment of Death*, was a rather pedestrian work, which was divided into two parts. Part I reproduced the social arguments against the death penalty put forward in recent works by Thomas Upham, John L. O'Sullivan, and E. H. Chapin. In Part II, Spear repeated the same scriptural arguments that Rush had advanced back in 1787. The main tenets of Universalist theology—the idea of a benevolent God, free will, and universal salvation—were very familiar to Americans in the 1840s. While Spear added little that was new, he was a competent advocate, helping to found the Massachusetts Society for the Abolition of Capital Punishment in 1845 and publishing and editing *The Hangman*—a magazine that printed essays, stories, and poetry condemning the gallows.[31]

Debate on the death penalty, Louis Masur has noted, "thinly masked a rancorous, sectarian civil war" between anti-Calvinists and orthodox Calvinist clergymen.[32] In Maine, for example, the Unitarian minister Sylvester Judd's arguments that the death penalty was contrary to the spirit of the New Testament provoked Reverend William T. Dwight, pastor of the Third Parish Church in Portland, to defend it in terms of the legitimation of retribution provided for in the Old Testament.[33] In Massachusetts, Spear took considerable delight in needling the Calvinist clergy, poking fun at their belief in a wholly inscrutable, arbitrary, and wrathful God. He even proposed that orthodox clergymen should be appointed state executioners and that hangings should take place outside their churches.[34]

Most northern jurisdictions had significantly reduced the number of capital crimes by the 1840s. Many states had eliminated public executions and degrading punishments such as branding, disfigurement, and whipping. And there was growing antipathy to the use of corporal punishment in prisons, schools, the home, and the United States Navy. Those who defended flogging and other forms of physical coercion in these settings were typically orthodox Calvinists, while opponents were Unitarians, Quakers, and Universalists.[35]

Patterns of child-rearing were also changing in the northern states as parents began to reject traditional methods that relied on physical pain to curb presumed depravity. Pain and fear had long been central ingredients in Calvinist child-rearing practices. For the orthodox Calvinist of the eighteenth century, as Bertram Wyatt-Brown puts it, "heaven was simply a place where beatings did not occur."[36] For the Arminian Christian of the early nineteenth century, whether Unitarian reformer or Methodist circuit rider, attempts to discipline children by harsh beatings denied the promise of ultimate perfectibility. In Massachusetts, for example, Horace Mann (1796–1859) campaigned to remove the rod from all classrooms, arguing that the Calvinist view of innate depravity contradicted the very idea of education. If children lacked "a capacity for all that is good and noble," Mann asked, how could they possibly be educated?[37] Rejection of the doctrine of original sin not only stimulated efforts to educate children, but also, as Gerald Grob has noted, efforts to cure lunatics.[38]

Slavery, a cult of honor and a tradition of localistic republicanism suspicious of central authority, explains why the South did not pursue criminal law reform.[39] North Carolina's statutes of 1837 listed twenty-two capital crimes, and South Carolina had thirty-two capital crimes on the books in 1838.[40] In 1831 Matthew Carey, Philadelphia's well-known Irish Catholic political economist and prison reformer, confessed that he was sickened to learn that South Carolina had enacted a law "for burning alive slaves who murder their masters."[41]

One reason, although obviously not the main one, why southern states failed to revise the bloody penal codes of the eighteenth century was that the evangelical revival in this region did not foster the same kind of intense anti-Calvinism that it did on the northern and western frontiers. Evangelical clergymen in the South were more likely to accept Calvinist orthodoxy. Even Methodists in the Old South, Anne C. Loveland points out, "were no believers in the perfectibility of man and society as that notion was defined in the North."[42] A commitment to the morality of the Old Testament and a "deep-seated pessimism about the reformability of man" prompted southern Christians to resist and ridicule missionaries from northern benevolent societies.[43] In 1851 Francis Lieber, then a professor of political economy at South Carolina College, informed Massachusetts's eminent social reformer Dorothea Dix that he had "not yet been able to interest one solitary minister in the cause of prison discipline or penal law reform."[44]

In the North, the remarkable success of the campaigns against cruelty led by Arminian Christians is all the more surprising in that these campaigns were fiercely opposed by orthodox clergymen. Evangelical Calvinists staunchly defended the need for both capital and corporal punishments. In 1843 an influential Presbyterian pastor in New York City, Reverend George Barrell Cheever (1807–91), confronted the radical Democrat, John L. O'Sullivan, in a debate on capital punishment in the Broadway Tabernacle. The year before, the New York House of Assembly had narrowly defeated O'Sullivan's bill calling for the total abolition of capital punishment. Cheever, who graduated from Andover in 1830 and served as pastor of the Allen Street Presbyterian Church between 1838 and 1844, performed eloquently in the debate and became the leader of the retentionists. His book, *A Defence of Capital Punishment*, is worth examining briefly because it reveals the lingering influence of Calvinism on New School Presbyterian thought.

Cheever based his defense of the gallows on the governmental theory of the atonement developed by Joseph Bellamy and his pupil Jonathan Edwards, Jr. According to that theory, Christ's death established God's "moral government" over the universe. In order to avoid national calamity, civil government must always enact God's moral orders and enforce his divine laws. Since the Old Testament demanded retribution for sins committed against God, the gallows was a necessary social institution. To think otherwise would be to deny that civil government was divinely ordained.

Cheever pointed out that the Universalists and others who claimed to be "transcendently Christian" rested their case against the gallows on exactly the same false assumptions as did the utilitarians. "Are these men aware, when they assert that government is only a human compact and nothing more, that they are denying religion?" Is the state an expression of divine will? Or is it "nothing more than a joint stock company formed simply for the ends of an utilitarian expediency?" Is penal law an "expression of the voice of God in the soul of man?" Or is it "nothing more than the expression of the volition of a majority as to what constitutes the convenience of the mass?" Is a judge someone who "provides a low, Bentham-like estimate of the amount of counter-inconvenience which would be just enough to deter the seducer, the adulterer, the procurer of abortion, the brutal, ruthless ravisher?" Or is he someone who "stands in the place of God and represents no merely human justice?"[45]

Arminians appealed to the merciful God of the New Testament in their attacks on the gallows. Cheever countered by saying that "the New Testament cannot stand without the Old. We must take the Bible, the whole Bible, the Bible in its plenary inspiration, as the voice of God to be listened to." In the Old Testament God "speaks mainly as a law-giver and judge" and directs his advice not just to individuals, but to individuals who are members of a community. "Wherever the Old Testament is honoured, and children are early taught to love it," Cheever remonstrated, "there will be a strong, an abiding, a conscientious and conservative morality."[46] The crime of murder must be avenged because it represents not just a violation of the Scriptures, but an attack on God's community. Moreover, lawful executions should always be held in public, since the public ceremony itself, Cheever argued, allows people to express "righteous feelings of indignation" so that "what would otherwise be revenge becomes purified and elevated into that sacred feeling of justice."[47]

Evangelical Unitarians like Charles Burleigh (1810–78) and the Universalist Charles Spear tried to undermine Cheever's argument that the death penalty must exist to vindicate violations of sacred communal norms by claiming that there was no such thing as a cohesive community. The existence of poverty divided the community and poverty, not innate depravity, caused crime. The unequal distribution of "the good things of life," Burleigh noted in his *Thoughts on the Death Penalty*, drives men to crime. Being "deprived of bodily comforts and necessaries and the means of improvement for mind and heart" makes men "reckless and desperate."[48]

Cheever, in the appendix to his book, accused Burleigh of having no more belief in the sixth commandment than "Thomas Paine or Theodore Parker." The "wretched sentimentalism" of "pseudo-philanthropists" like Burleigh had, according to Cheever, caused legislators to commit the great mistake of allowing the death sentence to be inflicted privately. "All punishments should be public," Cheever reasoned, "for it is their privacy which takes from them the healthful moral impression of law, and gives them that odious appearance of private revenge."[49] One of the chief arguments against the death penalty put forward by Burleigh was that innocent victims might be put to death. Dismissing those who protested that capital punishment rendered a false verdict irreversible, Cheever said that "ten innocent persons killed by mistake in two hundred years are more than a balance against the lives of a hundred persons who would have been killed by the murderer, had it not been for the penalty."[50]

Cheever was prompted to develop his views on capital punishment by O'Sullivan's attempt to get an abolitionist bill through the New York State legislature. Another well-known New School Presbyterian, Reverend Dr. George Duffield (1794–1864), was similarly prompted to defend capital punishment because of the actions of Michigan's legislature. In 1843 a proposal for abolition was passed by the Michigan House, but turned down in the Senate. Opponents of the proposal were much influenced in their thinking by a sermon that Duffield delivered in the same year. His two-hour sermon, which was eventually published in 1848 as *The Divine Organic Law*, was a typical statement of the New School position on the gallows.

Duffield was installed as pastor of the First Presbyterian Church of Detroit in 1838. From his pulpit, he championed a host of popular evangelical causes, including antislavery, temperance, and educational reform. But, like Cheever, he vehemently opposed efforts to abolish capital punishment. Duffield is probably best known as a zealous exponent of New School Presbyterian thought. In 1832 he published *Spiritual Life: or Regeneration*, in which he argued that "human depravity consists in the misdirection and inappropriate exercise of faculties, not in *wrong faculties inherited*."[51] Duffield denied inherited sinfulness in order to promote evangelical methods of reaching out to sinners. He did not go all the way in adopting Taylor's revised theology, however, and he criticized Congregationalism for not being scriptural enough. "It is," he wrote in his diary in 1848, "Loco Focoism in the church."[52] His criticism no doubt reflected the fact that the Congregationalists, who had invited Charles Finney to preach in Detroit in 1847, were drawing away members of his own church. In a review of Finney's *Lectures on Systematic Theology*, he argued that the Arminian notion that human beings could achieve a state of "sinless perfection" could not be squared with the biblical concept of human depravity.

Duffield maintained that public officials must address the problem of human depravity, since civil government itself is ordained by God. "The civil magistrate, be he who he may, when selected, deputed and installed in his office is as truly the image of God, as he is the representative of the people. His right and authority to govern and punish comes not from man or human compact, but from God."[53] The divine law mandated capital punishment for murder because the murderer attacks "the very sovereignty of God, the Great Creator and Moral Governor."[54]

Like Cheever, Duffield ridiculed the merciful, human-centered outlook of the Universalists. Yet his views were generally less severe than Cheever's. Noting that "the essays of Mr. Spear, and the views of Mr. Upham or Mr. O'Sullivan or the Editor of the *New York Tribune* are mainly founded on an overweening sympathy for a worthless and dangerous member of society," Duffield nevertheless proclaimed that he did not object to showing sympathy toward lesser criminals, and even admitted the benefits of "a healthful penitentiary system" for them.[55] However, Duffield categorically opposed imprisoning the murderer who "has degraded the rationality of his nature and sunk himself to the level of the wild bull, or tiger, or lion or hyaena, or ravenous beast." Until the day comes when "we are prepared to build prisons for murderous beasts of prey," he reasoned, "we must not do it for murderous men."[56]

The abolition of the death penalty would mean lynch law, since the outraged public would have no recourse but to take venegeance into their own hands. "The governmental execution of the murderer represses the spirit of vengeance (and) allays the tempest of passion in the anguished bosoms of the wretched sufferers who have lost a child, a parent, brother, friend or protector." Vengeance must always be divine, never human. Thus Duffield, unlike Cheever, objected to public hangings. "Executions before a popular crowd of curious gaping spectators who run to see strange sights, however dreadful, is no necessary part of capital punishment."[57]

In the final paragraph of his twenty-seven-page sermon, Duffield addresses the causes of crime, concluding that "at least three-fourths of all the murders and homicides that take place in the United States, grow out of the use of intoxicating liquors." His relatively subdued plea for capital punishment in the case of murder gives way to a bombastic attempt to link "the alarming increase of murder" to "the floods of liquid damnation, legalized or flowing in dreadful devastating streams through the length and breadth of our land."[58] Murder and drunkenness were together expressions of the human depravity, which no sensible person would deny. Michigan's legislators, however, ultimately ignored the postulate of human depravity. In 1844 a majority of the select committee in the house concluded that capital punishment was not "applicable to this era of intelligence and christianity," and in 1846 the legislature abolished the death penalty.[59]

CALVINIST PRISON DISCIPLINE

The writings of Cheever and Duffield reveal that the revival did not immediately extinguish Calvinist thinking. The evangelical turn within Puritanism was, nevertheless, accompanied by the theological revisions of Hopkins and Taylor, who tried to reconcile the doctrines of predestination and unmerited grace with an evangelical program of preaching based on the expectation of human ability to respond. Nowhere is the tension between orthodox theology and evangelical practice better illustrated than in the career of the evangelical Congregationalist, Louis Dwight (1793–1854). Dwight promoted the system of prison discipline developed at Auburn and Sing Sing prisons, the so-called silent system according to which convicts slept in separate cells at night and worked together in silence during the day. His proselytizing on behalf of the Auburn or silent system made him perhaps the most influential penologist in the country prior to the Civil War.

Dwight was first drawn into the orbit of Boston's benevolent societies after participating in the revival at Boston's Park Street Church in 1819. Schooled in Hopkinsian theology, Dwight believed that disinterested benevolence was required of all devout Christians. "Our usefulness," he wrote to his future wife in 1823, "is the chief end of our being, since by this alone we can promote the glory of God."[60] In 1824 he became an agent of the American Bible Society and was charged with distributing Bibles to prisons throughout the country. His horseback visits made him aware of "the abuses and terrible neglect of prisoners," and this experience motivated him to join with others in founding the Boston Prison Discipline Society. He issued the society's first report in 1826, then served as its agent and secretary until his death in 1854, earning a beginning salary of $1,000, which was later increased to $1,700.[61]

Bertram Wyatt-Brown has observed that evangelical Congregationalists and Presbyterians thought of religion primarily in terms of "things to do rather than things to think about."[62] God's saving grace was earned during a long career of service. This was certainly true for Louis Dwight, who proclaimed, "I had rather be immersed in prisons, contending against sin, than to receive the honors of Lafayette."[63] Dwight's doctrinal commitment to Auburn prison discipline and his zealous efforts on behalf of the Prison Discipline Society only make sense in the context of the evangelical turn in the established churches. The revival supplied the manpower and organizational resources needed to manage a society uniquely dedicated to improving and monitoring prison conditions throughout the country. If Nathan Hatch is right about evangelical Calvinists feeling "impotent in the face of an explosive growth of unschooled preachers," then Dwight's desire to bring about a disciplinary revitalization of society through prison discipline can be seen as an attempt to relieve some of the anxiety he and others like him felt in the face of the tremendous success of the Methodists and Universalists in recruiting new members.[64]

Not just the established churches, but an entire way of life was being challenged by the democratic impulses of a people who elected Jefferson to the presidency in 1800 in the hope that he would guarantee their continued enjoyment of the fruits of liberty. Evangelical Presbyterians like Lewis Tappan (1788–1873) and Gerrit Smith (1797–1874) were profoundly threatened by the changes in society occurring around them.[65] These changes were real, for by the 1820s, as Gordon Wood writes, "America had become the most egalitarian, individualistic, and money-making society in western history." The fact that, as Wood says, "everything seemed up for grabs" in the United States of the 1820s deeply disturbed religious men and women.[66] Evangelical reformers attributed intemperance, idleness and crime to the nation's wealth and prosperity. Certainly Dwight's writings in the annual reports of the Boston Prison Discipline Society can be read as a jeremiad—a catalogue of social decay, a lament over the passing of a purer, more devout Commonwealth. There is even a sense in which Dwight can be regarded as the archetypical Puritan who, as Michael Walzer writes, "feels himself to be living in an age of chaos and crime and seeks to train his conscience to be permanently on guard, permanently at war against sin."[67]

Donald M. Scott has noted that evangelical clergymen during the 1820s tended "to see all social situations as dangers, snares to trap the unwary and lead them to sin and eternal damnation."[68] Evangelical prison reformers experienced this same fear, for, as David Rothman writes, they were "convinced that deviancy was primarily the result of corruption pervading the community."[69] Grogshops, theaters, and brothels, unwholesome entertainments and unsavory friendships, profane habits like smoking and coffee drinking, marital breakdown and parental neglect, grandiose financial ambitions, the lack of trust between people and the unwillingness of the fortunate to care for the needy—these were some of the causes of crime. The evangelical fear of society's contaminating influence on behavior persisted long after the first penitentiaries were built. The zealous Unitarian, Dorothea Dix (1802–87), concluded in 1845 that "it is to the defects of our social organization, to the multiplied and multiplying temptations to crime, in fact, it is to our wealth and prosperity, and to our very civilization, that we chiefly owe the increase of evil doers."[70]

Calvinist values are discernible in the organization of Auburn prison discipline—in the uniformity of treatment, in the strict rules governing communication, and in the reliance on public-spirited citizens to serve as prison inspectors. The lives of Puritan saints and Auburn prisoners were similar in that both were highly regimented. Idleness was the cardinal Puritan sin—hence the centrality of hard labor to Dwight's program. Prisoners sentenced to hard labor were expected to learn habits of industry and become skilled tradesmen by working in well-managed shops. It was hoped that prison industry would eventually defray all the costs of building and maintaining prisons. John Cray and Elam Lynds, the nonreligious wardens who first developed the Auburn system, undoubtedly drew on their experience as soldiers.[71] But the military aspects of Auburn prison discipline—the rule of silence, the continuous watchfulness by the turnkeys to prevent prisoners from communicating, lockstep marching to and from the shops, downcast eyes while at work in the shops, and the general emphasis placed on strict obedience to authority—also reflect the militant character of the Puritan struggle against sin. Even the moral and religious instruction in these prisons was regimented. Convicts were asked to memorize long passages from the Bible. In their yearly reports to Dwight, Reverend B. C. Smith at the state prison at Auburn, New York, Reverend Gerrish Barrett at the penitentiary in Wethersfield, Connecticut, and Reverend Jared Curtis at the Massachusetts State Prison in Charlestown invariably stated that considerable progress had been made in teaching prisoners to read and memorize the Bible. Typical of the orthodox chaplain's approach to religious instruction was Reverend Smith's boast, in a letter written from Auburn on 29 May 1830, that several convicts "can repeat whole books of the New Testament."[72]

Dwight's penology was shaped by both the Puritan covenantal worldview and the evangelical revitalization of the established churches, a revitalization that called traditional Calvinist postulates into question. His belief that criminals could be saved reveals that his Puritanism was becoming liberalized, unraveling and evolving unwittingly in the direction of Arminianism. Dwight viewed prisoners as fellow sinners—"creatures of the same glorious Creator with ourselves"—who should be treated with kindness and forbearance.[73] His efforts to nurture programs of convict reformation through religious training and Bible reading indicate a radical rejection of the predestinarian view of salvation. Indeed, it is the synergy between the jeremiad and the evangelical expectation that the criminal could be redeemed that accounts for the resonance of Dwight's penology throughout the country. By 1850 Maine, New Hampshire, Vermont, Maryland, Ohio, Kentucky, Tennessee, Upper Canada, Michigan, and Indiana as well as the traditionally Puritan states of Massachusetts and Connecticut had adopted the Auburn system.

Although Dwight believed in the reformability of convicts, he was not able to distance himself sufficiently from his Calvinist heritage to endorse the abolition of capital punishment for murder. The tenth report of the Boston Prison Discipline Society deals with the question of capital punishment. In the report, Dwight prints a letter, written on 30 May 1835, from Wethersfield's chaplain, Gerrish Barrett, which discusses a convict named Southwick—originally sentenced to the penitentiary for putting poison in the water well of a community of Shakers. Southwick attacked and wounded one of the officers of the prison, and then killed a fellow convict by "beating his head with the night bucket." Barrett concludes that "here is a clear case, in which a most depraved wretch (will) produce a very bad impression on the minds of others, unless the punishment of death be inflicted." Dwight concurs and offers an essentially Cheeverian rationale for executing such a heinous criminal.[74]

Also indicative of the tension between Calvinistic assumptions about human incorrigibility and the evangelical belief that all sinners could be saved was Dwight's ambivalence toward Warden Lynds's disciplinary methods. Although Dwight insisted that whipping should never be a regular part of prison discipline, he conceded that there was a place for the lash. So too did one of his proteges, Reverend Jared Curtis, who after a three-year stint as Auburn's chaplain went on to serve for over two decades as chaplain of the Massachusetts State Prison.[75] When Frederick Robinson, the warden of the Massachusetts State Prison, let it be known in 1843 that he opposed corporal punishment of any kind, Chaplain Curtis complained facetiously that the warden would next be giving prisoners their freedom.[76] When Massachusetts enacted a statute abolishing whipping in 1849, Curtis again protested, fearing that, without the lash, prison officials would have to rely on the soul-destroying expedient of solitary confinement to maintain order:

> That the affairs of a prison may be conducted without a resort to stripes I have no doubt; but, after careful observation and much deliberate consideration in regard to this delicate and much agitated subject, I am clearly of the opinion that, in some cases, stripes may be resorted to with a more ready effect and a far happier result, both to the individual punished and to the institution, than can be secured from solitude with its customary privations.[77]

Curtis in Massachusetts and Barrett at Wethersfield Penitentiary in Connecticut were doctrinal believers in Auburn prison discipline. The reformation of the prisoner depended on an explicit set of disciplinary procedures. Auburn prison discipline represented the moral and organizational model of a perfect society, a Christian utopia.[78] These men, therefore, expressed the hope that a system of discipline not unlike Auburn prison discipline would soon be implemented in schools, academies, mechanics' shops, factories, and even families.

Dwight created a Calvinistic system of discipline. Yet his disciplinary program, precisely because its chief goal was the reformation of prisoners, testifies to the influence of the evangelical ferment of this period in liberalizing his Calvinism. Although hard labor was the key defining element of Auburn prison discipline, its purpose was to elevate and train the prisoner, not degrade him.[79] Thus the evangelical Congregationalist businessman, Lewis Tappan, rescued from Unitarianism by Lyman Beecher in 1828, complained:

> This very day at the State Prison at Charlestown, we saw a gang of convicts in their disgraceful uniform, working on the granite from the canal boats, with four men over them, armed with guns and bayonets; and that too, in sight of the public road. . . . To see fellow men in this republican Christian land, thus driven like beasts of burden, to labor perchance on the very stone that is to constitute a monument of triumph over vindictive and tyrannical power, is insufferable.[80]

The idea that prisoners were human beings, not work animals, reveals that Auburn prison discipline, despite the Calvinist character of its daily routines, sought to achieve a purpose consistent with the evangelical, anti-Calvinist direction in which American Christianity was moving.

Lewis Tappan's revulsion against physical coercion was an indication of how quickly Calvinist attitudes were being transformed. Tappan recalls that, when he was growing up in Northhampton in western Massachusetts, "the boys were let out of school" on execution days so that the rising generation should learn that wrongdoing always "received a just recompense of reward."[81] Several decades later Tappan, now a young man, was dismissing public punishments as remnants of a barbaric age untouched by the mild and benevolent spirit of Christianity. "Although civilization has effected much independently of Christianity to render criminal law less severe," he wrote in 1826, "this divine system alone is entitled to the praise of inculcating the sentiment that prison should aim at reforming character."[82]

METHODIST PRISON CHAPLAINS

The very notion that criminals could through their own exertions attain salvation is of course traceable to Wesley's repudiation of the Calvinist idea of an elect.[83] The tremendous growth of Methodism during the first half of the nineteenth century was due in large part to the fact that Methodist preachers could, as Nathan Hatch has observed, "embrace the forlorn and the uprooted far more intensely than any political movement and offer them powerful bonds of acceptance and hope."[84] The Methodist system of itinerancy was based on the belief that preachers should not only cater to the needs of ordinary people, but also know and understand the experience of people of low estate even to the point of sharing in their suffering. Itinerants, accustomed to ministering to the fallen woman, the wretched drunkard, and the untutored Indian, also volunteered their services as prison chaplains, using their knowledge of how criminals lived to ripen their souls for conversion.

While the directors of prison discipline societies and the members of penitentiary boards of inspection were likely to belong to the older denominations, the men who worked in prisons as chaplains were quite often Methodist itinerants.[85] This was especially likely in frugal frontier states that refused to pay for the services of a chaplain. In his annual report for 1833, Dwight singled out those prisons that had no resident chaplain. He reported that in Maryland religious exercises were being performed on a voluntary basis "by preachers belonging to the Methodist society, the Penitentiary being one of their regular appointments." There was no chaplain in the Kentucky Penitentiary, but the place "was attended by Methodist preachers." In Ohio there was "no chapel, nor any room in which it would be possible to assemble, and, therefore, no chaplain."[86] Methodists began visiting Ohio State Penitentiary in the early 1830s and this institution, like the Baltimore Penitentiary, became an important station.[87]

Like the state prisoners they preached to, Methodist itinerants were typically poor, propertyless, and informally educated. And they earned very little money from their work, barely enough to survive on.[88] Preachers who could no longer endure the rigors of riding a circuit because of age or poor health were often stationed at the penitentiary. Thus prison chaplains were frequently elderly men. Nathan Emery was fifty-six when appointed chaplain at the Ohio State Penitentiary in 1836. His replacement, Russell Bigelow, was a man in feeble health who had served as missionary to the Wyandott Indians. In 1845 Reverend James Bradley Finley (1781–1856) took over as chaplain. Finley, who was converted at Cane Ridge in 1801, was sixty-four years old at the time of his appointment. He found time to enlarge the penitentiary library and to write an important account of daily life inside the walls, *Memorials of Prison Life*.

The Arminianism of the Methodist chaplains was, to use Perry Miller's word, unabashed.[89] John Luckey, who was appointed chaplain at Sing Sing in 1839, set out to win souls for Christ by establishing a Sunday school and library and by visiting prisoners in their cells. His memoir, *Life in Sing Sing*, provides detailed descriptions of the conversion experiences of quite a number of prisoners. Luckey kept in touch with as many converts as he could, inviting them back to Sing Sing to preach. He not only ministered to the men while in their cells, but also accompanied released inmates back to their hovels in the Five Points district of New York City, and helped them find shelter and jobs. Helping discharged prisoners, he wrote, "opened up an immense missionary field."[90]

Prayer and Bible study figured prominently in missionary work with criminals. Methodist doctrine allowed for the possibility of backsliding, and hence there was always a chance that the consummate backslider—the recidivist felon—could be reached. Penitentiary sermons aimed to arouse the inmate's "obdurate and sin-steeled conscience." Reverend Finley reminded his readers that "criminals incarcerated within the gloomy walls of a prison are not lost to hope and heaven."[91]

Finley and others challenged established prison routines that hardened the prisoner's heart. During the 1820s and 1830s the Sunday service within prisons administered on the silent plan was highly regimented. At Auburn convicts marched in lockstep to a room on the upper west story of the south wing where they sat "facing the minister on narrow seats with backs" that prevented them from "looking in each others' faces," and listened as "the sermon was delivered and usual Divine service performed, except singing." During the service the turnkeys sat on "small platforms erected at the sides and ends of the Chapel" that were "so elevated" as to permit these officers "perfectly to overlook every convict."[92] With the appointment of Methodists as chaplains in the late 1830s, the staid, highly regimented Sunday services organized by the evangelical Congregationalist ministers gave way to more exuberant forms of worship. Both James Finley and John Luckey maintained that the rule of silence inhibited prisoners from declaring themselves for Christ. Inmates ought to be permitted to shout and cry out spontaneously when touched by God's saving grace. Whereas Dwight's chaplains sought to reach prisoners by making them memorize long passages from the Bible, John Luckey sought to reach prisoners by getting them to sing hymns.

Methodist chaplains could be counted on to speak out against all forms of organized oppression—the regimented Sunday service, and the contract system of convict labor whereby inmate labor was contracted out to local mechanics who established shops within the prison. Luckey called this system "a miniature slavery." Finley complained that the directors of the Ohio State Penitentiary overworked prisoners. "There is something degrading in the idea of a community endeavouring to enrich itself by the labor of the unfortunate convicts." Something is very wrong when greedy contractors "regard the prisoners as so much capital" and when wardens "do not believe the convict can be converted."[93]

The Methodist belief in the spiritual equality of all human beings provided legitimacy for democratic political arrangements and corroded popular respect for the opinions of the well-born and privileged members of society. Nevertheless, Methodist circuit riders espoused very conservative social philosophies, speaking out against the many "liberal" influences in society. Chaplain Luckey feuded with Eliza Farnham, the free-thinking matron of the women's prison at Sing Sing. He also disagreed with the radical democrat and powerful penitentiary inspector, John Bigelow, over such things as phrenology, the presence of Dickens's novels in the library, and the prisoner's right to chew tobacco.[94]

Historians have been puzzled by the conservative outlook of Methodist leaders, since a conservative politics seems inconsistent with a psychological identification with the oppressed and a commitment to help them overcome their difficulties. Sean Wilentz has written that "a tension between submissiveness and egalitarianism lay at Methodism's core."[95] The roots of this tension were in large measure doctrinal, for Methodist preachers "explicitly taught that divine insight was reserved for the poor and humble rather than the proud and learned."[96] Organized into societies rather than churches and subdivided into classes for intensive Bible study, Methodists might have channeled the economic frustrations of marginal groups into political protest.[97] However, this could never happen as long as Methodism individualized redemption—the circuit rider's message to the disadvantaged members of society was that spiritual awakening was a uniquely personal experience, with the Holy Spirit sometimes making his presence felt in visions and dreams.

Methodist evangelical strategy aimed to harvest the souls of the excluded for inclusion in Christ's everlasting body, not for social revolution. Hence the leaders of the Methodist Episcopal Church encouraged missionary efforts to bring southern slaves into the church, but did not promote the abolition of slavery.[98] Similarly, chaplains sweated hard to rescue the individual criminal from sin, but had little to say about the social and economic causes of crime. John Luckey was less interested in eradicating the deplorable housing and sanitary conditions in the Five Points than in converting the men who lived there. He rejoiced that the men who had converted while at Sing Sing gave him a "hearty welcome." He reports "having knelt with this unfortunate class of our fellow beings in the hovel and in the parlor, in the cellar and in the garret and even in the low grogshop."[99] Luckey's personal experiences of life in the seedier parts of the city are easily comprehensible in terms of the Methodist requirement that all itinerants partake of genuine apostolic suffering.[100] Personal salvation was contingent on the renunciation of secular ambition.

QUAKER PRISON DISCIPLINE

The enormous contribution that the Quakers made to society as pioneers in penology was perhaps inevitable, given their distinct religious vision and their social and economic power in post-Revolutionary Philadelphia. True, the Philadelphia Society for Alleviating the Miseries of Public Prisons was interdenominational and included such prominent clergymen as George Duffield's grandfather, who was Presbyterian chaplain to the Continental Congress, and Reverend William White, the society's first president, who was Episcopal bishop of the diocese of Pennsylvania from 1787 until 1836.[101] Nevertheless, Quakers were unquestionably the dominant group within the society, and several exceptionally wealthy Quakers carried forward the process of reform.[102] To a considerable extent this was because, as David Brion Davis has shown, Quaker philanthropy was a transatlantic project fertilized by fortunes derived from banking, insurance, shipping, mining, breweries, and the pharmaceutical industry.[103] Quakers in Philadelphia were far more open to the world than Quakers in more remote sections of the country, and they were also quite receptive to the evangelical orientation of an elite group of Friends who had begun to take an interest in prison reform in England.

Great wealth made it possible for Quaker merchants in the new republic to devote time and energy to the cause of prison reform. For example, Richard Wistar (1727–81), who amassed a fortune from managing a glassworks and other businesses, brought soup to Philadelphia's imprisoned debtors during the 1770s. Wistar's four sons, who worked for the prison society in Philadelphia during its early years, decried the deplorable conditions in the city's jails.[104] In 1790 the wealthy Quaker iron merchant, Caleb Lownes, began to renovate the Walnut Street Jail, transforming it from an overcrowded, unsanitary congregate prison into a well-managed, three-storey brick prison fitted with sixteen solitary cells. This institution, dubbed the cradle of the penitentiary by one historian, attracted visitors from all over the world and became the model for penal reform elsewhere.[105]

One such visitor was Thomas Eddy (1758–1827) who, after making a lot of money from currency trading and the insurance business, decided to devote himself to philanthropy in New York State. Eddy, whose philanthropic attitudes were shaped by both his Quakerism and his republicanism, maintained that the criminal laws of colonial New York conformed to "monarchical principles" and were therefore "imperfectly adapted to a new country, simple manners, and a popular form of government."[106] Eddy was instrumental in getting the legislature to pass a bill authorizing a penitentiary in 1796. He personally oversaw the construction of Newgate Prison and served as an inspector until 1803.[107]

In 1825 a good friend of Thomas Eddy's, John Griscom (1774–1852), founded New York's House of Refuge, the first reformatory for juvenile offenders in the country. Griscom was a chemistry professor at Columbia and a devout Quaker. Roberts Vaux (1786–1836), the man who planned and oversaw construction of the Eastern State Penitentiary at Philadelphia during the 1820s, was another wealthy Quaker. Vaux inherited considerable wealth in trust at the age of four. At eighteen he joined the Philadelphia counting house of John Cook. By twenty-one he owned his own mercantile business. Three years later, he retired and devoted himself full-time to public service, working with myriad organizations seeking both economic and moral goals.[108]

The philanthropic orientation of the Quakers in Philadelphia and New York was unusual in that, despite their deep spirituality and ascetic lifestyle, they did not reject rationalism, but rather prided themselves on their mastery of various sciences and their openness to European systems of thought. It would be a mistake, however, to attribute the Quaker interest in prison reform to Enlightenment humanism alone, and ignore the influence of their unique spiritual vision. Certainly the peculiar features of the Pennsylvanian system of prison discipline, especially the insistence on absolute solitude and the complete separation of prisoners, are comprehensible in terms of the Quaker belief that individuals could attain inward light without the aid of an ecclesiastical guide.

The Quaker way of life, according to Thomas O. Hamm, "differed radically from the dominant evangelical religious culture of the United States prior to 1850."[109] We should not, therefore, be surprised if the Quaker approach to punishment was also significantly different from that of the evangelical Calvinists who promoted the Auburn system. For the Quakers, salvation was not a single event of rebirth, as it was understood by many evangelical Christians, but rather a gradual spiritual awakening—a long, tortuous process of growth through suffering toward holiness. Quakers withdrew from the world in order to foster spiritual awakening. Prayer meetings were typically held in silence, for, as one Quaker noted, "it would be strange to think that God needed to hear one speak aloud in order to be worshipped."[110] Quakers rejected water baptism, but operated with a notion of baptism as the inward experience of God's Light, seeking absolute solitude as the condition under which they could prepare themselves to achieve total communion with God.

These features of the Quaker religious vision explain the policy of complete solitary confinement introduced at the Eastern State Penitentiary. The founders of this institution were obsessed by the need to keep prisoners isolated from each other. As is well known, Roberts Vaux and his fellow inspectors went to great lengths to ensure that prisoners did not communicate with each other. They spent an enormous amount of money building extra-thick, soundproof walls. Each cell had its own separate exercise yard. To prevent communication, the prison staff actually required prisoners entering the penitentiary to wear a hood over their heads.[111] Prisoners were to spend their entire sentence in solitary confinement. Cut off from all contact with others, without news of the wider society, criminals would reflect on their conduct and see the error of their ways. If no labor was provided—and the initial plan favored by Roberts Vaux precluded labor—prisoners would have nothing to do but introspect and ruminate. Eventually the directors of the Eastern State Penitentiary introduced labor, but restricted it to trades at which prisoners could work alone in their cells.[112] Because association with other inmates was an unhealthy distraction, the Pennsylvanians acted against their own financial interest in refusing to establish congregate workshops.

Life inside the sombre penitentiary was a time of trial and tribulation during which prisoners would experience remorse for their crimes and grow little by little through suffering toward holiness. The interior of the Eastern State Penitentiary was an exceptionally melancholy place, prompting Charles Dickens, who visited in 1842, to conclude that solitude was a punishment worse than death. For the Quakers, however, solitude was not an unnatural condition. Quiet reflection and daily Bible reading opened the soul to God's soothing, cleansing power. The process whereby sinners were led to repent could not be hurried or induced by boisterous singing. The ascetic sensibility of a man like Roberts Vaux would have been offended by the hell-fire preaching of Chaplain Luckey.

The German refugee Francis Lieber (1800–1872), who became one of the country's foremost liberal philosophers and perhaps its first scientific political economist, wrote a detailed comparison of the Auburn and Pennsylvanian systems in 1838. His *A Popular Essay on the Subjects of Penal Law* is of interest because it not only defends the Pennsylvanian system but also shows how this system was the product of Quaker values.[113] Lieber points out that, for both Quakers and Episcopalians, "the essence of religion lies in peace and not in excitement."[114] According to Lieber, the Pennsylvanian system of uninterrupted solitary confinement improves on the Auburn system because it produces "that state of calm resignation without which no deep-rooted and steady reform is possible."[115] Solitary confinement calms the mind, whereas congregate labor excites it. No matter how closely prisoners are watched and no matter how severely whipped, communication occurs under the Auburn plan. And the very presence of whipping ensures that the officers of a prison can never truly reform the inmate. For the pain that results from whipping "galls, irritates, exasperates and makes the chasm between the convict and society still wider."[116]

With their emphasis on asceticism and personal sobriety, Quakers demanded a stern but not harsh punishment. Solitude "is stern in its character," Lieber writes, "especially so to men, who nearly without exception have spent their lives in boisterous intercourse with fellow criminals." Full solitary confinement allows "the religious adviser, assistant and comforter to enter the solitary cell at any time, and, as all religious conversations with a convict must have much of the character of a confession, the undisturbed cell, overheard by no one, is the very place for this converse."[117] The defenders of the Auburn plan were naive to think that public worship can have a beneficial effect on prisoners. In this connection Lieber quotes William Crawford, the English commissioner who visited all but two American prisons in 1833. Crawford was a member of the Quaker-dominated London Prison Discipline Society. His remarks nicely capture the theological dimension of the Quakers' opposition to collective public worship inside penitentiaries. "In the great assembly, the tear of penitence and the sigh of a broken heart are suppressed by the reproachful frown or the contemptuous sneer of others. But the prisoner in his solitude feels no such restraint. His thoughts are undistracted by the presence of others.... *he is alone with God*."[118]

Lacking the zeal of the evangelical Presbyterians and the exuberance of the Methodists, Quaker penologists designed a penitentiary system which, according to Tocqueville and Beaumont, succeeded in "producing the deepest impressions upon the soul of the convict."[119] Prisoners were subjected to the discipline of solitude that Quaker seekers might impose on themselves. A frugal but wholesome diet, coarse clothing, and silence—these aspects of prison life were equally features of what the Quakers called the plain life. Francis Lieber felt that "an organ so placed that all prisoners can hear it might have a salutary effect, if hymns and otherwise pure music were played," but acknowledged that "most of his valued Quaker friends" would differ from him on this point.[120]

Quakers had an absolute abhorrence of whipping. Thomas Eddy made sure that corporal punishment was prohibited at New York's Newgate Prison, relying on solitary confinement on stinted rations to control disorderly inmates.[121] Although impressed with many aspects of the Auburn system, Eddy was ashamed that inmates were flogged. "I am mortified," he wrote, "to find that my friend Captain Lindes (*sic*) advocates (and practices) inflicting corporal punishment for violating any part of the prison discipline."[122] In objecting to whipping, Quaker reformers prided themselves on their humanity. Whether the Pennsylvanian approach was more humane than the Auburn system is not a question that can be easily answered. What it is possible to conclude, however, is that the Quaker approach to convict reformation was more detached, chillier than that of the Auburnites: the thick, sombre walls of the inmate's cell existed to ignite a spark of light in his heart that would gradually develop into a true and constant glow.

UNITARIAN PRISON DISCIPLINE

Like the Quakers of Philadelphia, Boston's Unitarians were men of considerable wealth and prestige.[123] In 1826 Lyman Beecher observed that "all the elite of wealth and fashion crowded Unitarian churches."[124] Readers of the Harvard-based *North American Review*, which published several important articles on prison discipline, were typically men "of influence, talents, wealth and learning."[125] Joseph Tuckerman (1778–1840), Josiah Quincy (1772–1864), and Francis Gray (1790–1856), the author of *Prison Discipline in America*, were very rich men. Samuel Gridley Howe (1801–76), Joseph Story (1779–1845), and Robert Rantoul, Jr. were the offspring of sturdy middle-class parents. But the well-to-do were not the only ones to propose reform. Dorothea Dix, Horace Mann, and Frances Bowen (1811–90) faced economic hardship in youth. For these men and women, reform was a vocational opportunity as well as a spiritual calling. Their activities were financed by some of the wealthiest men in the Northeast.[126]

Daniel Walker Howe has shown that there was a definite evangelical strain within Unitarianism.[127] William Ellery Channing actually credited Samuel Hopkins with "turning my thoughts and heart to the claims and majesty of impartial, universal benevolence."[128] However, Channing went far beyond the Hopkinsian commitment to disinterested benevolence in advocating a program of social reform based on the doctrine of human perfectibility.[129] One manifestation of the Unitarian commitment to social reform was the formation in 1831 of the Philanthropic Society of Harvard Divinity School. Students who had been conducting Sunday school classes at the state prison in Charlestown formed the society in order to ensure that the prisoners received permanent religious instruction.[130]

Although an evangelical impulse led Unitarians to take an interest in the sorry plight of prisoners, the Unitarian approach to prison reform was powerfully shaped by the value orientations that defined Unitarian theology—its rationalism, individualism, perfectionism, and voluntarism. Like the Quakers, Unitarians "prided themselves on their rational investigations of society's ills."[131] Unitarian penologists like Dorothea Dix, Samuel Gridley Howe, and Francis Gray gathered statistics on crime and intemperance, and based their policy recommendations on hard evidence that included rates of death, insanity, and recidivism among prisoners.

In light of the rationalistic character of Unitarian theology, it is not surprising that most, although not all, Unitarian reformers favored the Pennsylvanian over the Auburn plan.[132] Howe voted against a Massachusetts bill funding the Boston Prison Discipline Society, asserting that "the broad seal of the state (should not) be used to give currency to false ideas."[133] In his *Essay on Separate and Congregate Systems of Prison Discipline*, he lampooned the congregate system. His objections derived from his commitment to individualism and voluntarism. The congregate system was flawed because it treated prisoners as a mass rather than as unique individuals. The great fallacy in Dwight's thinking was the idea that convict reformation could be brought about by external pressure. True reformation, according to Howe, must instead involve an interior psychological process whereby the individual freely chooses good over evil.

The rivalry between the proponents of the Pennsylvanian and Auburn systems of prison discipline revealed the deeper philosophical conflict between the Congregational-Presbyterian and the Unitarian worldviews. The Pennsylvanian system, which made each felon responsible for his own reformation, was consistent with Channing's doctrine of personal reformation according to which God's grace would be bestowed only on those who chose to reform. Someone who did not in his heart want to change could never be forced to do so. The objective of Unitarian philanthropy should therefore be to aid human beings in their personal search for moral perfection, not frighten them into obedience by reminding them of their innate depravity. As Channing himself noted, drunkards "cannot be driven into temperance."[134]

Unitarians criticized the exploitation of prison labor in congregate prisons. Dorothea Dix wrote that "penitentiaries should not be a cost to government, (but) they should not be a source of profit either."[135] Howe went further and suggested that prisoners should be free to choose whether to work, although he doubted if any prisoner held in solitary confinement would refuse work. Living in solitude will teach the prisoner "how much pleasanter labor is than idleness" so that he "will in time form a voluntary habit of labor," whereas the prisoner who "feels that he is coerced to labor is naturally less inclined to it on that account."[136]

It is possible to locate within Unitarian evangelical reform a conservative, antidemocratic stance and a more radical, progressive position. The issue that divided Unitarian reformers was whether government should intrude into the affairs of its citizens. During the 1820s it was still taken for granted that public officials had an important role to play in fostering moral improvements.[137] Hence in 1826 Lewis Tappan could call on the legislators of the Commonwealth of Massachusetts to "discard all shortsighted economy and use a wise liberality" in constructing an addition to the state prison.[138] By the 1830s and especially during the recession of 1837–43, however, a new attitude of less government was forming. Socially conservative Unitarians, influenced by the doctrine of personal reformation espoused by Channing, insisted that associations of benevolent Christians, rather than governments, should take the initiative in preventing crime. Channing himself asserted that "great enterprises can better be accomplished by the voluntary association of individuals than by the state."[139] The less government the better, since governments, according to Channing, were prone "to intermeddle injuriously with human affairs and obstruct the processes of nature by excessive regulation."[140]

Socially conservative Unitarians promoted private charity, but objected to public relief schemes on the grounds that such schemes perpetuated dependence and pauperism. The ministries established by the Unitarians to visit the poor in their homes emphasized moral and religious instruction, not the redistribution of material wealth. Their purpose was essentially to inculcate those habits of industry, sobriety, and thrift that would enable the poor to become economically self-sufficient. The attitude of the philanthropic ministers was often patronizing. Thus Joseph Tuckerman, Boston's first minister to the poor, recommended that the philanthropic minister ought to take advantage of "daily opportunities for calling forth the kindly affections of the poor toward the rich."[141]

At Harvard, philanthropy was deemed to be a branch of theology. Whereas the evangelical Presbyterian admonished himself because of the greater suffering of prisoners or slaves, the Unitarian minister, as Daniel Walker Howe puts it, "recommended only that the fortunate *contemplate* suffering."[142] Students at Harvard were encouraged to visit prisons, hospitals, and plantations as part of their moral education. To make their own lives uncomfortable or deliberately mortify themselves because of the suffering of others was something that the Unitarians regarded as impractical, irresponsible, and inconsistent with the principles of reason. And in fact the Philanthropic Society at Harvard did not do much for the prisoners at Charlestown beyond preaching to them.[143]

Liberal theology led to social conservatism, but also, in the case of Theodore Parker (1810–60), to radicalism. Parker approached the question of punishment with both a religious heart and a scientific mind, the one inspiring him to preach at Charlestown Prison, and the other directing him to carry out a comprehensive demographic study of the prison population. Parker found that "nine-tenths of all prisoners came from the 'perishing classes', and seventeen-twentieths of all crimes were crimes against property." He concluded that criminals were not just spiritually wayward, but also members of an economically oppressed segment of society. "How can it be justice to punish as a crime that which the institutions of society render unavoidable?" he asked, while visiting the Tombs in New York City.[144] In pointing out that the community itself was often the cause of crime, Parker anticipated the arguments of late nineteenth-century reformers who argued that real reform would be achieved by limiting the use of custody.

The linking of spiritual regeneration to social criticism represents a culmination in the liberalization of Protestant theology. Parker made Christianity as scientific as it could be without becoming something other than religion. What unifies both Quaker and Unitarian philanthropy is not a political philosophy, but rather the belief that Christian benevolence would work best if it was guided by rational principles. The strain toward rationality in Quaker theology explains why the Pennsylvanian system has struck so many historians as modern, its reliance on solitary confinement prefiguring modern techniques of behavior modification. Similarly, the scientific attitude of the Unitarian reformers explains why so many of their ideas—home visiting and aftercare, moral counseling and job training—prefigured the penological developments of the late nineteenth century.

During the long decade prior to the Civil War, evangelical Protestantism lost some of its fire. The waning of enthusiasm coincided with a definite shift in penological emphasis from reform to custody, a subordination of religious objectives to administrative and fiscal concerns.[145] During the next significant period of reform beginning in the 1870s, reformers would self-consciously draw on the language of science rather than religion.[146]

CONCLUSION

The transformation that occurred in penal attitudes and practices during the early decades of the nineteenth century was made possible by an ongoing theological shift according to which the doctrine of inherited sin gave way to a more subtle theory that specified that sin, although it was inevitable as a universal feature of human action, was the product of sinning, and not a quality inherent in the individual prior to action. Although theology was important, theological differences of opinion nevertheless occasionally dissolved in the face of powerful similarities in social attitudes forged by the revival. Thus Calvinistic Presbyterians and Arminian Methodists came to rely on and even admire each other. Dwight, for example, praised the work of the Methodist prison chaplains. The underlying commonality here was not theology, but rather a fundamental social conservatism.

Methodists and Calvinistic Congregationalists shared an identical suspicion of the ideas and programs being advanced by Deists and radical Unitarians. The Methodist circuit rider, James Finley, linked crime to the increasing number of "renegades from Christianity," notably the followers of Saint-Simon, Fourrier, and other "crazy Frenchmen who have undertaken to make a settlement in Texas on the no-marriage principle."[147] Similarly the Calvinistic George Barrell Cheever asked, "What shall we do with the *tender consciences* of such disciples as Fourrier and Owen when summoned to serve as jurors on an indictment for bigamy and adultery?"[148] Cheever also praised the zeal of Methodist missionaries, even going so far as to suggest that these humble messengers of God were so busy "diving into cellars and mounting into garrets, exposing themselves to revolting forms, and encountering scenes of the most soul-sickening nature" that they hardly had time to think about complex issues like capital punishment. Among men who spend their days, Cheever fervently wrote,

> carrying the advice and consolation of the religious tract to the victims of vice and poverty, will be found very few indeed, if any, advocates of the abolition of capital punishment, very few, if any, socialists or Fourrierites, or sentimentalists of that

class who are ever obtruding *upon the public* their irrepressible sympathies for suffering humanity, and ever indulging in the most self-complacent camparisons of their own exquisite philanthropy and most transcendent Christianity with the alleged coldness, worldliness, narrowness and even want of faith of the professed churches of Christ.[149]

Although the social attitudes of Calvinistic evangelicals may have resembled those of Methodists, theological differences were essential points of reference in popular thinking about punishment in the new republic. The idea of redemption, which presupposed a belief in free will, was at the root of the belief that the penitentiary should reform the criminal. But Calvinist influences nevertheless shaped Dwight's penal philosophy.

The Puritan ideal of a unified, ordered society based on shared norms and a common discipline persisted right up until the Civil War. The Auburn prison system endured as the embodiment of that ideal. By the time of the Civil War, however, religions that affirmed the individual's spiritual freedom were in the ascendant, and Puritanism, with its collectivist, coercive bias, was losing popular appeal. During the last third of the nineteenth century, the Auburn system was just an empty shell, its original philosophy evident only in the skeletal structure of the tiered cellblock. Furthermore, the penologists of the Gilded Age, who hoped to reform the large, overcrowded penitentiaries in the urbanizing North, were already drawing on science to devise disciplinary strategies that revolved around release procedures and individualized treatment.

Perhaps the theological differences outlined here shaped more general orientations to social policy. Whereas the Calvinist concept of the reprobate translated into an acceptance of class differences, the revolt against Calvinism fostered an image of a classless society in that it presented a view of society as a collection of autonomous individuals. Methodist chaplains sought to convert individual felons rather than change an unjust social order. The Quakers, who were even more insistent than the evangelical Congregationalists and Presbyterians that society exerted a contaminating influence on the soul, developed a system of total solitary confinement in order to facilitate the individual prisoner's growth toward godliness. Unitarians offered sympathetic counsel and urged the individual criminal to mend his ways or be thrown back onto the mean streets of the antebellum city.

Whether the Arminian turn in American Protestantism helped to shape the general concept of the "monadic individual" which, according to a distinguished student of capitalism, "is foundational for many aspects of bourgeois ideology," is beyond the scope of this chapter.[150] This chapter does, however, corroborate Daniel Walker Howe's view that evangelicalism exerted a definite modernizing influence on American society.[151] The reformers of the Jacksonian period, as David Rothman concludes, "fully anticipated that their work behind prison walls would have a critical significance beyond them. By its discovery and verification of proper principles of social organization, the penitentiary would serve as a model for the whole society."[152] The prison reform societies, in applying Christian principles to solve the problem of crime, were unquestionably a modernizing force in society. What this chapter shows, in addition, is that the social transformation of punishment in the early republic was powerfully conditioned by theology.

NOTES

I would like to acknowledge the support of the Centre of Criminology, University of Toronto. Thanks also to John Beattie, Nicole Rafter, Mark Noll, and anonymous reviewers for their comments on this chapter.

1. William W. Sweet, *Religion in the Development of American Culture, 1765–1840* (Gloucester, 1963), 190–233; William G. McLoughlin, *Modern Revivalism* (New York, 1959); George M. Marsden, *The Evangelical Mind and the New School Presbyterian Experience* (New Haven, 1970); Nathan O. Hatch, *The Democratization of American Christianity* (New Haven, 1989); Daniel Walker Howe, *The Unitarian Conscience* (Cambridge, 1970).

2. See John R. Bodo, *The Protestant Clergy and Public Issues, 1812–1848* (Princeton, 1954), 184; Negley K. Teeters, *They Were in Prison* (Chicago, 1937), 89; Boston, *Reports of the Prison Discipline Society* (hereinafter *BPDS*), 6 vols. (1855; repr. Montclair, N.J., 1972); M. J. Heale, "The New York Prison Association, 1844–62," *New York Historical Society Quarterly* 59 (Oct. 1975): 330.

3. Quoted in George W. Pierson, *Tocqueville in America* (New York, 1959), 70.

4. Perry Miller, *The Life of the Mind in America* (New York, 1965), 7.

5. Daniel Walker Howe, "Religion and Politics in the Antebellum North," in *Religion and American Politics,* ed. Mark A. Noll (New York, 1990), 131. On the blurring of theological distinctions in the evangelical reform movement, see Charles I. Foster, *An Errand of Mercy. The Evangelical United Front, 1790–1837* (Chapel Hill, 1960), 122; Timothy L. Smith, *Revivalism and Social Reform* (New York, 1957), 32, 92; Ralph V. Harlow, "Gerrit Smith and the Free Church Movement," *New York History* 18 (July 1937): 274.

6. Hatch, *Democratization of American Christianity*, 63. See also Lois W. Banner, "Religious Benevolence as Social Control: A Critique of an Interpretation," *Journal of American History* 60 (June 1976): 23–41.

7. The separatist Baptists and Quakers persecuted in New England objected not to Calvinist doctrine, but rather to the emphasis that the Congregational clergy placed on an institutionally ordered religious life. See William G. McLoughlin, *New England Dissent, 1630–1833* (Cambridge, 1971).

8. Nicholas Tyacke, *Anti-Calvinists: The Rise of English Arminianism, c. 1590–1640* (New York, 1987), 245.

9. Conrad E. Wright has pointed out that theological liberals in New England were not directly influenced by Arminius but were called Arminians because their reaction against Calvinism was essentially similar to his. See *The Beginnings of Unitarianism in America* (Boston, 1955), 6.

10. It is important to remember, however, that Methodists did not attack "Calvinism in a narrow sense, as if Arminianism or Lutheranism were the preferred reading of scholastic theology. Instead, these attacks were directed against forms of Christianity that were preoccupied with theology" (Hatch, *Democratization of American Christianity*, 173).

11. The Methodist Episcopal Church grew from about 15,000 members in 1784 to over 250,000 in 1820 and almost 500,000 by 1829. In 1776 Congregationalists, Episcopalians, Presbyterians, and Baptists were the dominant religious groups, accounting for 20.4 percent, 15.7 percent, 19 percent, and 16.9 percent, respectively, of all religious adherents in the colonies. By 1850 the Congregationalists had dropped from 20.4 percent to 4 percent of all church adherents, the Episcopalians from 15.7 percent to 3.5 percent, while the Baptist share increased slightly from 16.9 percent to 20.5 percent. In dramatic contrast, Methodists increased their share of the religious market from 2.5 percent in 1776 to 34.2 percent in 1850. With over 13,000 congregations and more than 2.6 million followers, Methodism was by far the largest denomination, accounting for more than a third of all church members in the United States in 1850. See Richard Carwardine, *Transatlantic Revivalism* (Westport, 1978), 10; Roger Finke and Rodney Stark, "How the Upstart Sects Won America: 1776–1850," *Journal for the Scientific Study of Religion* 28 (1) (1989): 31. See also Robert E. Cray, Jr., "Forging a Majority: The Methodist Experience on Eastern Long Island, 1789–1845," *New York History* 67 (July 1986): 285–303.

12. Sweet, *Religion in the Development of American Culture*, 198.

13. Marsden, *Evangelical Mind*, 34.

14. Quoted in ibid., 50.

15. Bradley Chapin, "Felony Law Reform in the Early Republic," *Pennsylvania Magazine of History and Biography* 113 (Apr. 1989): 168.

16. Thomas Eddy, *An Account of the State Prison or Penitentiary House in the City of New York* (New York, 1801), 9.

17. Gordon S. Wood, *The Creation of the American Republic, 1776–1787* (Chapel Hill, 1969), 108.

18. The influences of the Enlightenment and Christianity cannot easily be disentangled in explaining a process as complex as the humanization of punishment. Many prominent early reformers couched their arguments for a humane penal code entirely in the language of republicanism, not Christianity. For example, the peripatetic Edward Livingston (1764–1836), John Breckinridge (1760–1806) in Kentucky, Virginia's George Keith Taylor (1769–1815), Massachusetts's Robert Rantoul, Jr. (1815–52), and New York's John L. O'Sullivan (1813–95) drew almost exclusively on the secular ideas of Beccaria and Bentham in attacking the sanguinary legacy of British criminal jurisprudence. These republican lawyers rested their case for the abolition of the death penalty and the elimination of the discretionary power of judges on the rationalist premises of Enlightenment humanism.

19. Patricia U. Bonomi, *Under the Cope of Heaven* (New York, 1986), 98.

20. In 1530 the belief in original sin was a pivotal idea in English cultural thought. By 1780 the Arminian belief in humanity's goodness and holiness had revolutionized cultural life. See Christopher Hill, *Reformation to Industrial Revolution* (New York, 1969), 287; Lawrence Stone, *The Family, Sex and Marriage in England, 1500–1800* (New York, 1982), 178. On predestination as a theological

warrant for harsh punishment in seventeenth-century New England, see Kai T. Erikson, *Wayward Puritans* (New York, 1966), 190.

21. A doctrinal shift was also taking place in Anglican theology during the period when Englishmen became intent on mitigating the inhumane treatment of criminals. See Randall McGowen, "The Changing Face of God's Justice: The Debates over Divine and Human Punishment in Eighteenth-Century England," *Criminal Justice History* 9 (1988): 63–98. On the opposition to the gallows and disfiguring punishments between 1660 and 1800, see John Beattie, *Crime and the Courts in England, 1660–1800* (Princeton, 1986), 619.

22. Pennsylvania abolished capital punishment for all crimes except first-degree murder in 1794. Virginia and New York restricted the death penalty to murder and treason in 1796. In the same year New Jersey enacted a new code that was not quite as lenient as that of its neighbors, prescribing the death penalty for murder and treason but also for a second offense of manslaughter, sodomy, rape, arson, burglary, robbery, and forgery. See Harry E. Barnes, *The Evolution of Penology in Pennsylvania* (1927; repr. Montclair, N.J., 1968), 106; *A History of the Penal, Reformatory and Correctional Institutions of the State of New Jersey* (1918; repr. New York, 1974), 57; Arthur A. Ekirch, Jr., "Thomas Eddy and the Beginnings of Prison Reform in New York," *New York History* 24 (July 1943): 300.

23. Quoted in David Robinson, *The Unitarians and the Universalists* (Westport, 1985), 55.

24. Ohio reduced the list of capital crimes from four to two in 1815, then in 1824 limited the death penalty to first-degree murder. See Albert Post, "The Anti-gallows Movement in Ohio," *Ohio State Archaeological and Historical Quarterly* 54 (Apr.–June 1945): 105.

25. William Crawford, *Report on the Penitentiaries of the United States* (1835; repr. Montclair, N.J., 1969), 6.

26. David Brion Davis, "The Movement to Abolish Capital Punishment, 1787–1861," *American Historical Review* 63 (Oct. 1957): 33.

27. Philip Mackey, " 'The result may be glorious'—Anti-gallows Movement in Rhode Island, 1838–1852," *Rhode Island History* 33 (1) (1974): 30.

28. Edward W. Bennett, "The Reasons for Michigan's Abolition of Capital Punishment," *Michigan History* (Nov.–Dec. 1978): 42–55.

29. Ballou was particularly critical of Samuel Hopkins. See Robinson, *Unitarians and the Universalists*, 65–66.

30. After studying the reformer's personal diary, Louis P. Masur concludes that Spear saw a career in reform as an opportunity to acquire "fame and income, as well as a chance to reshape the world according to religious principles." See *Rites of Execution: Capital Punishment and the Transformation of American Culture, 1776–1865* (New York, 1989), 125.

31. Ibid., 135–36. *The Hangman* was later renamed *The Prisoner's Friend.*

32. Ibid., 138.

33. Edward Schriver, "Reluctant Hangman: The State of Maine and Capital Punishment, 1820–87," *New England Quarterly* 63 (June 1990): 178.

34. Masur, *Rites of Execution*, 138.

35. Myra C. Glenn, *Campaigns Against Corporal Punishment* (Albany, 1984), 103–26.

36. Bertram Wyatt-Brown, *Yankee Saints and Southern Sinners* (Baton Rouge, 1985), 80.

37. Quoted in Glenn, *Campaigns*, 108.

38. Gerald Grob, *Mental Institutions in America* (New York, 1973), 49.

39. Edward L. Ayers, *Vengeance and Justice* (New York, 1984), 34–72.

40. See Michael S. Hindus, *Prison and Plantation* (Chapel Hill, 1980), 196; Davis, "Movement to Abolish Capital Punishment," 34.

41. Matthew Carey, *Thoughts on Penitentiaries and Prison Discipline* (Philadelphia, 1831), 12.

42. Anne C. Loveland, *Southern Evangelicals and the Social Order* (Baton Rouge, 1980), 162. See also Samuel S. Hill, Jr., *The South and the North in American Religion* (Athens, 1980), 70–73. Baptists do not occupy a prominent place in the history of efforts to reform prisons. Their lack of interest in prison reform may not be due so much to their traditional ties to Calvinism as to their lack of the financial resources needed to promote reform.

43. Bertram Wyatt-Brown, "Religion and the 'Civilizing Process' in the Early American South, 1600–1860," in *Religion and American Politics*, 182.

44. Quoted in Frank Freidel, *Francis Lieber* (Baton Rouge, 1947), 259.

45. George Barrell Cheever, *A Defence of Capital Punishment* (New York, 1846), 5, 84, 12, 84, 36, 22.

46. Ibid., 77, 79, 80.

47. Ibid., 94.

48. Quoted in *Voices against Death*, ed. Philip E. Mackey (New York, 1976), 96.

49. Cheever, *Defence,* 337, 350.

50. Ibid., 282.

51. Quoted in Marsden, *Evangelical Mind*, 55.

52. L. G. Vander Velde, "The Diary of George Duffield," *Mississippi Valley Historical Review* 24 (June 1937–38): 33.

53. George Duffield, *The Divine Organic Law* (Detroit, 1848), 8.

54. Ibid., 7.

55. Ibid., 13, 25. Duffield opposed the death penalty for property offenses, arguing that life is no longer sacred "if it is valued by property."

56. Ibid., 10.

57. Ibid., 24–25.

58. Ibid., 27.

59. Bennett, "Reasons for Michigan's Abolition of Capital Punishment," 52.

60. Quoted in William Jenks, "Memoir of Louis Dwight," in BPDS, *First Annual Report* (1826), 1:15.

61. Dwight's missionary chaplains earned considerably less. Gerrish Barrett earned $200 while chaplain at Sing Sing, and $400 while at the Massachusetts State Prison. Reverend Jared Curtis was paid $500 as chaplain at Massachusetts State Prison. On Dwight's salary, see Albert Hess, "Introduction," in BPDS, *Reports* (1972), 1:xix.

62. Bertram Wyatt-Brown, *Lewis Tappan and the Evangelical War against Slavery* (Cleveland, 1969), 29.

63. Quoted in Jenks, "Memoir of Louis Dwight," 29.

64. Hatch, *Democratization of American Christianity*, 133.

65. For a discussion of the business and benevolent careers of Lewis Tappan and Gerrit Smith, see Wyatt-Brown, *Lewis Tappan, passim*; Ralph V. Harlow, *Gerrit Smith, Philanthropist and Reformer* (New York, 1939), 22–45; Keith J. Hardman, "Charles G. Finney, the Benevolent Church and the Free Church Movement in New York City," *New York History* 67 (Oct. 1986): 411–35.

66. Gordon S. Wood, "The Significance of the Early Republic," *Journal of the Early Republic* 8 (Spring 1988): 18. Donald Mathews has argued that the revivals created much needed small-scale social organization in a society that was undergoing conflict-producing economic and demographic change. The Second Great Awakening, he writes, should be seen "not as the result of a threat to religious institutions so much as the appeal of a religious movement for men troubled by social cleavage." See "The Second Great Awakening as an Organizing Process, 1780–1830: An Hypothesis," *American Quarterly* 21 (Spring 1969): 43. Fred J. Hood has argued that the "community-organizing" function of revivalism fostered anti-Calvinism, especially in new communities and unsettled areas. "Ideas about salvation evolved from the concept emphasizing conversion as the work of God through a process of orthodox religious instruction to one featuring conversion as a human decision requiring little knowledge." See *Reformed America: The Middle and Southern States, 1783–1837* (University, 1980), 178.

67. Michael Walzer, *The Revolution of the Saints* (Cambridge, 1965), 301.

68. Donald M. Scott, *From Office to Profession: The New England Ministry, 1750–1850* (Philadelphia, 1978), 48. Paul Boyer has suggested that the urban Sunday school was created as "an actual attempt to recreate the moral order of the village." See *Urban Masses and Moral Order in America, 1820–1920* (Cambridge, 1978), 34.

69. David J. Rothman, *The Discovery of the Asylum* (Boston, 1971), 83.

70. Dorothea Dix, *Remarks on Prisons and Prison Discipline* (1845; repr. Montclair, N.J., 1967), 25.

71. John Cray, a British army officer who may have deserted his army post during the War of 1812, became deputy keeper of Auburn Prison in 1816. Elam Lynds (1784–1855), perhaps the best known warden in the United States prior to the Civil War, succeeded in making the silent regime work by relying on whipping. Believing that the criminal could be disciplined, but not redeemed, Lynds forced prisoners at Auburn and Sing Sing to work to the point of physical exhaustion, and boasted that his methods transformed the prisoner into "a silent and insulated working machine." Quoted in W. David Lewis, *From Newgate to Dannemora: The Rise of the Penitentiary in New York 1796–1848* (Ithaca, 1965), 88.

72. BPDS, *Fifth Report* (1830), 1:20. In 1829 Reverend Gerrish Barrett reported that convicts at Sing Sing had recited "770 chapters containing 19,328 verses during a period of 18 weeks" and that one man had committed "49 chapters or 1605 verses to memory during a 17 week period." See O. F. Lewis, *The Development of American Prisons and Prison Customs* (1922; repr. Montclair, N.J., 1967), 112.

73. Quoted in Lewis, *From Newgate to Dannemora*, 108.

74. BPDS, *Tenth Report* (1836), 2:49–50.

75. Reverend Jared Curtis began his career as a prison chaplain in 1825 when the Boston Prison Discipline Society sent him to Auburn. For a discussion of the religious program there, see Gershom Powers, *A Brief Account of the Construction,*

Management and Discipline of the New York State Prison at Auburn (Auburn, 1826), 17.

76. Hindus, *Prison and Plantation*, 172.

77. Quoted in Gideon Haynes, *Pictures from Prison Life; An Historical Sketch of the Massachusetts State Prison* (Boston, 1869), 66.

78. Tocqueville and Beaumont could have been thinking of Dwight when they wrote that Americans had "caught the monomanie of the penitentiary system which to them seems the remedy for all the evils in society." See *On the Penitentiary System*, 80.

79. Beyond the fear of crime, there was the economic worry that there would be a dearth of skilled and motivated workingmen in society. This explains why so much emphasis was placed on teaching prisoners a skill and instilling in them the habits of industry required of journeymen apprentices and wage laborers. See Christopher Adamson, "Toward a Marxian Penology: Captive Criminal Populations as Economic Threats and Resources," *Social Problems* 31 (Apr. 1984): 435–58.

80. Tappan, "Remarks on Prisons and Prison Discipline," *Christian Examiner* (Boston, 1826), 3:212.

81. Quoted in Bertram Wyatt-Brown, *Yankee Saints and Southern Sinners* (Baton Rouge, 1985), 88.

82. Tappan, "Remarks," 205.

83. On Wesley's influence on John Howard, see Sean A. McConville, *A History of English Prison Administration* (London, 1981), 79; Michael Ignatieff, *A Just Measure of Pain* (New York, 1978), 50–56.

84. Hatch, *Democratization of American Christianity*, 58.

85. Methodist missionaries began visiting American jails, poorhouses, and plantations in the 1770s. See James D. Essig, *The Bonds of Wickedness* (Philadelphia, 1982), 32. Terry Bilhartz notes that, during the first decade of the nineteenth century, Methodist preachers in Baltimore "held weekly services at the almshouse, Powhatten Factory and the penitentiary." See *Urban Religion and the Second Great Awakening* (Rutherford, 1986), 91.

86. BPDS, *Eighth Report* (1833), 2:12. See also *Thirteenth Report* (1838), 3:58; *Fifteenth Report* (1840), 4:26–33; *Sixteenth Report* (1841), 4:35.

87. Between 1828 and 1832 the ministers of the synod of the Presbyterian Church of the region raised the money to keep James Chute as penitentiary chaplain on a salary of $30 a month. When the governor condemned the prison in 1832, Chaplain Chute resigned. The directors of the penitentiary then tried to raise money for a chaplain by charging prison visitors an admittance fee. There was no chaplain in 1834, 1836, 1837, or between 1842 and 1844. See Clara B. Hicks, "The History of Penal Institutions in Ohio to 1850," *Ohio Archeological and Historical Quarterly* 33 (1924): 403, 421. Dorothea Dix observed that Ohio's failure to provide for a salaried chaplain created an opportunity for "those voluntary preachers who make disinterested and self-sacrificing labors in this field." See *Remarks on Prisons and Prison Discipline*, 59.

88. Methodist itinerants earned around $100 during the 1830s, at a time when the official salary for Presbyterian and Congregationalist ministers in large towns was between $1,000 and $4,000. See Finke and Stark, "How the Upstart Sects Won America," 39.

89. Miller, *Life of the Mind*, 61.

90. John Luckey, *Life in Sing Sing Prison* (New York, 1860), 127. Lewis dubbs Luckey "New York's pioneer penal case worker." See *From Newgate to Dannemora*, 213.

91. James B. Finley, *Sketches of Western Methodism* (Cincinnati, 1856), 412, 336.

92. Powers, *Brief Account*, 9.

93. James B. Finley, *Memorials of Prison Life* (Cincinnati, 1850), 302.

94. See Lewis, *From Newgate to Dannemora*, 230–55.

95. Sean Wilentz, *Chants Democratic* (New York, 1984), 80. On Methodists' identification with those of a lowly status, see also Donald G. Mathews, *Religion in the Old South* (Chicago, 1977), 37.

96. Hatch, *Democratization of American Christianity*, 35.

97. Methodists posed an obvious political threat when their religious freedoms were interfered with. In the province of Upper Canada where Anglicanism was still the established religion during the 1830s, the Anglican elite suspected Methodists of disloyalty. See Goldwin French, *Parsons and Politics* (Toronto, 1962); William Westfall, *Two Worlds: The Protestant Culture of Nineteenth Century Ontario* (Montreal, 1989). It was well known that Upper Canadian Methodists were in the habit of visiting criminals and debtors in jails throughout the province. Prior to 1850, however, only Anglicans served as chaplains at Kingston Penitentiary.

98. See Donald G. Mathews, *Slavery and Methodism* (Princeton, 1965).

99. Luckey, *Life in Sing Sing*, 127.

100. Hatch, *Democratization of American Christianity*, 83.

101. See Negley K. Teeters, *They Were in Prison* (Philadelphia, 1937), 89–116. Quakers played a dominant role, even though Philadelphia's elite in the early national period was heterogeneous. See E. Digby Baltzell, *Quaker Philadelphia and Puritan Boston* (Boston, 1979), 151.

102. Ibid., *passim.*

103. See David Brion Davis, *The Problem of Slavery in the Age of Revolution, 1770–1823* (Ithaca, 1975), 230.

104. On the Wistars and others, see Teeters, *They Were in Prison*, 118; Francis R. Packard, "Caspar Wistar," *Dictionary of American Biography* (hereinafter *DAB*), 10:433.

105. See Teeters, *The Cradle of the Penitentiary* (Philadelphia, 1955), 19.

106. Eddy, *Account*, 9.

107. Eddy was also a founding member of the New York Society for the Prevention of Pauperism in 1816 and a manager of the Society for the Reformation of Juvenile Delinquents. For a full account of his career in public service, see Samuel L. Knapp, *The Life of Thomas Eddy* (1834; repr. New York, 1976), 14. See also Ekirch, Jr, "Thomas Eddy and the Beginnings of Prison Reform," 376–91.

108. On Vaux's philanthropic career, see Teeters, *They Were in Prison*, 153. On his penological career and ideas, see Roberts Vaux, *Notices of the Original and Successive Efforts to Improve the Discipline of the Prison at Philadelphia* (Philadelphia, 1826).

109. Believing that the real purpose of Christianity should be to facilitate an inward experience of the divine light, the Quakers developed their own unique style of worship, refusing to proselytize, failing even to systematize their religious vision

into any kind of theology. See Thomas O. Hamm, *The Transformation of American Quakerism* (Bloomington, 1988), 10.

110. Ibid., 7.

111. The black hood, ridiculed by Charles Dickens in his *American Notes* (1842), was still being used in 1872. See Richard Vaux, *A Brief Sketch of the Origin and History of the State Penitentiary for the Eastern District of Pennsylvania* (Philadelphia, 1872), 69.

112. Legislation enacted in 1818 and 1821 ordering construction of the Eastern and Western State penitentiaries specified that no labor would be provided. Clearly the idea behind this legislation was that work would prevent prisoners from reflecting seriously on their sins. When work was eventually introduced, it was manual activity that prisoners could do in isolation, like weaving or furniture making.

113. Francis Lieber, *A Popular Essay on the Subjects of Penal Law* (Philadelphia, 1838), iii. In the introduction to the essay, Lieber defines penology as that "science which will necessarily treat of punition theoretically, practically and historically; of its relation to the political community, as well as to the psychologic state of the offender."

114. Ibid., 5

115. Ibid., 83.

116. Ibid., 51.

117. Ibid., 63.

118. Quoted in ibid., 82.

119. Tocqueville, *On the Penitentiary System*, 91.

120. Lieber, *Popular Essay*, 77. Devout Quakers frowned on hymn singing and social amusements. While in Europe in 1818, John Griscom recorded feeling ashamed by the unnecessary comfort provided for him by his hosts. He spent his days visiting prisons, hospitals, and other institutions of learning and charity, and in the evenings he retired in order to pray, refusing to attend the "theatres, ball-rooms, dinner parties and spectacles of amusement" to which he was invited. See John Griscom, *A Year in Europe*, 2 vols. (New York, 1824), vii. See also John H. Griscom, *Memoir of John Griscom, LL.D.* (New York, 1859).

121. Lewis, *From Newgate to Dannemora*, 32.

122. Quoted in Knapp, *Life of Thomas Eddy*, 316.

123. Ronald Story, *Harvard and the Boston Upper Class* (Middletown, 1980), 7; Jane H. Pease and William H. Pease, "Whose Right Hand of Fellowship? Pew and Pulpit in Shaping Church Practice," in *American Unitarianism, 1805–1865*, ed. Conrad E. Wright (Boston, 1989), 182–85.

124. Sweet, *Religion in the Development of American Culture*, 192.

125. Story, *Harvard and the Boston Upper Class*, 67.

126. Tuckerman broke family tradition by becoming a minister rather than a merchant. Quincy inherited wealth at a young age. Francis Gray inherited a fortune from his father, an extremely wealthy Salem merchant who owned the largest fleet of trading vessels in the world. Gray studied law but devoted his life to business and philanthropy. His money was tied up with "the Merchant's Bank of Boston, the Western Railroad, a Boston machine shop, a Boston ropeworks, a New Hampshire textile mill, and the New England iron manufacturing firm of his brother, Horace Gray." See Story, *Harvard and the Boston Upper Class*, 47.

127. Howe, *Unitarian Conscience*, 151.

128. Quoted in Joseph Conforti, "Edwardians, Unitarians and the Memory of the Great Awakening, 1800–1840," in *American Unitarianism*, 42.

129. In various writings, including an essay entitled "The Moral Argument against Calvinism" published in 1820, Channing challenged the doctrine of moral inability and called on his followers to spread the message of God's intrinsic goodness. Although Unitarianism did not develop as much more than a loosely organized association of congregations after 1825, its moral influence expanded during the 1830s. Younger, zealous Unitarians believed that, rather than consolidating themselves as a formal denomination with a distinct creed, they should spread the Unitarian message through philanthropic work, including anti-slavery, temperance, and prison reform. It is significant that the youthful Lewis Tappan actually wrote his essay on prison reform during the brief period of a year or two when he had fallen under the influence of Unitarianism. See Howe, *Unitarian Conscience*, 161, 173, 215–17.

130. Gary L. Collison, "A True Toleration: Harvard Divinity School Students and Unitarianism, 1830–1859," in *American Unitarianism*, 216.

131. Howe, *Unitarian Conscience*, 239.

132. Francis Bowen, "Prison Discipline," *North American Review* 66 (1848): 145–90. Bowen argued that the Pennsylvanian system produced unacceptably high rates of insanity.

133. Samuel G. Howe, *An Essay on Separate and Congregate Systems of Prison Discipline* (1846; repr. New York, 1974), iv.

134. Quoted in Samuel M. Crothers, "William Ellery Channing," *DAB* (1958), 2:7.

135. Dix, *Remarks on Prisons and Prison Discipline*, 10.

136. Samuel G. Howe, *Essay*, 53.

137. See Oscar and Mary F. Handlin, *Commonwealth: A Study of the Role of Government in the American Economy, 1774–1861* (Cambridge, 1969); Louis Hartz, *Economic Policy and Democratic Thought: Pennsylvania, 1776–1860* (Cambridge, 1948); Harry N. Scheiber, *Ohio Canal Era: A Case Study of Government and the Economy, 1820–1861* (Athens, 1969).

138. Tappan, "Remarks," 210.

139. Quoted in Howe, *Unitarian Conscience*, 223.

140. Quoted in Gordon A. Riegler, *Socialization of the New England Clergy* (Greenfield, 1945), 92.

141. Quoted in Howe, *Unitarian Conscience*, 253.

142. Ibid., 160.

143. Collison, "True Toleration," 217.

144. Quoted in Henry S. Commager, *Theodore Parker* (Boston, 1967), 171.

145. Rothman, *Discovery of the Asylum*, 249.

146. Blake McKelvey, *American Prisons* (1936; repr. Montclair, N.J., 1977), 88.

147. Finley, *Memorials of Prison Life*, 148.

148. Cheever, *Defence*, 106.

149. Ibid., 112.

150. Robert L. Heilbroner, *The Nature and Logic of Capitalism* (New York, 1985), 120.

151. Howe, "Religion and Politics in the Antebellum North," in *Religion and*

American Politics, 130. See also "The Evangelical Movement and Political Culture in the North during the Second Party System," *Journal of American History* 77 (Mar. 1991): 1216–39.

152. Rothman, *Discovery of the Asylum*, 84.

Children, Urbanization, and the Chances of Imprisonment in Mid-Victorian England

John A. Stack
University of Missouri, Kansas City

In 1851 the compilers of the English census noticed for the first time the country's mushrooming "public institutions." Near the end of their analysis of "Families and Houses" in their first report, the compilers observed that "Besides that large proportion of the population in families, some fractions of the people are for various reasons lodged in detached buildings, under the rule of one or more men or governing bodies."[1] On census day, 31 March 1851, the enumerators discovered 240,023 inmates in 1,758 barracks, work-houses, prisons, lunatic asylums, hospitals, and other charitable institutions in England and Wales.[2] Ten years later (in 1861) the census reported that the number of inmates had climbed to 276,458, although the number of public institutions had dipped somewhat to 1,696;[3] while twenty years later (in 1871) the census revealed that the number of inmates had increased to 362,295, and that the number of public institutions had jumped to 2,479.[4]

The authors of the 1851 census—as well as the authors of the 1861 and 1871 censuses—took considerable satisfaction in the spread of these asylums:

> One of the most unerring tests of the civilization of a State is to be found in its Public Institutions. A stranger arriving in a country where the most conspicuous objects consisted of edifices for religious worship, schools and colleges for the education of the young, almshouses and asylums for the aged or helpless, workhouses for the poor, hospitals for the sick, barracks for the soldiery, and prisons for the custody of offenders, would be at no loss in coming to the conclusion that he was in the midst of a highly civilized and enlightened community.[5]

Until fairly recently, most histories of these public institutions have been equally uncritical. These early accounts usually starred dedicated reformers who were said to have been inspired by the Enlightenment, or humanitarianism, or evangelical religion, and who were said to have struggled against the indifferent and cruel practices of the past and toward the concerned and humane methods of the present. As Michael Ignatieff has recently argued, these older studies "had an implicitly teleological bias, treating the history [of reform] as a progress from cruelty to enlightenment."[6]

During the early 1970s an influential group of revisionist historians inflicted numerous telling, if not mortal, blows on the old views. The revisionists suggested that the promoters of the new asylums were motivated by self- and class interest, as well as by conscience, and that the new institutions were frequently more like arrogant Leviathans than heavenly retreats. Furthermore, some of the more ambitious revisionists sought to understand and explain the asylum by exploring its role in such eighteenth- and nineteenth-century transformations as the rise of industrial capitalism,[7] the spread of democracy,[8] the emergence of new structures of power,[9] and the development of new perceptions of deviance and dependence.[10]

Although the revisionists advanced more complex—and more negative—interpretations of asylums and their promoters, and although they advanced exceedingly provocative ideas about the origins and shapes of asylums and their relationships to wider trends, they—like the earlier historians—exaggerated the influence of the reformers and their reforms. Hence, in the 1980s the revisionists came under attack from a diligent band of "new" revisionists who looked more closely at the actual administration of both the prereform era institutions and the reform era institutions. The "new" revisionists argued that the prereform institutions were "neither as squalid nor as incompetently administered" as the reformers had made them out to be, and that there were significant discrepancies between what reformers advocated and what officials in charge of local institutions in the reform era did.[11]

Absent from most of these accounts—the old histories, the revisionist histories, and the new revisionist histories—was any systematic attempt to reconstruct and explain the experiences of the inmates of the mushrooming asylums. This omission was curious because, as Peter Stearns reminded us in 1980, the upsurge in social history during the 1960s was "fueled" by an enthusiasm to see history " 'from the bottom up', through the experiences and perceptions of ordinary rather than extraordinary actors in the past."[12] The new social historians, however, were primarily concerned with capturing and sympathetically recreating the lives of working-class people in civil society, and did not concern themselves initially with the task of reclaiming the experiences of the inmates of the asylums that spread across Europe and America during the late eighteenth and nineteenth centuries. In 1970 the social welfare historian Robert Bremner noticed the resulting vacuum: "In the past, social welfare history has been written from the standpoint of (and usually by) the givers of assistance; in the future it will very likely be written by and from the point of view of the recipients and beneficiaries."[13] Ten years later, J. F. C. Harrison could still complain that a great deal of social reform history was "(dare one confess it) very unexciting," because "We hear little about poor relief from the voices of the recipients, and even less as to how labouring people viewed prison or elementary education."[14] During the 1980s a few historians became conscious of this void and worked to fill it. At a 1983 conference on "Life in Total Institutions" organized by the Social History Society, "one urgent plea which came from several of the discussions was the need to know far more about the experiences of life in total institutions through the eyes of the 'inmates' themselves."[15]

Missing from these debates and discussions was any consideration of the varying chances of being sent to one of these new "total institutions." The chances of being sent to a work house, for example, were greater than the chances of being sent to an insane asylum or prison. Furthermore, the chances of being sent to an insane asylum or prison or work house varied according to one's sex, age, ethnic background, and social background. Finally, the chances of any given individual, or group of individuals, being institutionalized in a particular type of institution might vary according to place. In order to illustrate these points we will examine the varying chances of children being sent to prison in mid-Victorian England.

DEFINING CHILDREN AND PRISONS

In 1857 the criminal registrar, Samuel Redgrave, indicated that for the purposes of the newly reorganized Judicial Statistics, "children are calculated at from seven to sixteen years of age."[16] Children in mid-Victorian England were sent to three kinds of "prisons": "lock-ups," "convict prisons," and "local prisons." Those suspected of crime were frequently taken by the police or private persons to lock-ups to await a hearing before a magistrate. Although many children accused of crime in the mid-nineteenth century found themselves incarcerated in lock-ups, it is unlikely that many of them spent more than a day or two in these institutions. On the other hand, children sent to one of the relatively uncommon convict prisons were normally given quite lengthy sentences of imprisonment. Children were only sent to these institutions, however, if they had been convicted of serious offenses. The number of children incarcerated in them was always small, and in the mid-Victorian period it became minute. This chapter concentrates on the children sent to local prisons, which were less common than lock-ups but much more common than convict prisons. The local prisons also kept children for longer periods than lock-ups, but for shorter periods than convict prisons.

Every county in mid-Victorian England had at least one local prison, and in every county authorities sent children to these institutions.[17] Between 1856 and 1875 there were in England—at one time or another—143 local prisons that received child prisoners.[18] Most of the children committed to these prisons had probably been committed to serve short sentences of imprisonment; a smaller group had probably been committed to await trial at either quarter sessions or assizes; and a few probably had been committed on remand or for want of sureties. It seems unlikely that many, if any, children were committed for the two other considerations for which persons were sent to local prisons (debt and military offenses).[19] Finally, it must always be kept in mind that the prison authorities counted "commitments" and not "individuals." In other words, if a child was committed to prison twice or more in a given year, each commitment was counted even though it was the same child on each occasion.

IMPRISONMENT RATES FOR CHILDREN, BOYS, AND GIRLS

In order to determine the risk of a child being sent to a local prison, it is necessary to consider both the number of children in the society and the number of child commitments to prison. Between 1856 and 1875 the average annual child population was 3,944,720,[20] and the average annual number of child commitments to prison was 9,373.[21] This means that there were on average 238 child commitments to prison per 100,000 children in the population annually between 1856 and 1875. It should be stated, however, that we are not dealing with children from all social groups. It seems highly likely that the children sent to prison were drawn almost exclusively from the working class. Although middle-class criminality was more common in the Victorian era than is usually appreciated,[22] middle-class children who committed crimes probably were protected by their families and their families' connections: "Mary Carpenter [a social reformer and child welfare advocate] reckoned that up to 10,000 children of the lower classes were sent to prison annually for 'robbing garden apples' and other minor offences for which upper class boys received only parental correction."[23]

The chance that a child might be sent to prison in the mid-Victorian period varied enormously by sex as well as by class. Relatively few girls were committed to prison. Between 1856 and 1875, of the 187,452 child commitments to prison, only 25,846 (14%) were female, whereas 161,606 (86%) were male. Analogously, between 1856 and 1875, only 65.9 girls p.a. per 100,000 were on average sent to prison in contrast to 408.62 boys.

The risk of child imprisonment also varied considerably according to ethnic background. Here the crucial contrast was between the Irish and the non-Irish, most of whom were English. Proportionately, many more Irish children were sent to prison than English. Unfortunately, the task of determining what proportion of the child prison commitments was Irish is only partially aided by the Judicial Statistics. These give the birthplaces of all those committed to prison, but do not provide the places of birth of the prison commitments in each of the various age stages. It is also impossible to obtain from the prison statistics any data on those committed to prison who were born in England of Irish parents, or of mixed Irish and English parents. Although most of these persons are probably best understood as being "Irish," they are all considered to be English in the prison statistics (as in the census). To obtain a true estimate of the number of "Irish" committed to prison, the number of Irish-born commitments should probably be doubled.[24]

Despite these very real difficulties, it is still worthwhile to compare total Irish-born commitments (i.e., all ages) to total non-Irish-born (i.e., mainly English of all ages) as a way to get at the relationship that Irish child commitments bore to non-Irish (i.e., mainly English). If one averages the population figures and the commitment to prison figures for the census years 1861 and 1871, and then works out the rates of Irish-born and non-Irish-born (i.e., mainly English) commitments to prison per 100,000, one discovers that the two rates were quite different. The Irish-born were sent to prison at a rate of 3,200.88 per 100,000 Irish-born, whereas the non-Irish-born (i.e., mainly English) were sent to prison at a rate of 551.51.[25] Another way to look at the disproportionate risk of Irish children being sent to prison is to look at the reformatory school statistics. Between 1856 and 1875 some 23,990 children in England and Wales were convicted of various offenses and given sentences of between two and five years in state-licensed reformatory schools.[26] These children were simultaneously sentenced to at least fourteen days' imprisonment in a local prison. Consequently, they were part of the total number of child commitments to prison.[27]

The 23,990 children who served short sentences of imprisonment, and longer sentences of reformatory detention in England and Wales between 1856 and 1875, formed 12.6 percent of the 191,090 child commitments to prison in England and Wales during these same years. According to the 1881 Report of the Reformatories and Industrial Schools Commission, 5,441 (23%) of these 23,990 children were Catholic, while 18,549 (77%) were Protestant.[28] Most of the 5,441 Catholic children were probably born in Ireland or were the children of Irish-born parents.[29] Since the ethnic Irish community in England and Wales formed approximately five percent of the mid-Victorian English and Welsh population, Irish children were roughly four times more likely to end up in a prison *and* a reformatory school than was statistically warranted by their numbers in the total population. Once again, however, the risk of incarceration for girls was considerably lower than for boys. Of the 5,441 Catholic commitments to reformatory schools, only 1,017 (19%) were girls, whereas 4,424 (81%) were boys.

IMPRISONMENT RATES BY LOCALITY

The chances that a child might be sent to prison in the mid-Victorian period also varied greatly according to locality. To take the extremes, there were on average 556.88 child commitments to prison p.a. per 100,000 children between 1856 and 1875 in Middlesex, but only 53.19 such commitments in Cornwall. Children were approximately ten times more likely to be committed to prison in Middlesex as in Cornwall. An analagous, although less dramatic, contrast emerges if one compares the five counties with the highest number of child commitments per 100,000 children with the five counties with the lowest number. There were on average 400.00 child commitments to prison p.a. per 100,000 children between 1856 and 1875 in the former, but only 75.98 such commitments in the latter.[30] Thus children were 5.26 times more likely to be sent to prison in the five counties with the highest number of child commitments per 100,000 as in the five counties with the lowest number.

When one breaks down child commitments into boys and girls, similar differences in the chances of imprisonment according to locality can be seen. Taking the extremes again, there were on average 1,000.08 boy commitments to prison p.a. per 100,000 boys between 1856 and 1875 in Middlesex, but only 82.99 in Cornwall. A similar contrast emerges when the five counties with the highest number of boy commitments per 100,000 boys are compared with the five counties with the lowest number. There were on average 706.55 boy commitments to prison p.a. per 100,000 boys in the former, but only 122.19 such commitments in the latter.[31] Thus boys were approximately 5.8 times more likely to be sent to prison in the five counties with the highest number of boy commitments per 100,000 boys as in the five counties with the lowest number.

The risk of imprisonment for girls also varied according to locality, but the differences between the extremes were significantly less for girls. Girls were only eight times more likely to be sent to prison in Middlesex (the county with the highest girls' rate) than in Bedfordshire (the county with the lowest girls' rate). Second, girls were only 4.35 times more likely to be sent to prison in the five counties with the highest number of girl commitments per 100,000 as in the five counties with the lowest. There were on average 101.02 girl commitments to prison p.a. per 100,000 girls in the former, but only 23.20 such commitments in the latter.[32]

What might explain these very considerable county differences? It has long been accepted that nineteenth-century England was fundamentally transformed by a series of radical changes such as industrialization, urbanization, population growth, immigration and emigration, and religious revival. In the last few years it has also been increasingly understood that these forces did not affect all of England equally. They influenced some places radically while other places were affected much less perceptibly. Furthermore, this uneven development so increased the differences among places that, as Olive Anderson has recently suggested, "In the nineteenth century, and even in the early twentieth, England was an immensely varied land, indeed, in Victoria's reign it was probably less homogeneous than ever before or since."[33]

The implications of this widespread regional diversity are enormous, and are only now being systematically explored. Hence Stephens has recently suggested that literacy rates varied by place,[34] Marsden that the provision of schools varied by place,[35] and Hunt that wages varied by place.[36] The procedure followed in most of these studies was to divide the nation, or a region within the nation, into distinct areas and then to determine if these different areas exhibited different patterns as regards the phenomenon being studied (literacy, provision of schools, wages, etc.). The "distinct area" could be a city, a registration district, or an ancient county. Obviously, the more distinct the "distinct area," the more precise the correlations that can be made.

Influenced by these studies, we tried to determine if there was any relationship between place and the commitment of children to prison. Unfortunately our unit of analysis had to be the rather unwieldy ancient county because the prison commitment statistics were only collected and published on an ancient county by ancient county basis. Counties were differentiated by degrees of urbanization, and degrees of urbanization were determined by calculating the percentage of the population of each county that lived in towns of 20,000 or more. The forty counties were then scaled and divided into six groups, and the average number of child commitments to prison p.a. per 100,000 children between 1856 and 1875 was then determined for each of the six groups. The results are quite revealing and are contained in Table 1.

It is evident from Table 1 that children in the most heavily urbanized county (i.e., group one: Middlesex) were more than five times more likely to be sent to prison than were children in the least urbanized counties (i.e., group six: ten rural counties). There was also a significant difference between the rate of the counties in group two (Surrey and Warwickshire), and the rate of the counties in the lowest group (i.e., group six). On the other hand, the differences among the rates of the counties in groups three, four, five, and six are less considerable, although the children in the counties in group three were still twice as likely to be sent to prison as were the children in the counties in group six.

When one shifts from child commitments to boy and girl commitments, the chances of imprisonment once again correlate very closely with degrees of urbanization, but there are also some interesting variations. It is evident from Tables 2 and 3 that both boys and girls in the most heavily urbanized county (i.e., group one: Middlesex) were much more likely to be sent to prison than were boys and girls in the least urbanized ones. But there were differences. Boys in Middlesex (i.e., group one) were 5.5 times more likely to end up in prison than were boys in the least urbanized counties (i.e.,

Table 1
Prison Commitments of Children, 1856–75

Column A	Column B	Column C	Column D	Column E
% of population in cities of 20,000 or more (1861 and 1871 censuses averaged)	Counties	Average child population p.a., 1856-1875	Average number of child commitments p.a., 1856-1875	Rate per 100,000 children
(1) 80.1 - 100	Middlesex	416,828	2,321.25	556.88
(2) 60.1 - 80.0	Surrey	182,334	963.10	
	Warwickshire	116,998	312.45	
		299,332	1,275.55	426.13
(3) 40.1 - 60.0	Lancashire	505,696	1,391.05	
	Yorkshire	437,891	599.15	
	Kent	152,663	308.45	
	Northumberland	71,537	158.70	
	Staffordshire	164,054	265.55	
		1,331,841	2,722.90	204.45
(4) 20.1 - 40.0	Gloucestershire	99,839	298.90	
	Durham	121,410	179.50	
	Leicestershire	50,656	101.05	
	Hampshire	96,228	256.35	
	Cheshire	104,290	149.35	
	Sussex	78,271	151.40	
	Devonshire	114,202	188.30	
	Nottinghamshire	60,410	120.10	
	Norfolk	86,544	162.55	
	Worcestershire	65,208	105.15	
		877,058	1,712.65	195.27
(5) 0.1 - 20.0	Essex	91,314	169.00	
	Somersetshire	91,573	133.50	
	Oxfordshire	35,614	53.70	
	Northamptonshire	47,451	72.15	
	Cambridgeshire	37,035	53.30	
	Berkshire	37,594	74.90	
	Cumberland	42,208	31.15	
	Monmouthshire	36,288	53.35	
	Derbyshire	71,407	70.50	
	Suffolk	70,619	100.85	
	Shropshire	48,479	56.80	
	Lincolnshire	86,029	122.90	
		695,611	992.10	142.62
(6) 0.0	Herefordshire	24,168	32.40	
	Bedfordshire	29,310	33.45	
	Westmorland	12,446	11.65	
	Wiltshire	52,333	67.10	
	Dorsetshire	38,514	42.40	
	Cornwall	76,328	40.60	
	Hertfordshire	37,600	62.85	
	Buckinghamshire	35,432	40.10	
	Huntingdonshire	13,408	14.30	
	Rutland	4,511	3.30	
		324,050	348.15	107.44

Sources: Census of England and Wales, 1851, 1861, 1871, 1881; Judicial Statistics of England and Wales, 1856–76.

Table 2
Prison Commitments of Boys, 1856–75

Column A	Column B	Column C	Column D	Column E
% of population in cities of 20,000 or more (1861 and 1871 censuses averaged)	Counties	Average boy population p.a., 1856-1875	Average number of boy commitments p.a., 1856-1875	Rate per 100,000 boys
(1) 80.1 - 100	Middlesex	205,349	2,053.65	1,000.08
(2) 60.1 - 80.0	Surrey	90,561	861.50	
	Warwickshire	58,600	269.70	
		149,161	1,131.20	758.38
(3) 40.1 - 60.0	Lancashire	251,645	1,188.85	
	Yorkshire	219,251	503.15	
	Kent	77,051	270.55	
	Northumberland	36,245	131.00	
	Staffordshire	82,605	206.50	
		666,797	2,300.05	344.94
(4) 20.1 - 40.0	Gloucestershire	49,624	259.70	
	Durham	61,641	145.00	
	Leicestershire	25,416	87.60	
	Hampshire	48,636	223.05	
	Cheshire	52,102	125.75	
	Sussex	39,539	124.45	
	Devonshire	57,306	160.80	
	Nottinghamshire	29,831	106.30	
	Norfolk	43,554	146.35	
	Worcestershire	32,564	83.65	
		440,213	1,462.65	332.26
(5) 0.1 - 20.0	Essex	46,468	153.15	
	Somersetshire	46,032	112.35	
	Oxfordshire	18,200	45.50	
	Northamptonshire	23,747	61.80	
	Cambridgeshire	18,695	46.10	
	Berkshire	19,123	65.10	
	Cumberland	21,356	24.90	
	Monmouthshire	18,411	35.75	
	Derbyshire	36,131	58.95	
	Suffolk	35,785	88.75	
	Shropshire	24,379	44.75	
	Lincolnshire	43,399	97.65	
		351,726	834.75	237.33
(6) 0.0	Herefordshire	12,336	26.95	
	Bedfordshire	14,654	31.10	
	Westmorland	6,262	9.50	
	Wiltshire	26,588	54.90	
	Dorsetshire	19,460	36.20	
	Cornwall	38,801	32.20	
	Hertfordshire	19,065	56.95	
	Buckinghamshire	17,934	36.25	
	Huntingdonshire	6,753	11.30	
	Rutland	2,365	2.65	
		164,218	298.00	181.47

Sources: Census of England and Wales, 1851, 1861, 1871, 1881; Judicial Statistics of England and Wales, 1856–76.

Table 3
Prison Commitments of Girls, 1856–75

Column A % of population in cities of 20,000 or more (1861 and 1871 censuses averaged)	Column B Counties	Column C Average girl population p.a., 1856-1875	Column D Average number of girl commitments p.a., 1856-1875	Column E Rate per 100,000 girls
(1) 80.1 - 100	Middlesex	211,479	267.60	126.54
(2) 60.1 - 80.0	Surrey	91,773	101.60	
	Warwickshire	58,398	42.75	
		150,171	144.35	96.12
(3) 40.1 - 60.0	Lancashire	254,051	202.20	
	Yorkshire	218,640	96.00	
	Kent	75,612	37.90	
	Northumberland	35,292	27.70	
	Staffordshire	81,449	59.05	
		665,044	422.85	63.58
(4) 20.1 - 40.0	Gloucestershire	50,215	39.20	
	Durham	59,769	34.50	
	Leicestershire	25,240	13.45	
	Hampshire	47,592	33.30	
	Cheshire	52,188	23.60	
	Sussex	38,732	26.95	
	Devonshire	56,896	27.50	
	Nottinghamshire	30,579	13.80	
	Norfolk	42,990	16.20	
	Worcestershire	32,644	21.50	
		436,845	250.00	57.23
(5) 0.1 - 20.0	Essex	44,846	15.85	
	Somersetshire	45,541	21.15	
	Oxfordshire	17,414	8.20	
	Northamptonshire	23,704	10.35	
	Cambridgeshire	18,340	7.20	
	Berkshire	18,471	9.80	
	Cumberland	20,852	6.25	
	Monmouthshire	17,877	17.60	
	Derbyshire	35,276	11.55	
	Suffolk	34,834	12.10	
	Shropshire	24,100	12.05	
	Lincolnshire	42,630	25.25	
		343,885	157.35	45.76
(6) 0.0	Herefordshire	11,832	5.45	
	Bedfordshire	14,656	2.35	
	Westmorland	6,184	2.15	
	Wiltshire	25,745	12.20	
	Dorsetshire	19,054	6.20	
	Cornwall	37,527	8.40	
	Hertfordshire	18,535	5.90	
	Buckinghamshire	17,498	3.85	
	Huntingdonshire	6,655	3.00	
	Rutland	2,146	0.65	
		159,832	50.15	31.38

Sources: Census of England and Wales, 1851, 1861, 1871, 1881; Judicial Statistics of England and Wales, 1856–76.

group six), whereas girls in Middlesex were only 4.0 times more likely to end up in prison than were girls in the least urbanized counties. Furthermore, differences among the six groups of counties were greater for boys than for girls. For example, boys in group one (Middlesex) were 2.9 times more likely to end up in prison than were boys in group three (Lancashire, Yorkshire, Kent, Northumberland, and Staffordshire), but girls in group one (Middlesex) were only 2.0 times more likely to end up in prison than were girls in the counties in group three (see Tables 2 and 3).

The unequal distribution of the Irish helps to explain the differences in child imprisonment rates. In 1861 there were 580,487 Irish-born persons living in England, or .031 percent of the population,[37] while in 1871 there were 551,453, or .026 percent.[38] The Irish-born, however, were overwhelmingly concentrated in the large urban centers. In 1861, seventy-nine percent of the Irish-born in England (460,146 of 580,487) lived in the ten most heavily urbanized counties, whereas only fifty-seven percent of the total population in England (10,853,923 of 18,954,444) lived in these same ten counties.[39] Furthermore, forty-five percent of the Irish-born in 1871 were located in the nine English cities with more than 125,000 people. These same cities accounted for only twenty-five percent of the total population of England in 1871.[40]

Because most of the Irish-born living in England resided in the heavily urbanized counties, and because the Irish-born were four or five times more likely to end up in prison than were their non-Irish-born neighbors, it seems reasonable to assume that part of the difference between the rate of commitment in the more and less urbanized counties was due to the larger Irish-born presence in the more urbanized ones. What is not clear is how much of the difference between the two rates can be attributed to the presence of the Irish-born group. Some indication of this can be obtained by looking at total commitments to prison during the 1861 and 1871 census years, and then subtracting the Irish-born to see what effect the inclusion and the exclusion of the Irish-born group has on commitment rates (see Table 4).

When the Irish-born are subtracted from both the population figures and the commitment figures for the six groups of counties, there is a decline in the commitment rate of all six groups of counties. But the decline is very uneven. In the least urbanized counties (i.e., group six) the decline was only three percent, whereas in the most urbanized county (i.e., group one, which contained only one county, Middlesex) the decline was eleven percent. The largest decline, however, was in group three. This group contains Lancashire, which had a higher proportion of Irish-born than any other county in England. Indeed, of the 18,116 Irish-born commitments to prison in 1861 and 1871 (averaged), 7,607 (42%) were committed in Lancashire.

The subtraction of the Irish-born also affected the difference between the commitment rate in the most heavily urbanized county (group one) and the least urbanized (group six). The former had a commitment rate 2.73 times

Table 4
Irish-born and Commitment Rates

Column A Percentage of population living in cities of 20,000 or more (1861 & 1871 censuses averaged)	Column B Number of Counties	Column C Total commitments to prison per 100,000 (1861 and 1871 population figures and prison commitment figures averaged)	Column D Total commitments to prison per 100,000 with Irish-born subtracted (1861 and 1871 population figures and prison commitment figures averaged)	Column E Percentage decline between Column C and Column D
(1) 80.1-100	1	1,011.03	900.23	-11%
(2) 60.1-80.0	2	690.98	645.14	- 7%
(3) 40.1-60.0	5	705.19	580.18	-18%
(4) 20.1-40.0	10	515.58	472.85	- 8%
(5) 0.1-20.0	12	432.00	408.84	- 5%
(6) 0.0	10	370.85	359.29	- 3%
England	40	625.65	551.51	-12%

Sources: Census of England and Wales, 1861 and 1871; Judicial Statistics, 1861 and 1871.

Total Commitments to Prison per 100,000 in the Counties of England (1861 and 1871 population figures and prison commitment figures averaged), with the counties arranged by the percentage of their populations living in cities of 20,000 or more, and the same thing with the Irish-born subtracted.

greater than the latter with the Irish-born included (i.e., 1,011.30 versus 370.85), but this figure sank to 2.51 when the Irish-born are subtracted (i.e., 900.23 versus 359.20). And if those born in England of Irish parents could also be included the difference would presumably be even less. It is important to remember, of course, that these figures relate to total commitments rather than to child commitments. It seems reasonable to assume, however, that child commitments would respond in a roughly similar way to the inclusion or exclusion of the Irish-born as did total commitments.

Although the facts that the Irish were disproportionately likely to be sent to prison, and that the Irish were disproportionately concentrated in the cities, help to explain why boys and girls living in urban counties were so much more likely to be imprisoned than were their rural counterparts, these facts are not enough in themselves to account for the wide differences in the rates. It is also necessary to look more closely at the possible effects of urbanization on three groups of actors: the children who were sent to prison; the victims and the police who apprehended and prosecuted them; and the magistrates and judges who gave the sentences. And the most obvious starting point is with the children themselves. What had they done to justify their being sent to prison, and how might urbanization help explain why they did what they did?

Unfortunately, it is impossible to identify the crimes for which children

Table 5
Crimes and Commitment of Children, 1858–75

Category	Number of children committed	Category as a percentage of total child commitments (i.e. 21,547)
1. Larceny and petty theft	12,499	58.0%
2. Larceny in dwelling house	3,272	15.2%
3. Larceny by a servant	990	4.6%
4. Larceny from a person	987	4.6%
5. Housebreaking, shoplifting, etc.	773	3.6%
6. Vagrancy	576	2.7%
7. Other offenses	538	2.5%
8. Attempts to steal	416	1.9%
9. Unlawful possession of goods	238	1.1%
10. Fraudulent offences	227	1.1%
	20,516 of 21,547 total child commitments	95.3%

Source: Judicial Statistics of England and Wales, 1859–76.

were sent to prison from the prison statistics alone. These list the crimes of the total number of commitments to prison, but they do not identify the crimes of the prison commitments in each of the age stages into which the prison commitments were divided. On the other hand, the reformatory school returns do provide data on the crimes of those children who were sentenced both to a short stay in prison *and* to a longer stay in a reformatory school. Between 1856 and 1875 children were sent to prison *and* reformatory school in England and Wales for twenty-nine categories of crimes that are enumerated in the reformatory school returns. Four of these twenty-nine categories were not listed in 1856, while four others were listed only in 1857. Between 1858 and 1875, however, there is a consistent yearly list of twenty-five categories of crime.

Almost all of the 21,547 children in England and Wales simultaneously given prison *and* reformatory school sentences between 1858 and 1875 were sentenced for relatively minor crimes against property (see Table 5). The most common category of crime was larceny and petty theft, which accounted for fifty-eight percent of all child commitments to prison *and* reformatory school. It far outdistanced its three nearest rival categories, all of which were also larcenies: in a dwelling house (15% of all commitments); by a servant (5% of all commitments); and from a person (5% of all commitments). These four types of larceny (i.e., categories of crime one through four) accounted for eighty-two percent of all commitments. On the other hand, hardly any children were sent to prison *and* reformatory school for crimes against persons.

There were differences, however, in the crimes for which boys and girls were imprisoned. First, boy commitments were spread more widely among the twenty-five categories of crime than were girls. There were boy commitments in each of the twenty-five categories, whereas there were girl commitments in only twenty-one. Furthermore, while the five categories of crime that accounted for most boy commitments accounted for an impres-

Table 6
Crimes and Commitment of Boys, 1858–75

Category	Number of boys committed	Category as a percentage of total boy commitments (i.e. 17,417)
1. Larceny and petty theft	9,886	56.8%
2. Larceny in dwelling house	2,803	16.1%
3. Larceny from a person	767	4.4%
4. Housebreaking, shoplifting, etc.	682	3.9%
5. Larceny by a servent	604	3.5%
	14,742 of 17,417 total boy commitments	84.7%

Source: Judicial Statistics of England and Wales, 1859–76.

Table 7
Crimes and Commitment of Girls, 1858–75

Category	Number of girls committed	Category as a percentage of total girl commitments (i.e. 4,130)
1. Larceny and petty theft	2,613	63.3%
2. Larceny in dwelling house	469	11.4%
3. Larceny by a servant	386	9.3%
4. Larceny from a person	220	5.3%
5. Vagrancy	96	2.3%
	3,784 of 4,130 total girl commitments	91.6%

Source: Judicial Statistics of England and Wales, 1859–76.

sive eighty-five percent of all boy commitments, the five categories of crime that accounted for most girl commitments accounted for an even more impressive ninety-two percent (see Tables 6 and 7).

Second, girls were more likely than boys to be sent to prison *and* reformatory school for relatively minor offenses against property. The five categories of larcenies accounted for ninety percent of all girl commitments, but only eighty-two percent of all boy commitments. Third, the more serious crimes against property (horse stealing, sheep stealing, cattle stealing, house- and shop breaking, burglary, and arson), although extremely infrequent for both boys and girls, were more infrequent for girls. These offenses accounted for only three percent of their commitments, compared to six percent for boys. Unfortunately, it is not possible to determine from either the prison or the reformatory school statistics if Irish children were sent to prison for a distinctive set of crimes.

The boys and girls sent to prison *and* reformatory school formed only about thirteen percent of all those children committed to prison. What about the "crimes" of the remaining eighty-seven percent? Most of the children sent only to prison were probably accused of lesser offenses than most of those sentenced to both prison and reformatory school. The authorities tried—not always successfully—to restrict reformatory school admissions to the so-called most difficult cases, to the "leaders in crime." Hence, the government inspector of reformatory schools argued that reformatories should concentrate on recidivists and on "the class of young offenders really living by crime, and professionally engaged in it."[41]

CHILD CRIMINAL ACTIVITY AND URBANIZATION

Although most children sent to prison had been accused or convicted of petty theft or some other minor offense, why children committed these offenses and how urbanization might have influenced child crime are still unknown. In 1967 J. J. Tobias provided highly controversial answers to both questions. Relying primarily on contemporary social commentators, Tobias suggested that the population explosion, the Industrial Revolution, and urban growth combined to break down the old face-to-face social relations of the preindustrial rural world, and to force more and more adults and children into the rapidly expanding towns and cities, where the adults remained basically honest but their children did not. Abandoned by their disoriented and exploited parents and with few significant socializing institutions yet in place the children fell prey to the criminal class that was expanding and responsible for most crime.[42]

Most subsequent historians of crime have questioned the significance of a distinct and separate criminal class. In 1980 V. A. C. Gatrell argued that, "The error of ascribing most Victorian crime to a professional class is now well established."[43] Revisionists like Gatrell argue that most crime was not committed by a "criminal class," or even by professional criminals, but by the working poor. According to the revisionists, crime was an endemic part of working-class life. The working poor lived very close to the margins of survival and regularly committed crime to help make ends meet. Most recent historians also stress that most crime was "opportunistic."[44] By this they mean that most crime was committed more or less spontaneously by amateurs, rather than after calculation and planning by professionals. Finally, revisionists have suggested that so many working-class persons engaged in some kind of crime that these people probably regarded at least some crime as legitimate. Gatrell argues that the court records of the nineteenth century were swelled not by professional criminals, but by "an unnumbered host of 'ordinary' men and women whose depredations upon each other had been built into an immemorial way of life and survival, and whose depredations upon their betters, when these were possible, were legitimized by the brutal facts of existence."[45] And Davis takes this argument one step further, suggesting that "perceived opportunities [for crime] were shared by such large numbers of the population that any claim that such perceptions were seriously deviant would be misplaced."[46]

The revisionists, however, are somewhat divided about the role that cities and urbanization played in nineteenth-century crime. Douglas Hay, for instance, has suggested that "urbanization as an explanatory category" is an "American obsession" of questionable value.[47] On the other hand, in his research on crime in eighteenth-century England, Beattie effectively contrasted crime in urban and rural parishes in Surrey and Sussex, finding that "more crimes were committed by both men and women in urban than in rural areas."[48] His explanations for these regional differences are suggestive, if somewhat speculative. Beattie maintained that there was more crime in the London parishes of Surrey than elsewhere because "Targets and temptations were more abundant there"; because "informal controls... could not work there as effectively"; and because "poverty pressed with particular urgency in London, especially when the large population of men and women who lived at the margins of security suffered from shortages of work."[49] Finally, Beattie also suggested that "London contained the largest concentration of men who were likely to be concerned about crime and the loose habits of the working poor."[50]

The revisionists are also somewhat skeptical of Tobias's argument that criminal children played a critical role in nineteenth-century crime. By making crime an almost inevitable feature of adult working-class life, they have not only reduced the significance of the so-called criminal class but have also reduced the relative significance of child crime. Nonetheless, revisionists such as Gatrell continue to acknowledge that juvenile crime remained "as serious a problem as ever,"[51] while David Jones has insisted that "The extent of juvenile crime in the nineteenth century is a major problem."[52] Furthermore, Jones has explicitly linked juvenile crime with "the major cities, notably London and Liverpool": "From a wide variety of historical evidence it appears that there was a high level of illegal activity by juveniles in such places well before the flowering of periodical literature on the plight of the urban young."[53] The specific characteristics and causes of children's crime in cities, however, are still largely unexplored. How did it differ from adult crime, for instance, and how important were such forces as parental instigators and child gangs? And, did Irish child crime differ from the English?

VARIATIONS IN THE PROSECUTION OF CHILDREN

Although it is obviously important to determine what criminal children did, and why they did it, it is equally, if not more important, to determine why these children were prosecuted by their victims and/or the police, and why some of those were sent to prison by the courts. Recent work has suggested that much crime in the past was ignored or dealt with informally.[54] And because child offenders were normally guilty of relatively minor offenses, it seems reasonable to assume that they were even more likely candidates for informal methods than their adult counterparts. Why then did victim-prosecutors in the mid-Victorian period so frequently involve the formal powers of the state instead of simply punishing child offenders themselves?

In 1974 Pamela Horn pointed out that in rural areas in the nineteenth century many victims of petty offenses were still "unwilling to press formal charges against children. They preferred to deal with the wrong doers in their own way—if necessary by taking the law into their own hands."[55] Horn then cited the example of a Somerset clergyman who caught a little girl biting one of his fallen peaches and who made her "spend all day on the lawn with a placard round her neck bearing the word 'thief' in large letters."[56] On the other hand, in 1836 William Crawford and the Reverend Whitworth Russell (newly appointed inspectors of prisons for the Home District) observed that "the youth who would a few years back on detection have been summarily chastised, is sent to gaol and arraigned before a criminal tribunal."[57] Similarly, in his study of juvenile delinquency in Oxford between 1890 and 1914, John Gillis found that "types of juvenile behaviour previously dealt with in informal ways became the subject of prosecution."[58]

Three factors probably encouraged victims and authorities in the mid-nineteenth century, especially in urban areas, to prosecute "criminal" children rather than to correct them informally: the increased likelihood of being prosecuted for administering informal correction or chastisement; the growing availability of formal methods of prosecution; and the expanded activity of the police. Although the right to chastise children in the nineteenth century was legally limited to parents, officials of the justice system, and school teachers acting *in loco parentis*, it was also widely believed that all adults were entitled to chastise children who had offended them.[59] And the courts were frequently lenient on adults who did so: "One J.P. [in Kent] told a boy who had been knocked down for saying, 'Holloa, Mr. Cole, you are off to cricket,' that he had brought the assault on himself by being impertinent."[60]

On the other hand, when the courts believed that extra-legal chastisement had been neither moderate nor deserved they could be harsher. When a beer house keeper in 1863 was convicted of kicking a teenager for throwing a stone at his dog, the bench fined the man 20 shillings and said it "considered it a very aggravated case and one in which the greatest possible injury might have been inflicted, perhaps maiming the boy for life."[61] Given the occasional willingness of courts to convict adults who informally punished children, more adults probably thought twice before informally chastising children, and some probably resorted to formal prosecution. Furthermore, as child protection societies grew stronger, the risks of administering informal punishment probably increased.[62]

The changing character of the mid-Victorian criminal justice system also affected the likelihood of children being prosecuted. In the past it frequently had been very time-consuming and expensive to prosecute offenders. Victims had to pay part, or all, the expenses of prosecution, and courts were often neither conveniently located nor especially helpful. This situation changed during the nineteenth century. Increasingly money was made available to pay the costs of prosecution, and the reformed courts were made more accessible and accommodating than their predecessors. This was especially true in the urban areas. In mid-Victorian London, for example, there were thirteen police courts operated by twenty-three stipendiary magistrates, and these courts were in session six days a week, closing only for Christmas and Easter. Furthermore, "the stipendiary magistrates were not merely to be entrusted with the essentially negative task of enforcing the law once it had been broken. They were also charged with the responsibility of providing 'a system of poor man's justice', which would 'encourage in the common people a habit of looking to the law for protection.' "[63] Parents were among the "victims" of crime who sometimes used the increasingly available courts to prosecute children. According to Jennifer Davis, parents in mid-Victorian London would occasionally prosecute their own children in order that they might be sent to reformatory schools. In 1862, for instance, a postman in London who "could do nothing" with his daughter, "charged her with theft and asked the magistrate to send her to a reformatory."[64]

Paralleling the reform and extension of the judicial system was the more well-known reform and extension of the police. According to Gatrell, by mid-century "England was approximating to what Allan Silver has termed a 'policed society' " in which the police "were permeating the nation's everyday life."[65] In 1864–65, for instance, there was one policeman for every 863 persons, while in 1874–75 there was one policeman for every 770.[66] The extension of the police, however, did not affect all parts of the country equally. Urban areas were much more carefully policed than rural ones. By 1874–75 there was one policeman for every 398 persons in the Metropolitan Police district, one policeman for every 738 in the boroughs (excepting the city of London and the Metropolitan Police district), and only one policeman for every 1,244 persons in the counties (exclusive of the boroughs, etc.).[67] After 1850 the police also became more and more involved in the prosecution, as well as the apprehension, of offenders. In the eighteenth century virtually all prosecutions were initiated by private persons, but by the mid-twentieth century the tables had been reversed and it was the police who initiated virtually all prosecutions. According to Hay, "How and when that [change] occurred is not yet clear. But most of the change probably occurred in the second half of the nineteenth century."[68]

VARIATIONS IN THE SENTENCING OF CHILDREN

What "criminal" children did, and how their victims and the police responded, clearly affected the likelihood of children being sent to prison in mid-Victorian England. Ultimately, however, the decision whether to send suspected or convicted children to prison belonged to the courts. Were courts in the urban counties more likely to send children to prison than their counterparts in the rural counties? Unfortunately, it is very difficult to answer this question. Little work has been done on sentencing practices in the nineteenth century, and even less has been done comparing and contrasting sentencing practices in different regions. There are, however, two variables that suggest that sentencing practices might have differed by region: the wide range of available sentencing alternatives, and the significant range of sentencing agents.

Because of the considerable amount of legislation dealing with child offenders passed from the 1840s to the 1860s, the options open to the courts were significantly expanded. For example, there were at least five alternatives open to the courts when dealing with children accused of petty larceny. The 1847 and 1850 Summary Jurisdiction Acts allowed the courts: (1) to dismiss the charges against such offenders, before or after conviction, with or without sureties; (2) to fine such convicted offenders a sum not exceeding 3 pounds; (3) to whip such convicted male offenders who were fourteen or under, in or out of prison; (4) to imprison such convicted offenders for a period not to exceed three months, with or without hard labor; or (5) to commit such accused offenders to prison for trial at quarter sessions or assizes.[69] These statutes also allowed the courts to sentence such offenders to combinations of these alternatives. Hence, on 26 May 1858, J. A., aged twelve, was convicted of stealing three ducks and sentenced by two Somerset justices to seven days hard labor and thirty-six lashes with a cat-of-nine tails made with twine.[70]

Furthermore, in 1854 Parliament increased the sentencing alternatives for children when it passed "An Act for the better care and Reformation of Youthful Offenders in Great Britain." Under this statute courts were allowed to sentence any child "convicted of any offence punishable by Law, either upon an Indictment or Summary Conviction" to a certified reformatory school for between two and five years, provided that the child was simultaneously sentenced to at least fourteen days' imprisonment.[71] Finally, as a consequence of legislation passed initially in 1857, but amended and extended in 1861, courts were allowed to sentence four different categories of children to certified industrial schools: (1) children under fourteen who were found begging or receiving alms; (2) children under fourteen who were found wandering and had no home or visible means of subsistence, or who frequented the company of reputed thieves; (3) children under twelve who had committed an offense punishable by imprisonment, or some less punishment; and (4) children under fourteen whose parents were unable to control them.[72] No preliminary term of imprisonment was required for any of these children.

Paralleling the wide range of sentencing alternatives for accused children were the rather different kinds of magistrates who might hear the cases involving them. Because most accused children were accused of relatively minor crimes, the inferior courts were the critical actors. But there were three types of inferior courts, and the magistrates in the rural counties were quite different from the magistrates in the urban ones. According to the 1871 census the forty English counties contained 602 predominately rural petty sessional divisions.[73] Most of these petty sessional divisions were supervised by unpaid and unprofessional justices drawn from the landed class. As late as 1887, 74.3 percent of the magistrates in fifteen sample English and Welsh counties were drawn from the aristocracy and squirearchy.[74] On the other hand, there were also eighty-two boroughs that had separate commissions of the peace, and ninety-five boroughs that had both separate commissions of the peace and courts of quarter sessions.[75] The borough commissions of the peace, like their rural counterparts, were made up of amateur justices who were appointed by the Crown and unpaid. Very few of them were drawn from the landed class. In 1885, only 11.6 percent of the borough magistrates in seventy-four sample English and Welsh boroughs were drawn from the aristocracy and squirearchy, while 71.5 percent were drawn from the ranks of the "middle classes."[76] The "quarter sessions boroughs" also had a court of quarter sessions, but that court had only a single judge, the recorder of the borough. The recorder was not an amateur, but a barrister of five years' standing who was paid by the borough.[77]

Finally, in the metropolis of London there were professional stipendiary magistrates who were barristers of seven years' standing and paid by the national government. These stipendiary magistrates heard most cases tried in the metropolitan counties. In addition, various other large towns (such as Birmingham, Leeds, Liverpool, Manchester, Sheffield, etc.) acquired stipendiary magistrates. These also had to be barristers of seven (in some instances five) years' standing, but were paid for out of local funds. Given these differences in sentencing agents, and in methods of disposal of accused children, it seems at least possible that courts in different regions disposed of similar offenders differently. And this is what Carolyn Conley found in her study of crime in Victorian Kent. She makes the point that "Though rural magistrates in Kent usually fined [juvenile] offenders, the London magistrates often opted for brief jail sentences."[78]

CONCLUSION

Three conclusions can be drawn from the foregoing analysis. First, the finding that girls in mid-Victorian England were much less likely than boys to be committed to prison is consistent with earlier research. There is now a small, but significant, body of literature on female criminality since the Middle Ages that indicates that in the past females were much less likely than males to become subjects of the criminal justice system.[79]

While insisting "there is obviously no simple explanation" for this wide difference, and acknowledging that "differences in sheer strength" and "temperamental differences" might have had some influence, most historians suggest that "fundamentally it must have resulted from contrasts in training and expected behaviour and in general from the place of women in society."[80] Because female crime tended to be "much less serious" than male crime, however, and because victims, the police, and the courts might have been less willing to prosecute and/or convict female criminals, historians also acknowledge that female crime was more likely to be underreported.[81] Although these explanations were developed primarily to explain differences between male and female crime rates, they probably also explain the differences between boy and girl commitment to prison rates in mid-Victorian England.

Second, the finding that a disproportionate number of Irish children were sent to prison in mid-Victorian England is somewhat surprising, primarily because the Irish offender in England has been a largely ignored subject. As Roger Swift has recently pointed out, "the relationship between the Irish and crime in nineteenth-century Britain—a relationship which many contemporaries believed to be axiomatic—has yet to receive close scrutiny."[82] On the other hand, the disproportionate number of Irish children sent to prison is certainly easily explained. The Irish lived more desperate lives than their neighbors and consequently had more reason to turn to crime. Furthermore, the prevailing stereotype of the Irish in England probably inclined victims, the police, and the courts to prosecute, convict, and imprison the Irish more readily than the English.

Third, the finding that children in the most urbanized counties were much more likely to be imprisoned than children in the least urbanized counties, is, perhaps, unexpected. The concentration of the Irish in the most urbanized counties clearly helps to explain part of the difference. How to explain the remaining part is more difficult. In the past, historians and sociologists would probably have explained these differences by emphasizing the evil effects of "the urban way of life": as greater isolation, alienation, anomie, and neglect.[83] Such explanations are highly suspect because urban inhabitants created communities and networks that were just as supportive as that of their rural neighbors.[84] Is it possible, however, that the rejection of the old stereotype of the evil city has gone so far as to blur the very real urban-rural differences that existed? Beattie has suggested that "life in the city was on a different order from life in a village or even a market town. It was a difference that changed entirely the tasks of constables and magistrates."[85]

Ultimately, the greater likelihood of children being imprisoned in urban counties must be explained by the interaction of urban conditions and urban working-class children and parents, or by the interaction of urban conditions and urban victims and authorities, or by some combination of the two. The most obvious method of explanation is to look to the influence of urban conditions on urban children: greater opportunities for theft, greater opportunities for escape, greater real or perceived need, and less control by critical social institutions. It seems as likely, however, that urban victims and authorities related and reacted to urban children differently than their rural counterparts did to rural children.

NOTES

For their helpful comments and criticisms, I would like to thank my colleague Patrick Peebles, as well as the editor and the anonymous readers.

1. "Census of Great Britain, 1851. Population Tables. I. Numbers of the Inhabitants . . . Vol. 1, Report," *Past and Present* (1852–53), 85, xliv.
2. "Census of Great Britain, 1851. Population Tables. I. Numbers of the Inhabitants . . . vol. 1, Appendix to the Report, Table 44—Number of Persons in the Principal Public Institutions in Great Britain, and in the Islands of the British Seas," *PP* (1852–53), 85, cxxx.
3. "Census of England and Wales, 1861. Population Tables. Numbers and Distribution of the People of England and Wales. Vol. 1—Summary Tables—Table 12—Number of Persons in Workhouses, Hospitals, Lunatic Asylums, Prisons, Barracks, Orphan Asylums and Other Principal Charitable Institutions on April 8th., 1861," *PP* (1862), 50, xxix.
4. "Census of England and Wales, 1871. Population Tables. Area, Houses, and Inhabitants, Vol. 1, Counties, Summary Tables. Table 10—Number of Persons in Workhouses, Hospitals, Lunatic Asylums, Prisons, and other Public Institutions in England and Wales, on 3rd April 1871," *PP* (1872), 66, xl.
5. "Census of Great Britain, 1851. Population Tables II. Ages, Civil Condition, Occupations and Birth-Place of the People . . . Vol. I—Report," *PP* (1852–53), 88, cxv.
6. Michael Ignatieff, "State, Civil Society, and Total Institutions: A Critique of Recent Social Histories of Punishment," *Crime and Justice: An Annual Review of Research* 3 (1981): 154.
7. Michael Ignatieff, *A Just Measure of Pain: The Penitentiary in the Industrial Revolution, 1750–1830* (New York, 1978).
8. Christopher Lasch, "Origins of the Asylum", in *The World of Nations: Reflections on American History, Politics and Culture* (New York, 1973), 3–17, 313–16.
9. Michael Foucault, *Discipline and Punish: The Birth of the Prison*, trans. Alan Sheridan (New York, 1977).
10. David J. Rothman, *The Discovery of the Asylum: Social Order and Disorder in the New Republic* (Boston, 1971).
11. Michael Ignatieff, "State, Civil Society, and Total Institutions," 163.
12. Peter Stearns, "Toward a Wider Vision: Trends in Social History," in *The Past Before Us: Contemporary Historical Writing in the United States*, ed. M. Kammen (Ithaca, 1980), 212.
13. Robert Bremner, "The State of Social Welfare History," in *The State of American History*, ed. H. J. Bass (Chicago, 1970), 94.
14. J. F. C. Harrison, Book review of *Before the Welfare State*, *Journal of Economic History* 40 (1980): 193.
15. Report of the conference on "Life in Total Institutions," organized by the

Social History Society and held in Lancaster, England, 3–5 Jan. 1983, *Newsletter of the Social History Society* 8 (1983): 1.

16. "Judicial Statistics of England and Wales for 1856," *PP* (1857, Sess. 2), 35, vi.

17. Local prisons were owned and administered by a variety of local authorities, but were subject to central government inspection. There were borough gaols and houses of correction (or bridewells), owned and administered by borough justices and/or borough councils; county gaols and houses of correction (or bridewells), owned and administered by county justices of the peace; and liberty or franchise gaols and houses of correction (or bridewells), owned and administered by various liberty or franchise authorities. Despite the growing emphasis on centralization and uniformity, it seems likely that children sent to these various local prisons encountered a wide range of penal regimes: "In no two places does six months or a year's imprisonment mean the same thing, each term of punishment, to know its true signification, requiring to be translated locally." See Charles Measor, *Criminal Correction* (London, 1864), 10, cited by Sean McConville, *A History of English Prison Administration, I, 1750–1877* (London: Routledge and Kegan Paul, 1981), 375.

18. Determined from the prison statistics section of the Judicial Statistics of England and Wales, 1856–76.

19. Unfortunately it is difficult to be more precise than this because the reorganized Judicial Statistics did not break down types of commitments to prison by age. One can obtain a rough idea of the breakdown of child commitments, however, by looking at the breakdown of total commitments. For example, in 1856 there were 132,689 total commitments (all ages) to prison in England and Wales, of which 77,712 (58.7%) had been summarily convicted and were serving short sentences of imprisonment; 19,278 (14.5%) had been committed to await trial at assizes or quarter sessions; 13,952 (10.5%) had been committed on remand and discharged; 11,406 (8.6%) had been committed for debt and on civil process; 7,557 (5.6%) had been committed as military prisoners under the Mutiny Act; and 2,794 (2.1%) had been committed for want of sureties. "Judicial Statistics of England and Wales for 1856," *PP* (1857, Sess. 2), 35, xvi. Because most children were accused of relatively minor offenses, it seems likely that the category "summarily convicted" accounted for a larger percentage of child commitments than it did of total commitments, and that the categories "for trial at quarter sessions and assizes," "for debt," and "for military offences" accounted for smaller percentages of child commitments than they did of total commitments. It is not clear where the categories "on remand" and "for want of sureties" fit into these calculations.

20. The censuses of England and Wales, 1851–81. In order to determine the average annual boy, girl, and child populations of each county in England, as well as of England as a whole, between 1856 and 1875, some estimating is involved. The 1851 and 1881 censuses gave the total male and female populations of each ancient county, but do not provide data on the various age stages. On the other hand, the 1861 and 1871 censuses do provide such data, although for the age stages 5 to 9, 10 to 14, 15 to 19, rather than for 7 to 15. Hence the annual number of boys and girls in the age stage 7 to 15 for each county between 1856 and 1875 have to be reconstructed from the above data.

21. Judicial Statistics of England and Wales, 1856–76. The prison statistics section of the Judicial Statistics provided age data on four of the six categories of

offenders committed to prison: those who had been summarily convicted and were serving short sentences of imprisonment, those awaiting trial, those on remand, and those committed for want of sureties. No age data were provided for those committed for debt or military offenses, but these categories probably included few, if any, children.

22. See, for instance, Rob Sindall, "Middle Class Crime in Nineteenth Century England," *Criminal Justice History* 4 (1983): 23–40.

23. Jennifer Davis, "Law Breaking and Law Enforcement: The Creation of a Criminal Class in Mid-Victorian London" (Ph.D. Thesis, Boston College, 1985), 117 n. 1. The citation from Mary Carpenter is from her book *Our Convicts* (London, 1864), 2: 341–44.

24. "A survey of the Irish in Britain conducted by the *Nation*, a Dublin Weekly Newspaper, argued that the number of Irish-born indicated in offical statistics should be doubled in order to arrive at a more realistic enumeration of the ethnic Irish community in Britain." See Roger Swift, "The Outcast Irish in the British Victorian City: Problems and Perspectives," *Irish Historical Studies* 25 (1987): 264.

25. Judicial Statistics of England and Wales, 1861 and 1871; censuses of England and Wales, 1861 and 1871.

26. "Totals of the Number of Young Offenders Admitted into and Discharged from Certified Reformatory Schools in Great Britain, and the Mode of Discharge, Up to December 31, 1881," Appendix A3, to the Report of the Reformatories and Industrial Schools Commission, *PP* (1884), 45, lxxviii.

27. In his second report on the newly created Judicial Statistics the criminal registrar, Samuel Redgrave, explicitly stated that "all [children] so committed [to reformatory schools] undergo a previous short imprisonment, and are therefore included in the above numbers [detailing the ages of those committed to prison]." "Judicial Statistics of England and Wales for 1857," *PP* (1857–58), 57, xxiii.

28. "Totals of the Number of Young Offenders Admitted into and Discharged from Certified Reformatory Schools in Great Britain, and the Mode of Discharge, Up to December 31, 1881," Appendix A3, to the Report of the Reformatories and Industrial Schools Commission, *PP* (1884), 45, lxxviii.

29. The only other significant groups of Catholics were primarily middle and upper class, for example, the converts and the old Catholics. These two groups were also numerically insignificant compared to the Irish.

30. The five counties with the highest number of child commitments per 100,000 children were Middlesex, Surrey, Gloucestershire, Lancashire, and Warwickshire; while the five counties with the lowest number of such commitments were Cornwall, Rutland, Cumberland, Westmoreland, and Derbyshire.

31. The five counties with the highest number of boy commitments per 100,000 boys were Middlesex, Surrey, Gloucestershire, Lancashire, and Warwickshire; while the five counties with the lowest number of such commitments were Cornwall, Rutland, Cumberland, Westmoreland, and Derbyshire.

32. The five counties with the highest number of girl commitments per 100,000 girls were Middlesex, Surrey, Monmouthshire, Lancashire, and Northumberland; while the five counties with the lowest number of such commitments were Bedfordshire, Buckinghamshire, Cornwall, Cumberland, and Rutland.

33. Olive Anderson, *Suicide in Victorian and Edwardian England* (Oxford, 1987), 73.

34. W. B. Stephens, *Education, Literacy and Society, 1830–70: The Geography of Diversity in Provincial England* (Manchester, 1987).

35. W. E. Marsden, *Unequal Educational Provision in England and Wales: The Nineteenth Century Roots* (London, 1987).

36. E. H. Hunt, *Regional Wage Variations in Britain, 1850–1914* (Oxford, 1973).

37. "Table 123—Birthplaces of the Inhabitants of the Civil Counties of England and Wales, Appendix to the General Report of the Census of England and Wales for the Year 1861," PP (1863), 53, pt. 1, 153–54.

38. "Population Abstracts: Ages, Civil Conditions, Occupations, and Birth-Places of the People, Census of England and Wales for 1871," PP (1873), 61, pt. 1, 1–617.

39. "Table 123—Birthplaces of the Inhabitants of the Civil Counties of England and Wales, Appendix to the General Report of the Census of England and Wales for the Year 1861," PP (1863), 52, pt. 1, 153–54. The ten most heavily urbanized counties were taken to be the ten counties with the largest percentages of their total populations living in towns of 20,000 or more.

40. "Table 93—England and Wales—Natives of England, Scotland, Ireland, the Colonies, Foreign Ports, etc., Enumerated in the Undermentioned 63 Large Towns in 1871, in Appendix A to the General Report of the Census of England and Wales," PP (1873), 71, pt. 2, 76.

41. "Report of the Inspector of Reformatory Schools," PP (1859, Sess. 2), 13, pt. 2, 19.

42. J. J. Tobias, *Crime and Industrial Society in the 19th Century* (London, 1967), 251–52. Most Victorians were convinced that urban areas were more criminal than rural ones. See, for instance, Clive Emsley's useful discussion of Victorian ideas about crime in Chapter 4, "Environmental Perceptions," of his study, *Crime and Society in England, 1750–1900* (London, 1987).

43. V. A. C. Gatrell, "The Decline of Theft and Violence in Victorian and Edwardian England," in *Crime and the Law: The Social History of Crime in Western Europe since 1500*, ed. V. A. C. Gatrell, Bruce Lenman, and Geoffrey Parker (London, 1980), 265. For other critical assessments of the role of "the criminal class," see J. A. Sharpe, *Crime in Early Modern England, 1550–1750* (London, 1984), 94–120; Clive Emsley, *Crime and Society in England, 1750–1900* (London, 1987), 129–37; David Philips, *Crime and Authority in Victorian England: The Black Country 1835–1860* (London, 1977), esp. 126–27, 197–99; David Jones, *Crime, Protest, Community and Police in Nineteenth-Century Britain* (London, 1982), 6, 134–35; Jennifer S. Davis, "Law Breaking and Law Enforcement: The Creation of a Criminal Class in Mid-Victorian London" (Ph.D. Thesis, Boston College, 1984). The only recent defender of the "criminal class" interpretation of crime is John L. McMullan, *The Canting Crew: London's Criminal Underworld, 1550–1700* (New Brunswick, 1984).

44. In their recent surveys of crime in England between 1550 and 1750, and between 1750 and 1900, both Sharpe and Emsley argue that most crime was "opportunistic." Sharpe insists that "even in the capital, the typical law-breaker, whether thief or prostitute, was essentially opportunistic in his or her approach and modest in his or her criminal ambitions" (Sharpe, *Crime in Early Modern England*, 117). Emsley makes essentially the same point for the later period: "The statistics and the

court records suggest that the overwhelming majority of thefts reported and prosecuted were opportunistic and petty" (Emsley, *Crime and Society in England,* 132).

45. Gatrell, "Decline of Theft and Violence," 265.

46. Davis, "Law Breaking and Law Enforcement," 115, n. 1.

47. Douglas Hay, "Crime and Justice in Eighteenth and Nineteenth Century England," *Crime and Justice: An Annual Review of Research* 2 (1980): 69.

48. J. M. Beattie, "The Criminality of Women in Eighteenth Century England," *Journal of Social History* 8 (1975): 96.

49. J. M. Beattie, *Crime and the Courts in England, 1660–1800* (Princeton, 1986), 14.

50. Ibid.

51. Gatrell, "Decline of Theft and Violence," 306.

52. Jones, *Crime, Protest, Community, and Police*, 7.

53. Ibid.

54. See, in particular, the highly suggestive overview by Bruce Lenman and Geoffrey Parker, "The State, the Community and the Criminal Law in Early Modern Europe" in *Crime and the Law: The Social History of Crime in Western Europe since 1500*, ed. V. A. C. Gatrell, Bruce Lenman, and Geoffrey Parker (London, 1980), 11–48.

55. Pamela Horn, *The Victorian Country Child* (Kineton, 1974), 193–94.

56. Hesketh Pearson, *The Smith of Smiths* (1934), no page number given, cited by Horn, *Victorian Country Child*, 194.

57. "Report of the Inspectors of Prisons of Great Britain, I—Home District," PP (1836), 35, 82, cited by Susan Magarey, "The Invention of Juvenile Delinquency in Early Nineteenth-Century England," *Labour History* 34 (1978): 18.

58. John R. Gillis, "The Evolution of Juvenile Delinquency in England, 1890–1914," *Past & Present* 67 (1975):98.

59. Carolyn Conley, "Crime and Community in Victorian Kent" (Ph.D. Thesis, Duke University, 1984), 116.

60. Ibid.

61. *Maidstone and Kentish Journal*, February 3, 1863, cited by Conley, "Crime and Community," 117.

62. On the growth of child protection sentiments, see, in particular, George K. Behlmer, *Child Abuse and Moral Reform in England, 1870–1908* (Stanford, 1982).

63. Jennifer Davis, "A Poor Man's System of Justice: The London Police Courts in the Second Half of the Nineteenth Century," *Historical Journal* 27 (1984): 315. The quotation is from testimony presented to the 1837 Select Committee on the Metropolitan Police Offices.

64. Jennifer Davis, "Law Breaking and Law Enforcement," 301. The quotation from the postman was taken from the *West London Observer*, 9 Apr. 1862.

65. Gatrell, "Decline of Theft and Violence," 276.

66. "The Judicial Statistics of England and Wales for 1875," *PP* (1876), 79, v.

67. "The Judicial Statistics of England and Wales for 1875," *PP* (1876), 79, vi.

68. Douglas Hay, "Controlling the English Prosecutor," *Osgoode Hall Law Journal* 21 (1983): 174.

69. "An Act for the further Extension of Summary Jurisdiction in Cases of Larceny," 13 & 14 *Vict.*, cap. 37.

70. "A Return, from each Gaol and House of Correction in England and Wales,

of all Cases in which Corporal Punishment by Whipping has been inflicted . . . ," *PP* (1862), 45, 73.

71. "An Act for the better care and Reformation of Youthful Offenders in Great Britain," 17 & 18 *Vict.*, cap 86, sec. 2.

72. "An Act to make better Provision for the Care and Education of vagrant, destitute, and disorderly children, and for the Extension of Industrial Schools," 20 & 21 *Vict.*, cap. 48; and "An Act for amending and consolidating the law relating to Industrial Schools," 24 & 25 *Vict.*, cap. 113.

73. "Territorial Sub-divisions of England and Wales, Appendix C of the General Report of the Census of England and Wales for the Year 1871," *PP* (1873), 71, pt. 2, 184–93.

74. Carl H. E. Zangerl, "The Social Composition of the County Magistracy in England and Wales, 1831–1887," *Journal of British Studies* 11 (1971): 115.

75. "Territorial Sub-divisions of England and Wales, Appendix C of the General Report of the Census of England and Wales for the Year 1871," *PP* (1873), 71, pt. 2, 184–93.

76. Zangerl, "Social Composition of the County Magistracy," 115.

77. F. W. Maitland, *Justice and Police* (London, 1885), 95.

78. Conley, "Crime and Community," 106.

79. See, for example, Barbara Hanawalt, "The Female Felon in Fourteenth Century England," *Viator* 5 (1974): 253–68; Carol Weiner, "Sex Roles and Crime in Late Elizabethan Hertfordshire," *Journal of Social History* 8 (1975): 39–60; and J. M. Beattie, "The Criminality of Women in Eighteenth Century England," *Journal of Social History* 8 (1975): 80–116.

80. Beattie, "Criminality of Women," 96.

81. Ibid.

82. Roger Swift, "Crime and the Irish in Nineteenth Century Britain," in *The Irish in Britain, 1815–1939*, ed. Roger Swift and Sheridan Gilley (London, 1989), 164.

83. See, for instance, the classic statements by Wirth and Chevalier: L. Wirth, "Urbanism as a Way of Life," *American Journal of Sociology* 44 (1938): 1–24; and L. Chevalier, *Classes laborieuses et classes dangereuses a Paris pendant la premiere moitie du XIXe siecle* (Paris, 1958).

84. See, for instance, the influential work on working-class and ethnic urban communities by Anderson and Lees: M. Anderson, *Family Structure in 19th Century Lancashire* (Cambridge, 1971); and L. Lees, *Exiles of Erin* (Ithaca, 1979).

85. Beattie, "Criminality of Women," 99.

Kanaka Slaves or Willing Workers? Melanesian Workers and the Queensland Criminal Justice System in the 1890s

Mark Finnane
Griffith University, Brisbane
Clive Moore
University of Queensland, Brisbane

INTRODUCTION

European commercial activities spread through the Pacific Islands from the seventeenth century on. The first Islanders to become involved were Micronesians, who serviced the Spanish galleon trade, and Polynesians, who collected exotic products and supplied port communities, whaling, and other sailing ships. European use of indigenous labor spread west into southern Melanesia with the sandalwood and bêche-de-mer trades.[1] But by the second half of the century the main commodity traded was labor, not Pacific products: Between 1840 and 1942 around one million Pacific Islander laborers, mainly from Melanesia, were harnessed to the development of pastoral, plantation, and mining ventures in the islands and in Australia and New Zealand.[2]

The Queensland labor trade operated between 1863 and 1908, during which time more than 62,400 initial labor contracts were entered into by Islanders from more than seventy mainly Melanesian islands now included in New Caledonia, Vanuatu, the Solomon Islands, and Papua New Guinea, but also including a few Polynesians from outliers in Melanesia, and Micronesians from Kiribati and Polynesians from Tuvalu. Recruiting ceased in 1904 and partial deportation began in 1906 lasting until 1908, motivated by a widespread zealous xenophobic nationalism demanding a white Australia. Eventually about 2,500 of the immigrant laborers were allowed to stay; their descendants now number around 15,000.[3]

The literature on the Queensland labor trade and Australia's immigrant Melanesian people is vast.[4] One theme in need of closer examination is the place of the long-staying immigrant Melanesians within wider colonial society. Large numbers of the Melanesians worked in the colony more than once and often stayed for several years. Many were immigrants in the same sense that Europeans were immigrants. They stayed in the colony for a number of years, sometimes ten or even twenty, some choosing to return home of their own volition, others deported by the fledging Commonwealth government between 1906 and 1908. A substantial number became permanent settlers.

The sugar industry began on the coast near Brisbane in the early 1860s, spread to the Maryborough district in the mid–1860s, and then to the region around Bundaberg and northern New South Wales by the end of the decade. Also from the mid–1860s sugar plantations were established in the Pioneer Valley at Mackay and farther north around what is now Tully. By the late 1870s the southern region was losing prominence. The Mackay district became the main sugar-producing area, and by the early 1880s the industry had been established north of Mackay at Proserpine, in the Burdekin delta, at Innisfail (originally Geraldton), Cairns, Port Douglas, and Mossman, its northern extreme.

The industry boomed in the late 1870s and early 1880s, its inefficiencies cloaked by the high price of sugar on the world market. But the world sugar price, declining since 1881, fell by one-third in 1884, and continued to fall until a slight recovery in 1888–89. It was thirty years before the 1883 price was again equaled.[5] The sugar industry was depressed (as was the wider colonial economy),[6] and the industry went through a major transformation: In 1885 notice was given that recruiting of Pacific Islanders was to cease after 1891.[7] In 1885 government-sponsored restructuring of the industry—the phasing out of plantations and the establishment of central mills supplied with cane grown by European small farm operators—began. The 1890s were as crucial for the survival of the sugar industry as a whole as they were for the establishment of a permanent Melanesian community.

This chapter is an examination of the immigrant Melanesians during the 1890s. Its focus is their experiences with the Queensland criminal justice system in the Mackay, Bundaberg, and Port Douglas–Mossman districts. Using court records from the three widely spread areas provides a control on the overall pattern of treatment of Melanesians in the criminal justice system in the 1890s. Two types of records have been used in this analysis. The police watch-house and bench books are registers of persons arrested, providing a great deal of social information together with offenses charged and outcomes, including sentencing, fines, and the magistrate responsible. These watch-house books, which cover the field of indictable and summary offenses, provide a record of bureaucratic justice in the Queensland sugar districts. Persons arrested would be charged by the colonial police, governed from the metropolitan center of Brisbane, while their cases would most likely be heard and disposed by police (salaried) magistrates, public officials themselves.

A different record is that of the magistrates' court summons cases, which record proceedings in the courts of petty session in civil matters. The incidence of assault actions as well as other matters involving Melanesians in both plaintiff and defendant roles provides important evidence for the later arguments of this chapter. These records are more valuable than the watch-house books in so far as they are a record of proceedings in many cases. They are less valuable in their failure to record systematically any social details of the parties to an action. The use of both sets of records, however, provides a substantial overview of the uses of law in this colonial settlement and industry.[8]

Mill and regional histories exist for the three districts under discussion, which enables the Melanesian and legal focus to be placed in a wider historical context.[9] The basic hypothesis being tested arises from data collected from the Mackay region and its analysis by Clive Moore. The findings there suggest that prosecution of Melanesians, particularly under the Masters and Servants Act, became more frequent in the 1890s when the size of the Melanesian population was actually declining. The prosecutions differed in several ways from those of earlier years: Punishments for absconding became heavier; there was a pronounced increase in the severity of the fines; fewer Melanesians went to gaol for failing to pay fines; most either paid immediately, had their fines paid by friends, or arranged to have the fines deducted from their wages; and the cases were mainly brought by small farm operators. For several reasons it seems likely that the majority of the offenders were time-expired laborers and ticket-holders, or first-indenture laborers with previous colonial experience. Forty to sixty percent of the Melanesian laborers in the district were either time-expired or ticket-holders who preferred to work for small farmers, not on plantations. They had the money to pay the fines and the ability to confront the system.[10]

Much of the recent research into the history of Queensland's Melanesians has a strong statistical base. Clive Moore has produced a detailed account of migration by Malaitans from the Solomon Islands. Charles Price's study of the origins of the recruits,[11] and Patricia Mercer's detailed reconstruction of Melanesian settlement patterns in the late nineteenth century and the first half of the twentieth century in North Queensland[12] provide firm historical demographic data. Ralph Shlomowitz undertook an extensive investigation of the various subcategories and wage rates among the indentured laborers. His heavily statistical analyses range from study of the recruiting voyages,[13] analysis of the profitability and interrelationship of different categories of labor,[14] the development of the Butty Gang as a system of organizing labor,[15] to health and mortality.[16] He and other recent historians have also considered the place of the Melanesian laborers in the search for institutional equilibrium in the late nineteenth century as sugar production changed, from its early base on plantations that operated mills supplied mainly by their own cane and depending on an extensive workforce of immigrant Melanesians for labor in the fields and mills, to the present-day pattern of large mills owned cooperatively by large numbers of farmers.[17] These studies provide a firm underpinning for further research into the social and legal history of the immigrants. But one of the difficulties with this present chapter is that the court records do not differentiate between first-indenture and longer-staying offenders. They provide useful statistics but their final interpretation depends on less finite evidence as to the status of the offenders.

CATEGORIES OF MELANESIANS AND WAGES

The South Sea Islanders, as the major segment of the labor supply, were integral to the transformation of the sugar industry. Initially they were likely to be raw recruits to colonial capitalist ventures, with little exposure to the world outside their limited cosmological and geographic outlook. It is difficult to know how many were "kidnapped," or imported illegally in terms of the provisions of the law of the day. Probably about ten percent were imported before the 1880s, but as the labor trade progressed it became more and more a voluntary affair.[18] It is impossible to distinguish between recruits lured by beguiling recruiters, but really legally enlisted, and those obtained by a level of deception and false promises, who should be placed into the illegal category. And we have also to grapple with what Moore has termed "cultural kidnapping": Europeans taking advantage of Melanesia's small-scale societies, aspects of which coincided with the requirements of the labor trade.[19] But there can be no doubt that the majority enlisted voluntarily, many more than once.

The Queensland labor trade continued for more than forty years and in its final decades the typical Melanesian laborer was as changed as the farming-milling interface of the industry. During the several decades over which the labor trade operated most of the labor recruits served out their three-year contracts and returned to their islands. But from the mid–1860s other categories developed alongside the first indentured group.

Not all laborers were enlisting for the first time. Some of the first recruits to reach Queensland from southern Melanesia, particularly from the Loyalty Islands, had already participated in the bêche-de-mer and sandalwood trades.[20] And reenlistments in Queensland occurred from the 1860s. By the early 1890s about one-quarter of the first indenture arrivals had worked previously in Queensland, Fiji, or Samoa. After serving their first three-year contract, if laborers chose to stay rather than take advantage of the passage home, they could sign new more lucrative indenture agreements, for three years or a lesser term. They were called time-expired laborers. The proportion of time-expired laborers to those working under first-indentures increased steadily from the 1860s but no separate register was kept until 1884, by which time they were one-quarter of the total number of Melanesians in Queensland. The final category was an elite and ever diminishing group generally called ticket-holders who had entered the colony before September 1879, forever exempt from post–1884 legislation that limited the occupations of all future Melanesian immigrants to tropical agriculture. Expressed as a proportion of the overall Melanesian population of the colony between 1885 and 1906, in any one year ticket-holders constituted between seven and eleven percent of the immigrant Melanesian population.

The basic wage specified under the act remained set at £6 per year from 1863 until 1904, but this was not the average wage overall. The wage rates for rerecruiting laborers varied from £6 to £12, the amount increasing as the century progressed.[21] Wage rates for time-expired laborers varied depending on the nature of the contract as well as the previous experience and the negotiating skills of the laborers. The most popular durations for contracts were six and twelve months. Basing his conclusions on Maryborough and Port Douglas statistics, Shlomowitz has calculated that between 1884 and 1906, for twelve-month contracts taken up after three or more years in the colony Melanesian males[22] were paid between £18 and £23.[23] Shorter contracts were usually to meet the labor requirements of the crushing season. There was also a marked seasonal variation in the wages. In Maryborough this averaged £16.3 to £24.6 during the crushing season and £13.7 to £23.9 during the slack season.[24] Ticket-holders negotiated their own wage rates. They probably earned as much as European farm laborers, which over the same period as the Maryborough statistics would have been between £30 and £50 per year, plus board and lodging; many were self-employed, leasing farms, owning boarding houses, and carting businesses.[25]

Although *wantok* (same language or dialect) and descent group connections remained strong, long-staying Melanesian migrants underwent a slow assimilation process: The longer they stayed the further estranged they were from the "new chum" recruits, making their first venture away from the confines of their small-scale societies. They all shared similar origins but had different degrees of sophistication in handling colonial society. Against this background, and using data from the Queensland criminal justice system records, we examine the hypothesis that the 1880s and 1890s saw important changes in the status of Melanesian workers in Queensland. It is argued that beginning in the mid–1880s long-staying laborers, forty to sixty percent of the immigrant Melanesian population, formed a Melanesian segment of the general working class, distinct from the indentured servant category. They were skilled at negotiating with Europeans who considered them obstreperous. It seems likely, although it can not be proved conclusively without detailed reconstruction of the lives of individuals, that most of the Melanesians involved with the courts from the 1890s were multiple-enlisters and time-expired and ticket-holding Melanesians.

THE LAW AND MELANESIANS

European powers had very limited means of enforcing legal or any other official authority in the South Pacific islands before the proclamation of colonies and protectorates by Germany and Britain in the 1880s and 1890s. Investigations and raids by naval ships were the main means of keeping even rudimentary order, and Melanesia was the last area to be regularly patrolled. Early New South Wales was a maritime trading post with an economic focus as much out into the Pacific as inland. From the late eighteenth century Sydney received supplies from as far east as Tahiti.[26] Loyalty Islanders were employed on the Sydney docks in the early 1840s,[27] and Islanders worked on European ships all during the nineteenth century, roaming as far north as Torres Strait on bêche-de-mer vessels in the 1850s and 1860s.

The first legislation to control the exploitation of Islander labor in Australia came in response to Ben Boyd's disastrous importation of 140 Loyalty, New Hebridean, and i-Kiribati men and women to work on his pastoral properties in New South Wales. In 1847 the government amended the Masters and Servants Act to stop the employment of "Natives of any Savage or uncivilized tribe inhabiting any Island or Country in the Pacific Ocean or elsewhere."[28] Queensland separated from New South Wales in 1859. When Robert Towns recruited the first Islanders to Queensland in 1863 there was no legislation specifically designed for them. Their contracts came under the 1861 Masters and Servants Act as with all indentured servants in the colony. Not until 1868 was an act introduced to specify conditions for their recruitment and work. The British government bolstered this with the *Pacific Islanders Protection Act* in 1872, amended in 1875, designed to limit abuses in the recruiting trade.

The conditions of employment laid down in the 1868 *Polynesian Labourers Act*[29] remained standard until the last recruits arrived in 1904. The indenture period was three years, after which the laborer could reengage or return home at the expense of the employer. The wage was set at not less than £6 per year with payments in kind of food, shelter, clothing, tobacco, and medical care. The employer had to pay for transport to and from the islands and pay a bond to the Queensland government to ensure that all contractual obligations were met. Under the terms of the Masters and Servants Act both parties to the indenture were liable to prosecution for default. Ostensibly the contracts of indenture set out the mutual rights and obligations of each party but in reality provided criminal punishment for breaches of contract by workers, while employers were dealt with by gentler provisions of civil law.[30]

During the remainder of the century further acts, amendments, and regulations modified or clarified the terms of the original act. In 1880 the 1868 act was completely redrawn, followed in 1884 by an amending act placing occupational restrictions on all Islanders who had entered the colony later than September 1879, and tightened government supervision of the island and plantation ends of the trade.[31] Any person supplying Islanders with alcohol could be prosecuted under the same legislation that made it illegal to supply alcohol to Aborigines. The laborers were also subject to the normal processes of the Queensland legal system.

By the 1890s the status of the long-staying Melanesian workers was increasingly comparable to that of the European or local-born working-class employee. There were still substantial numbers of first-indentured laborers working on the large plantations for £6 per year, with little knowledge and fewer means of confronting the system. But the long-staying laborers were more likely (than they had been earlier) to be employed on similar terms to other laborers. The operation of the legal system both reflected and constituted these changes. And Melanesian laborers increasingly demonstrated a knowledge of the potential of legal avenues for protecting their position. At the same time, the operation of the criminal justice system indicates the particular vulnerability of a population that was almost wholly of the laboring class and exhibited many signs of cultural difference from white society.

The central fact of the transition is the gradual shift from the status of indentured laborer to that of free[32] laborer. This shift entailed improved wages, implying among other things a greater capacity for meeting legal debts or fines. It also entailed a greater degree of participation in the forms of cultural life and practices of the white working class. Predictably, this was reflected in the greater incidence of public drunkenness, which was becoming an occasion of major concern by the late 1880s. Our evidence confirms the twofold legal consequences of the transition from indenture to free labor, a transition replete with cultural significance and opportunities that was truncated by the 1901 decision to end the Melanesian labor trade and deport as many as possible of those who remained.

Previous accounts of the Kanaka laborer experience of the law have tended to emphasize the repressive and discriminatory effects of a British legal system at the service of planters and white society. Although anecdotal and case evidence is patchy, we have drawn together a variety of statistical calculations of the impact of the law and the criminal justice system on the Melanesian laborers in Queensland.

Policing Offenses, Queensland

Although police statistics by birthplace are available only for fifteen years of the nineteenth century, the period covered is from 1877 to 1893. This was a period in which the most intensive use of migrant labor occurred in the sugar industry, and also a period during which there was a change in the nature of Melanesian employment.

Calculation of crime or policing rates in the absence of adequate demographic data for different sectors of the population is a hazardous business. Before noting the differences between Melanesian and other groups in policing rates in Queensland, some cautions are necessary. First, the differences

Arrests, Queensland Birthplace

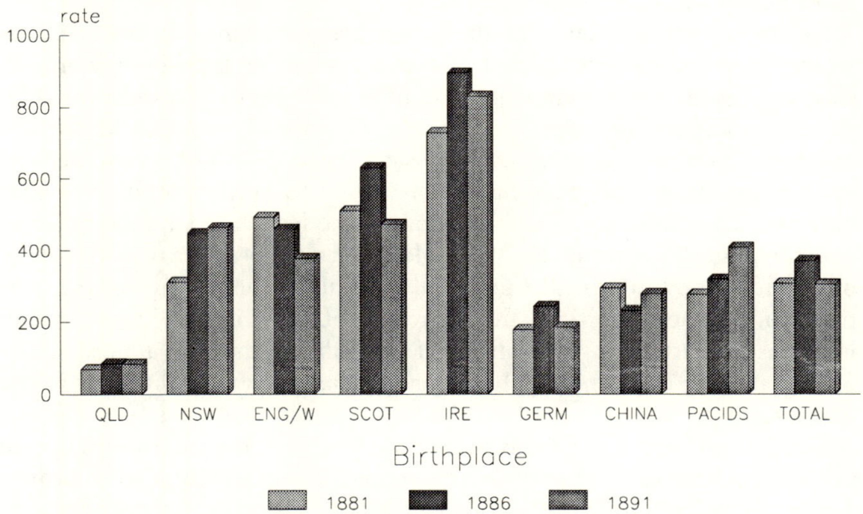

Source: Police Dept Annual Reports; rate per 100,000

between migrant groups and locally born is exaggerated by the very different age and sex structure of these populations. Chinese and Melanesian populations in Queensland were overwhelmingly male, and, therefore, most at risk of policing attention. Melanesian laborers were young, and came from societies where male aggression through a warrior persona was encouraged. Both factors were likely to increase their risk. Other immigrant populations, especially the Irish and British, had greater numbers of women, but tended to be more adult than the Australian-born population. These figures also include significant populations of those born in other colonies, principally New South Wales, whose age and sex structures were somewhere between those of the Queensland-born and the immigrant populations. A satisfactory comparison of Melanesian offending or risk of arrest would require age and sex-standardized rates, not possible in the context of this data. Nevertheless some trends for the whole colony are evident from the policing figures available in the annual reports, as illustrated in Figure 1.

Arrest of Melanesians for all offenses was initially somewhat below the colony rate and markedly below that for the major immigrant groups, the Irish and British. By 1891, however, Melanesian arrests were exceeding the colonywide rates. This is consistent with the transition we are arguing: As increasing numbers of Melanesians became ticket-holding and time-expired "free" workers on short-term contracts, their social experience was more like that of other working-class groups.

Melanesian vulnerability to the attentions of police was notably offense-specific. Charges against them for offenses against the person, above all for various forms of physical assault, were always notably high. There are substantial cultural reasons for this, as Moore has argued elsewhere.[33] The Mackay picture is confirmed in the more detailed locality studies discussed below. By contrast their appearance in court on property charges was infrequent in the early 1880s, although becoming more frequent by 1891. And in spite of the degree of colonial concern about their drinking, the rate of apprehension of Kanakas for drunkenness[34] and other public order offenses is lower than the colonial rate in the 1880s and early 1890s. Again the explanation is likely to be the degree of control of the majority of Kanaka laborers, limiting their access to town life and so restricting their opportunities to become police targets before the 1890s.

Besides offenses against the person, the other major category of prosecutions of Melanesians was under the Masters and Servants Act, invoked by police arrests and summons cases. Their arrests under this act were at ten times the rate of other groups, which is explained by their peculiar employment status. The greatest number of police charges under the act were for desertion from service, although a good number of charges were also brought for disobedience. As other historians have shown,[35] the act was a two-edged sword and an examination of police arrest alone does not exhaust their significance in Kanaka employment. A proper estimate of their use relies on access to the summons court records.

Police Arrests: Mackay, Bundaberg, Port Douglas

Previously Moore has shown, on the basis of newspaper reports of police court cases at Mackay, that there were significant changes in charging patterns over the whole period of Melanesian employment in the Queensland sugar industry. While the results were comprehensive, they could not be supplemented by police court or watch-house records.

Good evidence, however, survives for another main center of sugar production, Bundaberg. Mackay and Bundaberg had the largest populations of Kanaka laborers in Queensland. A study of surviving watch-house records, available for Bundaberg from 1884, has enabled comparisons of the patterns of policing on Melanesian defendants compared to other population groupings. All arrests for the Bundaberg watch-house during the years 1884–86, 1890–92, and 1900–1902 have been analyzed for a variety of social factors that were commonly entered in the watch-house books on the occasion of arrest.

As would be expected from the changing age-profile of the Kanaka laborers, as increasing proportions of time-expired laborers were reengaged in Queensland, initially the Melanesian defendants in Bundaberg were much younger than non-Melanesians. Ninety-four percent of the 124 laborers prosecuted between 1884 and 1886 were under thirty years, compared to

Bundaberg Arrests Age of defendants

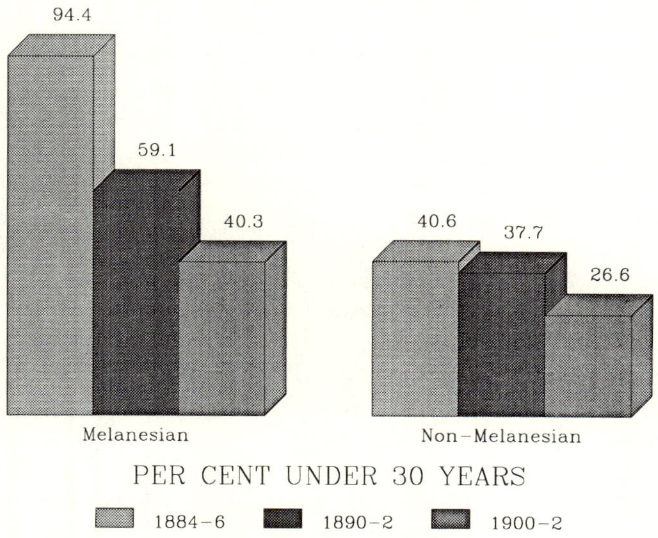

Source: Bench books, QSA

forty percent of the 512 non-Melanesian defendants. By 1900 the majority of Melanesians were over thirty years of age (see Figure 2).

Confirming Queensland and Mackay evidence, the charging patterns of Melanesian defendants in Bundaberg also changed over time. Arrests of Melanesians were much more likely to be for offenses against the person, principally assault, as well as Masters and Servants Act breaches, than was the case for non-Melanesians. But an important transition in the 1890s saw a much greater vulnerability of Melanesians to arrest for public order offenses.

As Figure 3 demonstrates, the proportion of public order charges preferred against arrested Melanesians in 1900–1902 (56.3%) approximated that for non-Melanesians (59%). Fifteen years earlier there had been striking disparities in significance for these two groups of public order charges, principally drunkenness. These patterns reflect the beginning of proletarianization of Kanakas in the sugar industry, involving a shift in social behavior to that more akin to European and Australian-born laborers.

The Kanaka experience of the hard edge of the criminal justice system reflected in some degree the specific nature of the offenses with which they were charged. With such a substantial number of assault charges it is perhaps not surprising that their conviction rates were higher than for non-Melanesians (see Figure 4).

But evidence of differential treatment is suggested by 1900 when, in spite

Bundaberg Police Court Public order charges, 1884–1902

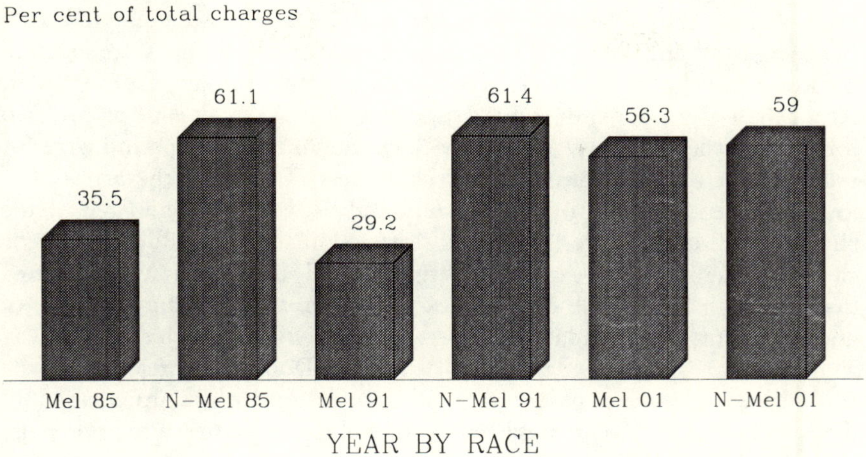

Source: Watch-house books,
QSA Mel = Melanesian; N-Mel = non-Melanesian

Bundaberg, 1884–1902 Convictions, per cent of charges

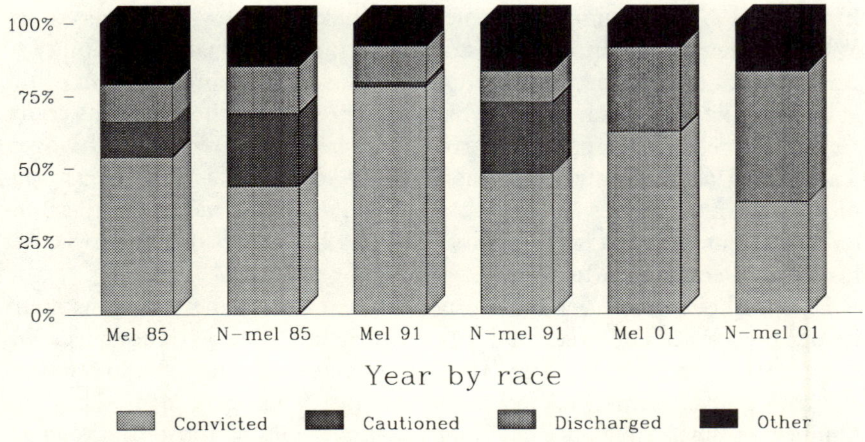

Source: Watch-house books, QSA; 'other' includes indicated to higher court
Mel = Melanesian; N-Mel = non-Melanesian

of similar charging patterns, conviction rates at some sixty-three percent of all charges against Melanesians were still much greater than the thirty-eight percent for non-Melanesian defendants. The implied leniency of the police court, which has been argued elsewhere,[36] was little evident for Kanakas, even as they became more familiar to the local society and economy.

A smaller sample of cases is available from the Port Douglas watch-house books for the 1890s. This district was the location of a third important (but much later) area of Melanesian labor in the Queensland sugar industry. Between 1888 and 1906 eighty-three Melanesian defendants were arrested by police and charged with a range of offenses from drunkenness to murder. Again there is a clear shift toward a greater risk of Kanakas being arrested for public order offenses. A majority of charges during this period were for public order offenses, principally drunkenness. Twelve of the arrests followed alleged breaches of the Masters and Servants Act, and ten of the charges were for absence from hired service. On such a small sample, little can be gained from an extended statistical analysis but it is worth noting that less than half of the drunkenness charges resulted in any sentence of imprisonment, the defendants being treated therefore in much the same way as non-Melanesian defendants. While the Port Douglas figures suggest the continuing relevance of indenture as a legal relation with punitive sanction, the Melanesian involvement with the criminal justice system was principally one that reflected the Kanakas' status as laborers in a cultural and social space that they shared with other non-Melanesian laborers.

The Summons Court: The Kanaka as Legal Subject

A different view of the Melanesian laborer in Queensland by the 1890s is highlighted by examining the role of Kanakas in the summons court. Whereas their appearance in arrest statistics indicates their vulnerability to certain types of policing, their status as objects of the repressive arm of the state, Kanakas appear in a somewhat different guise in the summons court. Actions were brought by them or on their behalf for recovery of wages. They could also use the summons court to seek satisfaction against employers or other whites for assaults on them. The evidence from the Bundaberg summons court for the years 1887 to 1906 relates to some 298 cases involving identifiable Melanesians (see Figure 5).

During this period over one-third of these cases in the summons court involved assault. The great majority of these involved Melanesian defendants. Sixty percent of these 102 defendants were fined, and another eighteen percent sentenced to various lengths of imprisonment. The high number of fines suggests the limited aggravation of most of these assaults.

In terms of the theme of the growing accommodation of the Melanesians to Australian society, one significant development of the 1890s was the emergence of the Melanesian complainant in the courts. Thirteen cases of assault were brought by Melanesians against European defendants in the Bundaberg summons court between 1889 and 1906. In three-quarters of these cases the assailant was convicted, with fines imposed, in some cases of significant amounts.[37]

Bundaberg Summons Court Actions involving Melanesians

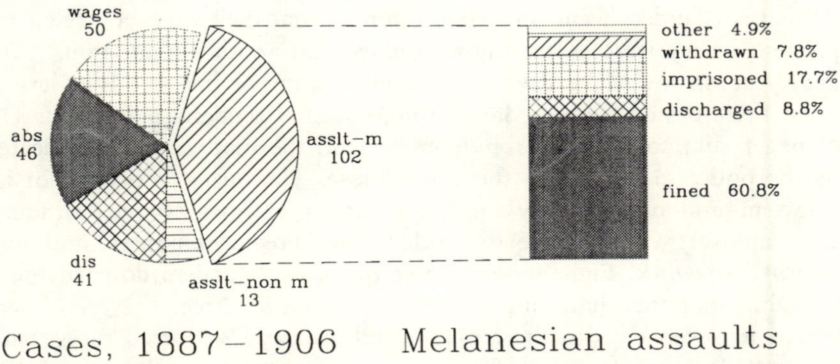

Source: Bench-books, QSA. 'Assit-m': Melanesian defendant; assit non-M: non-Melanesian defendant

Over one-third of the actions involving Melanesians related to these assault cases. About three-quarters of the remaining summons court actions were Masters and Servants Act cases. A good proportion of these cases were for absence from hired service or disobeying orders, the result of which was a fine or an order to return to work, although some of the absence cases were discharged or withdrawn. Another proportion of summons court cases—50 of the 298 cases for the period 1887–1906—were actions for nonpayment of wages. Over half of these resulted in a verdict in favor of the Melanesian laborer. These were more than nominal victories, for typically they were for substantial wages (10 and 12 pounds and more), and in most successful cases, costs and even compensation were ordered against the European employer. Melanesians in such cases demonstrated that they were not passive recipients of the employer's dictate but conscious of their rights and interests. Their position of course benefited from the bureaucratic structure that had been set up to oversee the labor trade. Many of these wage cases were actions taken up by the Inspector of Pacific Islanders. His intervention by way of summons frequently led to the action being quickly settled out of court.

OVERT AND COVERT RESISTANCE AND ACCOMMODATION

As was typical in the other Pacific colonies, Islanders in Queensland did not usually adopt overt methods of confronting their employers, such as taking action through the courts. When they did, overt resistance was normally small-scale, sporadic, and spontaneous.[38] Strikes were illegal, but small-scale Melanesian industrial action, recognizably strikes, did occur in Queensland from the 1860s, often motivated by desperation over living conditions and misunderstanding over the length of the period of recruitment. In 1867 on Nins plantation at Yahwalpah near Brisbane, Islanders went on strike, claiming that they were not being fed properly. They were eventually reemployed on another plantation.[39] The next year on the Mary River to the north some of the first Islanders to work there bolted from a Maryborough Sugar Company plantation. The manager summoned them for desertion and the matter was adjudicated by the police magistrate at the court house. The men complained of insufficient and poor quality food; the matter was sorted out, although the employers were unable to produce the agreement papers, and they returned to work. Eight months later the same Islanders downed tools, believing that they had enlisted for one year not three; they were sentenced to seven days in the lock-up, and afterwards refused to go back to work, foraging for food. They received support from the local European community, including the police who took up a collection on their behalf. Eventually two leaders of the strike were fined £3 each, and being unable to pay served a month in Brisbane gaol.[40]

Similar early cases can be found in all of the sugar districts, but from the late 1880s small groups of Melanesians began stopping work for more varied reasons. In 1889 and 1890 time-expired workers on Habana plantation at Mackay stopped work because they claimed that they were working longer hours than European laborers.[41] Strikes also occurred during the tussles over deportation. In 1905 in the Mossman district two gangs of Islander cutters refused to turn out for work on two or three occasions when no fresh bread was available for breakfast. And the next year Islanders at Mossman struck when asked to cut grub-damaged cane on a farm on which only white labor had been used previously. Sixteen were taken to court and fined £1 each plus costs. On hearing of the conviction all 143 Islanders employed by the mill went on strike. Their spokesman told the mill board that as they were not wanted in Australia they would choose which cane they cut.[42]

Large labor strikes did occur on plantations in the Pacific in the nineteenth century, but mainly within Asian and European segments of the labor force, and after indenture had been abolished. The only large-scale disturbances among Melanesians in Queensland were caused by excessive consumption of alcohol, or through aggression between different language and island groups, and in a few cases friction with Asian laborers.[43] Circular migration impeded the development of worker consciousness, and Melanesian laborers were far more likely to use covert methods of resistance and inward-focused social adjustment mechanisms to cope with life in their new land. There is evidence that they worked on a wide punitive front, involving violence, murder, sorcery, internecine fighting, malingering, working slow, sabotage, and generally recalcitrant behavior stopping short of breaches of the law.[44]

CONCLUSION

The suing for wages and the appearance of Melanesian complainants in assault cases may certainly be taken as symptoms of a broader change in the position of the Melanesians at law, and more reservedly within social life in Queensland in the 1890s. What we have is not the one-sided application of the law in defense of the master's and colonialist's interests. Rather, the Kanaka was assuming a position in relation to the law that was becoming more like that of other nineteenth-century workers. From our point of view today, the position of contract worker was not at all enviable. But recent social history accounts question an older view of the worker's position as one wholly subordinate. Typically, these accounts have stressed the contribution of such workers to the negotiation of workplace conditions and wages, in part through the occasional invoking of the law. In moving toward a revised view of their own capacities to seek remedy through the law we can see the Melanesian laborers in Queensland recognizing and taking advantage of the facts of a certain measure of legal power.

From another perspective, that of the criminal justice system, the experience of Melanesians in Queensland also confirmed their place as transitional. But here they experienced the law as not so much an instrument of their possible defense but as more conventionally repressive or reactive. Our review of the evidence of their policing for crime and public order offenses suggests that there were notable changes in their risks of arrests for particular offenses. By 1900 their appearance in the public order arrests is more on a par with non-Melanesian defendants in Queensland in this period. Paradoxically, these changes signified their greater freedom as time-expired laborers, participating increasingly in a colonial culture, particularly in imbibing its major drug, alcohol, which involved them in conflict with policing norms in the towns around which they resided.

Such changes occurred through a decade in which the Kanaka question again took on a political dimension that ensured that the future of the Melanesian laborers in Australia would be determined not by their possible future role in the local economy but only by their eventual exclusion.

There are substantial grounds for viewing the status of the Melanesian workers by the 1890s as increasingly comparable with the European- or local-born working class. What is not so clear is how to assess the development of class formation and consciousness among Melanesian workers in the colony, or how they combined their own cosmological system with the outside world system, or how much they affected their home communities in the islands when they returned.[45] We have argued that a process of proletarianization was beginning by the 1890s, but was truncated by the harsh mass deportation imposed by the Australian government in the 1900s, and that evidence of this is in part manifested through the court system.

These assertions are still open to debate. Care needs to be taken with using concepts like proletarianization, a peculiarly Western notion, which has yet to be satisfactorily applied to changes in the Pacific Islands over the last century. As Marshall Sahlins points out, "indigenous people struggle to integrate their experience of the world system in something that is logically and ontologically more inclusive; their own system of the world."[46] Melanesians in Queensland were between two cosmologies. In the main they used covert methods of resistance to confront the colonial regime rather than the courts or other overt action.

Yet, in seeming contradiction, they did enjoy a change in status over their decades in Queensland, and when it came to overt political action at the time of the mass deportation ordered in 1901, the Islanders were able to organize and run the Pacific Islanders' Association, the largest European-style political movement organized by Melanesians anywhere at that time.[47] There is no evidence of European participation in this organization, and although it was organized by an educated minority and was not a mass movement, nevertheless it was a significant politically centrifugal force.

Due regard also needs to be taken of other circumstances, such as the depressed economic conditions of the 1890s, which may have caused pressures on the criminal justice system that were independent of Melanesians. Small farm operators were at the cutting edge of the transformation taking place in the sugar industry, as plantations gave way to farms and central mills; long-staying Melanesians preferred to work on the farms. Disputes on the farms were usually handled by the employer-owner, not by an overseer. They may have resorted to the court system more readily than the planters with their more malleable, largely first-indenture laborers. And more work needs to be done on the life histories of the individual Melanesians who feature in the courts to ascertain their status within the labor system.

By the 1890s the status of half of the immigrant Melanesians was increasingly comparable with working-class Europeans, and by the 1900s they certainly confronted the Commonwealth government head on. But alongside this they also continued to operate their old cosmological and cultural systems. Class analysis in the Pacific is constantly confronted by similar dichotomies. Proletarianization of Melanesian immigrants was occurring, but has been obscured by earlier historians' lack of understanding of the work-categories that developed, of the degree to which Melanesians were active agents in shaping their own lives, and because of their concentration on the 1900s as the end of the Kanaka period in Australian history. By ignoring that 2,500 who remained after the mass deportation and continued to be slowly absorbed into the wider working class, historians have failed to see the transformation that was taking place, evidenced in part by their position in relation to Queensland's criminal justice system in the 1890s.

NOTES

Acknowledgment is due to Bryan Jamison, Julia Reid, and Martin Smith for assistance with research and data entry; and to Doug Munro and Bryan Jamison for perceptive comments on an earlier draft.

1. H. Morton, *The Whale's Wake* (Dunedin, 1982); C. Ralston, *Grass Huts and Warehouses: Pacific Beach Communities of the Nineteenth Century* (Canberra, 1977); G. L. Quimby, "Hawaiians in the Fur Trade of North-west America, 1785–1820," *Journal of Pacific History* 7 (1972): 92–103; M. Diamond, "Queequeg's Crewmates: Pacific Islanders in the European Shipping Industry," *International Journal of Maritime History* 1(2) (1989): 123–40.

2. D. Munro, "The Origins of Labourers in the South Pacific: Commentary and Statistics," in Labour in the South Pacific, ed. C. Moore, J. Leckie, and D. Munro (Townsville; 1990), xxix–li.

3. P. M. Mercer and C. R. Moore, "Australia's Pacific Islanders, 1906–1977," *Journal of Pacific History* 13(1–2) (1978): 89–101; C. R. Moore and P. M. Mercer, "The Forgotten Immigrants: Australia's Immigrant Melanesians," *Meanjin Quarterly* 37(1) (1978): 98–108; P. M. Mercer, "The Survival of a Pacific Islander Population in North Queensland, 1900–1940" (Ph.D. Thesis, Australian National University, 1981); C. R. Moore, *Kanaka: A History of Melanesian Mackay* (Port Moresby; 1985), 274–343.

4. See C. Moore, "Revising the Revisionists: The Historiography of Immigrant Melanesians in Australia," *Pacific Studies* 15(2) (1992) (in press). The main monograph studies are O. W. Parnaby, *Britain and the Labor Trade in the Southwest Pacific* (Durham, 1964); P. Corris, *Passage, Port and Plantation: A History of Solomon Islands Labour Migration, 1870–1914* (Melbourne, 1973); R. D. Bedford, *New Hebridean Mobility: A Study of Circular Migration* (Canberra, 1973); K. E. B. Saunders, *Workers in Bondage: The Origins and Bases of Unfree Labour in Queensland, 1824–1916* (St. Lucia, 1976); Moore, *Kanaka*; S. Gunder-Hock, *Mission und Wanderarbeit in Vanuatu: Eine Studie zum sozialen Wandel in Vanuatu, 1863–1915* (Munich, 1986).

5. A. G. Lowndes, ed., *South Pacific Enterprise: The Colonial Sugar Refining Company Limited* (Sydney, 1956), 443; J. H. Galloway, *The Sugar Cane Industry: An Historical Geography from Its Origins to 1914* (Cambridge, 1989), 238–39.

6. W. R. Johnston, *The Call of the Land: A History of Queensland to the Present Day* (Brisbane, 1982), 129–44.

7. Premier Griffith reversed his 1885 decision in 1892, a volte-face explained primarily in economic terms. The final phasing out of Melanesian immigration was left to the Commonwealth government in 1901.

8. The following records are held in the Queensland State Archives: Bundaberg, Police Charge Bench Record 1884–1912, vol. 3A/MI–34; Bundaberg, Summons Court, 1887–1906, CPS 3A/S2–8; Port Douglas, Police Watch-House Book, 1888–1907, CPS 12 E/6–7.

9. J. Kerr, *Southern Sugar Saga: Bundaberg Sugar Company Limited* (Brisbane, 1983); J. Nolan, *Bundaberg: History and People* (St. Lucia, 1978); Moore, *Kanaka*; J. Kerr, *Pioneer Pageant: A History of the Pioneer Shire* (Mackay, 1980); idem, *A Century of Sugar: Racecourse Sugar Mill, Mackay* (Mackay, 1988); F. Rolleston,

The Defiance: The Story of North Eton Co-operative Sugar Milling Association Limited, 1888–1987 (Mackay, 1987); K. W. Manning, *In Their Own Hands: A North Queensland Sugar Story* (Farleigh, 1983); J. Kerr, *Northern Outpost* (Mossman, 1979).

10. This argument is stated more fully in Moore, *Kanaka*, 188–97.

11. C. Price with E. Baker, "Origins of Pacific Island Labourers in Queensland, 1863–1904: A Research Note," *Journal of Pacific History* 11(2) (1976): 106–12.

12. Mercer, "Pacific Islander Population."

13. R. Shlomowitz, "Indentured Melanesians in Queensland: A Statistical Investigation of Recruiting Voyages, 1871–1903," *Journal of Pacific History* 16(4) (1981): 203–7.

14. R. Shlomowitz, "Markets for Indentured and Time-Expired Melanesian Labour in Queensland, 1863–1906: An Economic Analysis," *Journal of Pacific History* 16(2) (1981): 70–91; "Time-Expired Melanesian Labour in Queensland: An Investigation of Job Turnover, 1884–1906," *Pacific Studies* 8(2) (1985): 25–44; "Time-Expired Melanesian Labour in Queensland: The Measurement of Job Turnover, 1886–1906," *Journal of Pacific History* 20(1) (1985): 55–56.

15. R. Shlomowitz, "Team Work and Incentives: the origins and Development of the Butty Gang System in Queensland's Sugar Industry, 1891–1913," *Journal of Comparative Economics* 3 (1979): 41–55.

16. R. Shlomowitz, "Mortality and the Pacific Labour Trade," *Journal of Pacific History* 22(1–2) (1987): 34–55; "Epidemiology and the Pacific Labor Trade," *Journal of Interdisciplinary History* 19(4) (1989): 585–610.

17. R. Shlomowitz, "The Search for Institutional Equilibrium in Queensland's Sugar Industry, 1884–1913," *Australian Economic History Review* 19(2) (1979): 91–122; "The Profitability of Indentured Melanesian Labour in Queensland," *Australian Economic History Review* 22 (1982): 49–67; "Melanesian Labour and the Development of the Queensland Sugar Industry," *Research into Economic History: A Research Annual* 7 (1982): 327–61; A. A. Graves, "Crisis and Change in the Queensland Sugar Industry, 1862–1906", in *Crisis and Change in the International Sugar Economy, 1860–1914*, ed. B. Albert and A. Graves (Norwich and Edinburgh, 1986), 261–79.

18. Kay Saunders estimated that twenty-five to thirty percent were recruited illegally, but probably less than five percent were kidnapped. Using nineteenth-century assessments, Richard Bedford estimated a possible ten percent taken by force in 1871 and five percent in 1881, and double that number obtained by deceit and false promises. Clive Moore's detailed analysis of Malaitan recruiting provides reasonable support for Saunders and Bedford's findings. However, Bryan Jamison's study of recruiting in the Louisiade and D'Entrecasteaux archipelagos in the 1880s, examined by an 1885 Royal Commission and declared to have been illegal, has cast more doubt on the extent of the supposed predominantly illegal period. See K. Saunders, "Uncertain Bondage: An Analysis of Indentured Labour in Queensland to 1907, with Particular Reference to the Melanesian Servants" (Ph.D. Thesis, University of Queensland, 1974), 85; Bedford, "New Hebridean Mobility," 25. Moore, *Kanaka*, 23–100, esp. 45–64; B. Jamison, "Blackbirding in New Guinea Waters? The 1885 Voyage of the *Hopeful* and the Queensland Labour Trade" (BA Hons., University of Queensland, 1990).

19. Moore, *Kanaka*, 47–48. See also M. Jolly, "The Forgotten Women: A History

of Migrant Labour and Gender Relations in Vanuatu," *Oceania* 58(1) (1987): 123; and R. Adams, "Plantation Labour in Vanuatu," in *Labour in the South Pacific*, 141.

20. D. Shineberg, *They Came for Sandalwood: A Study of the Sandalwood Trade in the South-west Pacific, 1830–1865* (Melbourne, 1967), 193; K. R. Howe, *The Loyalty Islands: A History of Culture Contacts, 1840–1900* (Canberra, 1977), 90–91.

21. Moore, *Kanaka*, 156–57.

22. Females formed a very low proportion of the Melanesian immigrants (an average of 6.75%, 1871–1901). They received the same wage as males as first-indenture laborers but subsequently they received a lesser wage. See K. Saunders, "Melanesian Women in Queensland, 1863–1907: Some Methodological Problems Involving the Relationship Between Racism and Sexism," *Pacific Studies* 4:(1) (1980): 26–44. See also Jolly, "Forgotten Women."

23. R. Shlomowitz, "Time-Expired Melanesian Labor in Queensland: An Investigation of Job Turnover, 1884–1906," *Pacific Studies* 8:(2) (1985): Table 4, 32.

24. Moore, *Kanaka*, 172.

25. Ibid., 164–67.

26. H. E. Maude, "The Tahitian Pork Trade, 1800–1830", in *Of Islands and Men: Studies in Pacific History* (Melbourne, 1968), 178–232.

27. Howe, *Loyalty Islands*, 90.

28. M. Diamond, *The Seahorse and the Wanderer: Ben Boyd in Australia* (Melbourne, 1988), 131, and more generally, 119–40. See also K. R. Howe, "Tourists, Sailors and Labourers: A Survey of Early Labour Recruiting in Southern Melanesia," *Journal of Pacific History* 13:(1) (1978): 22–35.

29. Queensland, 31 *Vic.* No. 47.

30. Queensland, 25 *Vic.* No. 11.

31. See Moore, *Kanaka*, 344–45, for a list of all relevant legislation, Select Committee, and Royal Commission reports.

32. The only totally "free" immigrant Melanesians were the ticket-holders; most others were working in the sugar industry and still under indenture, although on a variety of contract lengths and remunerations.

33. Moore, *Kanaka*, 188–97, 361–64.

34. C. Moore, "'Me Blind Drunk': Alcohol and Melanesians in the Mackay District, Queensland, 1867–1907," in *Health and Healing in Tropical Australia and Papua New Guinea*, ed. R. McLeod and D. Denoon (Townsville, 1991), 103–22.

35. Australian research on the Masters and Servants Act has been divided on its role. Adrian Merritt and Robert McQueen stress the uses made by employees of the act's provisions covering employee conditions against a more conventional view. John Cashen, Martin Sullivan, and Jan Walker, for examples, stress the act's primary significance as an instrument of the employer. Kay Saunders has emphasized its use as part of a repressive apparatus against Melanesian workers, but her account of worker resistance also contains evidence of its use by Melanesians against masters.

See A. Merritt, "Forgotten Militants: The Use of the New South Wales *Master and Servant Act* by and Against Female Employees, 1845–1930," in *Law and History in Australia* (Bundoora, 1982); R. McQueen, "Master and Servant Legislation in Nineteenth Century Australia," in *Law and History in Australia*, ed. D. Kirkby (Bundoora, 1987), 4:78–110; M. Sullivan, *Men and Women of Port Phillip* (Sydney,

1985); J. Walker, *Jondaryan Station* (St. Lucia, 1988); J. Cashen, "Masters and Servants in South Australia, 1837–1860," *Journal of the Historical Society of South Australia* 10 (1982): 32–43; Saunders, *Workers in Bondage*, 126–40, 180–82.

36. M. Finnane and S. Garton, "The Work of Policing: Social Relations and the State in Australia, 1880–1914," paper presented at the Australia-Canada Labour History Conference, Dec. 1988, Sydney University; M. Finnane, "The Irish and Crime in the Late Nineteenth Century: A Statistical Inquiry," in *Irish-Australian Studies: Papers Delivered at the Fifth Irish-Australian Conference,* ed. O. MacDonagh and W. Mandle (Canberra, 1989), 77–98.

37. The highest fine awarded in the summons court (although not the highest penalty, as a number of Melanesians received prison sentences for their assaults) for any assault action involving a Melanesian in this period in Bundaberg was in fact against a European defendant in 1896.

38. There were no revolts in the Pacific colonies comparable with the large slave revolts that occurred in Jamaica and Brazil, and all big strikes, such as occurred in Hawaii and Fiji, came after the abandonment of the indenture system. Doug Munro has concluded that large-scale strikes, collective organized resistance, were not a viable option, despite just grievances existing. See "Patterns of Resistance and Accommodation", in *Resistance and Accommodation on Plantations*, ed. E. D. Beechert, B. V. Lal, and D. Munro (in press).

39. *Brisbane Courier*, 7, 28 Sept. 1867. We are indebted to John Kerr for this reference.

40. J. Kerr, *Sugar at Maryborough: 120 Years of Challenge* (Maryborough, 1987), 19–22.

41. *The Mackay Mercury*, 9 Nov. 1889, 10 June 1890.

42. Kerr, *Northern Outpost*, 42–43.

43. C. Moore, "Me Blind Drunk"; and "The Mackay Racecourse Riot of 1883," in *Lectures in North Queensland History*, ed. B. J. Dalton (Townsville, 1979), 181–96; K. Saunders, "The Workers Paradox: Indentured Labour in the Queensland Sugar Industry to 1920," in *Indentured Labour in the British Empire, 1834–1920*, ed. K. Saunders (London and Canberra, 1984), 231.

44. C. Moore, "The Counter-Culture of Survival: Melanesians in the Mackay District of Queensland, 1865–1907," in *Resistance and Accommodation on Plantations.*

45. Vijay Naidu and Jacqueline Leckie, "The Development of Class Analysis in the South Pacific," in *Labour in the South Pacific*, 244–55. See also M. Burawoy, *The Politics of Production* (London, 1983); M. Sahlins, "Cosmologies of Capitalism: The Trans-Pacific Sector of 'the World System,' " *Proceedings of the British Academy* 74 (1988): 1–51.

46. Sahlins, "Cosmologies of Capitalism," 4.

47. Moore, *Kanaka*, 274–85.

Índios, Fanáticos, Bandidos: Labeling the Millenarian Movement at Tomochic, Mexico

Paul J. Vanderwood
San Diego State University

The propensity for officially labeling enemies of the state is not particularly surprising; it is one of the tools most frequently used by dominant groups to discredit their opponents and enemies (and vice versa). Governments more or less routinely stigmatize rebels and revolutionaries as bandits and denigrate religious practices of which they disapprove as heresy or magic.[1] Howard S. Becker, a prominent labeling theorist, notes that "A major element in every aspect of the drama of deviance is the imposition of definitions ... by those powerful enough or sufficiently legitimated to be able to do so."[2] But while this is a common practice, similar labels carry a different significance in different cultures, not to mention changes in meaning over time, and therefore need to be examined for what they meant in a certain society at a particular time. At the same time, labels applied by the powerful tell us more about the accusers than the accused, more about the ambitions of the people who use them as well as the sort of society they mean to create than the recipients of such titles. In short, labels yield insights into the nature of the government at the time they are applied. In this instance, they reveal the heterogeneity of Mexican society near the turn of the century versus the endeavor of those who would sculpt such diversity into something called "nation." The basis for this case study in labeling lies in the events surrounding the emergence of a folk saint in the north of Mexico in 1890.

LA SANTA DE CABORA

A normally soft-spoken, rather plain-looking teen-age girl named Teresa, who claimed divine revelation while preaching the immediate need for the moral regeneration of society, rallied thousands of followers in northwestern Mexico in the early 1890s. Yaqui and Mayo Indians, mestizos, and Mexican-Americans flocked to hear her often caustic critique of their present conditions and her predictions of a better world soon to come. Enthusiastic crowds of common campesinos along with better-off citizens proclaimed Teresa their *santa*, witnessed her spectacular healings, and pledged their allegiance to her mission. Meanwhile, government agents probed the huge, emotional gatherings for signs of sedition, and alerted soldiers to the possible outbreak of public disorder. They did not have long to wait. In late 1891 residents of Tomochic, a pueblo on the Chihuahuan side of the Sierra Madre, vowed to obey no one but "Santa Teresa," a stance that led to armed conflict with local authorities. Some six months later in the name of the same *santa*, Mayos attacked a regional center in Sonora. Religious enthusiasm with potent political meaning began to sweep the sector and demanded an official response. Federal and state soldiers marched to the trouble spots, and at the same time the government unleashed the labeling, bias-building barrage of epithets that is the subject of this chapter. Specifically, we shall consider the three labels most consistently applied to the faithful at Tomochic: *índio*, *fanático*, and *bandido*.[3]

Teresa was the illegitimate child of Tomás Urrea, a reasonably well-to-do rancher and the descendant of a prominent Spanish family. The Urreas are well known to Sonoran and Sinaloan political, military, and social history. Tomás had fathered his daughter with the wife of one of his Indian workers and reared the child on his farm and cattle ranch at Cabora, located in the flat, dry countryside below the mountainous silver mining center at Alamos in southeastern Sonora. In 1889 Teresa, then sixteen years old, inexplicably lapsed into a coma and for three weeks hovered near death—or seemed to—until she abruptly awakened and began to describe a conversation with the Virgin Mary. The divinity commanded her to preach the urgent need for love and compassion among all humankind and the remoralization of society, a salvationist message that echoed the callings of the primitive church for brotherhood and equality. In tone, the communication, confirmed by a letter purportedly delivered by the Archangel Gabriel, suggested divine displeasure with certain fundamentals in Mexican society, urged immediate repentance and reform, and implied a formula for redemption.[4] No doubt each of the diverse ethnic groups listening in weighed Teresa's pronouncements through their own historical experiences, contemporary concerns, and respective cultural prisms. For the Tomochitecos, they seemed to resonate with moral concerns about recent events and longer-term alterations in village life.

For months Teresa wandered about in a kind of trance during which she seemed distracted from the normal activities of her daily life and periodically startled her friends and family by predicting a variety of happenings which then came to pass; she foretold the arrival of unexpected visitors and foresaw accidents at the rancho. Increasingly she effected miraculous cures. At times, Teresa simply laid hands on the afflicted; on other occasions, she mixed a paste of her saliva and plain soil and applied the balm to the sick. As a result, according to published testimonials and eye-witness reports, the lame walked, tumors and nervous disorders disappeared, barren women became fertile. Her fame spread as her audience grew, and as 1890 deepened, she attracted an increasing number of pilgrims, hundreds building into thousands, from the neighboring states of Chihuahua and Sinaloa as well as border people from the United States. Journalists arrived at Cabora to survey the spectacle, and their reports, even those scornful of the faithful and their practices, carried Teresa's reputation to Mexico City and implanted her message more firmly in the United States.[5]

Moreover, "Santa Teresita" could be quite specific and strident in her teachings. No longer in any sort of mystical trance, she unequivocally identified priests, money, and doctors as the three greatest evils in the world[6] and told crowds that they need no longer rely on priests to perform the sacraments of the Holy Catholic Church. They could baptize and marry themselves, a proposition once accepted by some early Christians disappointed with the official church. In fact, Teresa said, the rot in the church had spread to the pope himself—as close as she came to declaring the pope the Anti-Christ, the devil in disguise (itself an example of labeling), but advised that church reform was imminent. In fact, she claimed that a representative of the church reform movement (Pope León XIII soon pronounced the famous *Rerum Novarum*) was at that moment about to leave Italy to inform Mexicans about the forthcoming fundamental renovation of the church, which to many had strayed from the teachings of simplicity, justice, and egalitarianism embedded in primitive Catholicism.[7] "Priests, money, and doctors," common objects of complaint against Mother Church through the ages, suggest the social as well as religious discontent that meshed in the minds of the faithful. Priests, with their inattention to sacred duties, money grubbing, irreligious personal habits, and general slothfulness, hardly qualified as agents of God. Money was unequally distributed and immorally used to measure human worth. Doctors, some of them pretenders, practiced for money but ignored the poor. These, based on realities of those times in the region, seem to have been the specific evils attacked by Teresa in the name of God. But her teachings also indicated the Almighty's anger—a threatening anger—with an entire society gone bad. God's remonstrance seemed clear: Reform, or else.

TOMOCHIC AND ITS PEOPLE

Teresa's pronouncements registered with enormous impact in the small pueblo of Tomochic (pop. 300), situated on the eastern flank of the Sierra Madre, where it sloped down into the neighboring state of Chihuahua. The pueblo lay in a rather deep, fertile, square-shaped valley, by far the largest inhabitable spot in the immediate district. It was normally a two-day ride from the village down to the regional political and economic center at

Ciudad Guerrero. Ciudad Guerrero was situated in the fertile and relatively well-populated valley of the Papigochic River, which ran through the foothills to the Sierra, some eighty miles west of the state capital at Chihuahua City.[8] Tomochic's inhabitants were largely mestizos who starting in the 1840s had filtered in from surrounding areas to gradually displace the Tarahumara Indians who had originally lived in the valley. The 1890 government census showed the pueblo to be at least eighty-five percent mestizo, some of them apparently related to those *Norteños* who originally settled in the mining district.[9]

What shall we call these Tomochis: *rancheros*, *campesinos*, peasants, *medieros*, *serranos*? While the terms are neither parallel nor exclusive, none of these general labels designed by others seems to fit them very well. We had better stick to what most of them called themselves on census reports: *labradores*. Even the Tarahumaras are listed as *labradores*. That meant simply that they considered themselves to be small time farmers who owned and worked their own land.[10] Certainly they provided almost all of their own food, but the village also had petty merchants (often widows) who sold inexpensive clothing, cloth, and homemade foodstuffs, such as candy and baked goods, normally from the main room in their homes. The Tomochis could, if they chose to do so, earn additional income by catering to the voracious sustenance needs of the relatively nearby mining communities, or a villager might pick up a manual job in one of the perennially labor-short mines. Furthermore, they could work as muleteers or security guards for the commercial convoys that rolled through the Sierra. Or the better-off might engage in an enterprise down in the Papigochic, perhaps raise cattle on the ranch of a friend or relative. It was not unusual for a person who held public office in Tomochic to request leave from the political boss of the region—the *jefe político*—in order to attend to personal business elsewhere.[11]

Early in 1890 word of a prophet meandering through the Sierra reached the pueblo and aroused a group of perhaps a dozen Tomochis to investigate. Headed by Cruz Chávez, who in the absence of an ordained priest seems to have become the village's lay religious leader, the inquisitive group encountered at a fairly nearby rancho called Chopeque a humble, middle-aged man who called himself Joseph leading a mule that carried his pregnant wife named Mary. The "holy" man also carried a small wooden box which he claimed contained a sacred relic, an icon that confirmed his association with the divine. We are not privy to details of the conversation that occurred among Chávez, his band of a dozen or more followers, and Joseph that day, but the Tomochis soon began to revere "San José," who became known as the "Cristo de Chopeque," and to take instructions from him. It was as if they had been looking for, perhaps expecting, divine guidance for some time. Most likely, Joseph told them about "Santa Teresa" on the western side of the Sierra in Sonora and introduced them to her teachings. He also probably advised them that should their belief and practices lead to armed opposition, that the bullets of their enemies would not pierce their flesh, for their faith assured them of divine protection. Even if they died in combat, resurrection would soon follow. Such safeguards are the hallmarks of millenarian movements. Bullets may kill the faithful for the weakness of their belief or because of grave sins they have committed, but resurrection through God's mercy is normally assured.[12]

Cruz Chávez and his coterie of devotees traveled to receive the counsel of "San José" on a number of occasions, at one point under the wary eye of the regional priest, Padre Manuel Castelo, an itinerant representative of the official church who periodically performed religious rites, such as mass marriages, at the scattered population sites in the Sierra. The Mexican church was not rigidly adverse to prophecy. After all, as had occurred in the case of Lourdes, prophecy could be fashioned to unite the faithful on behalf of the church in its relentless struggle with the secular state. Therefore, Mexican church officials carefully tracked any modern-day prophets to learn what they had to say but did not normally denounce or interfere with them, at least not at first, or until they began to perform religious rites, such as administering the sacraments, reserved only for ordained priests. Following this procedure, Padre Castelo rejected the offer of civil authorities to break up the pilgrimages to "San José," apparently because he wanted to test the mettle of this *santo* and to know if José had any connections with Teresa, whose anti-clerical bombast had raised the ire of the church hierarchy and led to charges of heresy.[13] ("Heretic" is a label frequently applied by Mother Church against its detractors or disobedient members.)

At some point in late 1891 the priest had his answer; some inhabitants of Tomochic had begun to venerate "Santa Teresa," so the padre hurried to the pueblo to set matters straight. In his forceful sermon that fateful fall day (probably Sunday, 29 November), he admonished the gathering in the village church—most Tomochis seemed to be there—to desist at once from their veneration of Teresa under pain of excommunication. Cruz Chávez took up the gauntlet. He stood up among the congregation and, with his penetrating stare underscoring his commitment, resolutely declared: "We will obey no one but Santa Teresa." Then he led most of the gathering (six or seven families remained seated) past the stunned priest, whom he sarcastically mocked, and then out of the church and into his vision of a new world to come.[14]

From its vantage point, the state considered Chávez and his followers to be in rebellion against its authority, but whether the Tomochis saw themselves in revolt against the government is another question. Quite possibly not. Nothing in the documentation indicates that they considered themselves to be opposed to the government. In fact, in the strongest statement that we have on this point, Cruz Chávez, speaking to a government mediator in February 1892, insisted that he and his followers believed that society needed a government to direct it, and that contrary to reports that they had repudiated all government in favor of God's rule, they were then and still were disposed to obey the constituted local authorities, as long as the faithful were allowed to practice their religion as they saw fit, something they saw as a constitutional guarantee.[15] Whether this frank statement of loyalty to official government represented an aspect of the "hidden transcript" that subjugated peoples develop in their struggle with the powerful is difficult to assess. But once the armed struggle began, the millenarians did not even cut the telegraph lines that connected authorities in the state capital to major mining camps, such as Pinos Altos, in the Sierra, and their descendants still claim that the faithful had no quarrel with either state or national government.[16] Yet even while they openly swore no animosity toward official government, the faithful resolutely shunned reconciliation with civil authority. They intended to follow the guidance of Teresa toward the millennium. Such believers often ponder how to best bring about their new world, and some welcome, indeed invite, an armed confrontation with the state in order to induce the apocalypse needed to bring on the millennium. Religious martyrs have been known to do such things. Their actions, meaning their relative disinterest in active recruitment and their fatalistic steadfastness when approached by the state in both peace and war, suggest that the Tomochitecos expected, even desired, to do battle with the "Sons of Lucifer."

This is neither the place to examine the slow but inexorable consolidation of the millenarian movement itself nor to detail the encounters with the federal army that followed. Suffice it to say that after a brief but sharp encounter in December 1891, a small military force occupied Tomochic. Meanwhile, Chávez and his thirty-odd followers traversed the Sierra to consult with Teresa. Enroute they ambushed and routed a federal troop sent to arrest them. When the faithful arrived at Cabora, the *santa* was not at her chapel, so they returned in mid-January 1892 to Tomochic, where they vowed to die with their families.[17] Here we have another hint that they may have invited the apocalypse in order to usher in the millennium. Unfortunately, we cannot read their minds on this provocative possibility. All we do know is that they had ample opportunity to accept amnesty or to leave the region for the relative safety of the Sierra, or even refuge in the United States, which was common ground for political refugees, but that in any case the Tomochis chose to stand their ground and to die for their beliefs. They soon got their wish.

In September the federal army marched in force on the village but suffered a humiliating defeat that tested the ability and resolve of the national dictatorship to defend itself. Not only did citizens begin to question the strength of the dictatorship, but they wondered at the claims of the Tomochis to divine assistance and protection. Little so confounds and frightens secular governments as the power of religion to mobilize the masses against it. One month later the head-of-state, Porfirio Díaz, ordered a simultaneous attack by overwhelming forces from both Sonora and Chihuahua to subdue their foe. After eight days of military probings, forays, and siege, the defenders simply ran out of resistance. The army summarily executed the final six survivors, all grievously wounded, including Cruz Chávez.[18] Yet the dictatorship hardly triumphed, for the ashes of Tomochic settled everywhere in the republic and emphasized the government's propensity to use unmitigated brute force against the will of common people. And as the myth of Tomochic grew, its defenders became heroized in song, literature, and history as symbols of challenge to oppressive government.

CULTURAL LABELS AS OFFICIAL RESPONSE

Millenarian movements not only tell us a good deal about the communities that produce them but also about the nature of the state and state power that mean to control and frequently repress them. Fortunately, in the case under study we have substantial documentation, thanks to the correspondence between agents of the Mexican government who monitored and then repressed the social phenomenon unfolding in the nation's northwest. Such records naturally reflect the point of view of those who designed them, meaning elites and those empowered and determined to protect their dominant position in society. But it is not news to research scholars that such documentation may also yield important clues about the motives and goals of subaltern groups as well as the nature of those who mean to rule and exploit them. How one understands those clues is, of course, tied to the frame of mind and point of view with which one examines them.

As we analyze the official documentation covering rebellion, we encounter words and phrases and thoughts that lead us to wonder whether the state ever understood the challenge that it faced. However, elites are rarely so blinded by their own agenda or captives of such a myopic mind set that they reflexively limit their response to a simple and often brutal repression. Instead they seem to understand, even if imperfectly, the political nature of the menace they face and react in strategically developed and often rather sophisticated ways to defuse the threat to their hegemony. Of course, whether they succeed is another question. Mexican officials may not have responded to the outburst of religious enthusiasm represented by "Santa Teresa" as expeditiously and efficiently as hindsight now suggests to some, but they certainly understood the nature of the threat it posed to public order, and they respected the power of religion to mobilize the masses for whatever cause.

Authorities everywhere seem to understand how to handle civil disturbances based in obvious secular causation: Go in and nip them in the bud. But religious movements seem to give them pause, even though labels like *fanático* and *bandito* begin to creep into official communications. When the government mediator went to Tomochic late in the winter of 1892 to attempt to negotiate Cruz Chávez out of his intransigence, the official came away advising his superiors to treat the faithful with "prudence and moderation." He advised them to let the movement burn itself out. He hoped that once the promises of "Santa Teresa" and the "Christ of Chopeque" remained unfulfilled, the movement would dissipate by itself.[19] Moreover, for nearly two years Mexican government agents and army units prowled around the gatherings at Cabora but tolerated the "religious" preachings of Teresa. They hunted for signs of sedition but discovered only religious fervor. Still they could not have missed the political inferences; the mass gathering per se had political import. Teresa herself seems to have been guarded against making direct utterances against the state. Later on, even as armed bands marauded in her name, she denied any revolutionary intention or complicity.[20] Although some officials grew quite nervous about the potential for insurrection among the crowds who adored her, they declined to interfere, or were so ordered, mainly out of fear of inciting riot but also, it seems, because of a certain fascination (attraction?) for the spectacle unfolding before them. They would not have been the first nor the last public servants to ponder and then join millenarian activity developing in their midst. Díaz himself feared just such a possibility among the rank and file in his army, and we have the recent example of Uganda's well-educated, English-speaking former minister of education, who joined Alice, the Lakwena's, millenarian crusade in his homeland, all the while expounding the power of God to bring about immediate and radical change.[21]

Teresa's presence only became intolerable to Mexican authorities in June 1892 after Mayo Indians attacked the Sonoran agricultural center at Navajoa shouting, "Viva la Santa de Cabora." Leading village officials died defending Navajoa. Less than two years earlier, federal troops scouting the Mayo countryside had discovered that folk saints predicting the apocalypse in the form of the Great Flood had popped up everywhere among the natives. Now "Santa Teresa" had become their foremost inspiration, and the Mayo had begun to act on their visions.[22] So Teresa and her father, Tomás, had to be extirpated. But still how gingerly the government acted. It had no intention of arresting and trying them for sedition, which would have led at best to long imprisonment for the Urreas. Instead, the authorities made a deal with the pair: no more activities against the Mexican state in exchange for exile to the United States, but at some distance from the international boundary. Teresa and her father agreed, and amidst elaborate security measures, soldiers moved the pair at night to the port of Guaymas, where they were lodged, believe it or not, in the governor's house. How the state feared these folk saints. It suspected that Teresa's followers would fanatically defend her and carefully planned to avoid any such confrontation. Next day, troops moved her to the U.S. border at Nogales and urged her to move quickly toward Tucson or even farther into the interior. But Teresa and her father refused to budge from Nogales, supported by the merchants there who thought her presence good for tourism. Meanwhile, in Mexico, as aggressive Porfirian programs and authority increasingly asserted themselves and chafed segments of the populace, protests against the regime's suffocating oppressiveness, favoritisms, and blatant usurpations began to spout. So within a few years of Teresa's exile any number of armed bands made forays from border points such as Nogales, Arizona, into Mexico in the name of "La Santa de Cabora," some of them now openly vowing to overturn the dictatorship.[23]

ÍNDIOS

If the Mexican government for quite some time hesitated to repress these religious movements by overt force, it assuredly unleashed a labeling barrage aimed to discredit and ridicule them from the start. The intended audience of this official barrage seems to have been the populace-at-large—the mestizo and creole population, meaning the great majority of Mexicans, regardless of social status. Presuming to speak for a "nation" which did not exist but which they intended to design in their interests, the authorities assaulted their adversary on two broad but interrelated cultural fronts: its Indianness and its worldview.

The government—and this is absolutely clear in the documentation—deliberately and steadfastly labeled the religious participants from Teresa to the Tomochis as Indians, although it knew very well from the start that its antagonists were not Indians. Teresa, her father, many of her followers, and virtually all of the Tomochis were mestizos, just like the great majority of Mexicans, including those in government. Authorities knew that Teresa's father, Tomás, was a scion of the great Urrea clan, and a few days after the outbreak of hostilities at Tomochic, government representatives had interrogated villagers, including the mestizo wives of some of the faithful and verified that the participants, racially speaking, were like "US"; hence, the need of those in power to distance themselves from their dissident racial brethren by labeling them *índios*.[24]

As is rather commonly known, *índio* in Mexico (and elsewhere to be sure) is a term that is frequently used to denigrate. "Tu eres índio" means you are stupid. Parents tell their children: "No seas índio." Don't be gullible around strangers. Don't repeat the silly errors of those ignorant *índios* who welcomed the greedy Spanish conquerors into our midst. Or, "Que no te cambien espejitos por oro." Don't trade your valuable possessions for worthless mirrors like the dim-witted Indians who first encountered the Spaniards. This sort of discourse may well begin in a light-hearted way in the delivery rooms of Mexican hospitals, where doctors assisting in childbirth might tell a mother who has not yet even seen her child, "Mala suerte. Muy indiado," which means, "Bad luck. Your baby has the dark eyes and dark hair of an Indian," as opposed to, "Que suerte"—the good luck of a woman whose child "tiene ojos claros," or gray-green or otherwise light eyes and blond hair of an imagined Spaniard.[25] In 1890, the Mexico City newspaper *El Universal* wrote that children who tossed lighted matches and stones from balconies on pedestrians walking below were acting more like Indians on the frontier, like the Yaquis (followers of Teresa), than youngsters in the nation's capital.[26] So we can see that the negative image of *índio* is well embedded in Mexican culture and has been for some time, which is why the government moved quickly to stigmatize Teresa and the Tomochis as *índios*.

It is well beyond the bounds of this chapter to tread those pathways of power/knowledge/culture pioneered by Michel Foucault in his search for the technologies of power that originated and introduced labels such as *índio*. Nonetheless, a few signposts are indicated by Victoria Bricker's elaboration of the "Myths of Pacification and Ethnic Solidarity" that helped to mold the perceptions of Spanish colonizers toward the Indians, especially Indian rebellions. The "Myth of Pacification," she tells us, concerns the Spanish concept of "just war"—the idea that the Spaniards considered the natives to be vassals of the Castilian monarch, a relationship confirmed by an oath of allegiance demanded of the natives by the colonials. Indians who refused the oath were said to be in rebellion against the Crown and therefore the legitimate subjects of "just war." In this way, war against rebellious Indians became legitimate pacification. Within this same sort of cultural mind set, the Porfirian dictatorship justified its repression of Teresa and the Tomochis as part of the ongoing and legitimate pacification of Indians.[27] *El Monitor Republicano* expressed as much in late 1886 when it wrote that if reports of the war being conducted against the Yaquis in Sonora seemed "abominable, it is justified to war against the Yaqui, for it is flying the flag of a holy cause that far from destroying them [the Yaquis], regenerates and exalts them."[28]

Bricker's "Myth of Ethnic Solidarity" concerns the supposed ethnic or village homogeneity in relation to rebellion. Bricker informs us that "A belief of ethnic solidarity blinded conquerors and their descendants to the evidence of *considerable division* [my emphasis] within the Indian tribe or community."[29] Indeed, most Yaquis did not follow "Santa Teresa," just as most Sioux Indians did not participate in the ghost dance for cultural renewal about the same period in South Dakota.[30] Nevertheless in Mexico the myth of ethnic solidarity fueled the fear of caste war, which continued to prick mestizo consciousness deep into the nineteenth century (perhaps even further). Charles Hale discovered that just such concern permeated Liberal (albeit elitist) thought throughout the century. So we have José María Luis Mora, a leading Liberal protagonist studied by Hale, in 1848 asking for British assistance in crushing an uprising among the Maya, who are "pursuing with monstrous barbarity the plan for exterminating the white class."[31] So much for the Liberal doctrinaire proposition that in the name of egalitarianism the term *índio* must be abolished from public use. Instead, *índio* with all its potent meaning would not be eliminated from official discourse, because used as a label it so well served elitist concerns for public order and nation building, objectives that normally precluded Liberal regard for equality and social justice.[32]

While they certainly did not eschew the use of military power in resolving the "Indian problem," most leading Liberals preferred miscegenation. Justo Sierra, for example, sought Mexican nationality (meaning a Mexican state) in the "mestizo family," which is, of course, a fusion of Hispanic and Indian cultures. For Mora, that meant "the total extinction of the castes."[33] At the constitutional convention in 1856, a deputy from the state of Oaxaca, José Antonio Gamboa, suggested widespread intermarriage and the mass immigration of whites, so that "the Indians would be absorbed into our race," and "the threat of being absorbed by the Indian race" would disappear. Moreover, the deputy had a mathematical formula in mind: "five million Indians, ten million whites."[34] In sum, mestizo response to Indian recalcitrance and rebellion in the latter part of the nineteenth-century was much the same as that of creoles to Hidalgo's movement for independence in 1810 and the Maya caste wars at mid-century: Put political differences aside and extirpate the "barbarism" that seeded "social war" and impeded national progress.[35]

"Barbarism." Here we have powerful reinforcement, further cultural justification, for "just war" against *índios* rooted in Enlightened thought and confirmed by an all-out assault on "superstition" as the enemy of national progress. Mora tells us that Indians "in their present state and until they have undergone considerable changes, can never reach the degree of enlightenment, civilization and culture of Europeans nor maintain themselves as equals in a society formed by both."[36] Two Mexico City newspapers later confirmed that while the Indians might have had some legitimate local grievances, force was "the only recourse that civilization has against barbarism," and force must precede lawful adjudication of complaints and reform.[37] *La Libertad* warned in 1879 that once Indians lit the flame of rebellion, that whites had to use force to repress it or perish, that in such times Mexicans should seek foreign assistance to save themselves and the "cause of civilization."[38]

Even if *índios* did not threaten caste war, they impeded the nation's progress toward the modern (Western-style) world. Following the destruction of the Tomochic, Porfirio Díaz lamented the bloodshed but noted the necessity to rid the country of the enemies of progress.[39] In June 1893 *El Universal* carried photos of "characteristic Indians" who supposedly participated in the "rebellion" at Tomochic. The cutlines of that newspaper urge us to look carefully into those Indian faces, that contain not one trace of intelligence and which we are told are portraits of ignorance and backwardness. Seeing this, the newspaper assumed that the revolt at Tomochic carried no political aims or implications.[40] But of course it did, and no label could hide that fact.

Porfirians found (an unwitting?) ally in Pope León XIII, who reiterated Indian inferiority even as he sought to forestall racial conflict. In an encyclical issued in August 1892 to commemorate the 400th anniversary of the Columbus voyage, he reminded the natives of their supposed good fortune in becoming hispanized. The pope declared that a Mass of the Holy Trinity be celebrated the following 12 October (Columbus Day) to commemorate the "Discovery of America," when, as His Holiness pontificated, "thousands and thousands of mortals [meaning Indians] were delivered to human society, carried from a barbarous past to the sweet life and to civilization, and above all, to leave life to enter the eternal life."[41]

While His Holiness celebrated the arrival of the Spaniards in the New World to rescue the natives from perdition, others recognized that the Spaniards might have in some ways oppressed the natives. Still, the Indians should let bygones be bygones and recognize their new responsibilities as fellow Mexicans. At the inauguration of the famous monument to Cuauhtémoc in Mexico City in 1890, speakers reminded the crowd that while Indians might have been repressed by the Spaniards, many present Mexicans were descendants of those Spaniards. Therefore, the Indians should consider all Mexicans as brothers and should desist from waging caste war, "which is always latent, and that in this age would be disastrous."[42] It was up to the Indians to halt those ugly caste wars and to embrace all Mexicans as brothers, and in doing so help the country advance toward the ranks of the civilized. "Order and progress" was the slogan of those who drew up the blueprint for Mexico's march into modernity, and they made it clear that along the way "order" must take precedence over "progress."

FANÁTICOS

Fanático both underscored and broadened the stereotype promulgated by *índio* in the interests of the state. It concerned systems of belief and worldview, and while *índio* conveyed the idea of lethargic and benumbed thought (which in a contradictory sense still harbored thoughts of caste war), *fanático* connoted a head full of percolating emotions and ideas, which, from the viewpoint of the labelers, constituted outmoded, regressive, irrational, and even dangerous thought. Moreover, *fanático* was not ethnic-specific; it could be applied to anyone—mestizos, creoles, Indians—with no reference or inference to race or social standing. But because *fanático* referred mainly to religious notions, those who used the label to tar their enemies had to do so with considerable care, even some risk. Dominant groups certainly did not mean to discourage the "right kind" of religiosity, meaning that which adhered to the official dicta of the established church, which preached docility, even reverence, toward authority and promised that patience with pain and injustice in this life would, with heaps of penance and contrition, bring glory in the next. Such teaching helped to confirm the hierarchy, including the patron-client relationships, which characterized the structure of Mexican society and supported dominant groups in their positions of power.[43] On the other hand, *fanáticos* threatened such a status quo. They could be impatient people who looked for immediate change in the here and now.

As much as these elites wanted (and needed) official religion to serve them, they understood, perhaps better than a good many scholars today, that religion can also do quite the opposite: that it can encourage the faithful to examine their social condition, can heighten their expectations of a Golden Age and the anticipation of an immediate end of the world, and at certain historical conjunctures can fire their imagination, and inspire activities, even mass movements, which forcefully challenge the power of the state.[44] It was this kind of "radical" religious thinking that those in power sought to discredit and repress with the label *fanático*. When applied, it was meant to convey the idea that the wearers had crossed into irrationality, that such believers were not rational thinkers like modern people ought to be, that they were guided by superstitions and magic that enlightened and civilized people had long rejected as uncivilized. In sum, like *índios*, *fanáticos* were the opponents of Mexico's progress toward the modern world; they threatened to hold *US* (we Mexicans) back.[45]

Mexico's nineteenth-century state builders wove threads of Enlightenment thought into the liberalism, republicanism, and capitalism that became the ideological backdrop to nineteenth-century reformist movements. In the process dominant groups refigured religious belief etched by historical memory as the superstitious enemy of progress. Such a project did not come easily to Mexico's reformers, who wanted a secular state but valued the stabilizing effect of the institutional church on society. After much debate they worked out a compromise: Catholicism remained the country's official religion embedded in the constitution, while the state gained the right to monitor and control various activities of the church. In short, freedom of worship suffered a setback to domestic tranquility.[46]

This sort of pragmatism represented the type of arrangement that Mexican elites frequently worked out among themselves to foment political compatibility and social control. While elites (defined as those who control political, economic, and social power) may tailor an agenda to fit their perceived needs, there is no telling how others, even fellow elites, will receive and treat the recommended project. At times, it is rejected out of hand; more often, a probing process of negotiation occurs. This concept of "interchange" is at the heart of so-called labeling theory, which encourages us to study the "accusers as well as the accused."[47] Several chapters in this volume readily demonstrate how subaltern groups interpret, redefine for their own purposes, even refuse to play by the "rules of the game" as drafted and delivered by authority. The complexities of this process at every level are discussed in James Scott's *Domination and the Arts of Resistance*, which reveals the creativity, stubbornness, and often self-righteousness with which the subjects of programs promulgated by those in power are resisted. According to Scott, this resistance can be seen at all social echelons, at times overtly (tax protests or armed battles over electoral returns) but more frequently in covert and subterranean ways, which Scott locates in the "hidden agenda" of common folk and defines more explicitly in his *Weapons of the Weak*. For the researcher, surprises may be found everywhere, as the "logical" is subjected to human imagination, resourcefulness, whimsy, impulse, and self-interest. This realization was brought to my attention by the word under consideration here, *fanático*. The Tomochis were called *fanáticos*, and I wondered what that term meant at that time in the region where the movement occurred. To some, especially as reflected in the official correspondence, it clearly signified "religious fanatic," someone considered to be slightly berserk and relegated to a place on the outer fringe of acceptable society. This concept fit the official government line. But to most others, including a good many nonbelievers, skeptics, and elites (a Mexican lady from a family of notables provided this example[48]), it simply described people whose worldview openly admitted to belief in the presence of a supernatural good and evil, not to speak of the ceaseless struggle between the two, in a divine will and intervention, in the possibility of saintly intercession, and in the eventuality of the Second Coming. The widespread outpouring of deeply felt sympathy for the martyrs of Tomochic as well as the women and children who survived them on the part of the region's general citizenry suggests concurrence in such belief.[49] It indicates that for many religion continued to be an integral part of their belief system, and even if they did not become militant millenarians, they were not repulsed by the designation *fanático*. In its use of the label, the state meant to banish the practitioner to a distant, outmoded, foolish, traditional past, and damned the believer as an enemy to progress and modernity. But to many, at least in Mexico's northwest, *fanáticos* simply seems to have signified those who openly professed and practiced their faith in a world increasingly beset by state-inspired secularization.

We cannot be sure for lack of clear-cut evidence of precisely how the Tomochis wore the label *fanático*. Perhaps it was with pride, even arrogance; perhaps they ignored it. While we know little of how the "actors" themselves treated their label, we can only imagine the variety of ways in which other individuals and groups treated the term. Even some elites who sought to expose and criticize the government's repression of the movement sought to remove the label *fanáticos* from the participants. Others saw the religious fervor of the millenarians as an example of the kind of belief needed for the moral regeneration of Mexican society, which included overturning the political dictatorship at hand. So while we may have a rather clear impression of why, when, and for what purposes those people in positions of power designate labels for "deviants," we may be much less certain that others, even the audiences for whom they are intended, consider them legitimate or take them for granted. In fact, while the impact of Mexico's reform movement on religious institutions and privileges has been somewhat documented, its effect on religious belief has scarcely been recognized. When it is, we shall know more about the meaning of *fanático*, especially among the accused.

BANDIDOS

While the government at first labeled the Tomochis *índios* and *fanáticos*, it soon turned to *bandidos*, notoriously so after early February 1892, when the millenarians declined to accept official amnesty. Regimes and their adherents have for centuries tried to burnish rural troublemakers, dissidents, and rebels with the designation "bandits." It is a word with considerable elasticity, which stretches in meaning from common criminal to dedicated revolutionary. While in coded law it may obtain some specificity, in practice it has been employed by the state as needed to discredit activities deemed inimical to its interests. Says Eric Hobsbawm: "For the law, anyone belonging to a group of men who attack and rob with violence is a bandit, from those who snatch pay-rolls at an urban street corner to organized insurgents or guerrillas who happen not to be officially recognized as such."[50] Frequently the term has been employed by governments in an attempt to drain the politics from a movement against its authority; Tomochic is a case in point. Rosalie Schwartz tells us that during the long struggle for Cuban independence toward the end of the last century, "Cuban law enforcement officials and journalists blew sand across the bandit trail, lumping politically motivated lawbreakers together with the myriad robbers, petty thieves, cutpurses and assassins . . . , although government agents knew that members of some robber gangs met with [political] separatists and contributed the proceeds of their extortions and kidnapings to rebel officers [seeking independence]."[51] Spanish propagandists did the same during the Mexican wars of independence, when they, according to Brian Hamnett, "deprived them of a political existence and reduced them to the level of common criminals."[52] Scholars studying these events have not, in the main, taken the bait offered by the official documentation. Hence, in bandit studies we now have "social bandits," "bandit-patriots," and "bandit-guerrillas," a few of the new scholarly fashioned labels that purport to explain the motivations of these individuals and groups and to better locate them in the context of their place and time.[53]

Scholars such as Ranajit Guha, who studied peasant rebelliousness in colonial India during the nineteenth-century, would have us stand official reports of these happenings on their heads. So when a "document speaks of badmashes as participants in rural disturbances, this does not mean... any ordinary collection of rascals but peasants involved in a militant agrarian struggle." Or "contagion" as expressed by the state really means "the enthusiasm and solidarity generated by an uprising among various rural groups within a region" and "lawlessness" becomes "the defiance by the people of what they had come to regard as bad laws."[54]

As novel and useful as Guha's approach to test the official word may be, his broadly painted generalities threaten to mask reality. For instance, he encourages us to interpret references in the official correspondence to *dacoit* villages, meaning outlaw villages, as *the entire population of a village* [my emphasis] united in resistance to the armed forces of the state."[55] So in the official representations of the Tomochis as *bandidos*, or in the correspondence that finds the "pueblo of Tomochic" in the grip of superstition or even in rebellion, we could presume by Guha's reasoning that the entire pueblo, as a collective, had risen against the state. At least in the case of Tomochic, however, this was not the case; nearly half of the village declined to follow Cruz Chávez into his millenarian vision. In fact, the entire motivation for the movement and its explanation may more properly be found in the fissures within community life that existed well before any direct confrontation with the state. In short, the key to understanding crucial aspects of peasant consciousness in Tomochic lies within those fissures, and it is important that we *not* see the village as homogeneous. Indeed, historians (Steve Stern comes to mind), reinforced by the anthropological work of colleagues like María Teresa Koreck, Jane-Dale Lloyd, and Ana María Alonso, have begun to focus on village splits as seminal in understanding peasant rebellion and consciousness.[56] In my own work on rebellion in western Chihuahua over time, and even during the Mexican revolution in that region, one is struck by the village factionalism that underscores who does and does not join in insurrections against the state.

In its broad use of the label *bandido*, the state undoubtedly ran into similar problems of generalization. Simply put, a bandit to one person may well be a hero to another. There is plenty of evidence in bandit studies to support Hobsbawm's assertion that peasant outlaws labeled criminals by the state were regarded "by their people as heroes, as champions, avengers, fighters for justice and perhaps even leaders of liberation."[57] In Mexico during the 1880s, segments of elite culture as well as lower-class people apparently reveled in the antics of the bandit Chucho el Roto, who among other of his shenanigans, kidnaped priests and sued the bishops for ransom. A Mexico City newspaper, *El Correo de Lunes*, called Chucho a "civilized bandit," and in recognition of his daring independence and keen wit even nominated him to the national congress. When authorities captured him, another newspaper, *El Monitor republicano*, came to his defense and criticized the government for trying to saddle the brigand with unsolved crimes.[58] Another infamous Mexican bandit, Heraclio Bernal, the Lightning Bolt of Sinaloa, enjoyed widespread appreciation among all social classes in his home state.[59] Bandits throughout the world have been celebrated in stories, poems, and songs as well as folk traditions, admittedly a good many of them after they were safely dead.

Of course, bandits are not appreciated everywhere even by common rural people. In his investigation of criminality around Cuzco in the Peruvian Andes toward the end of the eighteenth century, Ward Stavig found that the natives disdained bandits, because the concept of banditry itself was negatively received in the group's culture. So that when bandits, social or otherwise, approached them, they were rejected, turned over to the Spanish authorities, or worse.[60] Certainly the case of Pancho Villa is a familiar case in point. In Villa we have a "bandit," both then and now, passionately revered by some and just as fervently detested by others. The truth is that "bandit" is capable of multiple interpretations even in specific situations. Take the example rendered by Hyam Mccoby in his book *The Mythmaker*. Mccoby argues that the two *lestai*, or supposed bandits who died with Jesus, were actually fellow rebels in his political movement. *Lestai*, according to Mccoby, frequently meant "rebels." So depending on one's translation and interpretation of the word *lestai*, it appears that either two rebels died along with their political leader or two bandits were crucified along with a religious zealot.[61] With the word evoking such random and powerful meanings and emotions, it is surprising that governments so regularly used and continue to employ it for their purposes.

The involvement of bandits in the movement at Tomochic further illuminates varied potential of the label in use, and at the same time its amorphous quality for scholarly analysis. A gang of some dozen bandits headed by one Pedro Chaparro had roamed the Tomochic region for some time before the millenarian movement erupted. The group was centered in the small village of Sisoguichic, south of Tomochic and somewhat off the beaten path to the mines of the Sierra. Chaparro's gang, at times only five or so and on other occasions perhaps twenty strong, sporadically raided ranchos along the southwestern fringe of the Papigochic and occasionally threatened traffic flowing to and from the mines. Origins of the group seem to lie in conflict among the leading families of Sisoguichic, where Chaparro enjoyed the support of some residents and the damnation of others. Apparently his clan had lost municipal power to another group, so he and his gang rode through town periodically, shooting up the place and reminding folks that he was still around, if not boss.[62]

In the summer of 1892, during that long spell between military actions against the millenarians at Tomochic, Chaparro offered his services and those of his band to Cruz Chávez. There is no evidence that he did so because of religious conviction; he does not seem to have participated in any of the utopian schemes of the faithful. He apparently only wanted to be part of the action, that is, to help defend Tomochic against the inevitable assault by the military. And how did the leadership of the millenarians receive this brigand? Certainly it welcomed his manpower and guns (Chaparro arrived with seven to ten followers), and Chávez specifically noted the man's "objectionable acts toward society," meaning his banditry, but under the circumstances proved willing to overlook them. Chávez only stipulated absolutely no stealing, even if the defenders were dying of hunger, and that when the going got tough, when the shooting began, Chaparro and his men agreed to stand firm; Chávez obligated them to defend the cause to death. "Only God can help us, and we will defend ourselves to the end," he said. "We do not expect to win, but to lose and to die." With those words, the leader of the movement gave Chaparro and his companions three days to decide their fate. The bandits decided to join up, pledging their loyalty to the cause.[63] They soon kidnaped a ranchero and held him for ransom, $500 pesos (about U.S. $400), which seems to have been paid.[64] Presumedly the money went to shore up the defense, although the written record is mute on this point, and there is no indication that the Tomochis purchased armaments and other supplies for their impending struggle. When in October the army closed its clamps on the pueblo, Chaparro with seventeen men (not all members of his band) resisted from a strategically located cave above the village to which they had been assigned by Chávez. But under pressure in the final days of the assault, survivors of the military attack on the cave reneged on their vow to the millenarians and fled for the safety of the surrounding forests. Only two seemed to have escaped, Chaparro and another. They pop up as hunted bandits in the historical record from time to time over the next year; the military captured some of the gang in late 1983, executed them, and hanged their bodies for public viewing in Chihuahua City.[65] About this time Chaparro himself disappears from the official report.

The detail about Chaparro illustrates the vagaries of banditry with which the populace and authorities—not to mention historians—have to struggle. Some evidently saw Chaparro as a kind of social bandit, others as an outright criminal, some a hero, others a rank opportunist who deserted his compatriots. One wonders just what was his interest in joining the ill-fated movement at Tomochic. Nonetheless, while we have no idea of how Chaparro wore or used the label "bandit," we have a good understanding of how the Tomochitecos considered the label when applied to themselves. It insulted them and made their blood boil, and it may well have nourished their millenarian response to their vision of a troubled world.

In January 1890, some ten months before the initial confrontation at Tomochic, sixteen brigands attacked a mule train carrying a substantial payroll of $45,000 pesos (U.S. $36,000) at a point called Puerto de las Manzanillas, along the route that connected the Papigochic to major mining centers and passed right through Tomochic. The mountain pass of Puerto de las Manzanillas lay only several miles north of Tomochic itself, and word got out that the bandits, who were driven off by the security guards that accompanied the shipment, had been identified as Tomochis. In fact, a local cacique, well paid to provide security for such transportation, directly accused the Tomochis of complicity, and as a result muleteers began to circumvent the village with their wares. Within two months regional security forces had identified, rooted out, and dispatched the genuine robbers with the Ley Fuga (Mexico's version of lynch law); the culprits had come from one of the villages in the Papigochic and as far as we know had no connection with any Tomochitecos.[66]

The reason why the cacique falsely (mistakenly or deliberately) linked the Tomochis to the assault on the mule train lies in a fuller discussion of those circumstances that propelled the millennial movement itself. Suffice it to say that the faithful not only considered the label a grievous mistake but a serious effrontery to their honor—and these people seemed to wear their honor on their sleeves. How dare anyone call them bandits? So ruffled were they by the accusation that they approached the authorities (apparently the presidente of the pueblo, but possibly even higher ups), and not only denied complicity in the attack but offered themselves as escorts for future mule trains carrying silver bullion and mining supplies and guaranteed their arrival at the appointed destination.[67] In other words, they would welcome (in a sense, they demanded) the opportunity to set the public record straight about the kinds of people that they were.

If the Tomochis responded with such vehemence to the charge of "bandit" even before their millenarian activities captured official attention, we can only surmise how they felt about the same label when unremittingly applied by the government, both state and federal, shortly thereafter and over an expanse of several months during the movement itself. Labeling theorists such as Howard Becker insist that labels do not necessarily cause what may be termed deviant behavior, but find that labels, once applied, can in important ways influence the thinking and behavior of the accused.[68] Concerning the instance at hand, we know that millenarian movements do not often come upon stage in full bloom; they pass through a building process during which the participants are increasingly bound to the cause; Tomochic provides a good example of this process. Official insistence that it was dealing with *bandidos* could have contributed to the consolidation of the movement at Tomochic. It may have helped to convince the participants, especially those who lacked the religious fervor and commitment of the Cruz Chávezes among them, that the government really was the Anti-Christ and needed to be confronted. Faced by the possibility that its labeling may backfire, plus the overall knowledge that the term "banditry" is endlessly malleable and can be turned into a weapon by one's enemy and rally support for the opposition, why is the state, in this case the government of Porfirio Díaz in the 1890s, so quick to use it? The answer to that question lies in the nature of the official project under way and the audience for whom the message is intended.

From its inception in the 1850s, Mexico's reform movement had been predicated upon the establishment of domestic tranquility—the famous "Orden y Progreso." Lawmakers debating the structure of the enterprise and the statutes that would hold it in place, compromised individual freedoms in the name of public peace. The organization of a national police force, the famous *Rurales*, was one result of this strategy. Its job was to rid the country of bandits, or better said, the image of a bandit-infested country which Mexico, with reason, held. Bandits, especially since independence, had played an important part in the country's political processes. During the period of intense regionalism, they had helped caudillos and caciques to defend their terrain. Later at mid-century when the country plunged into civil war, hired bandit gangs served contending parties. Some who sided with the winners became rural policemen, which allowed them to ride the fine line between law-enforcer and law-breaker. Travel accounts of the period made it clear that visitors to Mexico expected to be robbed.[69]

Porfirian modernizers meant to change all that. Foreign investment and political centralization, not to mention their personal social status among other things, depended on their success. Bandits became the enemies of progress; they impeded the country's march toward modernity. The sponsors of this program and their foreign supporters endorsed the all-out campaign against bandits. What the government could not in fact accomplish toward these ends, they shrouded in breast-beating propaganda, so that it *appeared*, especially to those who wanted to believe it, that Mexico was ridding itself of its infamous bandits. The dictator enjoyed virtual carte blanche (Díaz seems to have considered it a mandate from his powerful supporters) to extirpate bandits from the country, and so it became a standard tactic to label dissidents, such as those at Tomochic, as *bandidos* and thereby legitimize their removal. The label deliberately marginalized those who protested the Porfirian blueprint for progress; it pushed them from the symbolic boundaries of Porifiran society. Indeed, the word "bandit" stems from the Latin, meaning "banish."[70] Once excluded, they could be eliminated.

The Mexican constitution gave the congress the right to suspend in moments of perceived crisis specific civil rights normally guaranteed to individuals accused of certain crimes, such as kidnaping, tampering with railroads, or banditry. The official suspension denied citizens accused of those crimes their rights to trials and other legal procedures and placed their fates in the hands of the police forces, including the military, which arrested them. For one thing, it allowed for those caught in the act of a criminal activity to be shot on the spot.[71] The historical account is replete with abuses of this system, so much so that at times genuine brigands tried to work their way around it by posing as revolutionaries. During the great civil wars of the mid-nineteenth century Mexican bandits who sold their services to the contending sides, sometimes to both at the same time, carried political proclamations of the respective contenders, hoping that, if captured, they could flash the appropriate decree at their captors, plead political involvement, and escape summary execution as common criminals.[72] This is one reason why the government was so anxious to deprive the Tomochitecos of any political aims and their movement of political implications, but of course millennial activities are replete with political implications (many overtly so), and no label will hide that reality from anyone who cares to recognize it.

CONCLUSION

But something more seems to be at work here. Mexico's dominant groups were at the time of the outbreak of the disturbances surrounding "Santa Teresa" and Tomochic in the midst of nation building, in the process of "imagining" one of those communities about which Benedict Anderson writes.[73] There was little national consensus in Mexico, and even less nationalism, and so the nation had to be constructed through bureaucracy, law, education, language, and the creation of traditions, ceremonies, and rites, some of them actually celebrating Mexico's Indian heritage, and by the utilization of other mechanisms that serve such purposes.[74] Porfirian elites strove to invent a "community" of Mexicans that did not exist, and the garish image-enhancement that shrouded institutions such as the Rurales as well as the labeling, marginalization, and elimination of groups that declined the invitation to the banquet were all part of this grand design. While they may have employed such labels as *índio*, *fanático*, and *bandido* in an attempt to awe subordinate groups into compliance, to show them who is boss, the power-brokers seemed more interested in using such labels as symbols to indoctrinate the great mass of Mexicans in what they were expected to and ought to believe.

Lacking political legitimacy, Porfirians depended upon their outline for progress, their design of modernity and promise of progress to justify their rule, and labeling represented one means toward that end; it sought to define the approved membership of this planned community still very much in the making. Among the excluded were ethnic Indians (*índios*), such as the Mayo and Yaquis, who resisted in defense of their own culture; spiritually directed individuals and groups (*fanáticos*), including the Tomochis, who believed in the ultimate justice of God; and the dissidents and dissatisfied (*bandidos*), who either disputed the trajectory and shape of the new order or, more likely, utilized aggressive and "unauthorized" approaches to take advantage of them for personal gain. Among all of the outsiders, the "Santa Teresas" were the most dangerous to the schemes of the powerful, for not only did they symbolize the ability of religion to mobilize masses, but, more important, because their message directly challenged the morality, and therefore the legitimacy, of the *kind* of society envisioned for the new social configuration called "nation" being willed into existence by elites.

Labeling, it seems, speaks to political weakness; it signals the limits of government. All governments routinely use the technique to some degree, because it is one of the vast array of weapons in the arsenal of governing groups. The deliberate creation of bias is both its ally and its product. But the arrogant, reflexive manner in which the Porfirians utilized *índio*, *fanático*, and *bandido*, suggests the frailty of the structure on which the government stood. Indeed, personal dictatorships of the sort created by Porfirio Díaz are, despite their longevity, among the least stable of their genre (as Porfirians discovered when the revolution of 1910 erupted), and by the time of the events under study here it had already lost much of its claimed (largely invented?) legitimacy. Florencia Mallon tells us that the democratic aspirations of a good many common Mexicans unleashed by the promise of the reform had begun to sour by 1890 or so,[75] and opponents had started to hammer away at Porfirian arbitrariness in the conduct of its affairs as well as its disdainful abrogation of constitutional provisions that provided for free and fair elections and no reelections. At the same time, the program of secularization sponsored by the same reform enterprise seems to have encouraged religious believers unwilling to abandon time-tested practices, such as the Tomochis, to examine and critique the role of the official church in their lives. Teresa railed the Mother Church all the way to the pope. Protest was in the air, and some revolutionaries, like the intellectual Norteño Catarino Garza, were in the field.[76]

The Porfirians hoped that labeling would help to provide the national social cohesion and political cohesiveness that the geographical entity labeled "Mexico" so sorely lacked, and perhaps to some extent it did. Numbers of foreign investors and travelers professed to hold a new and positive view of the place. But labels cannot cover up the contradictions and injustices in a social system so deliberately designed to favor so few. Such labeling encourages the accused to develop some labels of their own, ones that may well expose the accusers to stern public scrutiny and serious debate, even confrontation.

NOTES

Sincere thanks to my friends and colleagues, Rosalie Schwartz and Eric Van Young, for their critique of an earlier draft of this essay.

1. Howard S. Becker, "Labelling Theory Reconsidered," in *Deviance and Social Control*, ed. Paul Rock and Mary McIntosh (London, 1974), 62.

2. James C. Scott, *Domination and the Arts of Resistance* (New Haven, 1990), 55.

3. The major published works on Teresa Urrea include William Curry Holden,

Teresita (Owings Mills, 1978); Mario Gil, "Teresa Urrea, La Santa de Cabora," *Historia mexicana* (Apr.–June 1957): 627–44; and Paul Vanderwood, "Teresa de Urrea: Mexico's Joan of Arc," in *The Human Condition in 19th Century Latin America*, ed. Judith Ewell and William Beezley (Philadelphia, 1989), 215–32. Brianda Domecq de Rodriguez, a Mexican historian and novelist, recently wrote a fascinating historical novel on Teresa, *La Insolita historia de la Santa de Cabora* (Editorial Planeta Mexicana, 1990). Also see Domecq's "Teresa Urrea: La Santa de Cabora," *Temas sonorenses: a través de los simposios de historia* (Hermosillo, 1984), 139–69. The folk saint is also prominently referred to in the books on Tomochic listed in n. 9. Main archival resources are the William B. Holden Papers, Southwest Collection, Texas Tech University, Lubbock, Texas; U.S. National Archives, Military Reference Branch, Adjutant General's Office, Record Group 94 (AGO); Mexico, Archivo de Relaciones Exteriores (ARE); Hermosillo, Sonora, Archivo del Estado de Sonora (AES); and Mexico, Universidad Iberoamericana, Archivo Porfirio Díaz (APD). Newspapers of the period, both Mexican and U.S., are also valuable. Material on Teresa Urrea in this chapter was drawn from these resources. Specific citations, as appropriate, appear in the text.

4. The letter itself, as printed in an undated and unidentified newspaper article (probably an El Paso, Texas, newspaper) may be found in AGO, Record Group 94, No. 34574, Brig. Gen. Wheaton to adjutant general, 14 Mar. 1896.

5. For examples of reports in a Mexico City newspaper, see *El Diario del hogar*, 9 Apr. and 23 Oct., 1890, and 18 Feb. 1892. For U.S. newspapers, see *El Tiempo* (Las Cruces, N.M.), 17 Apr. 1890; and *Arizona* (Tucson) *Daily Star*, 28 June 1892.

6. *El Diario del hogar*, 9 Apr. 1890.

7. *El Tiempo*, 17 Apr. 1890.

8. The physical description of Tomochic is based upon the author's multiple visits to the site, at specific times in the company of Rubén Osorio, an anesthesiologist from Chihuahua City who has written several fine historical pieces on the region; Victor Mendoza, a survey engineer also from Chihuahua, who has written important works on the Apaches and other aspects of Chihuahuan history; and Robert Schmidt, a physical geographer at the University of Texas, El Paso, who is an authority on arid regions and in particular the state of Chihuahua. I thank these three scholars for teaching me about Chihuahua and its environment.

9. The specific census is in the Archivo Municipal de Ciudad Guerrero (Chihuahua), Presidencia, Legajo 22, Expediente 235 (hereafter cited as ACG). It is difficult to be precise on the number of Tarahumaras residing in the pueblo proper, because any number of them included in the census actually resided on rancherías near, but outside, the village. The basic material on Tomochic in this chapter is taken from three books on the topic: José Carlos Chávez, *Peleando en Tomochi* (Chihuahua, 1955); Francisco R. Almada, *La Rebelión de Tomochic* (Chihuahua, 1938); and Plácido Chávez Calderón, *La Defensa de Tomochi* (México, 1964); as well as the author's article, " 'None but the Justice of God': Tomochic, 1891–1892," in *Rebellions in Mexico*, ed. Jaime Rodríguez O., (in press); and "Millenarian Movements a Century Apart: Mexico 1890—Uganda, 1990," paper presented at the annual conference of the American Historical Society, San Francisco, 1989. Major archival resources consulted include the Archivo Municipal de Ciudad Guerrero (ACG), as well as the Porfirio Díaz archive. Newspapers of the period were also consulted. Specific citations, when appropriate, are noted in the text.

10. These census reports are located in various legajos and expedientes in the Presidencia section of the municipal archive in Ciudad Guerrero, Chihuahua. For example, see Legajo 42, Expediente 380, for the 1900 census.

11. For examples, see ACG, Presidencia, Comunicaciones con inferiores, Leg. 8, Exp. 94, Lucio Mendoza, presidente seccional, Tomochic, to jefe político, 12 Nov. 1863; and Leg. 8, Exp. 93, Jesús María Ortiz, juzgado civil, to jefe político, 12 Feb. 1881.

12. For Chopeque, see Ahumada, *Rebelión en Tomochic*, 37–38 and 47; *El Diario del hogar*, 10 Feb. 1892; APD, Leg. 50, Caja 12, Nos. 006722–006726. The notion that the Tomochitecos were seeking a symbol that pointed toward redemption and salvation is embedded in the way in which Norteños (the specific evidence in this case pertains to inhabitants of the Lower Rio Grande Valley) celebrated their pastoral Christmas pageant. In their songs the shepherds say they are headed for Bethlehem "to see a great miracle," where "the Divine Redeemer is born." And most important, this Messiah "will set them at liberty." Unfortunately, the ethnographic report does not tell us "liberty" from what? See John G. Bourke, "The Miracle Play of the Rio Grande," *Journal of American Folk-Lore* 6 (Apr.–June 1893): 89–95. For ways in which such pageantry spurred millenarian movements that fed into the Filipino independence movement, see Reynaldo Clemeña Ileto, *Payson and Revolution: Popular Movements in the Philippines, 1840–1910* (Manila, 1979).

13. *El Monitor republicano*, 2 Nov. 1892.

14. This incident is related in Chávez, *Peleando*, 56–57. The eye-witness was Reyes Domínguez, a central figure in these events.

15. Mexico, Archivo General de la Nación, Archivo Histórico de la Revolución Mexicana, Serie Manuel González Ramírez, Vol. 3, Folios 141–45. The Mexican constitution of 1857 made Catholicism the official religion of the country and specifically did not guarantee freedom of worship. My gratitude to Osorio for bringing this important document to my attention.

16. The concept of "hidden transcript" is taken from James Scott, *Domination and the Arts of Resistance*.

17. ACG, Presidencia, Comunicaciones de inferiores, enero 1892, B. Ledesma, comisario de Tomochic, to jefe político, 25 Jan. 1892.

18. The battle sequences are detailed in the printed works of Chávez, Almada, and Chávez Calderón. See n. 9.

19. AGN, Archivo Histórico de la Revolución, Serie Manuel González Ramírez, Vol. 3, Folios 141–45. For an excellent discussion of concerns for scholars in researching and interpreting the official record, see Gilbert M. Joseph, "On the Trail of Latin American Bandits: A Reexamination of Peasant Resistance," *Latin American Research Review* 25 (Summer 1990), esp. pp. 15, 21, 24–25, and 41 n. 87, and 42 n. 90. For a book that assiduously examines and is a model for use of official documents in relation to a millenarian movement, see Karen E. Fields, *Revival and Rebellion in Colonial Central Africa* (Princeton, 1985).

20. *El Paso Herald*, 11 Sept. 1896; and Holden, *Teresita*, 149–50.

21. The author conducted research on the Lakwena movement in East Africa in 1989. The reference here is to Issac Newton Ojok. See two Nairobi newspapers: *The Kenya Times*, 27 Oct. 1987, and *The Nation*, 1 Nov. 1987. In the case of Mexico, no federal soldiers, save possibly one, seems to have defected either to the cause of Teresa or that of the Tomochitecos. Cruz Chávez attempted to convince

the enemy soldiers he held prisoner to join his movement but the federals declined. Of course, to do so would have been tantamount to suicide. Governments may also have political or economic reasons for not immediately squelching a mass movement headed by a folk saint. For example, we have the case of Niño Fidencio in the state of Nuevo Leon in the late 1920s. Fidencio's preaching made authorities uneasy, but they declined to intervene—not because they feared to attack profoundly held beliefs, but because business interests near the site of the religious activities would suffer a serious loss of patronage and because a government-run railroad earned substantial profits carrying pilgrims to Fidencio. See Barbara June Macklin and N. Ross Crumrine, "Three North Mexican Folk Saint Movements," *Comparative Studies in Society and History* 15 (Jan. 1973): 103.

22. Francisco P. Troncoso, *Las Guerras con las tribus Yaqui y Mayo* (México, 1977), 181–83, 196–99.

23. *Arizona* (Phoenix) *Gazette*, 10 Feb. 1901; *Arizona Daily Star*, 4 and 9 June and 6 July 1892; Holden, *Teresita*, 141–48; APD, Leg. 17, Caja 24, No. 011526, Gov. Rafael Izábal to Porfirio Díaz, 25 June 1892; Mexico, Archivo de Relaciones Exteriores, María Teresa Urrea, Exp. III, Nos. 513–890-Z and 11–19–11, 9–14.

24. A few examples among many include APD, Leg. 50, Caja 12, Nos. 006607–34, [?] Almada to Porfirio Díaz, 9 Dec. 1891; Telegramas, Leg. 50, Caja 11, 006595–600, 6 Dec. 1891; Leg. 50, Caja 12, 006673–75, Lauro Carrillo, governor, to Porfirio Díaz, 10 Dec. 1891; Leg. 16, Caja 34, 016578, Miguel Ahumada to Porfirio Díaz, 10 Dec. 1891; and J. R. Ramos et al., *El Indio en la prensa nacional mexicana: catálogo de noticias*, 3 vols. (Mexico, 1987), 3: 196, 204.

25. Osorio, who participated in hundreds of deliveries during his long career as an anesthesiologist at hospitals in Chihuahua, related this practice to me.

26. Ramos, *El Indio*, 180.

27. Victoria Reifler Bricker, *The Indian Christ, the Indian King: The Historical Substrate of Maya Myth and Miracle* (Austin, 1981), 6.

28. Ramos, *El Indio*, 2:160.

29. Bricker, *Indian Christ*, 177.

30. The classic study of the ghost dance is James Mooney's account in the *Fourteenth Annual Report of the Bureau of Ethnology . . . 1892–93* (Washington, D.C., 1896), reprinted with a fine introduction by Bernard L. Fontana by Rio Grande Press, Glorieta, N.M., 1973. A splendid, but not generally known, account of these same events is David Humphreys Miller, *Ghost Dance* (Lincoln, 1959).

31. Charles A. Hale, *Mexican Liberalism in the Age of Mora, 1821–1853* (New Haven, 1968), 239–40.

32. The themes expressed by Mora carried on into the Porfiriato. See Martin S. Stabb, "Indigenism and Racism in Mexican Thought: 1857–1911," *Journal of Inter-American Studies* 1 (1955): 418. Benedict Anderson posits that upper-class fear of political mobilization by lower groups actually spurred the independence movement in places like Mexico, Venezuela, and Peru. See his *Imagined Communities: Reflections on the Origins and Spread of Nationalism* (London, 1983), 51. Nor did Anderson find Mora's attitudes toward Indians peculiar to Mexico. He quotes Pedro Fermín de Vargas, an early nineteenth-century Colombian liberal, to this effect: "To expand our agriculture it would be necessary to hispanize our Indians. This idleness, stupidity, and indifference toward normal human endeavors causes one to think that they come from a degenerate race which deteriorates in proportion to the

distance from its origin.... It would be very desirable that the Indians be extinguished, by miscegenation with the whites" (Anderson, *Imagined Communities*, 21).

33. Hale, *Mora*, 223.

34. Quoted in Richard N. Sinkin, *The Mexican Reform, 1855–1876: A Study in Liberal Nation-Building* (Austin, 1979), 130.

35. Charles A. Hale, *The Transformation of Liberalism in Late Nineteenth Century Mexico* (Princeton, 1989), 252.

36. Hale, *Mora*, 223. For the manner in which dominant Liberals in the state of Oaxaca (including the future president, Benito Juárez), considered the "Indian problem," see Brian Hamnett, "Benito Juárez, Early Liberalism, and the Regional Politics of Oaxaca, 1828–1853," *Bulletin of Latin American Research* 10 (1991): 14–15. While Mexico's intellectual community had its share of racists, it was not bereft of Indianists who sought to regenerate (as opposed to incorporate or eliminate) the natives through education and even private landholdings. See T. G. Powell, "Mexican Intellectuals and the Indian Question, 1876–1911," *Hispanic American Historical Review* 38 (Feb. 1968): 19–36.

37. Hale, *Transformation*, 224.

38. Stabb, "Indigenism," 418.

39. APD, Leg. 17, Caja 35, No. 0177418, Porfirio Díaz to General Rosendo Márquez, [?] Nov. 1892.

40. Ramos, *El Indio*, 3:209. Criminologists of the period studied photographs of those arrested for supposed physical criminal characteristics. For typical photos, see Robert M. Levine, *Images of History: Nineteenth and Early Twentieth Century Latin American Photographs* (Durham; 1989), 29–31. While the Tomochic movement had no stated political agenda, the apparent intention of the faithful to celebrate their religion (to practice their lives) as they saw fit, in effect—to obey no one but "Santa Teresa"—is certainly a political act, and a revolutionary one at that. Whether *they* saw it as such is another question.

41. Ramos, *El Indio*, 2:366.

42. Ramos, *El Indio*, 2:282.

43. For a succinct statement on the manner in which officially sanctioned religious belief can reinforce the subordinance of ordinary people, see Patricia R. Pessar, "Masking the Politics of Religion: The Case of Brazilian Millenarianism," *Journal of Latin American Lore* 7 (Winter 1981): 256–60.

44. The point is forcefully argued by James C. Scott in *Weapons of the Weak: The Everyday Forms of Peasant Resistance* (New Haven; 1985), esp. 332–35.

45. Robert M. Levine, who writes on the famous Brazilian uprising at Canudos in the mid–1890s, notes that the Brazilian press and officials also referred to members of that religious movement as *fanáticos*, and also as *coboclos*, in reference to their dark skin. Those who actually participated in the fighting were labeled *juguncos*, meaning "hayseed," "ruffian," or "thug/" Captured children were called *jraguncinhos*, or little *jaguncos*. According to Levine, "all this fit the intention of coastal elites to portray the faithful as primitive crazies who rejected modernity and the benefits of Republican civilization" (personal letter, Levine to Vanderwood, 20 July 1991).

46. Sinkin, *Mexican Reform*, chap. 7.

47. Becker, "Labelling Theory," 61. For a discussion of this thesis set in a broader context, see Becker's *Outsiders: Studies in the Sociology of Deviance* (New York, 1963). The theory is critiqued in concert with other sociological explanations of

antisocial behavior in George B. Vold and Thomas J. Bernard, *Theoretical Criminology*, 3d ed. (New York, 1986). For interesting critical comments on labeling in the context of the Thailand peasantry during the 1970s, see Andrew Turton, "Patrolling the Middle-Ground: Methodological Perspectives on 'Everyday Peasant Resistance,'" *Journal of Peasant Studies* 13 (Jan. 1986), esp. 42–43. The major work from which questions of labeling draw much of their energy is Michel Foucault's *Discipline and Punishment: The Birth of the Prison* (New York, 1979), in which Foucault demonstrates how the modern state has marginalized individuals with scientific discourse.

48. My initial interest in the word *fanático* stems from an interview I had with Sra. Guadalupe Machado at her home in Chihuahua City in 1983. Sra. Machado was born and reared in Moris in the Sierra around the turn of the century and recalled conversations with her parents and relatives about daily life in the region during the last decades of the nineteenth century.

49. For examples, see ACG, Leg. 1892, Comunicaciones con inferiores, J. González, presidente seccional, Rancho Colorado, to jefe político, 12 Nov. 1892; Pascual Escarcega, president municipal de Guadalupe, to jefe político, 12 Nov. 1892; Comunicaciones con superiores, gobernador to jefe político, 14 Nov. 1892.

50. Eric Hobsbawm, *Bandits*, rev. ed. (New York, 1981), 17.

51. Rosalie Schwartz, *Lawless Liberators: Political Banditry and Cuban Independence* (Durham, 1989), 3.

52. Brian R. Hamnett, *Roots of Insurgency: Mexican Regions, 1750–1824* (Cambridge, 1986), 59.

53. For a state-of-the-art analysis on scholarly bandit studies over the past decade or so, see Gilbert Joseph's "On the Trail of Latin American Bandits." The erudite Carlo Ginzburg further muddies the water on notions of banditry in his *Ecstasies: Deciphering the Witches' Sabbath* (New York, 1991), where he links banditry to ancient Roman mythology (p. 236). Robert Bartlett critiques this thesis in the *New York Review of Books*, 13 June 1991, 37–38.

54. Ranajit Guha, *Elementary Aspects of Peasant Insurgency in Colonial India* (Delhi, 1983), 16–17.

55. Ibid. 16. Guha notes in other portions of his book that peasant resistance is not monolithic.

56. Steve Stern, ed., *Resistance, Rebellion, and Consciousness in the Andean Peasant World, 18th to 20th Centuries* (Madison, 1987); María Teresa Koreck, "Space and Revolution in Northwestern Chihuahua," in *Rural Revolt in Mexico and U.S. Intervention*, ed. Daniel Nugent (San Diego, 1988), 127–48; Jane-Dale Lloyd, "Rancheros and Rebellion: The Case of Northwestern Chihuahua, 1905–1909," in *Rural Revolt*, 87–111; and Ana María Alonso, "U.S. Military Intervention, Revolutionary Mobilization, and Popular Ideology in the Chihuahuan Sierra, 1916–1917," in *Rural Revolt*, 199–228. Further caution along these same lines comes to us from three scholars—Frans Schreyer, Sally Humphreys, and John Fox—who examined individual variations in a recent peasant land-grab in the state of Hidalgo, Mexico. They note that researchers have tended to view "the political behavior of peasants as members of a single economic class, who may or may not rebel depending on specific historical circumstances." Then they ask: "Why . . . do some peasants from the same region and even the same village (and who also belong to the same generation and speak the same language), take part in violent protests or other forms

of radical political behavior, while others remain passive or even oppose such militant actions?" While the Mexican press reported the land invasions "as a struggle involving Indian peasants, united in a common effort," the authors emphasize that "Not all Indian peasants took part in this struggle; there were also severe conflicts *within communities* [my emphasis] where the majority of people not only spoke Nahuatl (Aztec) language but participated in traditional religious ceremonies thought to provide communal cohesion." See Frans Schryer, Sally Humphries, and John Fox, "Variations in Peasant Militancy: Land Invasions and the Civil-Religious Hierarchy in Tlalchiyahualica, Mexico," *Revista europea de estudios latino americanos y del caribe/European Review of Latin American and Caribbean Studies* (Dec. 1989): 21.

The warning about presumptions concerning collectivity in social movements is very forcefully argued by Suzanne Desan in her critique of the work of E. P. Thompson and Natalie Davis. While properly acknowledging our tremendous debt to the stimulating works of these pioneering giants, Desan urges more nuanced studies that recognize diversity in crowd activism. She applauds the ways in which Thompson and Davis have taught us how notions of legitimacy and justice can inform rebellious popular behavior, but she also reminds us that "Various members of the community have different attitudes toward symbolic systems as part of a struggle for control." See Suzanne Desan, "Crowds, Community, and Ritual in the Work of E. P. Thompson and Natalie Davis," in *The New Cultural History,* ed. Lynn Hunt (Berkeley, 1989), 71.

57. Hobsbawm, *Bandits*, 17.

58. Paul J. Vanderwood, *Disorder and Progress: Bandits, Police and Mexican Development* (Lincoln, 1981), 95–98.

59. Vanderwood, *Disorder and Progress*, 98–100. For Heraclio Bernal, see Nicole Giron, *Heraclio Bernal: Bandolero, cacique o precursor de la Revolución?* (México, 1976).

60. Ward A. Stavig, "Ladrones, cuatreros y salteadores: Indios criminales en Cusco rural a fines de la colonia," in *Bandoleros, abiegos y montoneros: Criminalidad y violencia en el Perú, siglos XVIII–XX*, ed. Carlos Aguirre and Charles Walker (Lima, 1990), 71–103.

61. Hyam Mccoby, *The Mythmaker: Paul and the Invention of Christianity* (New York, 1986), 213 n. 1.

62. ACG, Presidencia, Leg. 27, Exp. 274, Comunicaciones con inferiores, José D. González, presidente municipal de Bocoyna, to jefe político, 30 Apr. 1892; Leg. 25, Exp. 262, Comunicaciones con superiores, gobernador to jefe político, 3 May 1892.

63. Chávez Calderón, *Defensa de Tomochi*, 33–34.

64. ACG, Presidencia, Leg. 26, Exp. 268, Comunicaciones con inferiores, Sóstenes Beltrán, presidente de Pachera to jefe político, 2, 15, and 25 Sept. 1892.

65. ACG, Presidencia, Leg. [1893], Comunicaciones con inferiores, José Dolores González, presidente de Boycona, to jefe político, 17 May and 2 Aug. 1893; APD, Leg. 52, Caja 14, Gov. Ahumada to Porfirio Díaz, 20 Oct. 1893, No. 007962; and Gen. Hernández to Porfirio Díaz, 26 Oct. 1893, Nos. 008614–008616.

66. Noel Irrab, "Efemérides chihuahuenses," *Boletin de la Sociedad Chihuahuense de Estudios Históricos* 2 (June 1939): 37; Francisco Almada, *Tomochic*, 30–32; ACG, Presidencia, Leg. [1891], telegramas oficiales, Pimentel to jefe político, 25 Jan. 1891; Ramón Ochoa, Pinos Altos, to jefe político, 24 Feb. 1891; Gov. Lauro

Carrillo to jefe político, 9 Mar. 1891; Leg. 23, Exp. 241, Copia de comunicaciones con inferiores, 27 June 1890 to 19 Sept. 1891, 28 Jan. 1891; Leg. 23, Exp. 243, Comunicaciones con superiores, Governor to jefe político, 6 and 21 Feb. 1891.

67. AGN, Archivo Histórico de la Revolución Mexicana, Serie Manuel González Ramírez, Vol. 3, Folios 141–45.

68. Becker, "Labelling," 42–44.

69. Vanderwood, *Disorder and Progress*, esp. chaps. 3 and 4.

70. David Moss, "Bandits and Boundaries in Sardinia," 14 *Man* (Sept. 1979): 481.

71. For example, see Vanderwood, *Disorder and Progress*, 94–95.

72. Ibid., 4.

73. Benedict Anderson, *Imagined Communities: Reflections on the Origin and Spread of Nationalism* (London, 1983).

74. For creation of traditions in service of the state, see Eric Hobsbawm and Terence Ranger, eds., *The Invention of Tradition* (Cambridge, 1983). Elites tried to sell Mexico at international expositions as a technologically advanced society and a prosperous country. As Mariano Bárcena, director of Mexico's exhibit at the New Orleans World's Fair in 1885, put it: "A country which presents a well-organized display deserves the respect of the entire world." See Gene Yeager, "Porfirian Commercial Propaganda: Mexico in World Expositions," *The Americas* 34 (Oct. 1977): 232.

75. Florencia E. Mallon, "Peasants and State Formation in Nineteenth-Century Mexico, Morelos, 1848–1858," *Political Power and Social Theory* 7 (1988): 30.

76. For a good start on Catarino Garza, see Celso Garza Guajardo, *En Busca de Catarino Garza, 1859–1895* (Monterrey, 1989).

Law Enforcement and Crime in America: The View from Germany, 1920–40

Robert G. Waite
Department of Justice, Washington, D.C.

Law enforcement professionals in Germany have long turned to their colleagues in the United States for ideas and direction. Already in 1824, Nicholaus Julius, a leading criminologist, came to the United States to examine new prison theories and to identify models that would be appropriate for Prussia. After traveling throughout the country and visiting a number of penal institutions, Julius returned to Prussia an adherent of the program of absolute solitary confinement that he had viewed at the Cherry Hill Prison in Philadelphia. His advocacy of the so-called Philadelphia system gained widespread support in Germany, and it came to be incorporated into all of the major German prisons.[1]

Later in the century a number of other criminologists and penologists made the journey to investigate New York State's Elmira Reformatory, a recently established prison whose program was a major innovation in prison management. At Elmira the prison administration made the commitment to reform or rehabilitate young, first-time offenders. Germany's leading jurist, Carl J. A. Mittermier, and a colleague, F. N. Freudenthal, visited a number of prisons, and their reports enthusiastically endorsed the Elmira system. In fact, Freudenthal, director of Prussia's Krohne Prison, established a juvenile penal institution at Wittlich in 1912, which later became known as the "German Elmira." The Krohne Prison served as a model for penal reform throughout the country.[2]

Other law enforcement professionals demonstrated interest in the criminal justice system of the United States. Franz von Liszt and his students, who led the reform of Germany's juvenile criminal codes in the early 1900s, based their efforts largely on American models. While the outbreak of war in 1914 interrupted reform efforts, they were resumed with even greater energy and determination after 1918. The Weimar Republic, established along liberal and democratic lines, looked to the United States for models of judicial and legal reform it could use in revamping the criminal codes and prison system. From 1918 to 1933 the entire criminal justice system of the United States was scrutinized by German criminologists and penologists as they modified and reformed the legal codes and prison system. The American experience served as an important model. Furthermore, this interest remained strong even after the Nazi takeover in 1933. Until the outbreak of the Second World War law enforcement professionals from Germany continued to travel to the United States, and a number of them wrote on issues dealing with law enforcement and crime in America.[3]

The perceptions of the American experiences held by German law enforcement professionals during the years 1920 to 1940 varied as the entire judicial system—patterns of arrests, police methods, court practices, crime rates, and prison operations—came under careful review. Both the liberal Weimar Republic and the oppressive Nazi regime were keenly interested in the American criminal justice system, although for very different and not always consistent reasons.

The end of the First World War in 1918 led to a renewed German interest in the American legal system. But the professional contacts and exchanges, severed by the war, continued to be disrupted by the political and economic turmoil of Central Europe and the difficulties in establishing a stable and democratic political order in Germany. Although the animosity generated by the war lingered, the United States and Germany shared a number of legal assumptions and crime problems in the 1920s, and these heightened the interest of German professionals as they searched for solutions to new problems. It was furthermore natural for law enforcement officials to look to America for models of reform. Along with its long experience in prison and legal reform, the United States had already provided Germany with specific examples. In addition, each of these two nations based its legal system on the fundamental rights of the individual, a central element of the democratic state.[4]

There were additional similarities and even some causes for concern. Each country was organized on a federal system, and each based its political system on a written constitution, with the American Constitution having served as a model for the Weimar Constitution. A few German legal thinkers viewed the federal system as a disadvantage. For example, the chief justice of the Hanseatic Supreme Court in Hamburg, W. Kiesselbach, believed that the American Constitution restricted effective law enforcement, a concern shared by a number of police officials.[5] A differing opinion came from legal scholar Herman von Mangelt, who wrote in 1934 that the German constitution "does not possess all of the recognized advantages and guarantees" offered by the American Constitution.[6]

The discussions of constitutional government were overshadowed by other issues. Serious misgivings about the reform of the criminal justice system in Germany grew out of the sharp increase in crime during the 1920s.

In part, these reservations stemmed from a heightened concern with crime, as well as from the serious disruptions of economic and social life caused by the war and revolution that resulted in a real gain in the incidence of crime and violence.[7] The public was well informed as newspapers carried daily accounts of spectacular criminal exploits, brutality, and political violence. The growing awareness of crime on the part of the general public was also tied in with the emergence of a new kind of court reporter in Berlin. Led by "Sling," as Paul Schlesinger, foremost of these reporters, was known, they offered incisive criticism of the workings of the criminal justice system and its seeming inability to combat crime. Sling and his colleagues addressed the most pressing legal and crime issues of the day, ranging from sensational murder cases to patterns of law enforcement, and they were widely read.[8]

STREET CRIME

During the 1920s German law enforcement professionals looked cautiously at American models, as did the general public, which had read about the gangsters who terrorized or controlled major American cities. A frightening popular image of these criminals was created by accounts in the tabloid press and bolstered by criminologists' analyses in professional journals. To most observers, the full range of street crime in the United States had reached alarming proportions and no decline was in sight. This presented German reformers with a dilemma. On the one hand, they recognized the need for reform of the criminal justice system and the importance of American examples. On the other hand, they clearly hoped to avoid the crime wave that had hit America's cities.[9]

Among the criminologists examining these problems, Roland Grassberger, professor at the University of Vienna, produced one of the most incisive studies of serious crime and professional criminals in the United States. Published in 1933 and widely read, his book was a solid study that used models and research methods developed by his American colleagues. In this book, Grassberger provided German readers with an overview and an explanation of professional crime. He based his study on the assumption that "a nation's crime rate is intimately tied to the way of life and the various social tensions of that country." The extent of serious crime and the difficulty in combatting it would, he maintained, reveal much about the American criminal justice system and social structure.[10]

In conducting his research, made possible by a grant from the Rockefeller Foundation, Grassberger drew on a variety of sources. Police statistics from cities identified as major centers of serious criminal activity—New York, Chicago, and Philadelphia—proved to be valuable indicators of the crime problem, and were used heavily by Grassberger.[11] Along with his analysis of police data, Grassberger conducted extensive field work, accompanying police patrols and visiting underworld hangouts. By working with the police in New York City, for example, he gained entry into pool halls, which he considered "the most important gathering point for asocials." Frequented "almost exclusively by the least desirable members of the population," pool halls attracted a mixture of those most frequently involved in urban crime—young people, the unemployed, and prostitutes. Grassberger provided German readers with vivid descriptions and first-hand accounts of America's urban underworld.[12]

The bulk of Grassberger's book deals with the types of crime plaguing the cities, and this must have provided his German audience with fascinating reading, for, as a reviewer in an American journal wrote: "The American scene is so far as it may be observed in our major cities compactly, vividly and faithfully depicted."[13] For the first time, the exploits of gangsters as well as petty criminals were discussed in detail and analyzed by a German criminologist. Through his analysis, Grassberger recognized that the structure of crime was changing; it was becoming more sophisticated and the criminal more professional. He provided some examples: One of the most common offenses of the 1920s, robbery, had characteristically involved a vagrant youngster holding up a random victim late at night. By the end of the decade, this had given way to well-planned actions by criminal gangs. Whereas they had long targeted businessmen on the way to the bank with deposits, organized gangs now also hijacked mail trucks and shipments of illegal alcohol. The gains from these crimes had proven to be considerable.[14]

By the early 1930s, organized crime in the United States had, in fact, become widespread. Grassberger and other German criminologists concluded that the criminal underworld of the big cities was supported largely by bootlegging, prostitution, and illicit drug trafficking, the same conclusions their American colleagues had already reached. In particular, Prohibition attracted the attention of German criminologists, who were astonished by the outlawing of alcoholic beverages and the crime wave it generated. They argued that the existence of speakeasies, widely known and readily accessible, extensive bootlegging, hijacking of liquor shipments, and gang wars for control of this trade, bred contempt for the law. The widespread illegal activities and the vast profits they generated led to corruption among the police, courts, and even political leaders.[15]

Other types of crime attracted considerable attention, especially prostitution and drug abuse, two offenses on the rise in Germany as well as in the United States. American investigations of prostitution, the so-called white slave trade, and the passage of the Mann Act in 1910 attracted Grassberger's attention. He and other German criminologists observed that most prostitutes had begun working the streets while teenagers and that most pimps were foreign-born.[16] To a large degree, his conclusions echoed the charges made by the American press. But Grassberger was not in full agreement with American analysis of the problem or the nation's efforts to combat it. He disliked the fact that American law gave much of the responsibility for enforcement to the individual states, because this reduced its effectiveness. Grassberger pointed out, for example, that the western and southern states were more tolerant of prostitution and therefore did not enforce the law as vigorously as the northeastern states.[17] German criminologists also recognized that narcotics use, especially opium, was frequently associated with prostitution and other forms of crime. Grassberger provided his German readers with detailed descriptions of the extensive and sophisticated smuggling operations that were central to the narcotics trade. In addition, Grassberger and his colleagues noted correctly that most American cities had opium dens where an estimated 100,000 addicts sustained their habits. Drug abuse and the opium trafficking was clearly a serious problem, as American criminologists had already recognized.[18]

Studies undertaken in America and his own investigations into the problem led Grassberger to view the United States as a country permeated with crime. Virtually every kind of criminal activity could be found in the larger cities. Grassberger concluded that the cause of the widespread criminality was "instability in economic and domestic life." Frequent moves, changes in life-styles, economic hardships, and lack of a strong sense of right and wrong had created a serious crime problem in the United States. And this, he maintained, contributed to a "poor sense of law and a feeling of legal insecurity." Americans, he concluded, "lacked the legal consciousness found in Europe."[19]

Writing at a time when many in Germany were frustrated by the government's inability to curb crime, Grassberger wanted the American experience to serve as a lesson and a warning. "As long as the major causes of crime do not get a foothold on the European continent, the spread of American style crime will remain isolated, and the overall pattern of crime will not change," he wrote. Grassberger called for greater respect for the law and cautioned that "should our era lose its sensitivity for the purity of the law and should we adopt a system of protection and corruption" as in the United States, crime in Germany and in Europe would escalate. The lack of success in combating crime was caused in part by an additional factor, the American legal system's inability to "instill in the masses of the population a sense of law and order and a feeling of legal security."[20]

While Grassberger was critical of the United States' troubled dealings with street crime and professional criminals, he did not openly condemn the foundations of the criminal justice system. He was, however, critical of its operation and warned of the perils of excessive political influence. His book was more than a warning to Germany and Europe about the threatening "Americanization" of their societies and the ensuing crime problem. Crime had already begun to plague Germany, and now with its sharp increase due to the economic crisis of the Depression and with the growing Nazi demands for the wholesale revision of the criminal code, Grassberger urged caution when considering far-reaching changes in the German legal system.

PRISONS

Criticism of the American criminal justice system was not limited to criminologists and their investigations of street crime and gangsters. In the mid–1920s three influential German penologists visited the United States, and their accounts of the prison system were highly critical. Moritz Liepmann, the first of these prominent scholars, came in the summer of 1926 with a commission sent by the Hamburg senate. The commission's assignment was to prepare a report based on several months of travel to county jails, state prisons, reformatories, and training schools, a report to aid the senate in establishing a prison at Fuhlsbuttel that was to be based on the most modern penological concepts.[21]

The results of the commission's visit were other than expected, and Liepmann's ensuing book on American prisons expressed deep disappointment. The penal institutions, he wrote, were "a hundred years out-of-date" and offered neither "positive examples in the field of penology" nor "constructive suggestions for combatting crime." With the American emphasis on harsh punishment and retribution, rehabilitative measures, long viewed as the cornerstone of the legal system, had become meaningless. As Liepmann concluded: "over there they have taken the wrong path, relying as they do on the electric chair and merciless severity."[22]

Rather than learning from the prison practices observed, Liepmann argued that the United States could gain much from Germany. The Weimar Republic, in spite of "its lost war, revolution, inflation, and economic crises, did not combat crime by increasing the severity of punishment." On the contrary, "preventative measures, programs to deal with unemployment and juvenile delinquency fought the problem head-on." Liepmann added that, "at a time of rising crime, we have reduced the widespread use of incarceration and freed prisoners from its excessive and damaging severity. We have attempted to instill an inner sense of worth and rehabilitation. The result of this work has been a reduction in the incidence of crime."[23]

Liepmann's book surveys a number of prison facilities visited by the Hamburg commission, and it points out the weaknesses and strengths of each. By the mid–1920s, he determined, jails had become the most widely used element of the American penal system. Local jails held suspects as well as those sentenced to short terms of incarceration. Perhaps because of their large number and the local control, jails were "the worst part" of the entire system, and they were "desperately in need of reform." While acknowledging the efforts of some reformers, including Dr. Hastings, J. F. Fishmann, and the American Prison Association, Liepmann found that few improvements had been made. The alarming lack of progress led him to write: "I do not have the words to describe the backward state of the jails. All in all, I have to say that the jails stand in shocking contrast to the demands of a cultured people in the twentieth century."[24]

Liepmann and other members of the Hamburg commission did visit some well-run facilities. They were impressed, for example, by the work-house of the District of Columbia at Occoquan, the Erie County Penitentiary, and the Westchester County Penitentiary and Work house.[25] But on the whole, the commission members found that American jails and prisons were housed in outdated structures and badly run. In fact, most of the sixty-five state institutions visited were, Liepmann wrote, poorly administered. He blamed this on the lack of training for the staff and their lack of job security. In American prisons, guards and administrators received little recognition, unlike in Europe where these professions required special training and commanded respect. American jailers were often political appointees with no professional experience and inadequate supervision. Their pay was low and opportunities for professional training nonexistent. The overall condition of these jails, Liepmann wrote, "belongs to the most puzzling contrasts of this country." A system heralded as the leader in the world only decades earlier had lost its preeminent position because of what he identified as political influence and public indifference.[26]

In addition to the inadequate administration of most jails, Liepmann characterized the conditions within the prison facilities as "inexcusable." Decrepit buildings housed the inmates, and even the most recently constructed structures retained the "inside cells, something, fortunately, unknown in Europe." These cells, built back-to-back and opening onto an interior corridor, lacked windows, adequate light, and ventilation. They were cold, dark, and offered no privacy. As Liepmann wrote, the inside cells dated "from a time when the criminal was looked upon as a dangerous beast of prey." The structure of the cell blocks furthermore revealed "an extraordinary fear of criminals," and did little to reduce crime. In fact, Liepmann continued, "as long as the physical structure [of local jails] undermined the possibility of an effective reform minded treatment of the prisoners, a serious effort to combat crime in America cannot be realized."[27]

Liepmann and other members of the Hamburg commission also found fault with the rehabilitative programs of the state prisons. They found that employment and training opportunities at these institutions were inadequate and outdated. "Programs that are really instructive and productive" were rare, and many prisons offered no work at all. In some states, legislation prohibited the open sale of goods produced by inmates, for this would have been considered "coddling the prisoner" or "too lenient." In Liepmann's view, the state prisons were "characterized not by sentimentality but what to a European seems like shocking severity and harshness." Furthermore, the sentences handed down by the courts were "barbaric." As Liepmann pointed out, some crimes that carried sentences of one to five years in England or on the Continent meant terms of thirty to forty years in the United States. The death penalty was used too frequently. Two teenagers, aged sixteen and nineteen, had recently been executed at Sing Sing.[28]

Liepmann's study was not only a harsh critique of prison conditions in the United States; it was also a call to his German colleagues to rally behind the reforms being introduced by the Weimar government, measures emphasizing rehabilitation over retribution. From the outset, his book advocates this position, and it is a strong condemnation of America's severe techniques and outmoded facilities.[29]

Liepmann and his colleagues on the Hamburg commission concluded that American policies and practices showed them "how not to set up our prisons." While many of the same beliefs and legal assumptions were found in Germany, the severe and outdated principles guiding America's prison system "appeal only to the fear and the public's call for retribution," and they had to be rejected. Such practices "make impossible the essential rehabilitative work oriented toward the individual." Liepmann clearly hoped that the conditions exposed in his book would lead German officials to far-reaching and genuine reform.[30]

Liepmann was not alone in his condemnation of the American penal system. Another member of the Hamburg commission, Berthold Freudenthal, director of Prussia's state prison at Krohne and the creator of the "German Elmira" at Wittlich, echoed these criticisms. From August to October 1927, Freudenthal visited many of the same institutions as Liepmann,[31] and he published his observations in a lengthy article. Freudenthal's description of Sing Sing summed up what he identified as the problems of American prisons: "If I look upon America as a land of contradictions, Sing Sing is the typical embodiment of these contradictions. I have never seen anything more brutal on this earth than the old cellblock wings which are still in use. When you look at the narrow barred openings you would never imagine that these are the windows, the only fresh air openings for the cell in which humans live. When the cells are opened, you see a narrow slice of hell, dark, barren and without air." Freudenthal criticized the state of New York for permitting such conditions to exist: "It is a disgrace that the Empire State still uses these dark medieval cells."[32]

Freudenthal blamed the archaic conditions on the pervasive influence of party politics, a sentiment shared by a number of other scholars. Dr. Steinecke, a German criminologist who attended the meeting of the American Prison Congress in October 1930, stated that the demand for the elimination of political influence from the administration of prisons was still being made. Condemnation of political meddling also came from Edgar Foltin, a German penologist who spent nine months in 1927 and 1928 on a grant from the Rockefeller Foundation investigating American prison practices.[33]

On his research trip, Foltin visited eighty-five institutions across the country and later wrote a book on American prisons. Organized around the various institutional issues—administration, physical care of the inmates, rehabilitative measures, security, and work opportunities—his study is a comprehensive survey of the American prison system. Foltin concluded that the key to the smooth and effective operation of any penal institution was the warden, and for this crucial position he found that most states had "almost no qualification requirements." Appointment was based largely on political connections and on party affiliation. When political power changed hands, new wardens were appointed, and that led to a high turnover among the staff. As Foltin wrote, "In looking at the administration of federal, state, and county penal institutions I must constantly point out the harmful influence of party politics."[34]

That politics played an important role in prison administration led to a range of problems. Many facilities lacked funds to expand and became acutely overcrowded. With no training or recreational programs, inmates often spent thirteen hours at a stretch confined to their cells. Some prisons adopted rehabilitative measures, such as access to the library, not as part of a well-conceived program, but simply as a means of letting the inmates out of their cells to give them some exercise. Although the conditions viewed by Foltin were poor, he concluded that as "long as things go peacefully the actual affairs of the prison are of little interest" to the public. The possibility of meaningful reform was therefore slight.[35]

Among German observers, criticism of the conditions in American jails and prisons was widespread and harsh. Those penologists who came to the United States were reformers looking for practices and policies that could be adopted by the Weimar Republic. What they found was a system far different from their expectations. Outdated, overcrowded, and decrepit facilities run by poor administrators revealed to the German observers the problems of extensive political influence and public indifference. In large measure, their writings were designed as words of caution to a profession eager to reform its prisons while facing mounting pressure from the political right in the 1920s and early 1930s.

THE NAZI TAKEOVER

Soon after the Nazi regime came to power in January 1933, a marked shift in the views of German criminal justice professionals became apparent. The new government was openly committed not to the rights of the individual, but to the protection of society, the newly proclaimed *Volksgemeinschaft*, or racial community. And it promised to get tough on criminals who were harming community. Many law enforcement professionals were ready for such a change. Furthermore, they looked upon the problems of the American criminal justice system as stemming from its democratic political life. In spite of a widespread contempt for the American judicial system, criminologists in the Third Reich were, however, not unrelenting in their criticism of the American system, and some found aspects and measures worth emulating.

Most law enforcement professionals in Nazi Germany became convinced that street crime in American cities had worsened in recent years. At the end of the decade, criminologist Willy Gierlichs recounted the grim facts: By 1938 the annual felony rate in the United States had increased to nearly 4.3 million, or one serious crime every forty-three seconds and a murder every forty minutes. The misdemeanor rate also soared to a staggering figure of 14 million per year. The cost of this crime wave was estimated at $15 billion, or $10 a month for every U.S. citizen.[36] Another German criminologist, Hans Burchardt, found the incidence of crime growing and its structure changing, and he concluded that "the overall view was not good."[37]

According to Burchardt, these changes stemmed from the poor economic conditions in many American cities. He found that the unemployed committed the greatest number of crimes, and the areas with the highest crime rate were the slums. Burchardt held that the most effective means of combatting crime would be strengthening of the economy, creating more jobs, and improving housing conditions, measures which, he boasted, had already been undertaken in the "new Germany." Until similar measures were taken in the United States, he insisted, crime would persist.[38]

Burchardt considered an improvement in social conditions as a necessary step toward curbing crime in the streets. He also believed that an effective system of law enforcement was imperative, and he advocated a carefully regulated prison policy. The major problem with American prisons was, Burchardt wrote, the lack of differentiation between first-time and repeat offenders. In America's city jails, it was common practice to lock up all prisoners in the same cell without attempting to segregate the hardened offender. The impact of this practice on the first-time offenders was often disastrous. In addition, Burchardt called for fewer paroles and pardons, arguing that until reforms were made, no improvement could be hoped for and all of the public funds spent on fighting crime were simply being wasted.[39]

Other criminologists agreed with Burchardt's assessment and advocated tougher measures. Hans Schneikert described American jails as "only a stop on the way to more criminal acts." Frankwood Williams, an American criminologist speaking at a conference on juvenile delinquency in Hamburg, told his audience that a closer and more careful examination of convicted offenders was imperative. There was agreement on both sides of the Atlantic that too many repeat offenders were imprisoned for too short a period of time.[40]

POLITICAL INTERFERENCE

Criminologists in Nazi Germany did not hesitate to point out that the cause of many of these problems was the excessive political influence and the corruption it bred in the American criminal justice system. Willy Gierlichs blamed corrupt politicians, short prison sentences, and quick pardons for the crime problem.[41] Another observer, Roland Grassberger, held the widespread corruption among American police and judiciary responsible. As he put it, police corruption was "significant" on the local level where there was an extensive system of police protection. In addition, influence reached into the courts where judges were frequently bribed or subjected to political pressure. Judges were particularly vulnerable because most were elected and thereby dependent on the local political machine for support.[42]

The opinion that political influence was extensive and pernicious was strengthened by articles written by prominent American criminologists and published in German legal periodicals. Severe criticism came from Edwin Sutherland, a well-respected scholar, who described influence peddling in the United States. According to Sutherland, the boundary between the criminal underworld and legitimate society had never been clearly drawn. In American cities, criminals mingled openly with private citizens and received a great deal of help from the police and judges who provided what he termed "the fix." Sutherland wrote that professional thieves had developed an effective means of preserving their freedom. If arrested, the criminal would try to bribe the officer, a practice that was often unsuccessful. Increasingly, the professional thief would, upon arriving in a city, go to the local "fixer" who would guarantee protection for a price. The fixer had already bribed the police and the district attorney, making the handling of additional cases relatively easy.[43]

In another widely read article, Sutherland condemned the protection secured by professional criminals, and he outlined some of the steps necessary to curb crime. Machine politics and the spoils system, he wrote, "go farther than anything else in explaining the ineffectiveness of administrative actions taken by the police departments and the courts in the United States."Political corruption undermined police effectiveness and seriously reduced the effectiveness of the courts. For many readers in Hitler's Germany, the criticisms applied to all liberal political systems, including the Weimar Republic.[44]

The problems of political influence and protection in America were amplified by the fractured nature of police authority, Sutherland wrote. The skilled professional criminal had quickly learned how to take advantage of the system. He was, for instance, careful only to violate state law, and therefore came under the jurisdiction of state or local courts where corruption was widespread. The split of jurisdiction, a further weakness in a democratic state's fight against crime, resulted from what Sutherland termed "the American fear of monarchial or centralized government."[45] German criminologists closely examined several measures adopted by the American federal government to overcome the jurisdictional divisions. They were, for example, interested in the activities of the Department of Justice, Treasury Department, and the Post Office Department, each of which had its own enforcement branch. But the efforts of these various agencies remained uncoordinated and were therefore not especially effective.[46]

The problems caused by the fractured nature of police and judicial authority in the United States were of particular interest to German law enforcement officials in the Third Reich. Sutherland's critical observations were echoed by criminologist Roland Grassberger and legal scholar Franz Exner. Until the Hitler regime came to power in 1933, police matters in Germany had been dealt with on a strictly statewide basis. The criticism of the American system provided additional justification for the centralization of police authority taking place under Hitler. Also, the FBI, potentially an effective nationwide police agency and a potential model, was looked upon favorably by German criminologists and police officials.[47]

THE FBI

Police officials in Nazi Germany found much to applaud at in the FBI. Under the leadership of J. Edgar Hoover, the bureau had launched what German criminologist Hans Schneickert termed "an energetic war on criminality." Founded in 1908, the FBI had undergone numerous changes with the most far-reaching occurring after Hoover took command in 1924. Political influence was eliminated, officers were promoted on merit, and close cooperation with local and state police agencies became commonplace. Nearly 2,300 police agencies reported to the FBI each month. The FBI had divided the country into districts with each managed by an officer, chosen and supervised by headquarters in Washington, D.C. It was an organization discussed and admired by German police officials.[48]

Hoover's criticism of the American judicial system was of interest to law enforcement professionals in Nazi Germany. A speech in which he attacked parole was reported at length in a major police journal, and according to the article, Hoover began by discussing the more than 4 million criminals who were still on the streets. At fault, he insisted, were the overcrowded prisons and, above all, the parole system. Prison had become "just one step on the way to more crime." And once in jail the convicted criminal had "too many pleasures."[49] According to criminologist Hans Schneickert, Hoover's insistence that "a professional safe-cracker or a murderer be kept behind bars comes close to our proven methods." It is not surprising that police officials in Nazi Germany admired the FBI, but, Schneickert added, Hoover's organization "could learn a lot from some of the European countries."[50]

OTHER ANTI-CRIME MEASURES

Additional information on crime and police methods in the United States appeared in the popular press. For example, a Munich newspaper in the spring of 1933 described "the systematic fight against pornography" currently underway in the United States. "Numerous commissions have been established and bookstores and libraries are constantly checked" for offensive material, which was seized and the establishment closed.[51] A report on another crime-fighting method, the lineup, was described in a police magazine. The "lineup gallery," a procedure referred to as an American tradition, took place every night at 9 PM when those arrested during the day would be paraded before witnesses, victims, and detectives. A German expert noted, however, that similar weekly line-ups had already been established by the police in Berlin at the turn of the century. The purpose of the line-ups in both Germany and the United States was much the same. Along with the chance of a positive identification from a victim or witness, line-ups gave police authorities a final opportunity to have a close look at the criminals being released. Lacking effective means of recording and distributing detailed descriptions of suspects, the detectives' memory proved to be an important weapon. In America's fight against crime, German authorities recognized that the FBI's collection of fingerprints was a far more efficient tool than the line-up. As Hans Schneickert wrote, "nothing was easier than for a criminal to go underground," and "every time he is arrested a different name is given." The widespread use of fingerprinting would be an effective countermeasure.[52]

Other methods of detecting criminals employed by American police forces were also discussed. In October 1937, a popular magazine ran an article on the use of the "third degree," police coercion, in New York City. Its author, Robert Minner, described the procedure: A suspect in an important case is taken to a precinct house for further questioning. Then, two or three days later, the newspapers report that the suspect had in fact confessed to the crime, and another big case had been solved. How did the police gain the confession, Minner asked. It was through the use of what "Americans call the third degree," what he termed "secret interrogation by the police." While the third degree "was not in any law," it was, Minner insisted, widely used. In spite of the frequent calls for its abolition, it had proven "too effective a tool for the police" to abandon it.[53]

Throughout the 1920s and 1930s, German criminologists had scrutinized the American criminal justice system. What they found was rampant corruption, influence peddling, and outdated practices and facilities. The system was also plagued by jurisdictional quarrels and the lack of a unified policy in combatting crime. Roland Grassberger maintained that the crime problem stemmed from "the disorganization of American society. Victims and officials are more interested in protecting themselves than society as a whole." There was, he added, a "lack of a sense of unity in the community and the nation." Grassberger concluded, "if professional thieves are to be effectively combatted a new loyalty to society and the nation is needed. Until then other efforts will not have much meaning."[54]

FRANZ EXNER'S CRITIQUE

Further condemnation of the American criminal justice system came from Franz Exner, one of Germany's leading criminologists. The author of a number of studies of crime in America, Exner was a harsh critic who called America's measures to combat crime mild and too lax.[55] Exner's views are of considerable interest, for he was a prominent and influential scholar whose criticisms of the United States applied equally well to the Weimar Republic's troubled dealings with crime.

In discussing the crime wave in America, Exner claimed it was part real, part imaginary. The inordinate attention given to crime, with newspapers reporting sensational offenses daily, created an exaggerated awareness of crime, and became "one of the most favorite topics of conversation." According to Exner, this interest stemmed from the Puritan tradition in America as well as outright sensationalism. The free and open press of a democratic society simply heightened the fear of crime while the detailed reports prompted others to imitate the criminals gaining such attention.[56] Also at work were what Exner termed "real factors"—Prohibition, the widespread possession of firearms, and the use of the automobile. These factors had not received the attention in the press they deserved. In addition, he wrote, "it is also clear to me that the racial, biological and hereditary factors that characterize the American people are decisive factors" in the crime problem.[57]

Exner identified other problems in the American system. In his view, a society governed by liberal political ideals, with constitutional safeguards for the rights of the individual, prevented the police from effectively combatting crime.[58] The work of the American police was further hindered by political influence, the lack of cooperation among the law enforcement agencies, and federal law. Having learned from the American experience, Exner advocated already in 1934 the creation of a highly centralized police force in Germany, one that would not suffer from the constitutional restrictions imposed upon the FBI.[59]

Exner's criticism of the American criminal justice system included the courts.[60] "The most crucial factor that burdens the pursuit of criminals is the procedure of the courts," he wrote. "I have the distinct impression that we have in fact nothing to learn from the American criminal justice system. Above all, the trial [in the American court room] attempts to *develop the ##### dural elements of liberalism to their grotesque extreme* while we are striving to remove our procedure from that mode of thought." Additional factors "characteristic of the liberal structure of the American court procedure have led to a marked weakening of fight against crime."[61]

Exner explained that in about half of the American states, a grand jury indictment was required before starting criminal prosecution. He charged that this practice had seriously compromised the effectiveness of the courts, which are viewed as mere "rubber stamps of the district attorney." Furthermore, a grand jury was subject to public pressure, and Exner asserted this frequently resulted in "unjustifiable adjournments."[62] There were other problems with the courts, and he wrote that the legal system was characterized by "the constant interference of the constitutionally guaranteed rights of the individual, which have been extended widely through a liberal court procedure." When the Constitution operates in this fashion, protecting the rights of all individuals, he concluded that it "can readily be called 'the magna carta of criminals.' "[63]

There was, however, one area of the American court system where Exner saw "the liberal ideas fading away." This was the growing use of plea bargaining, which he viewed as an indication that jury trials were now "fading more and more into the background." In his survey of American courts, Exner found that "over 90 percent of criminal cases were taken care of without a jury." While he applauded the outcome because it minimized the impact of the defense attorney who also employed every means to gain an acquittal, he did not praise the procedure. Exner called plea bargaining "a highly regrettable trick," which actually tended to aid the accused who pleaded guilty to a lesser offense while minimizing the protection of state and society.[64]

Exner viewed with contempt these efforts of a liberal political system to streamline its judicial system. The "business transactions between the state and the plaintiff," as Exner termed plea bargaining, were introduced as a "means of possibly saving time and energy," and a way of reducing the burden on the already overloaded court system.[65] He concluded that "The results of this are clear: there often exists great disparity between the actual offense and the penalty meted out." In Exner's view, the procedure had gone far toward undermining the criminal justice system, and he wrote: "Regardless of what you think of trial by jury, this method of circumventing it is absolutely to be rejected." Exner offered some suggestions for change, concluding, for example, that, "Things can only get better when the position of the judge is raised above the exaggerated rights of the plaintiff."[66]

Exner's analysis of the American criminal justice system also led him to criticize sharply the role of attorneys. According to Exner, the "high point of every court case" was neither the testimony presented nor the verdict.

Rather, it was the cross-examination, the adversarial combat between the lawyers and the witnesses. Exner believed that the resolution of the trial depended more on cross-examination and the abilities of the respective attorneys than any other factor. And because of the drama of this "duel in the courtroom" the position of prosecuting attorney was a very attractive and important one. Many young lawyers found that this "political appointment offers more visibility than any other post," and "a sensational case had already "made a lot of men." Exner noted that more than forty percent of the members of Congress and a number of state governors began their careers as prosecutors. Prosecuting attorney was clearly an important stepping stone to higher political office.[67]

Exner and other criminologists also criticized the American judicial system for what they regarded as its exaggerated concern with protecting the rights of the individual. As Exner stated, "it is very apparent that the entire procedure is designed to protect the accused as far as possible while the protection of the state and society is sold short."[68] This was characteristic of a liberal criminal justice system, such as that of the Weimar Republic or the United States, and this practice was in marked contrast to the new procedures introduced by the Nazi regime, which placed the well-being and needs of the racial community above the rights of the individual.[69]

One of the changes in Nazi Germany was the increased use of indeterminate sentencing which, as Exner readily pointed out, had been used in America, but used inappropriately. While most American states had legislated some form of indeterminate sentencing, its use varied widely. The laws provided the courts with the power to set a minimum and maximum length of incarceration, and prison officials were given broad leeway. After observing a number of American courts, Exner concluded that the setting of the actual length of a prison term was in practice being removed from the jurisdiction of the courts. Other problems existed. Several German criminologists argued that the parameters of the sentence were set either too high or too low; sentences of thirty-forty years and even sixty-ninety-nine, "in effect a life sentence," were "by no means uncommon in America."[70]

The courtroom practices witnessed by Exner contradicted the intended purpose of indeterminate sentencing. Based on the assumption that the length of rehabilitation cannot be determined at the beginning of the prison term, Exner concluded that indeterminate sentencing offered a flexible alternative, one more responsive to the actual rehabilitation of the convicted criminal. The length of sentence was to be determined after the rehabilitative process had begun.[71] But, as Exner wrote, "In fact, the length of the time served has nothing at all to do with the rehabilitative progress." Convicted criminals with "no hope of rehabilitation" are sentenced to varying terms of imprisonment. The result was that "in many cases the use of indeterminate sentencing is practically meaningless." In practice, it had become more of a technique for maintaining prison discipline than an integral part of the rehabilitative process. While Exner was condemning the liberal criminal justice system of America, his warnings were also intended for his German colleagues. Nazi Germany had recently enacted similar legislation, and Exner called upon criminologists and jurists to act in accordance with its intended principles.[72]

AMERICA'S RACIAL LAWS

With the advent of Nazi rule in 1933, German criminologists and law enforcement professionals increasingly criticized American practices as misguided. The emphasis on the rights of the individual, they asserted, had prevented an effective campaign against street crime, and similar charges were levied against the Weimar Republic. There were, however, some American laws and legal practices that legal professionals in Nazi Germany found attractive. Discriminatory legislation and the sterilization laws of various states were discussed and applauded.

For Nazi jurists, these laws provided a useful model and convenient justification. According to the legal theory in Nazi Germany, the so-called racial community was viewed as the source and embodiment of the law. Racial purity, the element that allegedly held the society together, was hailed by leading Nazi jurists Roland Freisler and Curt Rothenberger as the highest goal of the state and any threat to that alleged purity would be a threat to the law and the very existence of the state. Increasingly after 1933, criminologists looked outside of Germany for models of legal change to support their arguments.[73]

The best statement of the preoccupation can be found in the 1936 book by Heinrich Krieger on America's racial legal system. As Krieger writes in his introduction, the "swift development of racial law in Germany and its growing importance calls for the examination of the experience of other nations" in this area. Of special significance, he noted, were "those countries with a genuine racial legal system—the United States, the German Reich, and South Africa."[74] Krieger initially found the existence of racial laws in American states to be "a highly surprising fact." After all, the legal system was supposed to be based on the rights of the individual as guaranteed in the Constitution. While his book was an encyclopedic coverage of American racial law, Krieger focused on the legal position of blacks, but also included information on Native Americans and immigrants, especially Orientals. In addition, Krieger's book went beyond being simply informative—it provided a model for the systematic exclusion of racial minorities. And in Nazi Germany this proved to be of considerable importance.[75]

Not only did Krieger's book offer a program of discriminatory legislation, it was also designed to expose what he called "the fiction of equality" found in America and to admonish Germany to remain true to its "racial consciousness." The American legal system had compromised too much in its refusal to openly acknowledge the concept of racial law, Krieger wrote. "The fiction of equality" is "typical of the exaggerated belief in the power of the law." Americans believe, he continued, that "because racial equality is called for in the Fourteenth Amendment to the Constitution, it in fact will be so."[76]

Krieger called "naive" what he identified as "the typically American faith in the power of the law" and the belief in the equality of all who come to its shores. These assumptions simply hid "fundamental racial differences," and they led to a "shift of political domination from the majority race to the minorities." "This split, already present, bears much of the responsibility for the demoralization of political life and is a threat to the roots of American democracy." Furthermore, he insisted that the dichotomy between state and federal law, especially between the northern and southern states, jeopardizes the nation. The political life of the United States, Krieger asserted, rests firmly on racial differences.[77]

AMERICA'S STERILIZATION LAWS

To a large degree, Krieger's study provided legitimacy for the racial policies of the Nazi regime at a time when they were under attack from abroad. A similar attempt to use the American experience to provide justification for unpopular policies can be seen in the numerous writings on sterilization. In Germany, an interest in sterilization as a means of maintaining racial purity emerged in the 1920s, and in the Third Reich forced sterilization was used increasingly more frequently.[78] American judicial decisions and state laws provided further justification for the practice. In 1938, for example, E. Schubart discussed a 1924 U.S. Supreme Court decision upholding sterilization, and included with his commentary was a copy of the decision in both English and German. Schubart admonished those in Germany who opposed sterilization to read this U.S. Supreme Court decision.[79]

In spite of the early calls for the expanded use of sterilization in Germany, no legal action was taken until the Hitler regime came to power and race became the political and ideological foundation of the new state. M. Staemmler summed up the new sentiment when he wrote that "National Socialism strives for the renewal of the *Volk* on racial foundations." In Nazi Germany, he continued, "there is to be no equality under the law. Each has as much right as he is of value to the *Volk*. That must be emphasized more strongly than in the past. And now the state has the right, indeed the obligation, to differentiate between those of great value and those of little value." This determination was to be made largely along racial lines.[80]

Staemmler's article embodied a widely held viewpoint that was enacted in several pieces of legislation. The new laws emerged in part out of a growing sense of urgency that action had to be taken to prevent the alleged racial destruction of Germany. Staemmler noted that racial selection had not previously been needed because of Germany's balanced population growth. The high death rate among those Staemmler considered to be of "little value" had provided what he called "natural selection," a "self-cleansing action." Recently, however, the fertility rates of the "down and outs" in the cities of Germany began to grow, while those of "full value" were not having as many children. What was widely referred to as "racial suicide" came to be seen as a serious danger.[81]

According to Staemmler, "something must be done, and this will decide if Europe is one day conquered by Slavs and if Germanic culture is destroyed by the Slavs." This alleged threat led other German criminologists to look to America, where sterilization had long been practiced. Alfred Hoffman, in a book on sterilization and crime, noted that the United States had faced a similar problem. "The prevention of further undesirable generations is essential, for the colored races through racial interaction are threatening the American *Volk* with the danger of racial disintegration," he wrote. The American experience had relevance for those in Germany with an exaggerated fear of what they termed "racial pollution."[82]

The interest in the American experience grew rapidly after the passage of "The Law for the Prevention of Hereditarily Ill Progeny" (14 August 1933). The law provided for the first time for the sterilization of those with hereditary disorders, and an ordinance of 5 December 1933, elaborated the procedural requirements. Looking to America for models was natural, for as J. H. Landmann wrote, the States "have been the pioneers in the sterilization movement and are still the foremost leaders in the world."[83]

There were good reasons for this turning toward America. According to an article in a major German legal journal, twenty-six American states had sterilization laws.[84] The U.S. Supreme Court had decided favorably on the constitutionality of the sterilization laws of California, Virginia, Michigan, and Maine. Copies of these state laws were published in German law periodicals, part of the broadening discussion of that country's recent legislation. Already in 1933, Johannes Lange argued that the new German law would not be used casually, and he cited the experience of the United States, where criminal offenses and mental conditions were sufficient grounds for sterilization, to show its infrequent usage. Lange, a psychiatrist, voiced his opinion that the law would be applied only to those with acute mental illness, which he identified as including retardation, schizophrenia, epilepsy, and severe alcoholism. These afflictions, he commented, "make those affected unable to meet the responsibilities owed to the racial community."[85]

According to Lange, the legislation was intended to be preventative, to protect society from future generations of the mentally deficient. Included were what Lange called "the shockingly high number of simple minded individuals in the racial community, a full 1 percent which included between 200,000 and 300,000 schizophrenics and 100,000 manic depressives and epileptics." As Lange concluded, "the law is concerned not with the individual but with the community. And it is concerned not only with the visibly ill, but with the continuation of such hereditary traits among their progeny."[86]

Remarkably similar concerns were voiced by American criminologists, and many of these views were presented in a series of articles appearing in a German legal journal. An American criminologist, Paul Popenoe, writing on the sterilization laws of California, felt certain "that these precautions will find an even greater use in the future. They offer a humane and practical protection from the feared racial degeneration." In practice this meant that the law was used widely; "Nearly every feeble minded person in a [California] state institution is sterilized before being released." This practice, Popenoe continued, "allows the patients to be successfully integrated back into society because they are not forced to bear the burden of parenthood, which in many cases would be too difficult for them." The number of feeble minded and mentally ill sterilized in California's state institutions had reached 8,500 by 1933. Those sterilized at the same institutions for eugenic reasons numbered more than 16,000.[87]

America's experiences and legislation provided guidance for German law makers and criminologists. They argued that it was necessary to take a hard look at those whose biological contribution to society was detrimental to the general good. Lange outlined a procedure for identifying those who in his opinion should be sterilized, and much of the decision-making responsibility lay with the administrators of the various institutions, whether they be mental hospitals, asylums, or prisons. The administrator was to carefully investigate all inmates, and those with any hint of mental illness were to be sterilized.[88]

By placing much of the responsibility in the hands of the institutions' administrators, Germany was following the practice developed in the United States where staff physicians had long been involved in these decisions. In contrast to Germany, however, several American states did have safeguards. Some states required written permission from the next of kin, or as in Kansas where a commission made the final decision. Still, some doctors in Kansas had voiced their dissatisfaction; going through a commission was too cumbersome. These doctors wanted the supervisory commission dissolved and the decision to rest in their hands alone. This change was of special importance, for "sterilization is the single means for preventing useless progeny."[89]

There was, these articles suggested, a strong uniformity of purpose between the practice of sterilization in Nazi Germany and its practice in several American states.[90] Sterilization was viewed simply as a tool for preventing the mentally ill from having offspring. Furthermore, some states used sterilization as a form of punishment, and, although four states did have such laws, they were seldom used after 1930. One German criminologist, Alfred Hoffmann, rejected the use of sterilization as a punishment, noting that in

Nazi Germany "the purpose of punishment is to resocialize the offender, to win him back to the racial community as much as possible." Writing in 1940, Hoffmann added that, "the use of sterilization as a means of punishment, above all, violates our present day ethical point of view and modern criminology. It would mean a retreat to the mutilation and punishments of the Middle Ages." Hoffmann looked upon the American practice as barbaric.[91]

CONCLUSION

It might appear strange for a criminologist in Nazi Germany to view an American legal practice as inhumane. But Hoffmann was certainly not the first to be disappointed and even shocked by what he found in the United States. Throughout much of the 1920s and 1930s, German criminologists, penologists, and jurists had been disappointed by American practices. The examples of reform, so important to nineteenth-century law enforcement professionals, were no longer available or valid. The disappointment of not finding a model for meaningful reform in the 1920s was particularly bitter. To the reformers of the Weimar Republic who came to the United States, the corruption, political influence, and crime wave in the cities proved to be harsh reminders of the perils of democratic rule. Their writings also reveal the often ambiguous attitudes toward criminal justice reform and democracy. While the Weimar Constitution and legal reforms did provide guarantees for individual rights, concerns over a rising crime problem and the antidemocratic tradition in the legal profession remained strong.

To the criminologists in Nazi Germany, the excesses and abuses, identified as endemic to democratic societies, provided further justification for their attacks on the liberal Weimar Republic and its criminal justice system. The soaring crime rates in the United States and Germany during the 1920s, the deteriorating prison system, the alleged softness on criminals fit Nazi propaganda very nicely, giving additional substance to the recent accusations. While it was natural for the Nazis to be severely critical of America's democratic political and legal system, the applauding of some American practices by Nazi criminologists casts these measures in different light. Scholars have in recent years been critical of America's use of sterilization and the racist legislation. But the fact that some American measures provided additional justification for the Hitler regime's brutal and antidemocratic methods has not received much attention, and provides a further basis for examining the mixed record of the United States in law enforcement.

NOTES

1. M. Liepmann, *Amerikanische Gefängnisse und Erziehungsanstalten. Ein Reisebericht* (Mannheim, 1927), 1–2; N. K. Teeters, *The Prison at Philadelphia, Cherry*

Hill. The Separate System of Penal Discipline: 1829–1913 (New York, 1957), 7:113–15, 224–29.

2. Liepmann, *Amerikanische Gefängnisse*, 1–2, Rudolf Seitler, "Elmira 1913–1924," *Blätter für Gefängniskunde* (hereafter *BfG*) 57 (1926): 1–25.

3. Liepmann, *Amerikanische Gefängnisse*, 1–2; Hermann von Mangoldt, *Geschriebene Verfassung und Rechtssicherheit in den Vereinigten Staaten von America* (Breslau-Neukirch, 1934), V–VII, 1–8. For the reaction to von Mangolt's book, see the review written by R. A. Reuss in *Juristische Wochenblatt* (hereafter *JW*) 63 (1939): 441. See also Ernst Freund, *Das öffentlichen Reich der Vereinigten Staaten von Amerika* (Tubingen, 1911); Hans Pohl, *Organisations- und Berufsethik der Anwälte und Richter der Vereinigten Staaten von Amerika und die deutsche Rechtsanwaltschaft* (Berlin, 1930), 11–12, 26–35.

4. Robert Fritz, *Aus dem amerikanische Rechtsleben* (Berlin, 1930); E. Bumke, "Europaische Strafrechtspflege in amerikanische Beleuchtung," *JW* 56 (1927): 2664–67; Ben B. Lindsay and Rube Borough, *Das gefährliche Leben* (Stuttgart, 1931); Hans von Hentig, "Amerikanische kriminalwissenschaftliche Literatur," *Monatsschrift für Kriminalpsychologie* 21 (1930): 677–89; Klaus Marxen, *Der Kampf gegen das liberale Strafrecht. Eine Studie zum Antiliberalismus in der Strafrechtswissenschaft der zwanziger und dreissiger Jahre* (Berlin, 1975), 17–41; Hinrich Rüping, "Zur Praxis der Strafjustiz im 'Dritten Reich,' " in *Recht und Justiz im "Dritten Reich,"* ed. Ralf Dreier and Wolfgang Sellert (Frankfurt am Main; 1989), 180–93.

5. W. Kiesselbach, "Die amerikanische Justiz. Vom Standpunkt eines deutschen Juristen," *JW* 61(1932): 70; Friedrich B. Sieveking, "Das Problem des ne bis in idem in der amerikanische Bundes- und Staatangerichtsbarkeit," *Zeitschrift für die gesamte Strafrechtswissenschaft* (hereafter *ZStW*) 53(1933): 297–300, 232–36, 332–33.

6. Mangoldt, *Geschriebene Verfassung*, 151–52; Thorsten Sellin, "Das American-Law-Institute und ein neues amerikanisches Strafgesetzbuch," *Monatsschrift für Kriminologie und Strafrechtreform* (hereafter *MSK*) 27(1936): 205–6; Frederick E. Blackly and Miriam E. Oatman, "Some Consequences of Judicial Review," *Zeitschrift für auslandisches öffentliches Recht und Volkerrecht* 1(1929): 500–511.

7. Ervin Hacker, "Die Ergebnisse der Strafrechtswissenschaft in Amerika und Europa," *BfG* 56(1924–25): 44–54; Franz Exner, *Kriminalistischer Bericht über eine Reise nach Amerika* (Berlin, 1935), 5–13.

8. Sling, *Richter und Gerichtete* (Munich, 1969); Exner, *Kriminalistischer Bericht*, 13–14.

9. Hentig, "Amerikanische Kriminalwissenschaftliche Literatur," 677–89; "Die Mörde in den U.S.A.," *Archiv für Kriminologie* 83(1923): 196–97.

10. Roland Grassberger, *Gewerbs- und Berufsverbrechertum in den Vereinigten Staaten von Amerika* (Vienna, 1933); Hans Schneikert, "Der Kampf gegen das Verbrechertum in Amerika," *Archiv für Polizeiwesen* (hereafter *AfP*) 18(1938): 41–42; Exner, "Amerikanische Strafgesetzgebung gegen das Gewohnheitsverbrechertum," *MSK* 25(1934): 436–40; Sieverts, "Amerika—ein abschreckendes Beispiel für übertriebene Humanität im Strafvollzug," *MSK* 21(1930): 622–24.

11. Grassberger, *Gewerbs- und Berufsverbrechertum*, 27–30.

12. Ibid., 31–37. On Grassberger's research methods, see the review of his book in the *Zeitschrift für die gesamte Strafrechtswissenschaft* (hereafter *Zstw*) 55(1935):

486; and the laudatory reviews in *Revue de droit penal et de criminologi* 30 (June 1933): 649–650, and *Tijdschrift voor Strafrecht* 43(1933): 328–32. On the problem of juvenile delinquency in America as seen from the perspective of a German criminologist, see Wilhelm F. K. Guderjahn, *Kampf gegen die Verwahrlosung und Entartung der Jugend in USA. Erlebnisse in nordamerikanischen Knabenerziehungsheimen und Jugendrepubliken* (Leipzig, 1935), 171–85.

13. *Journal of Criminal Law and Criminology* (hereafter *JCLC*) 24(1933–34): 832; Grassberger, *Gewerbs- und Berufsverbrechertum*, 50–59, 79–141, 197–226.

14. Ibid., 50–59.

15. Ibid., 62–78, 79–106, 197–225, 228–34, 239–309; Edwin Sutherland, "Wie der Berufsdieb der Bestrafung entgeht," *MSK* 27(1936): 449–56; Willy Bierlachs, "Zur Natur- und Sozialgeschichte des 'Gang' in USA. Die gesellschaftlichen Mächte Amerikas im Kampfe für und gegen das organisierte Verbrechertum," *Kriminalistik* 12(1938): 49.

16. Grassberger, *Gewerbs- und Berufsverbrechertum*, 109–19; Anna Papritz, *Einführung in das Studium der Prostitutionsfrage* (Leipzig, 1919); Ella Drescher, "Das verwahrloste Mädchen von Amerika. Ein Ausschnitt aus der Jugendfürsorge von Chicago," *Zentralblatt für Jugendrecht* 25(1933–34): 50–53, 76–84.

17. Grassberger, *Gewerbs- und Berufsverbrechertum*, 109–19.

18. Ibid., 125–41. On the problem of narcotics abuse in Germany, see Tobben and Rudolf Koch, "Der heutige Stand der Bekämpfung des Rauschgiftmissbrauches," *MSK* 27(1936): 522–529; and Erwin Kosmehl, "Die sicherheitspolizeiliche Einsatz bei der Bekämpfung der Betäubungsmittelsucht," a lecture delivered on 14 October 1942, National Archives, microcopy T–73, roll 17, frames 1064624–36.

19. Grassberger, *Gewerbs- und Berufsverbrechertum*, 298–99. See also "Die Morde in den USA," *Archive für Kriminologie* (hereafter *AfK*) 83(1923): 196–97; Harry Trommer, "Gefängnisstatistik des Staates New York für die Jahre 1928–1933," *MSK* 26(1935): 339–44.

20. Grassberger, *Gewerbs- und Berufsverbrechertum*, 299.

21. Liepmann, *Amerikanische Gefängnisse*, V–VII, 1–5.

22. Ibid., VI–VII; Sieverts, "Amerika-ein abschreckendes Beispiel," 623; Thorsten Sellin, "Todesstrafe in den Vereinigten Staaten," *Monatsschrift für Kriminalpsychologie* 31(1931): 102–5.

23. Liepmann, *Amerikanische Gefängnisse*, VI–VII.

24. Ibid.; Sieverts, "Amerika-ein abschreckendes Beispiel," 623.

25. Liepmann, *Amerikanische Gefängnisse*, 5–6, 8–9.

26. Ibid.; Berthold Freudenthal, "Tagebücher von Berthold Freudenthal über sein amerikanische-englische Studienreise (August bis Oktober 1927), *BfG* 61(1930) (Sonderheft): 138, 177, 182–84.

27. Liepmann, *Amerikanische Gefängnisse*, 8–11; W. Mittermaier, "Gefängnisse von Morgen," *BfG* 62(1931): 454–58.

28. Liepmann, *Amerikanische Gefängnisse*, 11–14.

29. Ibid., 64–71.

30. Ibid.

31. Freudenthal, "Tagebücher," 134–36, 177–84.

32. Ibid., 137.

33. Dr. Steinecke, "Der 60. amerikanische Gefängniskongress," *BfG* 61(1930): 444–46; Edgar M. Foltin, *Amerikanische Gefängniswesen* (Reichenberg, 1930), 31,

41–44. Foltin's book was well received; see reviews in *ZStW* 51(1931): 654–56, and *JCLC* 22(1931–32): 459–60.

34. Foltin, *Amerikanische Gefängniswesen*, 33–38, 41.

35. Ibid., 38, 50–52, 71–83.

36. Gierlichs, "Sozialgeschichte des 'Gang,' " 147.

37. Burchardt, "Verbrecherbekämpfung," 136–37.

38. Ibid.

39. Ibid.

40. Schneickert, "Kampf gegen das Verbrechertum," 4; Frank E. Williams, "Massnahmen zur Verhütung der Straffälligkeit in Amerika," in *Bericht über die 4. Sachverständigen-Konferenze des Deutschen Vereins zur Fürsorge für jugendliche Psychopathen e.V* (Hamburg, 13–15 Sept. 1928) (Berlin, 1929), 37–39, 71.

41. Gierlichs, "Sozialgeschichte des 'Gang,' " 148.

42. Grassberger, *Bewerbs- und Berufsverbrechertum*, 17, 24–25; Edwin H. Sutherland, "Die Bekämpfung des Berufdiebes in den Vereinigten Staaten von Nordamerika," *MSK* 28 (1937): 410–406.

43. Sutherland, "Wie der Berufsdieb die Bestrafung entgeht," 449–56.

44. Sutherland, "Bekämpfung des Berufdiebes," 401–2; Grassberger, *Gewerbs- und Berufsverbrecher*, 8–11.

45. Sutherland, "Bekämpfung des Berufdiebes," 405–6.

46. Grassberger, *Gewerbs- und Berufsverbrechertum*, 8–11.

47. Ibid., 405–6; Exner, *Kriminalistischer Bericht*, 15–17; Alois Osterkorn, *Kraftfahrzeug und Verbrechen* (Leipzig, 1938), 7, 47ff. See also Sieveking, "Das Problem des ne bis in dem," 297–233; Herman von Mangolt, *Rechtsstaatsgedanke und Regierungsformen in Vereinigten Staaten von Amerika. Die geistigen Grundlagen des amerikanischen Verfassungsrechts* (Essen, 1938).

48. Schneickert, "Kampf gegen das Verbrechertum," 41; Hans Schneickert, "Die grösste Fingerabdrucksammlung der Welt," *AfP* 18(1939): 43; Gierlichs, "Sozialgeschichte des 'Gang,' " 152–54; "Vereinheitlichung von amerikanischen Kriminalstatistik," *AfK* 83(1923): 73.

49. Quoted in Schneickert, "Kampf gegen das Verbrechertum," 41.

50. Ibid., 41–42.

51. "Der Kampf gegen Schmutz und Schund in Amerika," *Bayern Kurier* (25 Apr. 1933); "Gefangen-Ausbruch in USA," *Münchener Neuste Nachrichten* (3 June 1933).

52. Hans Schneickert, "Line Up Gallery. Zurschaustellung von Verbrecher," *AfP* 17(1938): 299.

53. Robert Minner, "Der dritte Grad. Wie die New-Yorker Polizei Kapitalverbrecher zum Geständnis bringt," *Koralle* 5(24 Oct. 1937): 1485–86.

54. Grassberger, *Gewerbs- und Berufsverbrechertum*, 8–11.

55. Exner, *Kriminalistischer Bericht*, 38.

56. Ibid., 5, 13–14.

57. Ibid., 11–13.

58. Ibid., 17, 19.

59. Ibid., 15–17; Boris Brasol, "Die Entwicklung der Naturwissenschaftlichen Kriminaluntersuchung in den Vereinigten Staaten, *AfK* 104(1939): 31–35.

60. Exner, *Kriminalistischer Bericht*, 17–18; idem, "Amerikanische Strafgesetzgebung," 437–40.

61. Exner, *Kriminalistischer Bericht*, 17–18.
62. Ibid.
63. Ibid.
64. Ibid., 19–20.
65. Ibid., 20–21.
66. Ibid.; Curt F. Rothenberger, *Der Deutsche Richter* (Hamburg, 1943), 7–16.
67. Exner, *Kriminalistischer Bericht*, 19; Kiesselbach, "Amerikanische Justiz," 71.
68. Exner, *Kriminalistischer Bericht*, 21–23.
69. Kurt Daluege, *Nationalsozialistischer Kampf gegen das Verbrechertum* (Munich, 1936), 9–17; Herbert Kruger, "Rechtsgedanke und Rechtstechnik im liberalen Strafrecht, I.," *ZStW* 54(1935): 591–664; Wilhelm Gallas, "Die Krise des Strafrechts und ihre Ueberwindung im Staatsgedanken," *ZStW* 53(1933): 11–28; Alfred Rosenberg, "Die nationalsozialistische Weltanschauung und das Recht," *Deutsche Justiz* (hereafter *DJ*) (1938): 357–60.
70. Exner, *Kriminalistischer Bericht*, 21–23. See also Exner, "Amerikanische Strafgesetzgebung," 436–39; Thorsten Sellin, "Todesstrafe in den vereinigten Staaten," *MSK* 21(1930): 102–5; and Sieverts, "Amerika-ein abschreckendes Beispiel," 622–24.
71. Exner, *Kriminalistischer Bericht*, 21–22.
72. Ibid., 23–25; Kiesselbach, "Amerikanische Justiz," 553–57.
73. William Ward Fearnside, "National Socialist Ideology in German Criminal Law, 1933–1945" (Ph.D. Thesis, University of California, Berkeley, 1949), 26–30; Rothenberger, *Deutsche Richter*, 13, 40–41; Heinrich Krieger, *Das Rassenrecht in den Vereinigten Staaten* (Berlin, 1936), 9–10; Mangolt, *Rechtsgedanke und Regierungsformen*, 226–300.
74. Krieger, *Rassenrecht*, 9–10.
75. Ibid., 22–54, 77–87, 110–41, 145–308. Krieger's book was well received in Germany; see the reviews in *DR* 6(15 Dec. 1936): 512; *Zeitschrift für Rassenkunde und ihre Nachbargebiete* 4(1936): 220; and *Rasse. Monatsschrift der Nordischen Bewegung* 3(1936): 496–97. For another discussion of American racial legislation, see Mangoldt, *Rechtsstaatsgedanke und Regierungsformen*, 226–312.
76. Krieger, *Rassenrecht*, 315, 349.
77. Ibid., 345–46.
78. Gisela Bock, *Zwangssterilisation im Nationalsozialismus. Studien zur Rassenpolitik und Frauenpolitik* (Opladen, 1986); Loren R. Graham, "Science and Values: The Eugenics Movement in Germany and Russia in the 1920s," *American Historical Review* 82(Dec. 1977): 1133–64.
79. Bock, *Zwangssterilisation*, 113–15; E. Schubart, "Die Unfruchtbarmachung minderwertiger vom obersten Gericht der Vereinigten Staaten bestätigt," *Archiv für Rassen und Gesellschafts-Biologie* 20(1938): 74–76; idem, "Bundesobergericht Washington über Unfruchtbarmachung Erbminderwertigen," *JWS* 62(1933): 2041; Alfred Hoffmann, *Unfruchtbarmachung und Kriminalität* (Leipzig, 1940), 31–32; Geza von Hoffmann, "Die Durchführung der Sterilisierungsgesetzt in den Vereinigten Staaten von Nord-Amerika," *MKS* 10(1913): 297–302.
80. M. Staemmler, "Die Sterilisierung Minderwertiger vom Standpunkt des Nationalsozialismus," *Eugenik* 3(1933): 97.
81. Ibid.

82. Ibid.; Hoffmann, *Unfruchtbarmachung*, 30.

83. J. H. Landmann, "Sterilisierung in den Vereinigten Staaten," *ZStW* 53(1933): 712; Schmidt-Klevenow, "Die nordamerikanische Sterilisationsgesetzgebung bis 1934," *JWS* 65(1936): 240.

84. Landmann, "Sterilisierung," 712; Schmidt-Klevenow, "Sterilisationsgesetzgebung," 240.

85. Johannes Lange, "Psychiatrische Bemerkungen zum Gesetz zur Verhütung erbkranken Nachwuchs," *ZStW* 53(1933): 699–702; Hoffmann, *Unfruchtbarmachung*, 29–30.

86. Lange, "Psychiatrische Bemerkungen," 704–6.

87. Paul Popenoe, "Eugenische Sterilisierung in Kalifornien," *ZStW* 53(1933): 727, 729, 731–32.

88. Lange, "Psychiatrische Bemerkungen," 709–10.

89. Frank C. Richmond," Sterilisierung in Wisconsin," *ZStW* 53(1933): 733–34; Mabel Elliott, "Sterilisierungsgesetze und ihre Durchführung in Kansas," *ZStW* 53(1933): 743–46.

90. Bock, *Zwangssterilisation*, 113–15.

91. Richmond, "Sterilisierung in Wisconsin," 723; Elliott, "Sterilisierungsgesetze in Kansas," 746–47; Hoffmann, *Unfruchtbarmachung*, 41–42.

Book Review Essay: Bobby, Tommy, and the Enemy Within

Clive Emsley
The Open University, Milton Keynes

Anthony Babbington, *Military Intervention in Britain: From the Gordon Riots to the Gibraltar Incident.* London and New York: Routledge, 1990. x + 242 pp. £35.00.

Tony Jefferson, *The Case Against Paramilitary Policing.* Milton Keynes and Philadelphia: Open University Press, 1990. xiv + 161 pp. £32.50 (hardback), £10.99 (paperback).

Richard Vogler, *Reading the Riot Act: The Magistracy, the Police and the Army in Civil Disorder.* Milton Keynes and Philadelphia: Open University Press, 1991. xii + 206 pp. £32.50 (hardback), £14.99 (paperback).

Barbara Weinberger, *Keeping the Peace? Policing Strikes in Britain.* Oxford, Hamburg and New York: Berg, 1991. ix + 229 pp. £27.50.

During the eighteenth century a British prime minister could boast that he had led a mob. Not that the authorities in eighteenth-century Britain were always greatly enamored of turbulent crowds, but the tolerance of a measure of crowd activity appears to have been greater and there seems also to have been a degree of moderation and reciprocity among rulers and ruled in such situations that has led John Bohstedt to describe riots in provincial England at the end of the eighteenth and beginning of the nineteenth centuries as "community politics."[1] There has been considerable debate amon historians about the extent to which, and the reasons why, during the ni teenth century, popular disorder declined; it is no longer academically pectable or, more important, respectable to dismiss all rioters as the "dr of society and as criminal elements motivated by the desire for pl But since the 1960s, when historians began looking seriously composition of crowds in history and their motivations, the incid crowd action on the streets of Britain has increased; p policemen, journalists, and other members of a law-and-order lobby, ignorant of, or just ignoring academic research, have reverted to the old descriptions of rioters and have begun to speak of "the enemy within" stirring up political or industrial disorder.[2] When seriously out of hand, eighteenth-century riots were controlled by the military. Soldiers have remained a last resort for such tasks, but during the nineteenth century the new police largely took over the duties of controlling crowds; it was confidently argued that policemen were better able to cope and less likely to kill offenders. Disorders in contemporary Britain, however, have led to paramilitarism among the police; with his Nato helmet, overalls, body armor, long truncheon, and shield, the modern British Bobby may not much resemble the modern Tommy Atkins, but he might well be taken for his medieval forerunner. Given the riots in Britian's inner cities in 1981, 1985, and 1991, and the anti-Poll Tax riot that paralyzed central London in March 1990, it is timely, but hardly surprising, that a clutch of books address themselves to different aspects of these issues both contemporary and historical.

Anthony Babbington's *Military Intervention in Britain* provides a general chronological survey of the deployment of troops for the maintenance of internal order since the eighteenth century. It is a lively book, taking the reader through the most well-known of such deployments—the Gordon Riots, Peterloo, the Bristol Riots, Chartism, Featherstone colliery, the industrial disorders just before the First World War, and on to the contemporary situation in Northern Ireland. But there are problems with the book. A retired circuit court judge, Babbington has read, and makes reference to, George Rudé's work on eighteenth-century crowds but he remains rooted within the traditional interpretation; thus the Gordon Riots were worsened "by criminals who had poured into the capital from the counties nearby"
. 26); disorders in South Wales in 1910 were "augmented by large numbers
roublemakers" (p. 139); the riots accompanying the 1919 Liverpool
strike were "augmented by the riff-raff from the dockland tenements
ity slums" (p. 147). In Babbington's view by the end of World
"social maturity" of the English made disorders "prompted by
ence or a criminal impulse . . . relics of a past age" (p. 147).
nakes it difficult to explain the resurgence of disorder after
erhaps as a consequence, while chronicling this disorder,
rious attempt to explain what Babbington sees as the
d the deliberate violence during demonstrations,
since then.
al view of rioters Babbington has a Whiggish
s police and his soldiers are rarely anything
riots of 1981 "evolved out of a single
t to assist a black youth who was being
no mention here of the insensitive policing

of Operation Swamp, which raised tensions immediately before the disorder, and while Babbington quotes Lord Scarman's inquiry to the effect that the police during the riots "acted wisely, coolly, and with commendable restraint," he ignores Scarman's strictures on "the ill-considered, immature and racially prejudiced actions of some officers" during the years before the disorders, which unquestionably contributed to the violence.[3]

The impression comes through that, like the majority in his profession, Babbington does not like criticism or controversy when it comes to the law and the forces of the law; this may account for several lacunae in the book. For example, if the deployment of troops in nineteenth-century Ireland can be discussed, together with the use of troops in the Belfast strike of 1906 and at the beginning of the disorders in 1969, why is there no mention of the use of troops in Ireland during the 1916 rebellion and in the troubles that resulted in the creation of the Free State? It might be argued that rebellion is something different from rioting, and that, of course, the army may have to replace the police in such instances. It might also be argued that the ferocious behavior of the military authorities in 1916 contributed significantly to transforming the way in which the people of Ireland viewed the rebels. The recruitment and behavior of the "Black and Tans" in 1920 scarcely fit with the moderate and impartial image that is traditionally given to British law enforcement.

Since the beginning of the twentieth century military intelligence has begun to play a role in investigating subversion within British society; the "M.I." of M.I.5 stands for "Military Intelligence." During the First World War especially the military and the police began to cooperate closely in this area and in others. M.I.5 believed that, without the Communist party, there would have been no General Strike in 1926 and contributed to the "Secret" analysis of the strike made by Scotland Yard.[4] To all intents and purposes in September 1931 M.I.5 took over the Special Branch of the Metropolitan Police.[5] None of this is mentioned, let alone analyzed by Babbington, yet surely it all fits within the theme of "military intervention in Britain."

While there has been an increase in disorder since the Second World War, troops have not been used to confront crowds on the mainland. They have been used extensively during industrial troubles. Writing in 1984, Steve Peak counted thirty-six disputes since 1945 in which troops had been deployed to maintain what the government deemed to be "essential services."[6] Babbington devotes two pages to such incidents, concluding that "many believe [that government] has a . . . right and duty to use the armed forces, if need be, to protect the community from harassment and victimization in the course of an industrial dispute" (p. 152). He cites Peak's work in his footnotes, yet he does not engage with Peak's concerns about the undemocratic nature of these deployments and his belief "that the law surrounding [them] is confused and open to challenge."[7] Perhaps Babbington's use of the words "many believe" in itself is an admission of the problems here, but it is a pity that a member of the judiciary, albeit retired, did not focus directly on the question.

Richard Vogler's *Reading the Riot Act* covers much the same ground, and while his theoretical framework drawn from the work of Nicos Poulantzas will not be to everyone's taste, this is a far more penetrating and rewarding study. Recognizing that "the state" has to be understood in local terms—the county and municipal centers of power—as well as in centralized/national terms, Vogler identifes three agencies within the state involved with the suppression of rioting—army, magistracy, and police—and charts their interrelationship and development since the late eighteenth century. The first two-thirds of the book constitutes a broad historical survey; the last part focuses in detail on the responses of the police and the magistracy to the inner-city riots of 1981.

Initially the principal responsibility for organizing the response to disorder lay with the magistracy; but during the eighteenth and early nineteenth centuries this could create problems for soldiers on the spot when riots occurred and when magistrates were reluctant to act. The development of the Metropolitan Police in London gradually pushed the magistracy into a marginal role when dealing with disorder, even though the London magistrates were increasingly paid functionaries of the state rather than lay justices. In the provinces, in contrast, a lay magistracy kept the new police in a largely dependent role until the early twentieth century; as Vogler rightly stresses, the relationship between the police and the magistracy in London was not something readily adopted in Victorian England. The acceleration of change after the Second World War meant that by the time of the inner-city riots of 1981, across the country, the magistracy stood in a relation of dependency to the police. However, Vogler argues, this change is not best understood simply in terms of a steady growth of police power and the inexorable march of centralization. While in London by the 1880s the police were exercising independent authority over the army, Vogler argues that, from about 1910 to 1926, the situation was reversed; moreover, this military dominance in questions of public order spread across the whole country. This latter is, perhaps, the most challenging aspect of Vogler's historical analysis, and also, perhaps, the most debatable. The assertion of military dominance is based largely on the role of the army during the South Wales coal strike of 1910. His case might have been made stronger had he considered the role of the Authorised Competent Military Authorities established during the First World War; curiously the impact of the war, and the suspicions about police loyalty after the strikes of 1918 and 1919, are ignored here.[8] Also Vogler's determined focus on theory and state agencies, while important and profitable, tends to marginalize the significance of individual actors. Colonel Sir Charles Warren, the commissioner of the Metropolitan Police when the force achieved ascendancy over the army in the 1880s, appears here as a fairly typical commissioner—which he was not. His military arrogance and his outspokenness rapidly cost him his job. Captain Lionel Lindsay, the chief constable of Glamorgan in 1910, is briefly sketched as if he was a typical county chief constable of his time, responding typically to a strike. This, to say the least, is highly debatable, and it would be difficult to find another incident in the pre–1914 period in which the army, and military officers, were given such a central role. Vogler appears rather to lose sight of his emphasis on the significance of local peculiarities at this point. But these caveats aside, this is an important and stimulating book; it should be read and discussed by many more people than Babbington's, but its uncomfortable conclusions, particularly the evidence it presents of many magistrates' courts surrendering to policing imperatives in the aftermath of the inner-city riots of 1981, will probably militate against that.

Barbara Weinberger's analysis of the policing of strikes in the first quarter of the twentieth century is equally astute and penetrating; but the historical actors here are rather more human, and the theory underlining the book is less dominant. The question in the title, *Keeping the Peace?* immediately draws attention to the fact that matters are not as simple as Babbington believes. During strikes enforcing the law, keeping the peace, and maintaining impartiality are extremely difficult for those involved in policing, particularly when blackleg labor is involved. In such instances police discretion is essential, and discretion might mean weighing the alternatives of keeping the peace as against enforcing the law to the hilt. Weinberger begins with the Trade Disputes Act of 1906, moving through the strike wave immediately before World War I, the war itself, the postwar disorders, culminating in the general strike of 1926. She makes good use of local material and the significance of local context noting, for example, how social relations in different cities, and different political commitment by the economic elites, could have an influence on the structure of watch committees and, consequently, on policing. She also indicates how the dynamism and/or perceptions of certain key individuals could equally affect policing, as Home Secretary Winston Churchill pushed his authority to the limit, and probably beyond, in moving police around the country during the strike wave of 1910–11.

Weinberger challenges Jane Morgan's argument that the Home Office had been developing the concept of a national police response to strikes from the beginning of the twentieth century.[9] She maintains, convincingly, that Home Office intervention was much more ad hoc, tentative, and experimental, with the exception of the hectic eighteen months during which Churchill was in charge. Nevertheless she also demonstrates that, over the period of her study, there was a steady increase in centralization under the veneer of no change. During World War I the power of local authorities over their police was greatly undermined by the links forged among the police forces, the Home Office, the War Office, and the Special Branch. Furthermore, the fear of the subversive power of German gold and then of

Bolshevik infection led to new anxieties when industrial unrest manifested itself. When peace was restored and relations among local police, local authorities, and central government were claimed to have returned to the situation before the war, the police strikes of 1918 and 1919 and other examples of industrial unrest ensured that the anxieties continued and that the police became more and more an integrated system looking to the Home Office. This process gradually reduced local control over local police, and particularly over chief constables. South Wales during these years offers three alarming examples of chief constables (including Captain Lindsay) holding reactionary views, acting partially, confronting elected Labour local authorities, and being supported by the central government.

Many of the incidents discussed by Weinberger are well known and have been well worked over by labor historians. But the book has the virtue of approaching these incidents from a new perspective—not that of the strikers and their leaders, but that of the police. This alone would make it significant, but it is also thoroughly researched and presents its case cogently. Its use for historians is assured; it should be also read by politicians, policemen, and practitioners in the English criminal justice system, but as with Vogler's book, this is probably unlikely.

Tony Jefferson's *The Case Against Paramilitary Policing* deals combatively with contemporary historical developments. At the outset he explains that he has "never seen the slightest point in getting involved with police research if one is not interested in the 'controversial features' " (p. xiv). Paramilitary policing has always been controversial in Britain. Much of the opposition to the new police in the early nineteeth century stemmed from the fear that it was a military body like the French gendarmerie; in consequence politicians and senior policemen went out of their way to play down the military aspects of policing and to give the Bobby a civilian appearance. Jefferson's concern is the way that paramilitary policing has emerged in Britain since the 1960s.

Initially during the 1960s concerns about rising crime and about the threat of disorder coalesced with the belief that nuclear war might require the development of some different kind of civil defense policing to generate discussions of the need to create a "third force" situated between the police and the army. After a decade of inquiry in 1971 a Home Office Working Party concluded that any such "third force" would be unacceptable to the public and recommended that the exisiting police be retrained and equipped to deal with emergencies. The conclusions fit with the kinds of organizational experiments that the police had been pursuing since the mid–1960s with the organization of Special Patrol Groups. Unfortunately, too, in Jefferson's analysis, they also coincided with a breakdown of consensus within British society; thus as crowds increasingly took to the streets to protest or to further the claims of an industrial dispute, they were confronted by police units trained in a different and more aggressive form of crowd control.

Successive confrontations led each side to increase the scale of intimidation and violence deployed. For Jefferson the key problem in the escalation of disorder has been aggressive policing involving squads of men trained to act as teams and whose superior officers shared with their men perceptions of demonstrators similar to those of Babbington: Demonstrators were frenzied mobs augmented by troublemakers and stirred up by agitators.

Jefferson makes his case forcefully and convincingly. He makes some brief but interesting comparative references to developments in Australia and the United States. The big gap in his book is Europe. Paramilitary policing existed in France before the Revolution with the old regime's *maréchaussée*; it has existed across continental Europe since the early nineteenth century, although remarkably little historical research has ever been directed toward the gendarmeries.[10] Taken in a European context Jefferson's case against paramilitary policing might lead to an old-fashioned, English, and Whiggish view of continental policing and disorder. Of course there has always been ferocious violence on the streets of Europe during popular unrest, because the European police are armed, paramilitary, and lack any form of democratic accountability.

It is a common plea at the end of review articles to urge that more research is needed; of course research is always needed, but so too is more thought, particularly, perhaps, of a comparative nature. Perhaps too historians need to be more committed publicly, and to engage with the often shallow assertions of law-and-order lobbies and the continuing, blinkered vision of many in the law-and-order bureaucracy.

NOTES

1. John Bohstedt, *Riots and Community Politics in England and Wales 1790–1810* (Cambridge, Mass., 1983).
2. The term "the enemy within" was used by Margaret Thatcher with reference to miners during the strike of 1984–85; see *The Times*, 20 July 1984.
3. Lord Scarman, *The Scarman Report: The Brixton Disorders* (London, 1981), 4.61, 4.68.
4. Barbara Weinberger, "Communism and the General Strike," *Bulletin of the Society for the Study of Labour History* 48 (1984).
5. Christopher Andrew, *Secret Service: The Making of the British Intelligence Community* (London, 1985), 513.
6. Steve Peak, *Troops in Strikes: Military Intervention in Industrial Disputes* (London, 1984).
7. Ibid., 16.
8. David Englander, "Military Intelligence and the Defence of the Realm: The Surveillance of Soldiers and Civilians in Britain during the First World War," *Bulletin of the Society for the Study of Labour History* 52 (1) (1987); idem, "Police and Public Order in Britain 1914–1918," in *Policing Western Europe: Politics, Profes-*

sionalization and Public Order 1840–1940, ed. Clive Emsley and Barbara Weinberger (Westport, 1991).

9. Jane Morgan, *Conflict and Order: The Police and Labour Disputes in England and Wales 1900–1939* (Oxford, 1987).

10. Clive Emsley, "Community Regulation and Imperial Regulation: Peasants, Gendarmes and State Formation," paper presented at the 16th Conference of the Social Science History Association, New Orleans, Nov. 1991.

Book Review Essay: Bookmakers, Bribery, and the Betting Tax

Mark Clapson
Luton College

David Dixon, *From Prohibition to Regulation: Bookmaking, Anti-Gambling, and the Law*. Oxford, Clarendon Press, 1991. 320 pp. $89.

Before the mid–1970s, the social, economic, political, and legal significance of gambling had received little serious historical study. Gambling, as an activity in itself, was largely scrutinized in other academic disciplines: by psychologists seeking causal explanations for it; by sociologists who sought to understand gambling in relation to money making and the stock market; by philosophers who explored gambling as an expression of instinct and play; and by voluntary and public sector social workers concerned at the harm done to individuals and families by compulsive gambling. What little history did exist was confined to brief background sketches in such studies, and also to antiquarian or journalistic paens to the hallowed turf or Regency Rakes. Although entertaining and sometimes informative, the latter works rarely got beyond a romantic portrayal of the high days of the Grand National or Beau Nash.

The first historians in the field during the 1970s were James Mott and Wray Vamplew. Mott's stimulating and wide-ranging paper, given in 1975 yet sadly unpublished, interpreted the development of popular gambling from the abolition of the state lotteries in the 1820s to the rise of the football pools from the 1920s as a form of bottom-upwards influence on the nature of popular culture: Illegal sweepstakes and other lotteries, the growth of off-course ready-money betting on horses despite prohibition, and the development of gentle and communal sports such as pigeon racing and whippet racing without live bait, reflected the adaptation of what he saw as working-class values and the evolution of popular leisure to an increasingly urbanized and consumerist society.[1] Next came Vamplew, primarily an economic historian of sport, whose *The Turf* (1976) contains a couple of insightful chapters on bookmaking and betting, both legal on-course betting, and illegal off-course ready-money betting, which was abolished in 1853 in the light of a moral panic over gambling. The "something-for-nothing" mentality was seen as a cause of loose habits and crime, a threat to the industrious poor and to the Protestant work ethic. As Vamplew shows, in the face of prohibition a network of illegal street betting came into existence, based upon the much-maligned working-class bookmaker, which enabled the humble betters to have a little flutter well into the twentieth century.[2]

In 1979, Ross McKibbin further explored the world of street betting from 1880 to 1939, a time of growing prosperity and free time for the urban working class, when the commercialization of many leisure activities proceeded apace. McKibbin argues that the accusations of improvidence and irrationality leveled at gambling by its Puritan critics misunderstood the rationale of gambling as a source of hope and occasional payouts for those living lives often undermined by economic insecurity. It was also an interesting hobby involving the studying of form of horses and results of races.[3] A number of social historians since, including the present writer, have owed much to McKibbin, and have developed some of his concerns in order to further open up the history of gambling.[4] Oral history has proved a useful tool in recreating the experiences of street betting, something that Dixon himself called for in his 1981 paper on the Street Betting Act of 1906. Social histories have provided narratives detailing the day-to-day experiences of street betting for the bookmakers, their agents, and the punters. They have shown how the laws failed in the difficulties posed for the police when attempting to enact this most unpopular piece of legislation. Moreover, like McKibbin, they interpret gambling as an expression of sociability and economy. Historiographically, this is significant and specific to the later 1970s and since. Such histories aim to retrieve and reinterpret the cultural and recreational practices that were either ignored, written off as false-consciousness, or over-theorized as heroic counter-cultural class expression, positions to be located within the Neo-Marxist debate over popular culture since the 1960s. Unfortunately, a fuller discussion of what might amount to a new revisionist perspective in the social history of popular culture is beyond the bounds of this review.

One thing is clear, however: Future historians not only of gambling, but of the processes of law making and of policing will turn again and again to Dixon's work. Although his is what social historians rather pejoratively call a "top down" approach, and while he is primarily a criminologist and sociologist, this is an important and deeply researched piece of history. His major contemporary sources are a wide range of anti-gambling materials, parliamentary debates on and parliamentary inquiries into betting and gambling, police reports, and Home Office papers. The book under review here also represents the culmination of over a decade of prodigious research, and the drawing together of many of his previous publications.[5]

From Prohibition to Regulation discusses the high days of the anti-gambling campaign in late Victorian and Edwardian Britain, the passage of the impotent Street Betting Act of 1906, and the wholly unteleological pattern of twists and turns in the government's and the police's attitude toward gambling since then, which led to the legalization of off-course ready-money betting in 1960, in the form of Licensed Betting Offices, and culminated in the Betting, Gaming and Lotteries Act of 1984. This introduced television sets, coffee machines, and soft seating, turning over after more than twenty years a rule that betting shops should provide nothing that might activate "unstimulated demand." As Dixon puts it, the postwar social/liberal democratic philosophy "came to challenge and replace its predecessor, a more authoritarian paternalism whose tool was prohibitory regulation. In turn, it is now being undermined by the new philosophy of neo-conservatism, relying on the operation of the market as the prime social and economic regulator" (pp. 354–55).

The authoritarian paternalism that passed the 1906 Street Betting Act was not a class alliance of the rich ruling class seeking to allow itself the luxury of betting while denying the poor. Rather, the act represented the qualified success of the National Anti-Gambling League (NAGL) and its Nonconformist and well-meaning allies in Parliament. The NAGL had originally aimed at abolishing the legal right to bet for all, claiming that the rich were setting a bad example for the poor, a view endorsed wholeheartedly by Ramsay Macdonald and other Labour leaders. Anti-gamblers used gambling as a scapegoat for a plethora of Edwardian social and economic insecurities, such as a cause of lost production while Germany and the United States rose to economic supremacy, as symptomatic of a retarded lumpen street culture, and also for the defeat of an Imperial army by a handful of Boer farmers, and so on, all of which contributed to a conducive atmosphere for the passage of the legislation. The police generally welcomed the new powers, but their view was soon to be undone by two developments, first and foremost being the imperviousness of the street bookmaker and his customers to the laws, which led to widespread defiance of the law. This in turn caused the police to adopt a number of strategies: either to press on regardless, which was Canute-like in its futility, or to adopt a variety of tactics varying from the "blind eye" to downright collusion with bookmakers who rewarded them with financial favors in return for a smooth-running business. A number of accusations of corruption, some of which were proven, most notably in London in 1908 and in Liverpool in 1928, and also the general unwillingness of the public to cooperate, led many but by no means all police spokesmen to call for regulation rather than prohibition by the time of the 1923 and 1932–33 parliamentary inquiries into betting and gambling. Moreover, police spokesmen often complained of the unwillingness of local magistrates to convict unless there was hard corroborative evidence, and criticized magistrates for leniency in sentencing; the option of imprisonment for bookmakers was rarely taken. Not surprisingly, by the time of the Royal Commission of 1949–51, they were unanimous in calling for the abolition of an unpopular law.

A second reason for the legalization of gambling was its promise as a source of potential revenue for the state. Dixon emphasizes the role of the 1923 Select Committee on Betting Duty, which was chaired by the Conservative M.P. and expert on gambling law, Charles Cautley. Cautley's skepticism toward the alarmist claims of anti-gamblers was a notable departure from the authoritarian paternalism of previous parliamentary inquiries. Cautley's report of 1923 also dismissed the accepted image of lowly street bookmakers as unrespectable and sharkish "because the nature of the business must be carried on with scrupulous honesty or the bookmaker's business will disappear" (pp. 204–5). A committee that had originally intended to "investigate the revenue potential of betting duty developed into a much wider investigation of the social effects of betting and its control" (p. 208). This was of course no carte blanche for a straightforward decriminalization, but it symbolized a small and significant departure from the Edwardian moral panic mentality, and a more instrumental attitude of the state toward gambling. The first practical development came in 1926 when Winston Churchill as Chancellor of the Exchequer tried to levy a betting duty, but the law was so ill-thought-out as to be inoperable. For a start, Churchill proposed only to tax legal credit bets, and thus unwittingly deprived the government's coffers of the far larger tax to be gained from illegal off-course betting. Bookmaker opposition and a disinclination to register their bets, along with howls of indignation from the anti-gamblers, who argued that the twin tracks of illegality and taxation were grossly hypocritical, undid it. Furthermore, ideological differences and departmental squabbles between the Home Office and the Customs and Excise, who were to monitor the collection of the tax, did not help. The bookies had more than both ideological and practical differences with the tax, and even supported the Labour cause in the 1929 election in the name of a tax-free flutter, which they were duly awarded by Snowdon's orthodox, clean money economics. The chief result of this farce was its deterrent effect upon the subsequent speculation over the taxation of horserace betting.

Yet in 1928 the government introduced the totalisator levy on horse racecourses in order to pump money from betting back into the sport. Dog track companies, despite the fact the tote was only intended for horse racing, also installed totes, and after a few legal wrangles they were legalized at the dogs in 1934, following the Report of the Royal Commission into Lotteries and Gaming the previous year. In 1947, with a glint in his eye, Labour Chancellor Hugh Dalton introduced a tax on dog race totes, much to the chagrin of the greyhound racing companies who complained bitterly about payment while horse race totalisators still drew no money for government. The football pools were also taxed for the first time by the postwar Labour government. Later, the introduction of what Harold Wilson termed the "squalid raffle" of premium bonds in 1956, and the taxation of on-course bookmakers from 1961 via the Horserace Betting Levy Board, were further steps along the road of liberalization. Although taxation of off-course cash betting was not a function of the 1960 Betting and Gaming Act, which introduced Licensed Betting Offices in 1961, it followed in 1963. Bookmakers' organizations representing legal credit bookmakers feared that betting shops meant that the era of the small street bookie was nigh, but they need not have worried. An antagonist such as William Hill was soon to become the boss of one of the big three bookmaking firms that owned forty-two percent of all betting shops by the mid–1980s.

As Dixon makes clear, none of these legal developments was a happy reflection of "post–1945 liberal modernization," but the result of insufficient government, ad hoc decision making emanating from an inadequate culture of information getting, and anachronistic reformers. These latter points were made in 1978 in the Report of the Royal Commission on Betting and Gambling under the chairmanship of Lord Rothschild. The anti-gambling lobby had consistently and willfully failed to make the distinction between turnover and expenditure on gambling in order to serve their cause by exaggeration, but as the statistics of gambling became more available from the time of the Willink Commission of 1949–51, their tactics were exposed. By the early 1950s even Benjamin Seebohm Rowntree, a lifelong anti-gambler, yet one who placed his trust in findings of scientific social investigation, was prepared by 1950 to acknowledge the moderation of most betting, and that not every act of gambling was "sinful."[6] Basically, it was this reality, and the lingering Victorian imperviousness of the law to it until the 1950s, that made the anti-gambling laws so unpopular, and therefore inoperable.

In criticism, it may be objected that Dixon says less about the profession of bookmaking and the bookmaking interest than is suggested by the title. For example, there is no exploration of the role of bookmakers in the race-gang violence of the interwar years and the mid–1950s, which reinforced the image of the profession as one in cahoots with the criminal subculture, undeserved of legal recognition. Moreover, although this goes for most histories of policing, there is room for more analysis on the personnel and political composition of the magistracy as factors influencing the varying positions that magistrates adopted toward different pieces of legislation. However, such omissions do not undermine the strength of the argument presented here, nor the synthesis of themes and issues with the primary and secondary sources. *Prohibition to Regulation* shows in depth how laws are made, why they often fail, and the slow process of reform. It is a highly readable, wide-ranging analysis that provides ample evidence for a tall theory of legislative history, while never ignoring the divisions within, and the problems and limitations that face the police, economic interests, and reforming groups who seek to influence legislation.

NOTES

1. James Mott, "Popular Gambling from the Collapse of the State Lotteries to the Rise of the Football Pools," paper presented at the 1975 History Workshop Conference on "The Working Class and Leisure."

2. Wray Vamplew, *The Turf* (London, 1976). See also *Pay Up and Play the Game* (London, 1989).

3. Ross McKibbin, "Working-Class Gambling in England, 1880–1939," *Past & Present* 82 (1979).

4. Carl Chinn, *Better Betting with a Decent Feller: Bookmaking, Betting and the British Working Class, 1750–1990* (London, 1991); Mark Clapson, *A Bit of a Flutter: Popular Gambling in England, 1820–1961* (London, 1992); Andrew Davies, "The Police and the People: Gambling in Salford, 1900–1939," *Historical Journal* 34 (1991); and Jerry White, *The Worst Street in North London: Campbell Bunk, Islington* (London, 1985). See also Stephen Inwood, "Policing London's Morals: The Metropolitan Police and Popular Culture, 1829–1850," *London Journal* 15 (1990), whose discussion includes gambling.

5. For example, " 'Class Law': The Street Betting Act of 1906," *International Journal of the Sociology of Law* (1980); "Gambling and the Law: The Street Betting Act, 1906, as an Attack on Working-Class Culture," in *Leisure and Social Control,* ed. A. Tomlinson (London, 1981); "The State and Gambling: Developments in the Legal Control of Gambling in England, 1867–1923," in *The Gambling Papers,* ed. W. R. Eadington (London, 1981), vol. 7; and "Illegal Gambling and Histories of Policing in Britain," in *The Gambling Studies*, ed. W. R. Eadington (London, 1985).

6. See both Dixon, *Prohibition to Regulation,* 311–13; and B. S. Rowntree and R. Lavers, *English Life and Leisure* (London, 1951). The latter work, based on the oral testimonies of 400 people, remains not only a rich mine of information on domestic life and recreation, but also a source of commentary from many people of all social classes whose statements clearly undermine the notion of a postwar consensus among the people.

Book Reviews

Carlos Aguirre and Charles Walker, eds., *Bandoleros, abigeos y montoneros: criminalidad y violencia en el Peru, siglos XVIII–XX*. Lima: Pasado y Presente, 1990. 393 pp. $25.

Do bandits matter for the historian? Certainly the very considerable attention they have received in recent years by Latin American specialists (e.g., Gilbert Joseph, "On the Trail of the Latin American Bandit," *Latin American Research Review* 25 [3] [1990]: 7–53) would suggest so. But how much of this interest results from the sedentary academic's admiration for the colorful man, or woman, of action? And has the work demonstrated any significant relationship between outlaws and the fundamental political, economic, or political forces at work in history? The answer depends on which bandit and when and where. The authors of this excellent collection detail a variety of bandits and banditries evident in the Andes over the last two centuries and demonstrate that, at least in most of these cases, the activity was an integral and important part of local society. The poor of Peru and Bolivia became bandits for economic reasons, in order to right wrongs done to themselves or to their patrons, as an alternative to slavery and other forms of coerced labor, and to demand political and social inclusion. They did not become bandits to defend a preindustrial moral economy (Hobsbawn's "social bandit"). For such a defense they found the community to be the more effective vehicle.

It would be impossible in a short compass to do justice to the research and thoughtful analysis evidenced in *Bandoleros*, just as it would be impossible today to replicate much of the research because of the ever-growing violence in the countryside. After a brief introduction by Carlos Aguirre and Charles Walker, Carmen Vivancio Lara, Alberto Flores Galindo, and Ward Stavig open the book with chapters on various aspects of banditry in the late colonial and Independence period. Vivancio Lara, in a survey that rehearses themes raised in subsequent essays, identifies many of the phenomenon's principal local characteristics: that banditry was one way the dominated classes "express[ed] discontent and [made] claims" (p. 29) but that at the same time most of its participants continued to exhibit a "colonial mentality." That is, far from rejecting the moral-social order of the dominant group, the outlaw typically sought to replicate or to participate in that order. Bandits tended to organize themselves into groups with hierarchial internal organization, and generally they received help from at least some segments of the popular classes. Flores Galindo, in his essay, finds that despite elite and popular myths of the bandits' "ferocity," in fact banditry around turn-of-the-century Lima if endemic was not particularly violent. It did, however, expose some of the cleavages of late colonial society: Most of the bandits were black and their victims Indians. Not surprisingly the Indians cooperated enthusiastically with agents of the Crown in attempting to eradicate their tormentors. For the region around Cuzco, Ward Stavig shows that the most common offense was animal theft and that here both the criminals and the victims generally were Indians. But here again most of the Indians saw the illegal activities not as social revindication but self-interested criminality and turned to the state for protection.

Independence altered the context of banditry. In one of the most interesting chapters, Charles Walker examines how bandits became *montoneros*, political irregulars of the Liberal armies in the post-Independence civil wars. Most were *castas* and blacks denied citizenship by the racist definitions of "nationality" advanced by Conservative ideology and who instead supported the—admittedly only marginally—more inclusive Liberal project. They sought integration into the dominant system, not its overthrow. This was true even for black slaves of Lima and the environs who Carlos Aguirre shows escaped their masters and resorted to crime not so much to protest exploitation as to protest excessive exploitation. The effect, however, was that blacks did not simply wait out the disintegration of slavery as some have suggested but instead contributed actively to its destruction. Resort to banditry was at once an "escape valve" for the more active or desperate among the slaves and a stimulant to slave resistance.

As it did in much of Latin America, greatly increased integration into world markets during the second half of the nineteenth century stimulated social and economic changes at all levels in Andean society, greatly exacerbating class and race tensions. Three essays address the effects of these changes. Eric Mayer deploys a mass of quantitative data to make the point that crime and rebellions tended to follow cycles linked to the international economy and to the local agricultural calender. Focusing on Cajamarca, Lewis Walker paints a Hobbesian picture of personalist political conflict intertwined with war and banditry in the years during and after the War of the Pacific. And, in the only essay on Bolivia, Eric Langer compares late nineteenth-century animal theft in two regions, one dominated by Indian communities and the other shared by mestizo-owned large haciendas and small holdings. Much as Stavig demonstrated for Cuzco, Langer finds that in the Indian area while theft was a minor irritant and oriented chiefly toward covering immediate necessities, genuine class or ethnic resistance most typically took the form of community action. In the mestizo area, on the other hand, and in the absence of cohesive communities, animal theft was large-scale and widespread, the work of organized gangs recruited from impoverished small holders and squatters and aimed at the large haciendas prospering in the newly commercialized economy.

Two of the essays reflect extensive anthropological field work, if not, one hopes, participant observation. Benjamin Orlove uses interviews with jailed peasants made during the early 1970s in the Cuzco area to place animal theft in its local social context. He finds that far from being marginal such activities in this case were fully integrated into Indian society, providing both needed income and a form of protest against the expansion of haciendas into common pasture lands and harsh working conditions. This sort of crime served as the vehicle of resistance for an oppressed population unwilling to accept passively its declining situation but yet unable to construct a basis for genuine structural change. In a tour de force of field work if not readability—they make extensive use of quotes heavily larded with local terms—Ricardo Valderrama Fernandez and Carmen Escalante Gutierrez describe the lives of the inhabitants of two highland towns that "specialize" in stealing animals from distant communities. Even here, though, theft was not full-time work but was combined with agriculture and in recent years has been replaced by migratory labor to the coast. The book ends with an essay by Deborah Poole analyzing Peruvian discourse on Indian criminality and "dangerousness" between the 1930s and 1950s, pointing out the racism underlying even *indigenista* writings on the subject.

Bandoleros merits the close attention of anyone interested in the history of crime in Latin America or more generally in the question of peasant society, banditry, and rural criminality.

David McCreery
Georgia State University, Atlanta

Joe Sim, *Medical Power in Prisons: The Prison Medical Service in England 1774–1989*. Milton Keynes and Philadelphia: Open University Press, 1990. xii + 212 pp. £32.50 (hardback), £10.99 (paperback).

W. J. Forsythe, *Penal Discipline, Reformatory Projects and the English Prison Commission 1895–1939*. Exeter: University of Exeter Press, 1991. 255 pp. £25.00.

The appearance within a few months of each other of these works by Sim and Forsythe, both dealing with aspects of the development of the English prison regime, presents an interesting contrast in interpretations of penal history. Although the scope of the two books is different—the one dealing with the more specific subject of the role and influence of the Prison Medical Service over the last 200 years, and the other investigating more generally prison policy and regime in a shorter time-frame of less than fifty years—both inevitably give rise to thorny theoretical questions of how the facts of penal experience and discourse should be understood. What is immediately striking in moving from one author to the other is the difference between the unremittingly sinister reading of events by Sim (his quoted material presents a very grim picture), and Forsythe's discovery within the same institution of a genuine official belief in the individual worth of prisoners. The different tenor of these authors is not surprising, however, when they are located in the surrounding literature and theory on penal history. Sim openly acknowledges his "theoretical debt" to Foucault and his clear concern with the totalitarian tentacles of penal and welfare agencies places his work alongside that of writers such as Michael Ignatieff and David Garland. Indeed, Sim never steps outside this tradition of argument, conceding that Foucault's "analysis of the disciplinary genesis of institutional medicine, resistance to domination and the non-reductionist nature of power has been central to this dissection of medical power in English prisons" (p. 177). Forsythe, on the other hand, while aware of the "revisionist" arguments, distances himself from this approach and recalls the recent skepticism of Radzinowicz and Hood about the "carceral archipelago." The agenda he sets for himself, then, is "to understand whether Foucault was right that [the reformatory endeavor] was merely a convenient way of extending carceral subjugation or whether the disinterested idealism which was claimed by its advocates was a significant part of prison discipline" (p. 5). Thus, oddly enough, although Sim's style is the more biting—his work is in effect an exposure of the Prison Medical Service—Forsythe's endeavor is the more challenging in theoretical terms since he sets out to test, in a fundamental way, assumptions that have become deeply entrenched in academic argument.

Stepping back for the moment from the wider tendencies in the literature in this area, it must be said that both books are useful contributions that should be read by those interested in penal history. Both contain much interesting archival material and both are written in a lucid and readable style. Sim's book is obviously a more specialized study, which traces in a critical way the development and consolidation of the Prison Medical Service from its origins in the late eighteenth century to the present day. This review is divided into four main periods with an additional and substantial chapter on the way in which medical power has been brought to bear on female prisoners. This chapter on the gender dimension is largely self-standing and makes for compelling and disturbing reading as an elucidation of the element of gender in the exercise of both penal and medical power. The general thrust of the book is to emphasize the significant role of medicine and psychiatry as tools of discipline and control within the prison system and the interest of the medical establishment in the penal situation. It is striking to discover how much has been written in such publications as *The Lancet* and the *British Medical Journal* about medicine in the context of imprisonment.

Forsythe's book is concerned with the "reformative endeavour" in English prisons in the earlier years of this century. It should be noted that this work is part of a larger enterprise, since the author had already published *The Reform of Prisoners 1830–1900* in 1987; in other words, this is a continuing story and Forsythe is sure that it will continue into the future (p. 242). The early twentieth century is a period of significant penal development that has only recently been opened up by serious academic investigation, and Forsythe's work usefully complements that of Garland and of Radzinowicz and Hood published in the last few years. His specific interest resides in the use of techniques of reform in the context of imprisonment. After locating the subject-matter of the present book in the wider context of prior nineteenth-century transformations in penal policy and the *fin-de-siècle* change of regime in the English prison administration, he settles down to explore a number of substantive aspects of the prison system in this period and different types of sentence (such as penal servitude, prevention detention, and borstal training) in the light of reformative policy. This is a full and well signposted treatment of the subject that extends to some largely lost-sight-of topics, such as the ill-fated experiment with inebriate reformatories.

But ultimately with both these works it is the underlying argument that leaves an impression as much as the informative content, and readers will inevitably reflect on the contrasting interpretations. This is especially so since there are some points of overlap as regards the use of medicine and psychiatry in the prison system in the first half of this century and here it is possible to compare their treatment of much the same material. Sim is careful to note the challenges to and contradictions within the development of medical power, referring to "challenges to the role of medicine" and a "critical tradition," yet in the end his argument is unshakeable as regards the inexorable growth of this power: "At the same time the influence of the medical profession . . . was legitimized by the social reconstructionist ideology of the period. Medical intervention into the social body was increasingly formulated, implemented and legitimized by the state" (p. 72). Yet compare Forsythe's summary of such developments: "On the face of it these trends among medical officers . . . suggest a radical shift towards positivist determinism. . . . However . . . psychotherapy was only practised with a very small minority of prisoners . . . although . . . Grace Pailthorpe desired an entirely new penal system allocating its inmates to treatment programmes on the basis of selective psychological assessment, this view was not generally held by prison doctors. . . . the great majority of Prison Medical Officers were, like Norwood East, unwilling to see radical changes in the classical basis of sentencing practice and prison discipline in punishment and culpability" (p. 167). For Forsythe, between 1910 and 1939, medical officers "did not dominate reformatory theory but rather achieved a greater credibility and influence" (p. 167).

Indeed, a close reading of Sim and Forsythe on the same subject reveals that in the latter's account there lies an implicit challenge to the thrust of Sim's argument. Granted that there was a great deal of discourse of the medical totalitarian kind and there is evidence of prisoners having been dealt with in an arbitrary and brutal fashion. But how widespread was such practice and to what extent was it accepted or approved by informed opinion and within the penal establishment? Sim's account is hazy on this question, whereas Forsythe is more informative on the extent of "resistance" and "contradictions." For instance, take the role of Norwood East, a leading figure in the prison medical establishment during this period. Of him, Sim says shortly, and rather ambiguously and darkly, that he attended a conference at Rampton Hospital in 1920 (p. 65) and that during the 1920s he was producing 700 to 800 reports a year on the mental condition of prisoners. Yet it is Forsythe who tells us something of the content of Norwood East's writing. For example, in 1923, writing in the *British Medical Journal*, he warned against "hyper-enthusiasts" who saw the great majority of criminals as victims of inherited mental deficiency; in 1933 he cautioned that "eugenic sterilization" was "previous, unwarranted and possibly harmful to the race;" and although enthusiastic about psychoanalysis, he was concerned to play down its wider claims. From Forsythe we gain a fuller picture of the balance of the debate, such as the vigorous challenge mounted by such people as Horatio Donkin, the retired prison medical commissioner, and Charles Mercier, president of the psychological section of the British Medical Association, against eugenists and others who emphasized the role of inherited predisposition. This evidence points to an active and complex debate that is rather obscured in Sim's account of a more monolithic discourse. The great virtue of Sim's study is that it provides a view from the bottom up, at the receiving end. Yet in doing so it may well have understated the extent and nature of the resistance to and contradictions within medical power in both the official realm and wider society.

Christopher Harding
University College of Wales, Aberystwyth

John E. Archer, *'By a Flash and a Scare': Arson, Animal Maiming, and Poaching in East Anglia, 1815–1870*. Oxford: Clarendon Press, 1990. 300 pp. £35.00 ($74.00).

John Archer's painstaking and detailed book breaks new ground in the study of English rural history and criminal behavior. It will also have much to offer those studying arson or animal brutality in other periods and cultures. It is one of three recent books that together decisively refocus nineteenth-century English rural history, the others being Barry Reay's *The Last Rising of the Agricultural Labourers* (OUP, 1990), and the debate first conducted in *Journal of Peasant Studies*, now edited by Mick Reed and Roger Wells as *Class, Conflict and Protest in the English Countryside* (Cass, 1990).

Drawing together intensive research among records relating to East Anglia (the counties of Norfolk and Suffolk), Archer concentrates mainly upon arson. His treatment of arson and maiming is both innovative and illuminating, although at twenty-eight pages, the chapter on poaching is relatively short and adds little to the existing literature. Poaching is important to Archer's overall argument, however, because of his conclusion that a combination of poverty, terror, and oppression led to a state of rural war throughout the period he describes. Poaching was endemic, "a commonplace crime committed by ordinary men. Its very ordinariness gives poaching its peculiar place in the history of rural crime. It was the social crime of the countryside before the 1870s." Poaching is better categorized as "social" rather than "economic" crime because of the consistent unanimity with which the rural poor regarded it as a legitimate pursuit. "It challenged the very basis of rural society." On East Anglian evidence, Archer argues that Rudé's suggestion that during the third quarter of the century poaching was losing this popular sanction is wrong. Desperate affrays became rarer, but casual poachers were still widely at work.

Reay points out that "it is the background noise of 19th-century protest that is important—the continual negotiation and the grumbling, the acts of 'self-help' and revenge." Most historians would regard poaching as the constant element in this context, viewing arson as an irregular form of protest confined to periods of greatest tension. Archer refutes this view. One of the great merits of this volume is that it eschews the familiar milestones of English rural history (Swing, Tolpuddle, the trade union movement of the 1870s) in favor of the difficult but ultimately more rewarding journey over the unfamiliar terrain between and beyond them. Arson is shown to be endemic to East Anglian society. During the 1860s, supposedly a decade of tranquility, the region experienced considerably more fires than during the depressed 1820s. Furthermore, Archer suggests, covert protest was not an alternative to overt collective action. The two could and did exist side by side, for example, during 1831–34 and then the period of implementation of the New Poor Law, in enclosure disputes, and during the depression of 1849–52. Archer also notes some correlation between incendiarism in the late 1860s and parishes that were shortly to be at the forefront of the agricultural trade union movement.

The author, however, goes beyond this to argue persuasively that arson was itself a form of overt and collective protest, especially until the early 1850s. The grievances of agricultural labor legitimized the actions of the incendiary, and the fact of legitimation was evident time and time again in the reactions of the crowds who gathered to witness, to celebrate, and sometimes literally to fan the flames. Onlookers cheered the blazes, fed the fires, obstructed firemen, or simply stood and watched in displays of sullen defiance—2,000 of them at one Norfolk fire in 1831. Archer's careful correlation of the incidence of arson against other data suggests that the fires were an expression against low wages and very high unemployment. They were seldom purely the product of personal pique. They may even be seen as a form of collective bargaining. After 1852, however, the nature of arson changed, and communal celebrations of incendiarism disappeared. The typical arsonist of the early period was an unmarried day laborer, residing in the vicinity of the fire, and the most vulnerable in his community to unemployment. Out-migration and high farming diminished the reservoir of these "loose hands" among the laboring population. Incendiarism diminished, and later arsonists were more likely children or vagrants.

Animal maiming, Archer concludes, should be seen as "an act of transferred or symbolic murder and as a weapon of psychological terror." "I shood verry well like to hang you the same as I hanged your beastes," wrote the slaughterer of two bullocks in 1844 to his master, who had recently acquired a scuffling plough and thus laid off workers previously employed in hand hoeing. Two days later a barn, stables, and four animals were burnt on the same farm. The purpose of animals was to create profits for farmers, and to suppose that laborers were at all sentimental about them, Archer suggests, is to impose anachronistic urban values. Killing livestock, then, was similar to other forms of protest involving the destruction of employers' property. Archer coins the term "animal luddism" in emphasizing this, since the perpetrators rarely revealed any economic motive (for, example, taking meat from a slaughtered carcass). The additional symbolic dimension involved in the taking of life, however, meant that compared to arson incidents of animal luddism were rare acts of particular desperation, whose occurrence in East Anglia during this period was never more than once a month, and was generally less. Like arson the incidence of maiming was greatest in the period to the early 1850s.

'By a Flash and a Scare' is a fine study of rural protest, but ultimately it also reveals the limitations of its subject matter. If maiming had the profound capacity to unnerve farmers that this book suggests, then it is perhaps a measure of the social stability of East Anglia that its incidence was not greater. As it is, poaching is made to bear much of the weight of the concept of a "rural war" persisting in the period after 1852. Archer's integrity as a scholar will not permit him to make larger claims for arson and maiming in the later period, but his adherence to a notion of continuing rural class

conflict means that he is nonetheless reluctant to conclude that the period of high farming may have been paralleled by the emergence of a viable class society. He is right to be reluctant, but the further evidence to support this thesis is not going to be found in the continuing study of protest crimes, even if these are widened beyond Archer's agenda to include, for example, offenses under the Malicious Injuries Acts of 1826–28. Agricultural laborers were first and foremost workers, and the perpetrators of social crime (if at all) only second. Rural protest is in danger of becoming a conceptual strait-jacket, excluding conflicts within the labor process and in relations of employment. These are conflicts to which historians will remain blind while they continue to operate with the conventional typologies of protest on the one hand, and of trade unionism on the other.

Malcolm Chase
University of Leeds

Carolyn A. Conley, *The Unwritten Law: Criminal Justice in Victorian Kent.* New York and Oxford: Oxford University Press, 1991. 244 pp. £22.50

In *The Unwritten Law* Carolyn Conley assesses the degree to which the regularization of the criminal law in Victorian England actually determined the practices of local administrators in Kent between 1859 and 1880. In essence, this book provides a microstudy of the values and assumptions of mid-Victorian England as revealed in the actual working of the criminal justice system, with particular reference to the influence of contemporary perceptions of class and respectability.

In her analysis of community law (chap. 1) Conley examines the methods, both official and extralegal, that were used to police mid-Victorian Kent, demonstrating that the law was largely defined by local magistrates and the police, whose power and effectiveness depended largely on the acquiescence of the local community. In return for public cooperation, magistrates were expected to respect local custom, including Guy Fawkes celebrations and incidents of rough music, and to preserve the rights and dignities of the "respectable" sectors of local society. Similarly, local control of policing ensured that relations between the police and the public were generally good, a consensus that was threatened only by the periodic incursions of the metropolitan police (who were regarded as an alien force and whose presence was strenuously opposed) in extrametropolitan Kent.

In her analysis of violent crime in Kent (chap. 2), Conley demonstrates that the administration of justice was influenced by local interpretations of the criminal law. With reference to 973 assault cases in the county during the period she explores the factors that determined which violent actions were perceived as criminal and which were regarded as excusable, concluding that Kentish judges established the limits on violence with considerable clarity. Thus occasional bouts of violence among equals in a pub or among relatives in private were perceived as understandable, while public assaults on inoffensive, "respectable" persons and violence directed toward social superiors were not, and were punished accordingly.

Gender and class also influenced the administration of justice in the county, and Conley provides a lucid analysis of the problems experienced by women who came before the male-dominated judicial system, either as victims or suspects, with particular reference to domestic violence, rape, and indecent assault (chap. 3). She shows how prevailing attitudes often undermined the legal sanctions against the domestic abuse of women. Judges were more likely to condone male violence in response to retaliation than they were to sanction female retaliation; magistrates often suspected women of bringing such attacks upon themselves; often the physical abuse of women, especially wives, was regarded as chastisement. Indeed, public officials, including the police, generally preferred not to involve themselves in domestic disputes and, even when cases reached the courts, much depended on the court's perception of the character of the accused and his victim. Hence a husband of perceived "good character" could chastise an "immoral" or "irritating" wife with impunity. Rape, an even more gender-specific crime, presented particular difficulties for the criminal justice system and, as Conley observes, rape victims were suspect on three counts: they were female; they had been temporarily outside the supervision of male guardians when the offense occurred; they were publicly announcing their loss of sexual innocence. In this context it is hardly surprising to discover that only twenty-one percent of men accused of rape actually stood trial in Kent, of whom only forty-one percent were convicted. Notions of class and respectability also influenced the courts in dealing with other sexual offenses against women: Significantly, only thirty-four percent of men who were described in court as "respectable" were convicted of indecent assaults on women, while fifty-nine percent of men who were not "respectable" were convicted.

Children were also at a distinct disadvantage before the courts (chap. 4). As victims of crime they could prosecute only through their parents, guardians, or the local Poor Law Board. Invariably their testimony was regarded as unreliable, unless corroborated by adults. Hence the Kentish authorities were generally reluctant to interfere in cases of child abuse and/or neglect, and only cases of gross and deliberate cruelty elicited a firm response. In their attitude to infanticide, a relatively frequent occurrence, the response of the authorities was ambivalent, while sexual assaults on children rarely resulted in committals for trial since the authorities wished to protect children from the strain and stress of the proceedings.

In view of the influence of middle-class perceptions on the interpretation of the law and on the administration of justice in Kent, Conley's revelation that "To the merchants, artisans and farmers who sat on Kentish juries there was a clear distinction between the innocent part of the community to which they belonged and the 'criminal class'—persons who lived outside the bounds of respectable society and who were inherently guilty" (p. 136) is somewhat predictable. Indeed, numerous studies of nineteenth-century crime have suggested that local communities were often quick to attribute much crime to the activities of a "criminal class" or to "outsiders" (terms not always perceived as mutually exclusive) and mid-Victorian Kent was clearly no exception. Thus Conley demonstrates (chap. 5) that much local criminality was attributed variously to the career criminals of London, who were perceived as a constant threat; to people from distant parts of the country; to the poor in general, and to vagrants in particular (although contemporaries distinguished between local beggars, who were tolerated, and the transient poor, who were not); to soldiers, who were associated with drunkenness and disruptive behavior; to local prostitutes. The Irish were also associated with the "criminal class" and there were manifestations of anti-Irish feeling in Kent during the period, notably during the harvest season when hundreds of Irish hoppers migrated to rural Kent from Kentish London. However, Conley notes that clashes between the police and the Irish were less frequent than might have been expected, in part due to the relatively sensitive policing of Irish communities.

Conley's study of the response of the criminal justice system to white-collar crime and to breaches of the Masters and Servants Act provides further evidence of the extent to which notions of class and respectability influenced the administration of justice in Kent (chap. 6). The perceived "respectability" of criminals often determined the initial decision to prosecute (or not to prosecute), the verdict, and the sentence. This did not always apply, however, in regard to poachers, for poaching was accepted by the authorities as a fact of life. Hence punishments for poaching were usually light except where gangs of poachers ("outsiders") had been at work and/or there had been violent confrontations between gamekeepers and poachers.

Conley's essential conclusion is that a sense of tradition and continuity was one of the most remarkable features of the criminal justice system and the men who ran it in mid-Victorian Kent. In practice, the law was determined as much by local tradition as by parliamentary statutes and older patterns of judicial discretion and extralegal community sanctions continued to be practiced with considerable support. Administrators regarded the law as an impartial entity and treated each case on its merits according to persons and circumstances. Thus the gravity of an offense depended very much on who was involved and why. Class and respectability thus played an important role in the administration of justice because Kentish magistrates and jurors defined crime and the law according to the standards of the respectable male members of the community and responses to criminality were measured in these terms.

Hence "the respectable men of Kent combined state and community law to protect their society and... the criminal justice system did what its constituents expected by providing protection and autonomy for local persons, property and sensibilities" (p. 204).

This is an interesting and informative study, concise, well-written and researched. This said, a more comprehensive presentation and analysis of the statistics of crime would have been useful; the contrasts between Kentish London and extrametropolitan Kent (and between rural and urban districts within extra metropolitan Kent) could have been explored more fully; and Conley's essential thesis is hardly novel. Nevertheless, the book illustrates effectively the value of the study of the local community in highlighting and exploring a range of key issues pertaining to the administration of justice in Victorian England. It also poses a number of questions of contemporary relevance. As such, *The Unwritten Law* constitutes a welcome addition to the historiography of crime in nineteenth-century Britain.

Roger Swift
Chester College of Higher Education

Alf Lüdtke, *Police and State in Prussia, 1815–1850*. Cambridge and Paris: Cambridge University Press; Editions de la Maison des Sciences de l'Homme, 1989. 320 pp. $59.90.

This book constitutes an abridged version of an original German text published at Göttingen in 1982. It seeks to expand upon Hans Rosenberg's pioneering analysis of German bureaucratic absolutism, *Bureaucracy, Aristocracy and Autocracy*, published in 1958. Additionally, Lüdtke attempts to compare the Prussian example to the recent study of *Policing and its Context 1750–1870* undertaken in 1983 by Clive Emsley for Britain. Since the English translation has eliminated Lüdtke's archival bibliography, one must surmise from the detailed notes that the majority of the research was undertaken in various regional archives in the Rhineland and in the former Prussian territories of Poznan (Posen) and Wroclav (Breslau).

Lüdtke's main thesis is that "bureaucratic rule" in Prussia from the Congress of Vienna to the revolutions of 1848 was based upon coercion in the form of both armed and symbolic force. The concept of "police" assumes two forms of analysis: first and foremost, the use of armed force by the ruling orders against the "lower popular classes"; and more sophisticatedly, the use of gendarmes as agents of a primitive early nineteenth-century welfare system. With regard to this "new police" as individuals "to whom resort could be made in a variety of troubles," Lüdtke's work tangentially touches upon Emsley's major findings with regard to the police in Britain. At a secondary level, Lüdtke argues that the "rule of law" in Prussia was driven by economic—read, class—distinctions. The "commercial bourgeoisie" based its intercourse with society on legal instruments. And the bureaucracy, as the only "universal estate," laid sole claim to manipulating these legal forms. In all cases, bureaucratic domination "is *necessarily violent*" (p. 204).

The strength of the book lies in the richness of detail. Lüdtke has tracked down documentary evidence for all sorts of major and minor cases wherein the Prussian police sought to establish and to enforce its view of order, public safety, and well-being. The advancement of the common good demanded economic and social mobilization, and this translated into safeguarding property and defending accepted forms of social intercourse. In Lüdtke's view, the all-pervasive role of the state in regimenting the legal, social, and economic mores of its citizens underscores the validity of the currently fashionable notion of "everyday history" (*Alltagsgeschichte*) practiced by his colleagues at the Max-Planck-Institute of History at Göttingen University.

The book's greatest weakness results from the author's insistence on equating police with bureaucracy in Prussia. In doing so, he ignores that other state agencies such as administration, economics, education, and the military also played major roles in shaping the nature of Prussian society in the early nineteenth century. Moreover, Lüdtke fails to note that the state's ability to shape society was highly limited in this pre-modern and pre-industrial era. To a larger degree than today, the state's power to enact and to enforce educational and taxational policies—to name but two—was determined largely by its ability to forge a local consensus for such measures.

The second major flaw of the book is that Lüdtke tries to adapt to Prussian social history Harold Lasswell's concept of the "garrison state" from military history. By "citadel practice," Lüdtke means the "militarization of police-administration in Prussia, and of the Prussian bureaucracy in general." The equation of the bureaucratic and the military state is accomplished through the "unmistakable permeation of military standards and professionalisation into the civil apparatus of coercion." And the police, the "sword of internal order," in time rendered direct military intervention in state affairs "largely superfluous" (pp. 190–92). What Max Weber termed "acquiescence to order" was brought about in Prussia by the constant threat of force, as symbolized in the various forms of "gentle violence." Its costs, according to Lüdtke, were revealed in 1914 and again in 1933: "mass capitulation and submission to authoritarian excesses" (p. 203).

In the final analysis, the Prussian state between 1815 and 1848 was highly complex, as could only be expected from a society undergoing transformation from an absolutist and agrarian to a semirepresentative and industrial system. To suggest that the police—which in Berlin in this period consisted of less than 200 persons, compared to a military garrison of 15,000—dominated the state and rendered the army "superfluous" is going beyond the limits of credibility.

Holger H. Herwig
University of Calgary, Alberta

Richard J. Evans, ed., *Kneipengespräche im Kaiserreich. Die Stimmungsberichte der Hamburger Politischen Polizei 1892–1914*. Rowohlt Taschenbuch Verlag: Reinbek bei Hamburg, 1989. 310 pp. DM 18.80.

In December 1892, a few months after the great cholera epidemic, the Hamburg political police initiated an intelligence-gathering exercise that was to last until the eve of the First World War. At the initiative of its head, Commissar Rosalowsky, a half-dozen police officers were allotted a new task. Dressed inconspicuously as workers, they were to spend their time in places where working people congregated, especially in pubs in working-class districts of the city, listen carefully to the conversations around them, and record what they heard. As a result of Rosalowsky's concern to keep a finger on the pulse of working-class opinion in Hamburg, roughly 20,000 handwritten reports about public opinion in Germany's premier port city during the two decades before the First World War were left behind in police files.

Richard Evans, who has spent much of his academic career hunting in the Hamburg State Archive, has edited a selection of these reports—348 of them to be exact. The edited reports are organized thematically, rather than chronologically, around a variety of social-historical themes and political subjects. The resulting volume is a gold-mine of information about the German urban working class and workers' opinions under the last kaiser, and social historians no doubt will find it a valuable source of juicy quotes for years to come. Although it yields few surprises, the collection provides as good a picture as we are likely to get of what working-class Germans were thinking long before the advent of public opinion polls. What emerges is a picture of a society that largely shared the values and categories of Social Democracy—of a class society that formed with industrialization in the nineteenth century and dissolved in the twentieth.

But what does this tell us about the police and the way they operated? Although Commissar Rosalowsky was convinced of the need to keep a careful watch on Hamburg's potentially dangerous classes, the reports yielded little that was of direct use to the police. (No doubt this was why they eventually were filed under the heading, "reports without value"). Rather than uncovering revolutionary conspiracy or specific occasion for police action, the reports demonstrated that workers generally rejected political violence. Yet, as Evans notes, the police failed to apply this intelligence when, confronted by political unrest in January 1906, they assumed they were faced with part of a secretly and carefully planned attempt at revolution. When one considers that no real use was made of these reports, perhaps the most remarkable thing about this impressive intelligence-gathering exercise is that it lasted so long. Not until the end of 1910—eighteen years and 20,000 reports after it had begun—was it stopped. The exercise had its origins in unfounded paranoia, was carried out with considerable professional skill, was applied to neither policy nor practice, and continued largely as a consequence of bureaucratic inertia—all of which says a lot about the police of Wilhelmine Germany.

The volume contains an informative introduction and is well illustrated with appropriate photos. Furthermore, and unlike so many German historical texts, it has a good index. However, the decision to present the material thematically rather than chronologically (together with the fact that even within the thematic sections the reports are not presented in chronological order) tends to transmit a rather static picture of Wilhelmine Germany. Although Evans provides much useful contextual information when introducing the material, readers without a clear idea of the political and economic changes that occurred in Imperial Germany may come away from the reports with a sense that conditions and opinions altered little between 1893 and 1910. Also, a map of Hamburg before the First World War would have been useful, if only to allow readers unfamiliar with the city to locate the pubs from which the reports were made.

Richard Bessel
The Open University, Milton Keynes

Philip Terdoo Ahire, *Imperial Policing: The Emergence and Role of the Police in Colonial Nigeria 1860–1960*. Milton Keynes and Philadelphia: Open University Press, 1991. xviii + 165 pp. £35.00.

In his introduction to this study of the history of policing in colonial Nigeria, the series editor, Colin Sumner, rightly reflects with regret upon the "Anglo-American, Eurocentric and even imperial character" of so much of the literature on crime and justice in the underdeveloped world. He might have gone further, to lament the long neglect of colonial policing by both historians and social scientists. The social history of policing, so well developed for Europe since the 1970s, is only now becoming a serious area of inquiry for historians of Africa and Asia. Earlier generations had to make do with the dubious pleasures of "official" institutional histories, augmented only by the published anecdotal reminiscences of former serving officers. Whether sounding a trumpet call for the alleged successes of "professional policing" or providing a cheerie narrative of "a job well done," this literature was hardly satisfactory to the serious scholar of policing or criminal justice and did little to situate policing within the context of a broader social (or even political) history. By contrast, Philip Ahire's study of the policing of colonial Nigeria is in the vanguard of a new wave of historical research that will at last give historiographical prominence to this crucially important aspect of the colonial experience.

The central thrust of Ahire's analysis is simple enough. He charts the establishment of a militarized police force, burdened more by its commitment to the defense of the realm than by any notion of combatting crime, and then exposes the reasons for the failure of the Nigerian colonial state to achieve its avowed aim of turning that police force into a body capable of conducting civil policing with the support and consent of the population. This failure had much to do with the nature of the state itself, asserts Ahire. Where other writers have viewed the emergence of policing in Nigeria in a predominantly Whiggish light, Ahire sees little in the way of "progressive improvement" in the Nigerian police force. Instead, he describes the durability of a deeply ingrained colonial model of policing that the modern state has been unable to throw off. Militaristic policing, although challenged by policies that sought to reform Nigeria's colonial police, was a necessary element in the maintenance of colonial authority and could not be effectively replaced. In common with many other police forces in Africa, in the public mind the Nigerian police were enemies rather than friends of the people.

Colonial policing thus remained coercive in practice regardless of any changes in the theoretical basis of police work over the colonial period. If militarism seemed to decline after 1914, this did not mean that the police gave up coercive tactics. After 1914 Ahire characterizes Nigerian policing as "demilitarised coercion." Quoting Cohen with approval, Ahire notes the emerging deployment of the police as the "moral entrepreneurs of public propriety." And of course, propriety was in this case set in the terms of the European (colonizer) and not the African (colonized). Policing accordingly reformed not in response to changing patterns of crime or public perceptions of law and order, but in the necessary adjustments the state sought to make in order to maintain strategies of domination over a subordinate population.

There is, therefore, much here that will seem familiar to students of policing history in Britain, Europe, and North America, but there is also much that was distinctive about the colonial context in general and Nigeria in particular. The creation of a "Native Authority Police" (called "Tribal Police" in some colonial territories), to operate in parallel with the colonial police but to be concerned with predominantly rural matters and to be under the control of local African authorities, marked one significant departure from British metropolitan practice. Another was the close and overt relationship between police power and the functioning of colonial capital. In the colonial world the police were prominent agents for the consolidation and legitimization of imperial authority: yet in their continued dependence upon coercion rather than consent lay perhaps the cause of their failure as the vehicles of hegemony.

While Ahire makes all these points, his account lacks the vibrancy that might have been provided by a closer scrutiny of the daily grind of police work, especially in the context of Nigeria's social history. There is disappointingly little here on the changing nature of crime, on the experience of the police themselves, or on the social perceptions of police authority. While the police enforced a colonial public morality, there was surely room for some discussion of how that might relate to existing African public moralities. The discussion of the activities of secret societies, oracles, and cults (pp. 124–28) takes us toward this terrain, but Ahire's insistence that "criminalisation" of such groups was merely a colonial convenience to facilitate the imposition of colonial values and goals surely ignores the deep and long-standing division of opinion within African communities over the social and political legitimacy of such groups. Given the sophistication of current writing on Nigeria's social history, these statements seem naively simplistic. The emphasis on the actions of policing in relation to theories of imperialism and the colonial state seems to have deflected Ahire's attention away from these other, and potentially more revealing, areas of inquiry. Africanists, and especially social historians of West Africa, may therefore find some of the generalizations about the impacts and limitations of colonial controls a little difficult to swallow. Redressing the previous biases of an "imperial" and "Eurocentric" literature need not have resulted in this glossing over of the cracks and contradictions within African societies.

Turning to the pedantic, but nonetheless important matter of sources and citation, it must be said that the author and publishers should have taken greater care in the presentation of the footnotes. Inconsistencies and oddities have crept into the many abbreviations used, and although the provenance of most unpublished sources can be deduced by the diligent reader, a clear indication of the particular archival location of materials (especially those in Nigeria, a country with several archive centers) would have been welcome. Readers might also have benefited from some discussion of the nature of those archival sources. After all, it is not every African state that has allowed the records of its police department to be opened to public scrutiny and it would be interesting to know more precisely the types and range of materials that were made available to Philip Ahire.

But this is merely to ask for amplification and elaboration from the author and to make the historian's customary plea for attention to the specifics of sources. Within the limitations of its political focus, Philip Ahire's book has made an important and timely contribution to a developing field of study, and deserves to be widely read.

David M. Anderson
School of Oriental & African Studies, University of London

Dorothy E. Chunn, *From Punishment to Doing Good—Family Courts and Socialized Justice in Ontario, 1880–1940*. Toronto: University of Toronto Press, 1992. 249 pp. $29.95.

American legal historians Julius Goebels Jr. and T. Raymond Naughton once wrote that the functioning of the legal system depended "upon three intensely volatile elements—human judges dealing with relations of human litigants in terms of ideas."[1] The essence of this dynamic is central to Canadian criminologist Dorothy Chunn's examination of Ontario's emergent family court system from 1880 to 1940. Focused on the process whereby state law and regulation forced its way into the sanctity of the home, Chunn has given us an illuminating portrayal of how half-formed ideals and contradictory notions often provided the backbone of what subsequently became the welfare state. Based on a convincing mixture of personal papers, government records, and secondary literature, Chunn's work is grounded in evidence documenting the considerable gap between the stated goals of reformers advocating socialized justice and the actual reforms that were eventually instituted and reaffirmed by the Canadian Supreme Court. In adopting such a view of both state law and the reform process, Chunn provides a realistic portrayal of the complex interaction between a society and its legal structures.

Divided into eight chapters, the book approaches Ontario's family court system by initially outlining possible theoretical perspectives and then weaving the abstraction of theory with the actions of reformers. While Chunn believes that the period from 1880 to 1940 was "a distinctive and fundamental period of transition from laissez-faire to welfare state" and that a "distinctive change" occurred during these years, it was not necessarily linked directly to efforts of reformers (p. 11). For Chunn the growing concern over the impact of industrialization and urbanization on the lower classes, and the desire of the middle class to regulate and control those lower sorts, was the prime motivation for the changes in Ontario's court system. These middle-class reformers focused their efforts on propagating their own visions of the central importance of the family in maintaining societal stability and thus it was to be on this plane, that of familial tension, conflict, and breakdown, that the battle to regulate the lower classes would be fought. Yet to accomplish this goal a mechanism was needed to provide both legitimacy and official sanction to those who thought it incumbent to intervene in what most thought was the sanctuary of the home. In Ontario, the ad hoc development of the family court system provided that mechanism.

The character of such a court system offered a number of problems for the reformers, the Ontario government, the judiciary, and eventually the Canadian federal government. While it eventually came to be accepted that there was a legitimate need for some form of family tribunal, there was no agreement as to whether it ought to be a distinct level of courts presided over by trained legal professionals, or within the existing county court structure, or at the level of magistrate's court under the supervision of nonprofessionals. This debate is central to Chunn's work as it was a key concern for those involved with what reformer Charlotte Whitton envisioned as a "court in social causes" (p. 140).

If these courts were viewed as legitimate their work might bring about relief for those families in turmoil, but if viewed with skepticism or outright hostility, these tribunals could exacerbate the situation they were supposed to alleviate. In the end, at the behest of the Ontario government and with the agreement of the Department of Justice in Ottawa, the status of Ontario's family courts was referred to the Canadian Supreme Court in 1938, which, in a unanimous decision, upheld the courts as falling within the jurisdiction of the Ontario provincial government. Yet as Chunn demonstrates in her discussion of the reference case, the affirmation of Ontario's family courts was not the product of an acceptance of socialized justice, but was rather the result of the give and take of the ongoing contest over interpreting the British North America Act.

While Chunn succeeds in depicting the idiosyncracies and inconsistencies of a process spanning sixty years, there are a few bothersome characteristics in her presentation. First, the incorporation of both in-text references to sources as well as the more traditional historical end-note style is, to say the least, extremely annoying. Undoubtedly most historians would prefer the traditional format, but even if the in-text reference style was preferred by Chunn and the University of Toronto Press editorial staff, a far wiser course would have been to adopt one or the other format. A more significant difficulty, however, is the almost complete absence of those people who found themselves in Ontario's family court system. It is unfortunate that a discussion of a court system chose not to discuss the substance of what that court actually did on a regular basis. Rather, Chunn's emphasis was on the creation of the system as opposed to its substantive operation. While it is always easy to review a book for what it did not do, it would seem that the inclusion of those who were using the family court system would have only strengthened Chunn's argument that a gap existed between the ideals of reformers, the system that was created, and the "law" that the system then administered. Recalling Goebel's and Naughton's description of the legal system, Chunn dealt with both the judges and the ideals, but overlooked the human litigants.

While some of Chunn's emphasis might be subject to debate, this certainly does not detract from a strong piece of work. Without doubt the most important contribution of her efforts is to reinforce the perspective that the interaction between legal remedy and society is multi-layered and very complex, and as a result, the interpretative perspectives we employ to understand that interaction must be capable of pulling back those layers. Having detailed the origins of Ontario's family court system, Chunn finds that it was "characterized by contradictions" (p. 192). While such a conclusion may be disappointing, naive, or frustrating for those who want to draw a straight line from cause to effect in sketching the relationship of law and power, Chunn's view offers compelling reasons to reconsider the real limits of reform and the reformers or, those who opposed change, in shaping the legislative agenda in any jurisdiction.

NOTE

1. Julius Goebel Jr. and T. Raymond Naughton, *Law Enforcement in Colonial New York*. (New York, 1944), 59.

Jonathan Swainger
University of Northern British Columbia, Prince George

Rosamund M. Thomas, *Espionage and Secrecy. The Official Secrets Acts 1911–1989 of the United Kingdom*. London and New York: Routledge, 1991 xvi + 304 pp. £40.00.

Although this is ostensibly a book about the history of the Official Secrets Acts, it is not a book for historians. As a historian, I feel a little diffident about reviewing it. Books ought to be considered on their own terms, and I'm not sure that I can do that. I thought at first of returning it to the reviews editor for this reason. On the other hand it is bound to get plenty of notices by lawyers in other journals, and a cross-cultural view of it, so to speak, may be useful. So I have decided to stick with it. This is just by way of warning, to lawyers who may rightly feel that I am not being entirely fair.

There are a number of trivial reasons why this book is likely to alienate historians. The dedication, which spreads over two pages and leads with "Queen and Country," is one. No historian would wish to appear to side so firmly with one party in the controversy over official secrecy in advance. The writing style, too, is duller and more stilted than historians are used to, and repetitive to an irritating degree. These may not be such grave faults to a lawyer. Stylistic elegance, for example, is not always consistent with precision, which must be a lawyer's first aim. Repetition may be necessary to avoid misunderstandings. The dedication is harder for historians to swallow; but that may be their problem, rather than the lawyers'.

A far more serious difficulty is this book's whole approach to its subject. Historians will find it narrow, to say the least, and intensely frustrating in some respects. That is because they are generally concerned to try to discover the reasons for things, and this book does not help in that regard at all. An example is the 1911 Official Secrets Act, which was the most important and controversial of all Britain's secrecy laws. No one knows for certain why it was passed. It was sprung on Parliament in a hurry, at the height of an international crisis, at the end of a week in mid-summer when many MPs had left for home. It was presented by ministers in a highly misleading, possibly deliberately duplicitous way. It was rushed through all its readings in the Commons in less than an hour. On the other hand, as Thomas rightly points out, it was not drafted in a hurry, but had been drawn up, waiting this opportunity to be passed, for many months and even years before. Between 1911 and 1989 it had (together with its amending acts) an enormous effect not only on the policing of foreign espionage, which was its ostensible purpose, but on a wide range of civil liberties in Britain.

This, therefore, was an event of great significance. Historians want to know why it happened. Who was responsible for it? What were their motives? Why did it need to be effected in this very underhand way? How was it able to be effected? We have been looking for answers to these questions for years. There are clues among the Public Records, although the main Home Office file on the passage of the Official Secrets Act, for example, is still (ironically) closed to scrutiny even today. Any new book on the subject is eagerly awaited, to see what light it can shed on the affair. Rosamund Thomas in her preface promises to trace the act's "origins." Alas, she does not. Her only primary sources for this affair are the statute itself, and the record of the (very short) debates in *Hansard*. So far as motives are concerned, she seems content with the ones given publicly by law officers at the time. When the attorney general tells the Commons that there is "nothing novel" in the bill, for example (*Hansard*, 5th series, Commons, vol. 29, c.2252), she accepts that this was said in good faith (p. 3). She may be right. What is puzzling—to a historian—is the fact that it does not occur to Thomas to question this, or any other aspect of the official version of this event. That is why as history—the historian's sort of history—this book is seriously flawed.

The same flaws—seen from a historian's point of view—pervade the rest of the book. It deals with the development of official secrets law in the narrowest conceivable terms. It is chiefly a record of legislation and cases, taken from statutes, law reports, *Hansard*, and occasionally *The Times*. Its only dramatis personae are government ministers, law officers, judges, barristers, and defendants. It nearly all takes place in courtrooms, with the occasional foray into Westminster when the law is being changed. The viewpoint is that of the legal establishment (Queen and Country, if you like), which of course is not a monolithic one, but is still very circumscribed. The outside world hardly impinges, unless it actually appears or threatens to appear in court. There is no sense in this book of the law's being an aspect of society, in both its formulation and its implementation: affected by pressures from "public opinion," or from government (except for poor Lord Havers under Thatcher), or by simple prejudice (what Thomas quaintly calls "first impressions" [p. 40]) on the part of judges. There is almost no awareness of the political context of much of this legislation: no conception—to give just one example—of the possible danger to democracy posed by the exemption enjoyed by the security services from the harm test (p. 216) in the 1989 Official Secrets Act, which is what all the recent fuss has been about. To understand this law properly, as a historian would wish to understand it, all these aspects need to be taken into account and discussed. To avoid nearly all of them, as Thomas does, creates a highly artificial impression of events.

But that, of course, is exactly what the law is: artificial, an attempt to impose simple order on what is in reality complex and disordered; in other words, on life. It is clearly necessary from a legal point of view (and from the point of view of all of us as citizens) to have this artificial creation, in order to prevent life degenerating into what is likely to be (unless you are an anarchist) sheer chaos. That is all right. But you have to realize that it *is* artificial. You must not mistake it for reality. In particular, you must not mistake it for *historical* reality. The history of law is not simply legal history just as the history of railways, for example, is not simply the history of the laying of lines and the building of trains and carriages. A book on the latter written in those terms would satisfy railway freaks, but not historians. In much the same way *Espionage and Secrecy* is likely to satisfy lawyers more than it does me.

Of course this really is unfair. The book was not written for historians. It was written primarily, one imagines, for practical lawyers, who are not interested in context, but only in the structure itself, and how it works. Despite its ahistorical nature it is far from being useless to historians, who have to take the artificial world of the law into consideration in their work, even if there appears to be no pressing need for lawyers to have much regard for reality. This book, consequently, is interesting and illuminating on the purely legal aspects of Section 1, in particular, of the old Official Secrets Acts—the one dealing with espionage proper: on its internal developments over the years; the legal problems associated with it (especially of evidence, and the role of the attorney general); and the ways in which it has been applied. Historians can learn a lot from it. I imagine that lawyers will also learn a lot from it. I still think, however, that even they would have learned a lot more if the author had been a better historian. (It is possible. Leon Radzinowicz is a shining example of a lawyer who managed to make the cultural jump.) But that is for them to say, in a proper review of this book, by Thomas's peers.

Bernard Porter
University of Newcastle-upon-Tyne

John L. McWilliams, *The Protectors: Harry J. Anslinger and the Federal Bureau of Narcotics, 1930–1962*. Newark: University of Delaware Press, 1990. 251 pp. Notes, bibliography, and index. $37.50.

This is a revisionist history that tries to remove Anslinger from the vituperative debate over marijuana policy. McWilliams seeks to present Anslinger as neither the demon behind the criminalization of marijuana, nor the heroic defender of his country from the assaults of the "killer weed," but as an exceptionally able bureaucrat engaged in a variety of activities over a very long career.

He starts with Anslinger's rise from railroad detective and state policeman, through the wartime Ordnance Department and the U.S. foreign service, to the Prohibition Bureau and the Federal Bureau of Narcotics. While McWilliams convinces the reader of the importance of Anslinger's early career, he provides only a sketchy outline. To the extent that this is a biography, it would help to know if Anslinger had any ties to the prohibitionist movement and culture before his bureaucratic involvement in prohibition via the consular service. Readers may also wonder how this child of a German-Swiss immigrant railroad worker came to marry into the Mellon family and how much his new ties had to do with his career.

After an analysis of the development of U.S. narcotics policy from the Harrison Narcotic Act of 1914 through the act that created the Federal Bureau of Narcotics in 1930, McWilliams describes Anslinger's appointment as the FBN's first commissioner. Anslinger created the FBN in the midst of the financial crisis of the Great Depression and the political changes associated with the shift from Hoover to FDR, but McWilliams postpones his analysis of these issues.

Instead, driven by the historico-political debate over marijuana, McWilliams jumps into an analysis of Anslinger's relation to the criminalization of the "killer weed." He presents Anslinger as a late convert to the cause (although a very important one). While he allows for bureacratic motivations for this conversion in the midst of sharply declining budgets, McWilliams accepts Anslinger's conversion to the anti-marijuana campaign as sincere.

Then, in the midst of the marijuana story, McWilliams inserts a discussion of the commissioner's policies relating to narcotics addicts and his hostility to scientific research.

Only after completing an effective presentation of the "Second Prohibition" does McWilliams turn to the fundamental organizational, administrative, and political issues that Anslinger and the FBN faced. He attributes Anslinger's renewed appointment by FDR to "Anslinger's Army," an alliance of drug companies and an anti-drug lobby. Given its importance to

Anslinger and the FBN, some further exploration of this lobby (including the WCTU and the General Federation of Women's Clubs) would have greatly enhanced the book.

Once again, however, McWilliams presents only a brief view of the administrative and political realities of the FBN before turning to the more colorful stories of Anslinger's fascination with drug use by entertainers and the FBN's campaigns to silence challenges to its drug orthodoxy from the New York Academy of Medicine and the AMA.

These aspects of Anslinger's career get a more thorough treatment, as does Anslinger's role in the increasingly punitive aspect of U.S. drug policies via the adoption of uniform state drug laws, the adoption of the Boggs Act in 1951, and the Narcotics Control Act of 1956. Anyone who still thinks that tough punishments for drug users are the solution to the drug problem would do well to review this section of McWilliams's study.

McWilliams's Anslinger is also distinguished by his early promotion of the concept of the Mafia, a nationally organized criminal syndicate whose existence was long denied by J. Edgar Hoover. Dealing with the international narcotics trade, Anslinger was soon convinced that there was a highly developed organization behind criminal activities. Successful FBN campaigns against Lepke Buchalter (of "Murder Inc.") and Lucky Luciano in the 1930s were capped in 1957 by the FBN's domination of the McClellan Committee hearings on organized crime and the coordination of the nationwide campaign that followed the discovery of a large meeting of underworld leaders at Apalachin.

Anslinger was prone to conspiracy theories. McWilliams traces their evolution from the nativist association between narcotics and a "Yellow Peril" of Chinese gangsters, to a Japanese plot to corrupt and prepare the United States for conquest by promoting drug use. After the war, Anslinger reverted to a Chinese conspiracy, this time one of communists who combined aspects of the two earlier versions. McWilliams effectively debunks Anslinger's fifteen-year campaign against "communist narcotics infiltration" and points out the irony of blaming Chinese communists when Chinese Nationalists, supported by the CIA, were heavily involved in the opium trade.

This leads McWilliams into the area of his current research, the relationship among the FBN, organized crime, and U.S. intelligence agencies. During World War II the drug trade was disrupted and Anslinger loaned several key agents to the military and naval intelligence agencies and to "Wild Bill" Donovan's OSS. After the war they returned to the FBN, but later they often worked for the CIA (with FBN salaries sometimes paid by the CIA).

McWilliams only whets the reader's appetite. We get full accounts of the FBN's joint operations with the OSS and the CIA in their searches for a "truth drug," and their experiments with LSD. But McWilliams is reduced to asserting well-founded suspicions when it comes to the wide range of

Cold War covert operations engaged in by FBN agents overseas. We can only look forward to his next book in that regard.

Thirty-two years after becoming the first head of the FBN, Anslinger retired, although he remained the U.S. representative on the U.N. Commission on Narcotic Drugs until shortly before his death in the early 1970s. Only six years after Anslinger left, the FBN was swept out of existence by an internal power struggle and a devastating corruption scandal. The logic of treating Anslinger and his agency together is thus apparent.

Nonetheless, this book really does not work. It has far too little on Anslinger's life and thoughts, and far too much about the agency he headed, for it to work as a biography of Anslinger. By the same token, the volume is far too brief and too focused on Anslinger's person to work as an institutional history of the FBN. The combination of biography and institutional history is certainly possible. Richard Powers's 1987 biography of J. Edgar Hoover must have encouraged McWilliams, but McWilliams should have noted that it is three times the size of his own work.

Despite these problems, *The Protectors* is an important book. It does begin to develop a much needed, balanced appraisal of Anslinger and it provides a much better evaluation of his role in American drug policy than was previously available.

The Protectors also begins an important process. While previous investigators have suggested that there is more to the history of crime and policing than simple opposition, and others have discovered ties between intelligence agencies like the CIA and criminal activities (especially the international drug trade), McWilliams begins to tie it all together. He thus opens up a whole new perspective on the relationship between organized crime and the state.

Stanley Nadel
Central Connecticut State University, New Britain

Charles M. Lamb and Stephen C. Halpern, eds., *The Burger Court: Political and Judicial Profiles*. Urbana and Chicago: University of Illinois Press, 1991. x + 513 pp. Photographs, tables, notes, bibliography, case index, and index. $49.95 (cloth); $19.95 (paper).

Some Supreme Courts of the United States are labeled by their chief justices; the man and his court become intertwined. Most notably was "the Marshall Court" headed by Chief Justice John Marshall (1801–35) with its ringing arguments about the power of the Supreme Court and the power of the nation versus the states. Another example where the Court and its chief justice became in the public's mind one and the same was "the Warren Court" headed by Chief Justice Earl Warren (1953–69).

But most chief justices and their courts leave no such indelible marks on the nation and on the history of the Supreme Court. Most leave only an ambivalent impression on the law, the nation, and the constitutional order. The Supreme Court of Chief Justice Warren E. Burger (1969–86) had just such an impact—so much so that one now wonders whether "the Burger Court" is an appropriate designation. Political scientists, constitutional historians, and court watchers have struggled to identify what was special and important about the Burger years. *The Burger Court* contributes to the process of assessment while calling into question the appropriateness of the label as well as the relative importance of Burger's Court. In fact, after completing its thirteen essays, one wonders whether the label "the Burger Years" would not be a more accurate description than the more honorific "the Burger Court."

The job of the judicial biographer is always one of achieving a balance between describing how a judge decided and wrote on cases and describing the justice's overall approach to the law, constitutionalism, and jurisprudence, deliberately downplaying the justice's case law production. It is a choice for the writer and editor between trees and forests, between case law and "judging." Editors Charles Lamb and Stephen C. Halpern chose to emphasize the case law, and although readers will profit from this decision, their opening and closing articles do not provide enough of an overview of the forest, the Burger years, and the essays they frame cannot make up for the lapse.

The Burger Court includes an essay on every Supreme Court justice who served during Chief Justice Burger's tenure on the Court. Arranged alphabetically beginning with Associate Justice Hugo L. Black and ending with Associate Justice Byron R. White, the essays describe and appraise the influence, power, and jurisprudence of the thirteen justices of the Burger years. The quality of each article varies, but no more so than usually occurs in such collections. Among the strongest is Stephen Wasby's article, "Justice Harry A. Blackmun: Transformation from 'Minnesota Twin' to Independent Voice." All penned by political scientists, the articles make their theses clear in their titles; for example, "Justice Hugo L. Black: The Enduring Effort to Realize Law over Judicial Discretion," by Howard Ball; "Chief Justice Warren E. Burger: A Conservative Chief for Conservative Times," by Charles M. Lamb; "Justice William H. Rehnquist: Right-Wing Ideologue or Majoritarian Democrat," by Sue Davis (why Rehnquist could not be seen as *both* a right-wing ideologue *and* a majoritarian democrat is not clear); and "Justice Potter Stewart: Decisional Patterns in Search of Doctrinal Moorings," by Tinsley E. Yarbrough.

Each essay begins with a historical/biographical sketch touching on its subject's legal training, legal experience, and appointment to the Court.

Then the article is usually divided into topical subsections. These subsections describe how the justice decided cases on such topics as civil rights and federalism, as well as how that justice agreed with or opposed the position taken by Chief Justice Burger. This method is, at times, unfortunate for two reasons. First, by comparing all the justices to Burger, the writers assume that Burger is the proper standard of measure and analysis for understanding the behavior of his Court. But using Burger as the standard skews the analysis of the structures of power within the Court and reveals little new about the justices' values. Second, the division of the articles into subsections breaks up the narrative of each article. For example, Beverly B. Cook's essay, "Justice Sandra Day O'Connor: Transition to a Republican Court Agenda," is divided into twelve subdivisions, some of which are themselves subdivided. What results is little more than an annotated outline of topics and cases. Although Cook and the other writers do attempt to step back and assess each justice, their attempts cannot overcome the avalanche of cases created by the book's structure.

In addition, each article touches upon the topic of criminal justice as seen in each justice's opinions in Fourth, Fifth, Sixth, and Eighth Amendment cases. From their discussions it becomes clear that the topic of criminal justice in the 1970s to the mid–1980s deserves a much fuller history and analysis than is possible in a book organized around the justices of the Burger years. Although some articles are suggestive on the topic of criminal justice history a topical history would likely yield a richer understanding.

The Burger Court advances the scholarly study of the Burger years, and the overall work will be mined by future scholars. For this contribution, editors Lamb and Halpern should be commended. But the history of the Burger years, in all its judicial complexities and social reactions, still awaits definitive study.

Thomas C. Mackey
University of Louisville

David Garland, *Punishment and Modern Society*. Oxford: Oxford University Press (in U.K.); Chicago: Chicago University Press (in U.S.A.), 1990. pp. iv + 312. $29.95.

Readers of David Garland's earlier work will expect much from *Punishment and Modern Society*: they will not be disappointed. It is a bold and scholarly attempt to review existing theories of punishment, and to suggest an alternative framework within which future theorizing might be conducted. Throughout Garland maintains a more historically informed approach to his subject than is customary in such studies, and it is this which makes the book especially relevant to historians.

The first two-thirds of the book is taken up with reviews of three of the existing approaches to the history of punishment: that of Emile Durkheim; what might most conveniently be described as the Marxist one, here exemplified by the work of Rusche and Kirchheimer; and that of Michel Foucault. Garland does not offer a mere textbook rehearsal of the main strands of each of these approaches. Each of the three approaches is treated to a chapter of exposition, and another of critique, always informed by the author's penetrating intelligence and firm grasp of the issues in question. His reassessment of Durkheim is especially interesting, while in this book as elsewhere Garland demonstrates his welcome ability to make the thoughts of Michel Foucault more accessible to empirically minded historians. Both historians of crime and punishment and their pupils will find much of value in these chapters.

The conclusion that Garland draws from his analysis of the grand theories of punishment is the not entirely surprising, if inherently sane, one that all of them have something to offer but that none of them provide a single pathway to understanding the subject. The author's objective is not "to find reasons for setting an approach aside, but rather to grasp what is important within a particular perspective and how it might be developed" (p. 111). This does leave us with the problem of which bits of a particular perspective to develop, and how we can be certain of doing the best job possible when fitting together various components from different theories when constructing a new paradigm: but it does emphasize the need to keep debate on punishment, in both its historical and its current forms, opened rather than closed.

In the last third of the book Garland turns to setting out his own ideas of how punishment as a social phenomenon might best be considered. His approach is, in brief, a "cultural" one. Punishment, he argues, is a cultural artefact, which embodies and expresses society's cultural forms. The work of Marx, Durkheim, and Foucault demonstrate this point, but each suffers from privileging only selected aspects of those forms. Garland suggests that a sociology of punishment needs "an analytical account of the cultural forces which influence punishment and, in particular, an account of the patterns imposed upon punishment by the character of contemporary sensibilities" (p. 197). Penalty communicates meaning, and hence helps account for shared values, shared meanings, and, in the anthropological sense, culture, in any given society. It is one of the many institutions that do so, thus helping people to evaluate conduct, make moral sense of their worlds, and to evaluate the moral worth of their fellow citizens.

Although this conclusion is in all probability correct, there are some problems with it. If punishment works in this way, it does so, for most of us, in very indirect ways. Arguably, the processes emphasized by Garland worked more obviously in the pre-industrial world than they do at present. Three hundred years ago, a fifteen-minute walk to the center of the city where I currently live would have allowed me to see petty offenders whipped in public, a longer walk would have allowed me to see serious offenders hanged a mile to the west of its walls. My opportunities of witnessing what currently goes on in prisons, or even in the offices of the probation service, are rather more limited. I accept that forces that work indirectly can be no less significant in forming culture than overt ones: it is just that, given the essentially covert nature of much of the operation of the "penal-welfare complex," I would have welcomed a fuller discussion of what exactly the symbols of penality are and how they operate. I must, however, express complete sympathy for Garland's fundamental contention that punishment is not just something that happens to offenders, but which also helps form, inform, and deform the social and political outlook of society at large.

Further problems arise from the concentration on the history of changing sensibilities, signposted for Garland by the work of Norbert Elias. Again, this seems a fruitful area of exploration, and is one which, perhaps due to the influence of a set of investigative priorities suggested by Marx, has not been much investigated by social historians. Yet measuring changes in sensibility is a notoriously difficult enterprise, and it remains unclear how much can really be explained by this approach. Thus Garland, like everybody else, attributes the replacement of earlier penal regimes by the advent of the penitentiary prison to changed sensibilities, but, again like everybody else, he has no means of explaining the striking suddenness of that transition.

But perhaps these criticisms are misplaced: Garland's main purpose is not to provide answers, but rather to help us in formulating the right questions. His use of historical writing (apart from putting too much trust in Lawrence Stone) is usually unexceptionable, and it is especially good to see the work of Pieter Spierenburg and John Beattie receiving due attention. Moreover, Garland manages to write for nearly three hundred pages on what are sometimes very technical matters in a style that loses neither clarity nor the reader's attention. This is an important book that deserves to be widely read by historians, sociologists, and criminologists alike.

James A. Sharpe
University of York, England

Research Note

THE POLICE ARCHIVES OF ENGLAND AND WALES

Ian Bridgeman and Clive Emsley (comps.), *A Guide to the Archives of the Police Forces of England and Wales*, N.P., Police History Society Monograph Number 2, 1989, iii + 242. £16.50.

In the 1960s, when this reviewer stumbled by chance into what would later be called criminal justice history, he encountered a great deal of difficulty tracking down and consulting English provincial police materials. They were extremely scattered—as they still are, unfortunately—between the Public Record Office, county archives and the police themselves. There were severe problems ascertaining what the police possessed and then gaining access.

Encounters with the police were often frustrating and occasionally hilarious. Puzzled or suspicious desk sergeants would be totally flummoxed by requests to view occurrence books or charge sheets from the 1850s. The wheels madly revolved in an attempt to put one safely into some standard police category. In the end, the expression softened and a condescending smile spread over the officer's face—a bad sign, since it meant that one had been pigeonholed as a harmless crank. One quickly learned not to pop in out of the blue and to write to the chief constable first; but even then one had to be prepared to be stonewalled. Sometimes, one was informed that nobody really knew what was retained (often true) so please don't come. But, occasionally, there would be an encounter with a long-serving officer with a proprietorial fondness for archives and an amateur interest in the institutional history of his force. And then you would be told: "Well, once we had such materials, but when the force moved headquarters five years ago, much of it was thrown out or destroyed," or "they were gone even when I joined up."

Ian Bridgeman and Clive Emsley discovered that a great deal of twentieth-century material is still in the custody of the English police although, as a glance through this volume sadly shows, the bulk of the nineteenth-century records has vanished through neglect, periodic purging or even, occasionally, the surreptitious "borrowing" of nice leather bound volumes for display on the shelf at home.

To be sure, the police collect statistics (and are not unaware that longitudinal studies can be based on them), and are deeply interested in the past records of criminals; but they are, of necessity, present-oriented—preoccupied with burglaries, riots, robberies, rapes, the state of their budgets, public opinion and the minds of their political masters *now*. They can be forgiven for considering the inquiries of historians a waste of time or thinking that keeping old charge books from the 1850s is a waste of space. Twenty-five years ago, there were few formal contacts between police and historians which would have increased police awareness of the importance of their records and mitigated the concern with secrecy that is part of the occupational culture. These problems have been largely remedied in England.

The compilation of the *Guide* was facilitated by the formation in 1985 of the Police History Society. The prime movers were police officers of senior rank, aided and abetted by scholars such as Clive Emsley who serves as academic advisor. The patron of the society is a former chief constable; the chairman a Deputy Assistant Commissioner of the Metropolitan Police; the president, the commandant of the Police Staff College. The society has helped to legitimize police history among the police themselves, and receives support from chief constables and the *Police Review*. Academics now present papers to its conferences and write for its journal.

In 1986, Emsley reported to the annual meeting that he hoped to survey all documents in police custody. According to the minutes, the project "was enthusiastically received." Other positive developments followed. Some forces have founded museums to house their archives and paraphernalia; others have transferred their holdings into the hands of professional archivists at county record offices.

The *Guide* includes those records of the Metropolitan Police not in the custody of the Public Record Office, as well as the entire archive of the British Transport Police. Forces which have disappeared due to recent consolidations are listed under the present force covering their old territory, but their records have been placed under separate headings. The materials are listed under the following master classifications: Administrative (organization, finances, etc.); Crime (charge and summons books, prisoners, informations, photos, etc); Force Instructions (orders, chief constables memoranda, etc.); Station Journals (occurrence books, beat books, constables' notebooks, etc.); Personnel (registers, discipline books, paybooks, sickness registers, etc.); Watch and Standing Joint Committee Materials (chief constables' reports, minutes of borough and county police authorities, etc.); Miscellaneous (newspaper cuttings, scrapbooks, handbooks, station building plans, etc.).

There is a great deal of material on policemen themselves—many forces having kept complete registers of recruits since their founding—on police discipline, crime and criminals, riots and public order, oversight by civilian authorities, daily life in the streets and country lanes, brothels, aliens policy, early traffic and motor vehicle policies, police activities in both world wars, and women police—even the suffragette movement.

Since the *Guide* lists all known police holdings, it is now possible for any student contemplating the use of such documents to consult the printed catalogues of the Public Record Office, county record offices, and this volume, and be fairly sure of what is extant and where it can be found. Future research will be greatly aided by the *Guide*, although it will be a bit duller. Much of the material will be microfilmed and kept at the European Centre for the Study of Policing at the Open University; scholars will no longer have to play the harmless crank at the sergeant's desk.

The *Guide* is itself the result of a heroic research effort. Bridgeman and Emsley visited and surveyed thirty five forces, logging thousands of miles on British Rail. This volume is an important and welcome resource for specialists in police and criminal justice history. It is available from M. Stallion, Police History Society, 18 Cornec Chase, Leigh-on-Sea, Essex SS9 5EW, England (sterling money order only).

Robert D. Storch
University of Wisconsin Center-Janesville

Index

Contributors

CHRISTOPHER ADAMSON is a policy analyst in Ontario's Ministry of Colleges and Universities. His principal research interest is the history and sociology of punishment. His essay, "Societal Punishment and Social Stratification: An Historical Perspective," is forthcoming in *Perspectives on Social Problems*, ed. Gale Miller and James A. Holstein (Greenwich, 1993).

DAVID M. ANDERSON is lecturer in history at the School of Oriental and African Studies, University of London. He is co-editor (with David Killingray) of *Policing the Empire: Government, Authority and Control 1830–1940*, and *Policing and Decolonisation: Nationalism, Politics and the Police 1917–1965*.

RICHARD BESSEL is senior lecturer in history and co-director of the European Centre of the Study of Policing at the Open University. He is author of *Political Violence and the Rise of Nazism: The Storm Troopers in Eastern Germany 1925–1934*, and is currently completing a study of the problems of demobilization in Germany at the end of World War I.

MARIA R. BOES is Assistant Professor at the West Chester University, Pennsylvania. Her present research projects focus on personal aspects of criminal adjudication in Early Modern Germany.

MALCOLM CHASE is a lecturer in the Department of Adult Continuing Education at the University of Leeds. He is the author of *'The People's Farm': English Radical Agrarianism 1775–1840*.

MARK CLAPSON is a lecturer in history at Luton College. He is the author of *'A Bit of Flutter': Popular Gambling in England c. 1820–1961*.

CLIVE EMSLEY is professor of history and co-director of the European Centre for the Study of Policing at the Open University. Among his publications are *Crime and Society in England 1750–1900*, and *The English Police: A Political and Social History*.

MARK FINNANE is senior lecturer at the School of Australian and Comparative Studies. He is the author of *Insanity and the Insane in Post-Famine Ireland*, and editor of and contributor to *Policing in Australia: Historical Perspectives*. He is currently working on a book on Australian policing history, and researching the history of imprisonment in Australia and the comparative history of the prosecution of violence in the late nineteenth century.

CHRISTOPHER HARDING is reader in law at the University College of Wales, Aberystywyth. He has published articles on penal history and other work on the criminal justice system. More recently, he is the co-author (with Richard W. Ireland) of *Punishment: Rhetoric, Rule and Practice*.

HOLGER H. HERWIG is Professor of History at The University of Calgary. A scholar of Modern German History, he has a recent book on *Germany's Vision of Empire in Venezuela 1871–1914* (Princeton, 1986), and is engaged in a study of "Modern Germany 1648–1992: A Reinterpretation".

DAVID McCREERY teaches Latin American history at Georgia State University and specializes in Central America. He is currently completing a book manuscript entitled "Rural Guatemala, 1760–1940."

THOMAS C. MACKEY, a specialist in American legal history, teaches at the University of Louisville. He is the author of *Red Lights Out: A Legal History of Prostitution, Disorderly Houses and Vice Districts, 1870–1917*.

CLIVE MOORE is senior lecturer in history at the University of Queensland. He has long been interested in the history of Queensland's immigrant Melanesians and has published numerous works on the Queensland labor trade, including *Kanaka: A History of the Melanesian Mackay*. He co-edited *Labour in the South Pacific*. His current research is connected with British New Guinea.

STANLEY NADEL teaches history at Central Connecticut State University. He is the author of several works on immigration and labor history and is currently working on the history of suicide.

BERNARD PORTER is professor of history at the University of Newcastle. He has published widely on political crime and secrecy in Britain, notably

The Origins of the Vigilant State: The London Metropolitan Police Special Branch before the First World War.

MARTIN K. SCHÜSSLER is a private scholar in Birkenfeld, Germany. His original research was in medieval England, for which he wrote a dissertation on "Die Gentry und das Verbrechen im England des 13. und 14. Jahrhunderts" (Stuttgart, 1989). He has recently turned to medieval Nuremberg, on which he has written an article in *Zeitschrift der Savigny-Stiftung für Rechtsgeschichte, Germanistische Abteilung* (1991).

JAMES A. SHARPE is senior lecturer in history at the University of York. He has published widely on crime and criminal justice in early modern England, notably *Crime in Early Modern England 1550–1750* and *Justicial Punishment in England.*

JOHN A. STACK is an assistant professor of history at the University of Missouri-Kansas City. He has written a number of articles on social policy and juvenile delinquency in nineteenth-century England.

ROBERT D. STORCH is Professor of History at the University of Wisconsin Center—Janesville. A scholar of the modern English police, and of numerous articles on policing late eighteenth and nineteenth century Britain, his most recent major study is on "Policing Rural Southern England before the Police, 1830–1850," in Hay and Snyder's *Policing and Prosecutions in Britain, 1750–1850* (Oxford, 1989).

JONATHAN SWAINGER is assistant professor of history at the University of Northern British Columbia, Terrace Campus. A recent graduate of Western Ontario University, he is working on a book-length study entitled "Governing the Law: Statecraft and the Canadian Department of Justice, 1857–1896."

ROGER SWIFT is senior lecturer in history at Chester College of Higher Education. He has published widely on aspects of crime, policing, and popular protest in Victorian Britain, and is the co-editor (with Sheridan Gilley) of *The Irish in the Victorian City* and *The Irish in Britain 1815–1939.*

PAUL J. VANDERWOOD is Professor of History at California State University, San Diego. He has written a major study of *Disorder and Progress: Bandits, Police and Mexican Development* and has published recent articles on this subject in *Rebellions in Mexico* (edited J. Rodriguez), and *The Human Condition in 19th Century Latin America* (edited J. Ewell and W. Beezley).

ROBERT G. WAITE is a Washington, D.C. based historian. He specializes in the history of law enforcement and crime in the United States and Germany. The research for this article was conducted while on a grant from the German Academic Exchange Service, to which he is grateful for its support.

Submissions

Notes on submissions:

The general rule guiding authors and editors is that submissions should follow as closely as possible the formats of the most recent publication. Therefore, the previous volume of *Criminal Justice History* should be consulted for guidance. The basic format used is the University of Chicago Style Manual.

Editorial correspondence and submissions:

Professor Louis Knafla
Department of History
University of Calgary
Calgary, Alberta
Canada T2N 1N4
FAX 403–289–8566

Books for review, proposals to review, and reviewer registrations should be sent to the appropriate review editor:

U.S.A. and Canada

Professor Julia Kirk Blackwelder
Department of History
University of North Carolina
Charlotte, NC 28223
U.S.A.

Other areas and transnational:

Professor Clive Emsley
European Centre for Policing
The Open University
Milton Keynes MK7 6AA
England